CITY POLITICS

CITY POLITICS

EDWARD C. BANFIELD
JAMES Q. WILSON

VINTAGE BOOKS NEW YORK

A DIVISION OF RANDOM HOUSE

Reprinted by arrangement with Harvard University Press
An original publication of the Joint Center for Urban Studies of the
Massachusetts Institute of Technology and Harvard University

Manufactured in the United States of America

VINTAGE BOOKS ARE PUBLISHED BY
ALFRED A. KNOPF, INC. AND RANDOM HOUSE, INC.

ACKNOWLEDGMENTS

We have made extensive use of the approximately thirty reports of the politics of particular cities that have been published in mimeographed form by the Joint Center for Urban Studies of the Massachusetts Institute of Technology and Harvard University. References to these reports appear here and there in the text, but our reliance upon them has been more extensive than the footnotes indicate. We wish to acknowledge a general debt to the authors of these reports and to the Joint Center, which sponsored them and aided us as well. Martin Meyerson, its director until July 1963, was both a lively critic and a patient friend.

We wish to acknowledge also the assistance of the following friends and colleagues who read parts of the manuscript: V. O. Key of Harvard University; Peter H. Rossi and Duncan MacRae of the University of Chicago; Alan Altshuler of Cornell University; Scott Greer of Northwestern University; Oliver P. Williams and Charles Liebman of the University of Pennsylvania; Lloyd Rodwin of the Massachusetts Institute of Technology; T. J. Kent of the University of California; David Greenstone of the Brookings Institution; and Saul Alinsky, Ben Bagdikian, Peter B. Clark, Martha Derthick, John Dinklespiel, Anthony Downs, and Wayne E. Thompson. Professor Charles Gilbert of Swarthmore College made certain data on city elections available to us.

We owe a special debt to Max Hall of the Harvard University Press, whose skill and care as an editor went far beyond the call of duty; to Wallace Sayre and Herbert Kaufman, whose book, *Governing New York City*, proved to be an invaluable resource; and to Roberta Wilson, who prepared the index.

CONTENTS

TABLES

FIGURES

CITY POLITICS

INTRODUCTION · A POLITICAL
APPROACH TO URBAN GOVERNMENT

THIS BOOK is based on the view that the day-to-day workings of city government in the United States are best understood by looking at the differences of opinion and interest that exist within the cities, at the issues that arise out of these differences, and at the ways institutions function to resolve (or fail to resolve) them. It is based, in short, upon a view of city government as a political process.

This is not the usual approach to the subject. City government is usually treated more as a matter of "administration" than of "politics." Those who write about it are, as a rule, more concerned with legal arrangements than with the informal devices by which things are actually done, more with the activities of appointed officials (bureaucrats) than with those of elected ones (politicians), and more with the procedures by which routines are carried on than with the large forces that determine the content of policy.

We have reversed the usual emphasis because we think the nature of American government requires it. In many other countries, it might be possible to identify some sphere—often a large one—that is almost purely "administrative," in the sense that matters are decided, as Max Weber said, according to rule and without regard to persons. But in the United States there is no such sphere. Our government is permeated with politics. This is because our constitutional structure and our traditions afford individuals manifold opportunities not only to bring their special interests to the attention of public officials but also —and this is the important thing—to compel officials to bargain and to make compromises. The nature of the governmental system gives private interests such good opportunities to participate in the making of public decisions that there is virtually no sphere of "administration" apart from politics.

To say that the government of American cities is to a high degree political does not necessarily mean that decisions are made on partisan grounds or by people who are called, or who think of themselves as, politicians. To be sure, many decisions *are* political in the rather narrow sense. But many equally important ones are made without regard to party or to electoral considerations and are made by people who are professional administrators. These decisions are nevertheless political. The governmental system affords special interests the opportunity to impose checks on administrators in much the same way that they impose them on politicians; and therefore administrators, even those of them who regard "politics" with abhorrence, are normally obliged to be responsive to the demands of special interests.

If the governments of American cities are political, so are the problems of the cities, and this, we think, is another reason for approaching the study of city government by way of politics. To the extent that social evils like crime, racial hatred, and poverty are problems susceptible to solution, the obstacles in the way of their solution are mostly political. It is not for lack of information that the problems remain unsolved. Nor is it because organizational arrangements are defective. Rather it is because people have differing opinions and interests, and therefore opposing ideas about what should be done.

In the United States, the connection between local and national politics is peculiarly close. This is a further reason why the study of city politics is important. The national parties, except for a few months every four years when they come alive to elect a President and Vice-President, are hardly more than loose congeries of local parties. Congressmen and Senators are essentially local politicians, and those of them who forget it soon cease to be politicians at all. One cannot understand the national political system without knowing something about how it works locally.

Another reason for studying city politics is that it affords exceptional opportunities to generalize about American political culture, American democracy, and democracy in general. The most important questions—the question of peace or war, for example—do not arise in city politics, to be sure. That city politics is never played for the highest stakes makes it in some ways an entirely different game. Nevertheless, the similarities are great enough so that one can learn something about the greater game from studying the lesser, and the large number of cities affords unique opportunities for comparison. There are only a few democratic nations, and all of them differ radically in culture. But there are several hundred democratic cities in the United States, and their culture is, broadly speaking, the same.

To say that city politics is worth studying for these reasons is not to imply, however, that the spread of knowledge about city politics is likely to lead to the solution of local or national problems. Knowledge about politics may indeed help one side of a controversy to gain an advantage over its opponents, but there is no presumption that from a social standpoint this will make any improvement in the situation. To increase equally the knowledge of *all* sides would put the competition on a somewhat different basis without changing the structure of the situation essentially.

The kind of knowledge about politics that might give one side an advantage over the others, it must be added, can seldom be got from books. Moreover, it is not a kind of knowledge that is intellectually worthwhile; it consists not of general propositions but of facts about particular circumstances of time and place (e.g., that the alderman of the tenth ward will switch his vote on the park proposition if the mayor applies pressure) and of a mysterious faculty for making good guesses.

The reason why knowledge about politics (whether in the form of general propositions or as practical wisdom) will not lead to better solutions of social problems is that the impediments to such solutions are a result of disagreement, not lack of knowledge. Knowing how disagreements arise, how the parties to them act vis-à-vis each other, and the rules and practices by which certain institutions mediate them is not likely to be of use either in preventing disagreements from arising or in bringing them to quicker or more satisfactory resolution. Thinking that a general increase in the level of knowledge about politics will promote better and faster solutions of social problems is something like thinking that a general increase in the skill of chess players will lead to shorter games or to a "solution of the problem of chess."

At least two important practical purposes may be served by a wider diffusion of knowledge about politics, however.

First, young men and women who enter the civil service may, if they understand the setting in which they work and the constraints that the system imposes upon them, work more effectively and with less strain to themselves. A city planner, for example, may learn from the study of city politics to be more aware of the limitations upon him and more tolerant of them. This may help him to make plans that are more likely to be carried into effect.

Second, the spread of knowledge about politics may also reduce the amount of well-meant but often harmful interference by citizens in the workings of political institutions. A public which understands the nature and necessity of politics may perhaps be more willing than one that does not to allow politicians to do their work without obstruction. Such a public may be more appreciative of the social value of the results of this work (but not necessarily more respectful of the motives of the people who do it; that is another matter). And it may be more aware of the risks it runs of damaging, or perhaps even of destroying, a tolerable system by attempting reforms the full effects of which cannot be foreseen.

The ultimate justification for the study of city politics, however, is certainly not a practical one. Perhaps the most intrinsically satisfying of man's activities is trying to understand the world he lives in. Politics, being one of the most difficult things to understand, is therefore particularly challenging. Responding to the challenge is, we think, its own justification and reward.

PART I
THE NATURE OF CITY POLITICS

CHAPTER 1 · THE CITY AS
A SETTING FOR POLITICS

POLITICS arises out of conflicts, and it consists of the activities—for example, reasonable discussion, impassioned oratory, balloting, and street fighting—by which conflict is carried on. In the foreground of a study of city politics, then, belong the issues in dispute, the cleavages which give rise to them and nourish them, the forces tending toward consensus, and the laws, institutions, habits, and traditions which regulate conflict. But these cannot be understood without some account of the factors conditioning them. The city is an arrangement of people in space. Certain developmental tendencies are inherent in it, and it is subject to external pressures as well. The nature of the arrangement (and of the pressures and tendencies) fixes in a general way the form and content of the conflict that goes on within the city.

To speak of "the American city" generically may strike the reader as implausible, even though it is only general features that we propose to discuss. To most Americans the differences among cities, especially the larger ones, are probably more conspicuous than the similarities. Boston, so it seems, could hardly be more different from Houston, or Atlanta, or even Cincinnati. Chicago is a world apart from Philadelphia and another world apart from Los Angeles. Everyone knows that New York is *sui generis*—a world city.

The differences are, indeed, striking. Nevertheless there are enough important underlying similarities to make discussion of a typical situation and a typical set of problems worthwhile. It must be kept in mind, however, that what is true of the "typical" city may not be true of a particular one and certainly will not be the *whole* truth about any city.

The typical city exists within a metropolitan area. The Census in 1960 defined 212 such areas in the United States for statistical purposes, ranging in size from the New York area with almost 600 local governments and 10,694,633 people to the Meriden, Connecticut, area with few local governments and 51,850 people. For our present purposes, a metropolitan area consists of a central city, several suburban cities (residential or industrial or both, and of various sizes) and, in the interstices between the cities, villages and unincorporated places. The metropolitan area is often coextensive with a county, but it may include parts of two or three (in a few cases even more) counties. What makes it a unity, to the extent that it is one, is a common orientation—cultural and political, perhaps, but mainly economic—toward the central city. The central city is called "central" because it is the object of this common orientation. Where there is a discontinuity in the pattern of settlement, it is this that usually fixes the boundaries of the metropolitan area: beyond a certain point urban settlement ceases and there is a gap of many miles to the next urban settlement. In some cases, however, there is no discontinuity: settlements extend without interruption, some being oriented toward one large city and some toward another. Rather arbitrarily in such cases (for the orientation of the cities is usually ambiguous and the line of demarcation between them is not clear), it is said that one part of the contiguous bloc of settlement constitutes one metropolitan area and another part constitutes a second.

No metropolitan area has a general-purpose government serving the whole of it. There are in many places governments which perform one or two functions (e.g., sewage disposal) for the whole of a metropolitan area, and there are two or three general-purpose governments (e.g., Dade County, Florida) that serve a considerable part of the metropolitan area. But one cannot at present speak of "metropolitan government" as a thing that exists in the United States. Government in the metropolitan area (not "of" it, for there is no government *of* it as such) consists of municipal corporations of various kinds. The most common are city governments, school districts and similar bodies organized to perform special functions, and counties.

DEVELOPMENTAL HISTORY[1]

As a rule, the central city is the oldest part of the metropolitan area. It is apt to be on a river or a well-protected harbor. Every sizable city requires a large flow of water to carry away its waste products (this is true even if the waste is nothing more than the effluent of a modern sewage disposal plant), and this would be a sufficient reason for cities to be located close to rivers, lakes, and oceans. But there is an additional reason why the larger cities are near water: most of them were

---

[1] For this account we owe a general debt to Raymond Vernon, *The Myth and Reality of Our Urban Problems* (Cambridge, Mass.: Joint Center for Urban Studies, 1962).

founded before there were railroads, and transportation was then mainly by water.

The oldest part of the central city, the point from which its expansion began, is closest to the river or harbor. This is where the core of the city is likely to be now. The central business district—"downtown"— the place where office buildings, banks, theaters, and restaurants are thickest and at which all transportation lines converge—is, if not the exact site of the first settlement, at least adjacent to it.

When the central cities were laid out, people traveled on foot. Accordingly, everyone—factory hands, clerks, and merchants—lived close to the center of things. Although there was limitless space to be had outside the city, the city was built at a very high density. Streets were narrow, lots were small, and houses were crowded together. The rich lived on the hills, a few minutes by carriage from their places of business. The poor were crowded together in the mudflats along the river front, close to their work, or in whatever open spaces they could find around warehouses and breweries. The middle class, perforce, lived on the edges of the city, a safe distance from the noise, confusion, and immorality of the waterfront.

Late in the nineteenth century, changes in transportation changed the form of the city. People began to travel on electric trolleys or trains rather than by foot. This meant that their residences could be farther away from their places of work. The growth of the railroads tended also to cause the city to spread out. Taking advantage of rail transportation, many industries left the waterfronts and located beyond what were then the city boundaries. Meanwhile central business districts were growing. The skyscraper was invented (following the invention of structural steel and of the electric elevator), and as great insurance, banking, and industrial empires came into being, the centers of the cities filled with offices and office workers. In its essential elements, however, the structure of the city remained as it had been. The rich and the poor continued to occupy the core (the rich in the desirable and the poor in the undesirable locations) and the middle class settled the outskirts.

The city's rapid growth required raising large sums in taxes. The burden was by no means intolerable, however, because it could spread over the real estate of the thriving central business district and the property of solid citizens in the outlying residential neighborhoods. Furthermore, municipal boundaries were flexible. The city annexed outlying neighborhoods as fast as they were populated; the residents of these neighborhoods were anxious to be annexed because they depended on the central city for services.

Beginning in the 1920's, another change in the technology of transportation accelerated the dispersion of the city. Widespread use of the automobile enabled the middle class to move outside the city. During the preceding decades this class, growing in numbers and income, had built new homes within the city. These were mostly three- and four-story row houses and single dwellings on very small lots, located along the lines of the electric railways. The density of population in these middle-class neighborhoods was high. The freedom of movement that the automobile gave encouraged the middle class to begin almost at once to leave the "crowded city" for the suburban countryside, where one could have "a place of one's own." Around the city "dormitory suburbs" sprang up, the populations of which commuted to the central business district of the city. This "flight to the suburbs" still continues.

To some extent the movement out of the central city expressed (and expresses) the desire of offspring of immigrant parents to cut themselves off both from the slum or semi-slum, and from status attributes that it more or less symbolized. To some extent, too, it expressed the desire for more living space and for the satisfactions of rural life. There was also an economic factor at work. It was more costly to create the kind of houses and neighborhoods that were wanted in the central city, where lots were too small and houses had to be rebuilt, than to start afresh in a new suburb. Central-city neighborhoods that were only twenty or thirty years old were, by the standards of the more prosperous 1940's and 1950's, obsolete. Nothing, therefore, could prevent the mass migration of the middle class from the central city and its abandonment of most of the housing built in the first decades of the century.

From the New Deal on, the flight to the suburbs was encouraged, although inadvertently, by the federal government. The Federal Housing Administration (created in 1934) and, since World War II, the Veterans Administration, have insured (and hence subsidized) loans for the purchase of houses. Because both agencies were concerned about the soundness of the loans they guaranteed, they virtually limited them to the financing of *new* homes, which meant, for all practical purposes, homes in the new suburbs. By 1959 the FHA had "helped to make it possible for three out of every five American families to own their own homes."[2]

[2] U.S. Federal Housing Administration, "The FHA Story in Summary, 1934–1959" (FHA 375).

The movement to the suburbs began long before expressways were built to make automobile travel convenient. No matter how congested the roads, there were plenty of people ready to commute. The heavy subsidization of expressway construction by the state and federal governments was intended in part to bring new life to the downtown business districts of the central cities. The cities tore themselves open to make way for new superhighways in order to attract shoppers back to their big department stores. The improvement in transportation, however, had the unintended effect of encouraging even more people to live outside the city while working in it, or—in more and more cases —to live *and* work outside it.[3]

The central-city housing left by the middle class has been taken over by the poor. The densest slums in the center of the city have lost population and the better neighborhoods in the outlying sections have gained it. This has been going on for many years, but the rate has been dramatic in the last decade or so. In Philadelphia, for example, a district between the two rivers, the oldest, poorest, and most overcrowded part of the city, lost almost 20 percent of its population between 1950 and 1960 and now contains 72 percent fewer people than it did a hundred years ago. Figure 1 shows the Philadelphia trend in the 1950's. A similar trend could be shown for many large American cities.

This rapid spreading out has made the slum increasingly visible in recent years and has given many middle-class people the impression that there is a new and growing "slum problem." Actually, the cities have fewer slum dwellers now than ever before. The difference is that the slums are now less dense and less centralized. From the standpoint of the poor, this is a very good thing. A family that used to live in a decaying tenement with fifty or a hundred other families thinks itself (and is) much better off in a place that is merely dilapidated and that is lived in by only two or three other families. But to those middle-class people who are not yet ready to move out of the transitional neighborhoods or who look back nostalgically from the suburbs at the "nice" neighborhoods where they grew up, the "invasion" of the slum dwellers seems a catastrophe.

That the slum dwellers are mostly Negroes (and, in a few cities, Puerto Ricans) makes the spread of the slum all the more conspicuous,

[3] For a summary of the effects of the highway program, see U.S. Department of Commerce, "Studies of the Economic and Social Effects of Highway Improvement," *Final Report of the Highway Cost Allocation Study*, part 6, House doc. 72, 87th Congress, 1st session, 1961.

FIGURE 1. Population changes in Philadelphia by Congressional district, 1950–1960

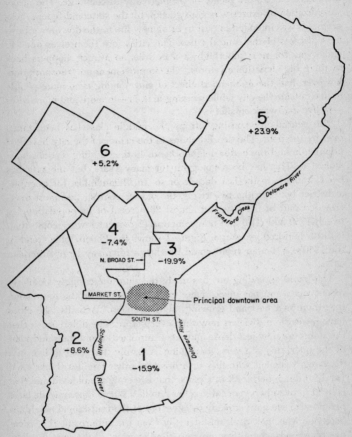

Source: U.S. Bureau of the Census, *Congressional District Data Book* (87th Congress), 1961.

and, for some people, all the more horrifying. The existence of large stocks of both jobs and poor housing (poor by middle-class standards, that is) has enabled a great many Negroes to come to the central cities from the small towns of the South. As Table 1 illustrates, migration and a high rate of natural increase have dramatically increased the number and proportion of Negroes in many cities.

TABLE 1. Percentage of nonwhites in large cities, 1950 and 1960*

City	1950	1960	City	1950	1960
Boston	5.3	9.8	Milwaukee	3.6	8.9
Chicago	14.1	23.6	New York City	9.8	14.7
Cincinnati	15.6	21.8	Philadelphia	18.3	26.7
Cleveland	16.3	28.9	Pittsburgh	12.3	16.8
Dallas	13.2	19.3	Richmond	31.7	42.0
Detroit	16.4	29.2	San Francisco	10.5	18.4
Houston	21.1	23.2	St. Louis	10.0	28.8
Kansas City	12.3	17.7	Washington	35.4	54.8
Los Angeles	10.7	16.8			

* In most places, the number of nonwhites who are not Negro is insignificant.

Source: 1960 Census of the Population, vol. PC (1)-1B.

Until recently, Negroes found it almost impossible to get housing outside of segregated slums. It was poor whites, not Negroes, who left the slums for the neighborhoods that the middle-class suburbanites vacated. Negroes got additional housing, if they got it at all, by "taking over," sometimes at the risk of life and limb, one block after another on the perimeter of their slums. Late in the 1950's, however, the supply of housing caught up with the backlog of demand that had been generated by the war and by the large number of new families formed in the postwar period. Furthermore, the United States Supreme Court ruled in 1948 that "restrictive covenants" in property deeds could no longer be enforced to prevent the sale of homes to Negroes. White sellers then had both an incentive and an opportunity to sell to Negroes. Negroes have since been increasingly able to spread out into declining areas everywhere in the central cities and older suburbs.[4]

About half the jobs in an urban area exist to supply wants that arise because of the presence of the urban dwellers. As people move to sub-

[4] See Davis MacEntire, *Residence and Race* (Berkeley and Los Angeles: University of California Press, 1961).

urbs, many jobs therefore go with them. Industry also tends to move outward when the central city ceases to be the only source of a labor supply. The central business district then becomes more and more a place for such businesses as require frequent face-to-face communication with a large and varied clientele. A businessman, for example, may find it indispensable to be where he can talk face to face with bankers, public officials, and other businessmen. But the record-keeping departments of his firm may very well be decentralized to the suburbs where land is cheaper and where many typists, business machine operators, and accountants live.

All these changes have created acute problems for the central cities. Their tax bases have shrunk from the loss of industry, business, and middle-class homeowners. But demands for city services have not decreased. Indeed, the replacement of the middle class by the lower has necessitated increased expenditures for fire, police, welfare, education, and other services.

The departure of the middle class from the central city is important in other ways as well. The middle class supplies a social and political leavening in the life of a city. Middle-class people demand good schools and integrity in government. They support churches, lodges, parent-teacher associations, scout troops, better-housing committees, art galleries, and operas. It is the middle class, in short, that asserts a conception of the public interest. Now its activity is increasingly concentrated in the suburbs.

Living in the suburbs does not, however, prevent the owners and managers of the largest enterprises of the central city from participating actively in its affairs. To members of this elite, the central city—or rather its central business district—is not only the locus of their wealth but also the center of their cultural lives and the symbol of values that they cherish. Although they continue as business and civic leaders, the members of this elite are as a rule disqualified by their residence in the suburbs for elective and appointive office in the city. For this reason, it is no longer easy to find wealthy and cultivated people to serve on boards of education, housing and redevelopment authorities, park boards, and the like.

The middle-class people whose stake in the central city was never so large—who do not own department stores or newspapers and are not trustees of its hospitals and museums—tend to lose all interest in it when they move to the suburbs. For many of them, it symbolizes a social status they have transcended. It is a place where "undesirables" live, and it is run by "corrupt politicians." The suburbanite commonly feels no responsibility to contribute to the financial support of the central city.

What has happened to the central cities has happened to many of the older suburbs and small cities as well. These have also begun to decay at the center as residents of old neighborhoods have moved out in search of more spacious, convenient, aesthetically satisfying, and prestigious places to live. Lower-class and lower-middle-class people, including, of course, Negroes, wait watchfully for housing to be "downgraded." Poor whites (but not Negroes) tend to "leapfrog" the newer suburbs to take root near the centers of the older suburbs, and to convert these neighborhoods that are obsolete by the standards of the middle class into slums and semi-slums.

It is often assumed that the flight of the middle class to the suburbs, urban sprawl, poor housing, unsatisfactory race relations and other characteristically urban problems exist chiefly in the large cities, especially such great metropolitan centers as New York, Chicago, and Los Angeles. Actually, as James G. Coke has shown with respect to Illinois, all of the same problems are to be found,[5] often in more marked degree, in many small cities. The difference is that in the large cities there is lively concern and protest about conditions that go almost unnoticed in the small ones. This, Coke very convincingly argues, is to be explained largely by political factors—especially the existence in the large cities of a larger number of highly organized and articulate special-interest constituencies, a larger number of policy-oriented professionals, and voluntary associations devoted to some form of community problem-solving.

Newburgh, New York, the city that broke into the national news in 1961 by defying the generally accepted standards for city welfare programs, is an example of a small place in the toils of these changes. Originally a whaling port on the Hudson River, it was long a predominantly middle-class trading center for the surrounding farm country. In recent years, prosperity and automobiles encouraged many of the better-off people to move out of town. This made it possible for less prosperous people to move into the places they had vacated. Eventually Negro

[5] James G. Coke, "The Lesser Metropolitan Areas of Illinois," *Illinois Government*, no. 15, November 1962, published by the Institute of Government and Public Affairs, University of Illinois, Urbana, Ill.

migratory fruit pickers settled in four ancient waterfront slums. Suddenly Newburgh found itself with a serious financial problem. The assessed value of its central business district, an important part of the tax base, declined $945,000 in three years. Meanwhile, welfare expenditures rose rapidly; in 1961 the city was spending about $1,000,000, one third of its budget, for welfare (federal and state grants reimbursed it for 55 percent of this). Two thirds of the persons now on relief are Negroes. Some Newburghers blame the city's troubles on the Negroes, and it was against the Negro, of course, that the stringent welfare code was directed in 1961. That the poor must live somewhere and that they may be better off in Newburgh than they were in other places is not something which Newburgh, occupied as it is with its own troubles, is likely to consider.[6]

In 1960, most suburbs were still almost entirely white. Whereas in 1930 three percent of the suburban population of the twelve largest metropolitan areas was nonwhite, five percent was nonwhite in 1960. In seven of these twelve areas, there was in these thirty years only a slight increase in the proportion of nonwhite to white in the suburbs. In five areas—Philadelphia, Pittsburgh, Washington, Cleveland, and Baltimore—the proportion of nonwhites in the suburbs declined.[7]

The differences between the central city and suburban populations is of profound importance politically.[8] The central-city populations, which are often heavily Catholic, Negro, and lower-class, tend to be Democratic and to tolerate or even favor the old-style machine politics of bosses. The newer residential suburbs (there are, of course, industrial suburbs as well) tend to be Republican, to favor high levels of public service, and to be devoted to "good government."[9] The suburbanite is as anxious to turn his back on the tradition of the "boss" as on the old slum tenement. But not all suburbs have the same political composition, and all are subject to rapid change. As the middle class empties into the new suburbs and the lower class into the deteriorating

---

[6] *Time*, June 29, 1961, p. 17, and *New York Times*, Sept. 17, 1961, p. 64.

[7] *New York Times*, May 7, 1961.

[8] Central cities, industrial suburbs, and old suburbs belong in one category in opposition to all the rest of the metropolitan area, i.e., newer suburbs and unincorporated areas. See Leo F. Schnore and Robert R. Alford, "Forms of Government and Socioeconomic Characteristics of Suburbs," *Administrative Science Quarterly*, June 1963, pp. 1–17.

[9] We have put "good government" in quotation marks here and elsewhere to indicate that we refer to the doctrines of the reform movement, not to what we ourselves regard as good government. The doctrines are discussed in Chapter 11.

portions of the older ones, the Republicanism of some suburbs is being diluted. In some cases this is at least partially offset by the tendency of those who leave the central city to be upwardly mobile individuals who adapt to the suburban environments by becoming Republican or "independent." Some suburbs will become Democratic, but others will become even more solidly Republican. The central cities, however, are likely to remain at least as Democratic as before. The relatively few people who move into them will be mostly lower-class whites, Negroes, and Puerto Ricans.

Even if these population differences did not exist, there still would be important political differences between the central cities and the suburbs. That some people live on one side of a boundary and some live on the other is enough in itself to make an important difference. Those who live in one place (say the suburbs) do not want to be taxed to support facilities and services in another place (say the central city).

The politics of almost every facet of urban government—of metropolitan organization, of housing, of race relations, of transportation, of finance—bears a close relation to the much larger question, which is often outside the view of the interests most actively concerned, of the future of the central city, and, indeed, of the structure and character of urban life. Not far below the surface in all of these matters lie the questions: Is the central city to become the possession of the lower class and of the minority groups or is it to be restored to the middle class? If it is to be restored to the middle class, where is the lower class to live? If it is not restored to the middle class, what will happen to the centers of economic and cultural life in the cores of the central cities? If these centers lose their vitality, how will the pre-eminent role that the central city has played in the creation and dissemination of culture be filled in the future?

CHAPTER 2 · THE POLITICAL FUNCTION

THE FUTURE of the city and the great forces affecting it are talked about in after-dinner speeches sometimes, but they rarely occupy the serious attention of practical men. The questions that *do* occupy their attention are usually of a more immediate and limited kind. Such questions may or may not matter to the community as a whole, but their importance to particular interests is usually great or even crucial, and it is this that brings them to the fore in a practical way. The questions that give rise to most city politics are the following: (1) Who is to be elected to office? (2) Where is some specific facility to be located? (Usually the struggle is between neighborhoods, each trying to *avoid* having the facility for fear that it will displace families, attract "undesirable" people, or depress local property values.) (3) How are taxes to be apportioned? (4) Which agency or official is to be in charge of a particular matter? (5) Is an existing policy or practice to be changed? (6) At what levels are certain services to be supported, and how is the budget to be distributed? (7) What is to be the bias of the police in its treatment of organized crime, labor disputes, and racial incidents?

MANAGING CONFLICT

A government serves two principal functions. One is that of supplying those goods and services—for example, police protection and garbage removal—which cannot be (or at any rate are not) supplied under private auspices. This is its "service function." The other function—the "political" one—is that of managing conflict in matters of public importance.

Since the two functions are performed at the same time by the same set of institutions, they are often concretely indistinguishable. A mayor who intervenes in a dispute about the location of a new public library manages a service at the same time that he settles a conflict, but he usually is thought of, and thinks of himself, as doing a single thing—"running the city government." One function may at times be much more conspicuous than the other. In some cities, the service function is decidedly subordinate to the political one; decisions generally turn on the struggle of politicians, parties, and interest groups for some advantage. In other cities, politics seems to be entirely absent; there are no conflicts and no struggles for power; matters are decided, at least seemingly, on purely technical grounds.

The city without politics is held up as a shining example by some writers on local government. Many people believe that politics in any sphere is pointless and wasteful, a pathological disturbance of social life.

This attitude may arise from a general distaste for conflict and a feeling that matters ought always to be decided reasonably and without contention. A writer on public school administration, for example, upholds this view in the following characteristic terms: "One criterion of how well a school board functions is the extent to which its members agree among themselves. If they are in fair agreement of what the school board should do and about what the duties of the superintendent should be, then, when it comes to making a decision, they will spend little time disagreeing about basic values, about what their jobs actually entail, and devote their energies to solving the problem at hand."[1]

Another reason for disliking politics is that political decisions are often based on considerations entirely unrelated to the merits of the issue. Of course the politician *claims* that his decision is based solely on grounds of efficiency: for example, he favors a certain site for the library "because it will be most convenient to users." But the observer suspects that the *real* grounds of the decision are self-serving or party-serving—that the politician wants the library there because its being there would gain him votes.

It does not necessarily follow, however, that if a politician acts from self-interest he inevitably sacrifices the public interest. Nor is it necessarily true that the public interest is best served by treating the service function of government as more important or more worthy than the political one. It is entirely possible that in some circumstances it is more important to manage conflict than to make the most "efficient" use of resources. If the politician's self-interest leads him to put the library in what the contending interests regard as an acceptable compromise site, he may serve a more useful social function than he would if he

[1] Neal Gross, *Who Runs Our Schools?* (New York: John Wiley and Sons, 1958), p. 85.

decided on purely disinterested grounds to put it where it would be most convenient. Many people's cast of mind is essentially unpolitical, however, and they find it hard to see how the politician's self-interest can serve the public or how any sacrifice of the service function can be justified by any gain in the political one.

City government especially, many people think, ought to be free of politics. In this view, the government of a city differs from other governments, or *should* differ from them, in that it exists solely for the sake of the service function. Cleaning streets, running schools, and collecting garbage ought to be no more controversial, and therefore no more political, than selling groceries. There will be politics in the city government (according to this view) only if it is "injected from the outside"; to prevent this, city government ought to be insulated from state and national government, which are bound to be affected with politics. This is the general idea behind nonpartisanship, and it is one which has greatly affected local government in the United States.

At least two good arguments can be made in support of this view. One is that because of the city's inferior position in the federal system (a matter to be discussed in Chapter 5), all conflicts of real importance must be settled at a higher level. The great questions of the day and, for that matter, most that are not great, cannot fruitfully be discussed by the city council. Such questions as can usefully be discussed by it (for example, the location of the new library) ought to be decided on their merits, which means that considerations of efficiency (the service function) ought to be paramount.

The other argument that can be made is that there are ordinarily no inherent conflicts in the city—no conflicts, that is, which are not the result of politics rather than the cause of it. This is indeed sometimes the case in fairly small, middle-class cities. Where everybody is pretty much agreed on fundamentals, there is certainly much to be said for leaving the choice of means to technicians. In sizable cities, however, there is rarely this agreement on fundamentals. Moreover, even in those places, small or large, where matters are left to technicians, conflict may arise, for the technicians themselves have different and more or less incompatible professional ends. Park, school, and traffic technicians, for example, may disagree about street layouts; and, in the end, politics—albeit generally not under that name—must decide.

Whether one likes it or not, politics, like sex, cannot be abolished. It can sometimes be repressed by denying people the opportunity to practice it, but it cannot be done away with because it is the nature of man to disagree and to contend. We are not saying that politics arises solely from the selfish desire of some to have their way, although that is certainly one source of it. The fact is that even in a society of altruists or angels there would be politics, for some would conceive the common good in one way and some in another, and (assuming the uncertainties that prevail in this world) some would think one course of action more prudent and some would think another.[2]

Whether it is generally desirable to try to repress conflict may also be doubted. Civilized people have a distaste for it because in the ordinary personal relations of life it involves selfishness, deceit, and strong and unpleasant emotions like hate. On the wider stage of political life, however, it does not necessarily involve these. Political struggle is often noble and highminded. To repress it, moreover, is to discourage or prevent some people from asserting their needs, wants, and interests. One can imagine a political system in which there is no struggle because the people in disagreement know that their efforts to exercise influence would have no effect upon events. In such a case politics is absent, but so also are the conditions of progress.

Where there exists conflict that threatens the existence or the good health of the society, the political function should certainly take precedence over the service one. In some cities, race and class conflict has this dangerous character. To govern New York, Chicago, or Los Angeles, for example, by the canons of efficiency—of efficiency *simply* —might lead to an accumulation of restlessness and tension that would eventually erupt in meaningless individual acts of violence, in some irrational mass movement, or perhaps in the slow and imperceptible weakening of the social bonds. Politics is, among other things, a way of converting the restless, hostile impulses of individuals into a fairly stable social product (albeit perhaps a revolution!) and, in doing so, of giving these impulses moral significance.

This suggests another reason why the management of conflict is a social function of the greatest importance. Political struggle, even the seemingly trivial kind that so often exists in the cities, is frequently a part of the rhetoric by which society discusses the nature of the common good and the meaning of justice and virtue. The location of a housing project may not be of much intrinsic importance. But such a question becomes endowed with very great importance when in the

[2] Yves R. Simon, *The Philosophy of Democratic Government* (Chicago: University of Chicago Press, 1951), chap. i.

course of controversy larger issues are connected with it symbolically or ideologically; then the housing matter is the vehicle for the discussion of, say, racial justice and ultimately of justice itself. Society creates its ideals, as judges make laws, by deciding particular cases in the light of general principles. It is only as general principles are brought into contact with particular cases that the principles have meaning.

Finally, politics is a way by which politicians and others get the power they must have to govern. In the American political system, legal authority is so widely distributed that an official—say a mayor—usually lacks authority to do very much. By "playing politics" he in effect borrows additional authority and he also acquires other means of exercising influence. Part II of this book describes at length the process by which power (that is, legal authority plus other means of exercising influence) is assembled in the city. It will suffice here to point out that generating some of the power without which the authorities could not govern is an indispensable function of politics.

POLITICS AS PLAY

In America, perhaps more than anywhere else, politics is also a form of play—a game. *Play* is any activity that is enjoyed for itself and not as a means to some end. A *game* is play that is carried on under rules. Much of our city politics fits these definitions. The ends that are in conflict are often not "really" valued by the players: they are not valued, that is, except for the purposes of the game. To put it still another way, the players value the ends about which they contend *in order that* they may enjoy the game. Much local office seeking, for example, cannot be understood on any assumption other than that people are having fun.

The origins of Tammany Hall, the once powerful Democratic machine in New York City, illustrate the point very well. At the end of the Revolutionary War, certain troops serving under Washington discarded their patron saint, St. George, and adopted instead "St. Tammany." Tamanend had been a noted Indian chief who was supposed to have died at the age of 107 after making a great record as a statesman. The soldiers put on a big celebration to mark the change of patrons. They erected a liberty pole and dressed themselves as Indian warriors with feathers and bucktails. According to Matthew Breen: "From the huge wigwam, which was adorned as befitted the abode of a great chief, came forth the representative of St. Tammany, dressed in the most artistic Indian fashion. To the assembled multitude, composed of civilians as well as soldiers, he gave a 'long talk' on the duty of the hour, dilating upon the virtues of courage, justice, and freedom; after which the warriors danced and caroused far into the night."[3]

Celebrations of this sort occurred in Pennsylvania and elsewhere for several years and then, in 1789, the Tammany Society was organized in New York City. It elected a presiding officer or Grand Sachem and twelve lesser sachems, adopted Indian ceremonies, divided the year into "moons," and issued calls for meetings "one hour after the setting of the sun."

There was an element of seriousness in the Tammany Society, but this does not mean that it was not mostly horseplay. Play is boring, even for little children, unless it can be made serious. Anyone who is a member of a fraternity or lodge knows that exalted purposes are essential to sustain the nonsense.

The "game" and "work" elements of a political incident may therefore be difficult or impossible to separate in some instances, but the distinction is important for analysis nevertheless, because it helps to explain behavior which would be otherwise inexplicable. It also points to a possible danger for society. For although it may be safe to treat make-believe as real, it probably is not safe to treat what is real as make-believe; a politics which is an "interesting game" may in some circumstances be radically unsuited to serve the most important function of politics, the management of conflict that is *real*.

ACTORS IN CITY POLITICS

It is characteristic of the American political system that everyone has a right and even a positive obligation to "get in on the act" of running the government. As heirs to the Protestant tradition, a great many Americans believe that they owe a debt of service to the community; participating in public affairs is one of the ways in which these Americans discharge their obligation to "do good." As heirs of the frontier and of Jacksonian democracy, they believe, too, that the ordinary citizen is qualified to decide any matter of public importance. And, as we have just seen, politics in America has always been a form of mass entertainment. For all these reasons and more, the public

[3] Matthew P. Breen, *Thirty Years of New York Politics Up-To-Date* (Boston, 1899), p. 34.

business is everybody's business to an extent that would astonish other democratic peoples, even the English.

However, most participation in the affairs of the city is by groups and organizations rather than by individuals. Or, to put it properly, it is by individuals acting in group or organizational roles. The individual appears as a "person" on election day to choose between this candidate and that and sometimes to say "yes" or "no" to a few propositions on the ballot. At most other times, "persons" are of little account; groups and organizations are the principal actors.

An exception must be made to this in the case of towns and very small cities. Here formal organizations concerned with governmental affairs may not exist. Informal groupings—crowds, cliques, and circles formed around leading men—take the place of formal organizations to some extent. Whether by themselves or in cliques, individuals are relatively more important in the politics of smaller cities, or else—the two possibilities are by no means exclusive—the level of participation is lower.

Arthur Vidich and Joseph Bensman found this to be the case in a village (which they called Springdale) in upper New York State.[4] Meetings of the village trustees are dull and almost meaningless. There is scarcely ever any new business, projects are rarely undertaken, and few decisions are made. The trustees do what they absolutely must, but avoid whatever they can. Far from seeking power, they seem to shun it. When the trustees act, it is always unanimously; no one ever dissents. Before the vote, however, the "debate" on the issue is long, rambling, uninformed, and inconclusive. No one wants to commit himself or to disagree with his colleagues.

Beneath the surface of Springdale, there are many matters about which some citizens feel concern. The tax assessments have never been reviewed, despite obvious inequities. Some homeowners and some farmers are disturbed about the lack of adequate roads and street lights, deficiencies in the removal of garbage and snow, and occasional failures in water pressure. Others want the town to try to attract industry, and still others are upset by certain school policies. These matters rarely develop into public issues, however, and they almost never lead to governmental action. The one opportunity effectively to challenge the system—the annual election of village trustees—is carefully controlled to prevent struggles for power. Local elections are held

[4] Arthur Vidich and Joseph Bensman, *Small Town Politics in Mass Society* (Princeton, N.J.: Princeton University Press, 1958), chaps. v–viii.

at different times from state and national ones; this reduces turnout and keeps partisan issues from affecting village affairs. The polls are open for only four hours; this further discourages participation, particularly by the commuters who work during the day in nearby cities and may not entirely share the village ethos. Out of about four hundred who are eligible, no more than thirty-five vote, and on occasion as few as fifteen. Slates are made up after consultation with everyone "who counts" and are rarely opposed.

This pattern is characteristic of many small places. It can be explained on several grounds. For one thing, there is not much at stake in small-town politics; no large formal organizations are concerned in it and, since the governing body spends very little, citizens and taxpayers have little to gain or lose by what it does. For another thing, the leaders of the town depend for support upon personal associations and friendships and being "good fellows," not upon interest groups and organized constituencies. The most important consideration, however, is probably that the intimacy of small-town life makes harmony, or at least the appearance of it, almost indispensable. Where everyone is in frequent face-to-face contact with almost everyone else, it is essential that all be on good terms. People in such a town have learned from experience that controversies are particularly bitter when they involve "persons" as distinguished from "representatives of organizations." Nothing in small-town politics is as important to most people, consequently, as the preservation of peace and harmony and the maintenance of easy personal relations. The style of this politics therefore reflects this view of things. The tacitly accepted rule of unanimity and the rambling, pointless character of public discussion, for example, are both functional; they insure that no one will be put on the spot, as they probably would be if there were split votes, firm positions, and clear arguments. To put the matter more generally, the function of politics in the small towns is less to resolve issues than, by suppressing them, to enable people to get along with each other while living together in very close contact. In sizable cities, of course, this need does not exist.

In a community which is relatively compact and homogeneous, the idea of a common good tends to be widely shared. Few citizens identify themselves with organizations having rival interests in community politics. There is little need for "interest balancing" and, in any case, it is considered wrong and even immoral. Since the maintenance of organizations is not at stake, there is more likely to be discussion of what is "best for the community." The views of people who are especially disinterested, well-informed, and intelligent, and who represent in a marked degree the ethos of the community, are considered particularly relevant and those of people who speak for special interests are considered irrelevant or are given little weight. Even in the largest and most heterogeneous cities, of course, some issues may be decided largely on the basis of what is "best for the community," and even there some individuals (though usually not many) hold themselves aloof from organizational identifications in order to have the authority that goes with impartiality.[5]

From time to time the search for the common good under arrangements designed to suppress conflict breaks down. When this happens, politics in the small community tends to be more bitter, more divisive, and more explosive than politics in the large city. Issues, once they "break through" social restraints, are likely to polarize the community into hostile camps. James S. Coleman has described the impact of such issues as fluoridation, desegregation, and school policy on various small communities. There are few, if any, large impersonal organizations which seek to mitigate the conflict in order to preserve themselves. There are no established channels for the expression of disagreement. Since organized interests are not involved, issues tend to become ideological and their settlement imposes heavy strains on the social fabric.[6] James G. Coke has noted that protests and calls for remedial civic action are "endemic in the large, but weak and episodic in the small" metropolitan centers; the larger the city, he says, the more likely it is to have its attention called to social problems and the more likely also to deal with problems by making rules rather than by treating cases individually; the application of rules, he thinks, is likely to lead to conflict.[7]

The participation of individuals in politics probably tends to be reduced where strong organizations exist, because organizations are apt to push individuals out and to pre-empt the field of controversy for themselves. This happens because organizations are impelled by a dynamic, immanent in the process of organization, to select and manage issues in ways that individuals do not.

[5] Edward C. Banfield, *Political Influence* (New York: Free Press of Glencoe, 1961), p. 250.
[6] James S. Coleman, *Community Conflict* (Glencoe, Ill.: Free Press, 1959), p. 4.
[7] James G. Coke, "The Lesser Metropolitan Areas of Illinois," *Illinois Government*, no. 15, November 1962, published by the Institute of Government and Public Affairs, University of Illinois, Urbana, Ill.

The organizations which participate in big-city politics are of two general sorts, permanent and *ad hoc*. The *ad hoc* ones are, of course, those that come into being to participate in a particular issue and then either dissolve or else convert themselves into permanent ones.

The permanent organizations which play continuing roles in city politics are of five general kinds: (1) the press; (2) other business firms, especially department stores and the owners and managers of real estate; (3) the city bureaucracies; (4) voluntary (or "civic") associations; and (5) labor unions. Each of these will be treated later in a separate chapter.

Except for the press, which concerns itself with the whole spectrum of civic activity, the permanent and *ad hoc* organizations which participate in city politics usually confine themselves to rather narrow ranges of subject matter. Wallace Sayre and Herbert Kaufman classify nongovernmental groups in New York City by frequency of intervention and scope of influence.[8] On their chart, the quadrant representing high frequency and broad scope is very sparsely populated, containing only the press, the League of Women Voters, and the Citizens' Union. That representing high frequency and narrow scope is heavily populated, and the organizations in it (concerned mainly with health, education, and welfare) tend to be permanent. That representing broad scope and low frequency is almost empty. The remaining quadrant, representing low frequency and narrow scope, is heavily populated with *ad hoc* bodies—letterhead organizations that quickly come and quickly go.

Any organization must offer a continuous stream of incentives to elicit the activities that it requires from its members or other "contributors" (taxpayers, customers, patrons). In large, permanent, formal organizations these incentives are largely pecuniary (e.g., salary) or at least material. But the maintenance of such organizations depends also upon their ability to offer certain nonmaterial incentives, such as prestige, association with pleasant or interesting people, and the opportunity to "do good." If it is to grow, or even to survive, every organization must offer a suitable mixture of such incentives—material, nonmaterial, or both—and it must offer them in sufficient quantity and without interruption.[9]

[8] Wallace S. Sayre and Herbert Kaufman, *Governing New York City* (New York: Russell Sage Foundation, 1960), p. 79.

[9] See Chester I. Barnard, *The Functions of the Executive* (Cambridge, Mass.: Harvard University Press, 1938).

Voluntary associations (such as welfare organizations and housing and planning associations) rely mainly upon nonmaterial incentives, especially opportunities to "serve the community," to mix with "important people," to engage in activity which is "interesting." Because they must provide such incentives in order to survive, associations of this sort are always in search of "good program material," that is, topics or issues which will bring the right people together and arouse in them the enthusiasm needed to sustain the organization. The range of suitable program material is in the nature of the case limited.[10]

HOW ISSUES ARISE AND ARE HANDLED

These considerations help to explain how political issues arise in the city and how they are handled after they arise. Sometimes an issue is created by a politician in the course of his effort to get or keep office. Sometimes they arise because a voluntary association has put in motion certain legal machinery—as, for example, when a civic group gets enough signatures on a petition to compel the city to hold a referendum on a new city charter. More commonly, however, they arise in response to the maintenance and enhancement needs of large formal organizations. These are not, as a rule, voluntary associations. Typically they are organizations which offer mainly material rather than nonmaterial incentives (i.e., which must meet a payroll). The manager of such an organization sees some advantage in changing the status quo. He proposes changes. Other large formal organizations are threatened by the proposed changes. They oppose them, and a controversy which involves public authorities takes place.

One of the authors of this book found that the six city-wide controversies that occurred in Chicago in a two-year period could be analyzed in these terms.[11] In one case, a large private hospital felt threatened by heavy demands for service from low-income Negroes. Its managers proposed that the county build a public hospital nearby. This idea was opposed by the existing county hospital, a very large institution on the other side of the city. The two principal antagonists, both large organizations depending mainly upon material incentives, gathered about them various allies. The private hospital, for example, was supported by the Welfare Council, an association of organizations dealing with

---

[10] Martin Meyerson and Edward C. Banfield, *Politics, Planning, and the Public Interest* (Glencoe, Ill.: Free Press, 1955), pp. 144–145.

[11] Banfield, *Political Influence;* see especially chap. ix.

welfare matters; by a civic-minded millionaire; and by the newspapers. In the other Chicago cases, the prime-mover organizations were the city and county welfare departments, a university, a forest preserve district, a transit authority, a department store, and a newspaper.

Sometimes an issue is created, so to speak, out of thin air by an organization that is searching for program material. One of the Chicago cases, for example, arose when the *Chicago Tribune*, anxious to demonstrate its power and to memorialize its late editor and publisher, Colonel Robert R. McCormick, fought a long, hard, and successful battle to have an exhibition hall built under public auspices on the lake front. When the editor was asked why the paper had made such a fuss about the hall, he replied:

Why did we put so much time into this? Because it's good for the city. But partly from selfish motives too. We want to build a bigger Chicago and a bigger *Tribune*. We want more circulation and more advertising. We want to keep growing, and we want the city to keep growing so that we can keep growing.

We think the community respects a newspaper that can do things like that. People will go by that hall and say, "See that? The *Tribune* did that single-handed." That's good for us to have them say that.

If it hadn't come off—if those lawsuits had turned out wrong—it would not have been good. It's good that people should think that their newspaper is powerful. It's good that it be powerful.[12]

When a large organization is the prime mover in a civic controversy, the chief executive of the organization normally plays a crucial role in development of the controversy. In the struggle between the private and the public hospital in Chicago, the chief strategists on both sides were the medical superintendents of the hospitals. In the case of the exhibition hall the strategists were the editor of the *Tribune* and the owner of a private amphitheater which would be damaged by competition from the new hall.

The chief executives of the prime-moving organizations do not ordinarily appear in the matter conspicuously. They much prefer the background. They are used to doing things through subordinates. Unless they are newspaper executives they are reluctant, for reasons of public relations, to have their organizations involved openly in controversies. For example, when the University of Chicago decided to do something drastic about the spread of blight in its neighborhood, it set up the Southeast Commission. This was largely controlled by

[12] *Ibid.*, p. 231.

the university—that is, by the chancellor and his subordinates—but it had a separate board of directors and a separate letterhead, and could at least claim to be "broadly based" and representative of "the whole community."[13]

This is what often happens. The principally affected, or prime-moving, organization sets up a "front" organization like the Southeast Commission, or else it gets voluntary associations to "front" for it. For the voluntary association there are usually definite advantages in such an arrangement; the prime-moving organization not only supplies it with good program material but, perhaps, with financial assistance as well.

Local government agencies—city departments and special-function districts, for example—are often the prime-moving organizations, and they therefore commonly foster close, continuing relationships with at least one voluntary association which can be depended upon to "front" for them when necessary. We are in the habit of thinking that pressure groups use public agencies, and of course they often do. But the influence commonly runs the other way as well, the public agency using the pressure group, and there are a good many cases where the "pressure group" exists solely to be used by the public agency.

The public agitation of a civic issue is likely, therefore, to be carried on by co-opted voluntary associations which pass resolutions, testify before legislative committees, issue press releases, wait on the mayor, and then at the end of the year give testimonial dinners to acclaim themselves for "civic leadership."

The elected officials, who of course have the authority to decide matters, watch the maneuvers of the prime-moving organizations and their co-opted agents with critical attention. They know well enough what is going on behind the scenes and they know approximately how many—if any—votes the organizations may be able to swing. Usually they wait as long as possible before making a decision. They know that as long as they do nothing they are probably safe, and, anyway, they want to allow time for public opinion to form. When a magazine writer suggested to Mayor Richard J. Daley of Chicago that the mayor had never in his whole life committed himself to anything whatsoever until he absolutely had to, the mayor laughed. "That's a pretty good way to be, don't you think?" he said. "Pretty good way to run any business."

[13] Peter H. Rossi and Robert A. Dentler, *The Politics of Urban Renewal* (New York: Free Press of Glencoe, 1961), pp. 72–84.

But this tendency to let proposals affecting city affairs arise and be fought over by nongovernmental organizations (or at any rate by organizations which do not have responsibility for the city government as a whole) is not merely an expression of the politician's shrewdness. In the United States, the public takes the view that the elected official ought not to make and impose a policy of his own; instead, he should preside over and exercise final authority in a struggle among private and partial interests in which they try to get their policies adopted. This explains, perhaps, why the mayor of Minneapolis, the politics of which is as different from that of Chicago as could be imagined, follows the same strategy as Mayor Daley. According to Alan Altshuler, the mayor of Minneapolis does not actively sponsor anything: "He waits for private groups to agree upon a project. If he likes it, he endorses it. Since he has no formal power with which to pressure the Council himself, he feels that the private groups must take responsibility for getting their plans accepted."[14]

Sometimes (and, as we shall suggest later, more frequently now than in the past) mayors do create issues. Several, for example, have taken the initiative on urban renewal. This seems to be most often the tactic of a mayor who takes office without much prior civic achievement to point to and without a strong party organization to produce votes for him. Sometimes it is an ambitious man's response to a situation in which general dissatisfaction with the local government has afforded an opportunity for spectacular, visible (and popular) innovation. But the advantages in being a bold, vigorous leader—if, indeed, they are real and not based on misconceptions—are fleeting; often, after a first wave of mayor-initiated programs, the situation returns to normal and the mayor finds that discretion is the better part of valor.

That the seriousness with which an issue is taken depends so much upon considerations of organizational maintenance and enhancement has wide implications for the political life of the city. What happens in those matters in which no organization's maintenance is involved? What happens in those which do not afford good program material to the voluntary associations and the press? Such matters are not likely to come to public attention at all. It is easy to think of examples of matters that might be issues but almost never are. Municipal justice is one. In several cities, large organizations have a stake in the enforce-

[14] Alan Altshuler, *Minneapolis City Politics Report* (Cambridge, Mass.: Joint Center for Urban Studies, 1959, mimeo), pp. 14–15.

ment, or non-enforcement, of building and housing codes, and accordingly this particular kind of court case is often in the news in these cities. But so far as we know there are no large organizations in any city with a stake in seeing that justice is done in, say, cases of breaches of the peace or vagrancy, and the quality of justice in these is therefore hardly ever the subject of a civic controversy.

For example, a study of vagrancy law in Philadelphia showed that it was seriously abused.[15] At certain times of the year, the police force conducted "drives" to keep "undesirables" out of some areas. In a typical day at the courts, fifty-five vagrancy cases were heard within fifteen minutes. Four defendants were tried, found guilty, and sentenced within seventeen seconds. "In each of these cases the magistrate merely read off the name of the defendant, took one look at him and said, 'Three months in the House of Correction.'" Some who were discharged were told to get out of Philadelphia or out of certain sections of it. After being discharged, some defendants were kept to mop up the building for a couple of hours because work was "good for them," but if one of them contributed a dollar or more to the magistrate's favorite charity (collected in a Heart Fund box), he was permitted to leave at once. These "drives" were given extensive newspaper coverage. The *Philadelphia Inquirer* in particular ran editorials and stories under headings like "Get the Bums Off the Streets and Into Prison Cells." When the newspaper publicity let up, magistrates became less harsh and would often dismiss the cases with a joke. Justice, however, was still largely hit or miss. "When you get tired of seeing their faces," one magistrate said, "you send them to correction."

The author of the study concluded that "the only reason such administration is tolerated" is that the defendants involved "are too poor or too weak to assert their obvious rights." No doubt this was the ultimate reason. But the proximate one was that no large organizations—except perhaps the newspapers, which were on the other side—had any maintenance or enhancement interest at stake in the situation.

[15] Caleb Foote, "Vagrancy-Type Law and Its Administration," *University of Pennsylvania Law Review,* vol. CIV (1956), p. 603.

CHAPTER 3 · CLEAVAGES

ISSUES arise out of, or at least are nourished from, the more lasting divisions in the society that we have called cleavages. These are conflicts that run from issue to issue, and which divide the community into "we" and "they."

In some communities there are few lines of cleavage and none that run very deep. There are many villages and small cities in the United States with extremely homogeneous populations; conflict occurs in these, of course, but the grouping of forces is *ad hoc*. It is necessary to choose up sides afresh for every conflict, because there are no lasting principles of division, or, to change the metaphor, no fault line along which a fissure opens when pressure is applied.

THE URBAN-RURAL CLEAVAGE

Historically the principal division affecting city politics has not been *within* the city, but between the countryside and the city. This cleavage goes back to the very beginnings of our history; since colonial days, Americans have cherished the myth that the farmer is morally superior to the city dweller. The view of the city as the harlot bent on corrupting the simple, wholesome countryman has been accepted not only by countrymen, but, to a surprising extent, by city dwellers as well.

In turn, some city dwellers, particularly liberals, have in recent years viewed with increasing dismay the "backward" and "selfish" attitudes of rural people. In part this is a reaction to the success of rural areas in frustrating the attainment of urban liberal objectives; in part it springs from the contempt in which the city slicker has always held the "country bumpkin."

The long-standing antipathy of "upstate" or "downstate" to the big city is in some cases a reflection of original differences in culture. Chicago, for example, was settled by immigrants from Ohio and New York, whereas "downstate" Illinois was settled by immigrants from the border states and the South. When Chicago was hardly more than a village and contained no "foreigners" to speak of, it was actively disliked by the rural hinterland. The downstate Southerners could see even then that eventually the city—the Northerners—would dominate the state. Today traces of this old hostility remain. Cotton is still grown in Southern Illinois, and a lobbyist who speaks with a trace of a southern accent gets a better reception in Springfield, other things being equal, than one who does not.

Historically, alcohol was the issue over which the rural hinterland was most generally at odds with the city. Rural Protestants—Methodists and Baptists—were much affected in the nineteenth century by evangelical preachers for whom abstinence from alcohol was almost synonymous with virtue. The city was the place of the saloon, and the Methodists and Baptists loathed the Papists and Lutherans who drank whiskey and beer there.[1]

Although some of the old distrust of the country for the city still exists, the farm population is now so diminished in numbers as to make it politically unimportant in most places. In Wisconsin, the voters recently instituted daylight saving time, something farmers detest. This may be taken as a sign of the times: it is not farmers but rural nonfarm and small-town people who now hold the power upstate or downstate. Such people may accept some of the old mythology about rural goodness and urban badness, but the conditions of life in small towns are today not so different as they used to be from the conditions of life in the city, and this tends to make for understanding and collaboration. A city administrator in Cincinnati recently told an interviewer: "The legislature is rural-controlled, but the character of the representation from former rural areas is changing; where those areas are becoming part of a metropolitan community, they are beginning to have the same industrial urban problems that we have. Their point of view is changing."[2]

The rural point of view is no doubt changing, but in many places it is still a good deal different from that of the city. By and large, the rural and small-town areas are unwilling to let the cities have high levels of public services even when it is the city taxpayer who will pay for them. Rural people are often inclined to think that the cities are spending more than they should for schools, police, and, especially,

[1] D. W. Brogan, in *An Introduction to American Politics* (London: Hamish Hamilton, 1954), chap. v, describes the saloon struggle at the turn of the century.
[2] Kenneth Gray, *A Report on City Politics in Cincinnati* (Cambridge, Mass.: Joint Center for Urban Studies, 1959, mimeo).

welfare services. The voters of upstate New York, for example, have repeatedly refused to allow New York City to increase its debt and to expand school and other such facilities.[3]

The cleavage between the hinterland and the city has probably tended (and probably still tends) to prevent mayors from rising to higher offices. Only a few mayors have been elected governor or senator;[4] and mayors—those from the largest cities least of all—are not seriously considered for the Presidency. Even La Guardia, who wanted the nomination very much, never had a chance of getting it, or for that matter of being nominated for governor or senator. To be President, a man must have some identification with the hinterland, or at any rate must not be too exclusively identified with the Big City. That city office is not a route to the great prize—the Presidency—must inevitably discourage some of the most able men from entering city politics. John F. Kennedy, for example, was too ambitious and too astute to begin his career by running for mayor of Boston.

URBAN CLEAVAGES

Within the cities and metropolitan areas the most important cleavages are those between (1) haves and have-nots, (2) suburbanites and the central city, (3) ethnic and racial groups, and (4) political parties. These tend to cut across each other and, in general, to become one fundamental cleavage separating two opposed conceptions of the public interest.

Haves and Have-Nots

Disparity in kinds and distribution of property, James Madison said, is the most fundamental cause of parties and factions in all ages and places. In the city, it is useful to think in terms of three income groups —low, middle, and high. Surprising as it may seem to Marxists, the conflict is generally between an alliance of the low-income and high-income groups on the one side and the middle-income groups on the other. The reason is not hard to find. The poorest people in the city favor a high level of expenditure for welfare, housing, and sometimes

[3] See Lyle C. Fitch, "Fiscal and Political Problems of Increasing Urbanization," *Political Science Quarterly*, vol. LXXI (1956), pp. 80–82.

[4] Governor David Lawrence of Pennsylvania had been mayor of Pittsburgh; Governor Michael DiSalle of Ohio had been mayor of Toledo; Governor and later Senator Frank Lausche of Ohio had been mayor of Cleveland; Senator Hubert Humphrey had been mayor of Minneapolis; Governor Frank Murphy of Michigan had been mayor of Detroit.

schools, and rarely oppose expenditure for any purpose whatever. They favor expenditures even for services that they are not likely to use— municipal opera, for example—because they pay no local taxes, or hardly any. Upper-income people also favor a high level of expenditures. They want good public services for the same reason that they want good private ones—they can afford them. But they also want good, or at any rate adequate, services for others, and they willingly support—although no doubt at levels lower than the poor would like— welfare services which they themselves will never use. Table 2 shows how our largest cities vary with respect to this upper-income group; the percentage of families with $10,000 or more income ranges from about 25 to 10 percent.

TABLE 2. Cities over 500,000 population ranked by the percentage of families with incomes of $10,000 a year or more, 1960

Rank	City	Percent	Rank	City	Percent
1	Los Angeles	25.1	12	Cincinnati	15.8
2	Seattle	22.9	13	Baltimore	15.0
3	San Francisco	22.6	14	Pittsburgh	14.3
4	Washington	21.7	15	Philadelphia	14.2
5	Chicago	21.3	16	Boston	13.6
6	San Diego	20.9	17	Buffalo	13.1
7	Dallas	18.9	18	Cleveland	13.0
8	New York	18.5	19	New Orleans	12.9
9	Detroit	17.8	20	St. Louis	10.8
10	Houston	17.5	21	San Antonio	9.6
11	Milwaukee	16.7			

Source: 1960 Census.

The middle-income group generally wants a low level of public expenditures. It consists of people who are worrying about the mortgage on their bungalow and about keeping up the payments on the new car. Such people are not especially charitable, no doubt partly because they feel they cannot afford to be, but partly, also, perhaps, because they feel that if others are less well off than they it is mainly because the others have not put forth as much effort as they. Many of these people want to spend their money in status-giving ways, and obviously a new car is more status-giving than a new school or a better equipped police force.

The United Auto Workers has tried for years without success to take control of Detroit's nonpartisan government. Detroit is largely a one-industry and one-union town, and the UAW has been extraordinarily successful in state politics, as evidenced by the fact that G. Mennen Williams, the workingman's friend, was elected governor five times. Nevertheless the mayor of Detroit for four terms was Albert E. Cobo, a conservative businessman who opposed public housing and favored economy and efficiency. Why did the working people who voted for Williams for governor vote for Cobo for mayor? The answer may be that Detroit is a predominantly lower-middle-class homeowning town. In partisan state and national elections, a UAW member votes as a "liberal" because the costs of measures he supports will not be assessed against his bungalow. In nonpartisan city elections, however, he votes as a property owner and taxpayer, and in all probability (if he is white) as one who fears that a progressive city government might make it easier for Negroes to move into his neighborhood.

Suburbanites and the Central City

The spectacular recent growth of the suburbs and the not unrelated deterioration of the central city have tended to deepen a long-standing line of cleavage between the city and its suburbs. Today many central cities find that their principal antagonist in the legislature is not the rural hinterland but an alliance of the hinterland and the suburbs.[5]

The suburbs are not all of one kind, of course; they are industrial as well as residential, lower-income as well as upper. Not very far from upper-class suburbs where garbage is collected in paper bags and put in fly-proof trucks and where high school teachers are paid as much as many Ivy League college professors, there may be communities (often unincorporated) in which most people cannot afford or else do not want even such basic amenities as sidewalks, police protection, and community sewage disposal. The upper-income suburbanite fears that by annexation or the creation of a metropolitan-area government he may be brought within the jurisdiction of the central city's government and receive a lower level of government service in consequence. The low-income suburbanite also fears being brought within the jurisdiction of the city, but for an opposite reason: it would insist upon providing

[5] See David R. Derge, "Metropolitan and Outstate Alignments in Illinois and Missouri Legislative Delegations," *American Political Science Review*, December 1958, pp. 1062–1065.

him with—and taxing him for—services that he would rather do without.

This is not the only basis for the cleavage between city and suburb. Central-city residents often think that the city is being exploited by suburbanites, who use its facilities without paying taxes to it. Because the suburbanite comes to the city to work and shop, the city must spend more than it otherwise would for certain public services—traffic control and police protection, for example—but none of this extra expense, the city resident points out, can be charged against the suburbanite. To this, the suburbanite may reply that by coming to the city to work and shop he creates enough taxable values to make the city a net gainer. He may even assert that it is the suburbanite who is the victim of injustice since suburbs must provide expensive public facilities, particularly schools, even though most of the tax base created by suburbanite spending is in the city.[6] When central cities try to annex suburbs or impose taxes upon the earnings of suburbanites who work in the cities, there is always a howl of protest and usually the effort fails.

Ethnic and Racial Groups

Ethnic and racial differences have been, and still are, basic to much of the conflict in the city. Here it will be convenient to speak of three such lines of cleavage: that between native Protestant and all others, that among the various nationality groups of foreign stock, and that between the Negro and all others.

Although the largest waves of immigration ended long ago, some cities, such as New York and Boston, still have, as Table 3 indicates, a sizable number of persons of foreign stock. Other cities, such as Dallas, have scarcely been touched by immigration at all.

Until the latter part of the last century, native Protestant industrialists and businessmen ran most cities. Then, in the Northern cities, when the tide of immigration swelled, the newly arrived ethnic groups began to challenge the natives for political control. For a time there was a sharp conflict, but in most cities the natives soon retired from the scene, or, more precisely, they transferred their activity from one sector of the scene to another.

[6] For some discussion of these claims by an economist, see Julius Margolis, "Metropolitan Finance Problems," in National Bureau of Economic Research, *Public Finances: Needs, Sources, and Utilization* (Princeton, N.J.: Princeton University Press, 1961), especially pp. 256–259.

TABLE 3. Cities over 500,000 population ranked by the percentage of persons foreign-born or with at least one foreign-born parent, 1960

Rank	City	Percent	Rank	City	Percent
1	New York	48.6	12	Philadelphia	29.1
2	Boston	45.5	13	San Antonio	24.0
3	San Francisco	43.5	14	San Diego	21.5
4	Chicago	35.9	15	Baltimore	14.8
5	Buffalo	35.4	16	St. Louis	14.1
6	Los Angeles	32.6	17	Washington	12.6
7	Detroit	32.2	18	Cincinnati	12.0
8	Seattle	31.4	19	Houston	9.7
9	Cleveland	30.9	20	New Orleans	8.6
10	Pittsburgh	30.3	21	Dallas	6.9
11	Milwaukee	30.0			

Source: 1960 Census. The term "foreign-born" does not, of course, include Puerto Ricans.

In Boston, for example, the Irish were able to command a majority beginning about 1890 and the native Protestants thereafter ran the city from the state house. Boston's police commissioner was appointed by the governor and so was its licensing board; a finance commission, also appointed by the governor, was set up to make continuing investigations of the city's affairs and was given the power of subpoena. Much of the interference of the legislatures in the affairs of other large cities at this time and afterward reflected the same cleavage between the outnumbered native Protestants and what Mayor James M. Curley of Boston used to call the "newer races."

In a good many cities, where several new ethnic groups competed for control, the old native Protestant elite might conceivably have retained its control by serving—as the Irish so often have—as a neutral force on which all elements of the ethnic struggle could agree. But the elite was incapacitated for this role by its distaste for the political culture of the new immigrant, a distaste that it did not try to conceal. As Peter and Alice Rossi have shown in an unpublished paper on "Bay City," Massachusetts, local politics, which was a source of prestige for the local industrialists until the immigrants became numerous, was "dirty business" afterwards. Accordingly, the old elite turned from elective office and took up instead the control of a relatively new set of institutions, the community service organizations. The local hospital, Red Cross chapter, Community Chest, and Family Welfare

Society became the arenas in which the "old families," who of course now asserted that there was no prestige in public office, carried on their public activities.[7]

One can see today in many places elements of informal government that have been produced by this cleavage between the "old family" Protestants and the "newer races." A study in 1947 indicated that in "Jonesville," Illinois, the Rotary Club was handpicking the members of the school board.[8] The interviewer was told: "This school board around here has been looked upon as the private property of the Rotary Club for about twenty-five years. The fact is, the school board has been kind of a closed corporation. . . . The boys decide who they want to run. The fact is, they invite them to run." For at least fifteen years prior to 1947, all members of the "Jonesville" school board were Protestant Republicans; only twice in that period did candidates for the board face any opposition.

The Rossis, who are sociologists, in their report on "Bay City" interpret the change in the character of the old elite's public service as a redirection of its drive for status and recognition. Unwilling to play the status game in the same set with the immigrant, the old elite (according to the Rossis) set up its own game and in effect said that henceforth that was to be *the* game.

We prefer a different explanation. The native middle-class Protestant inherited from his Anglo-Saxon ancestors a political ethos very different from that which the new immigrants brought with them. The ethos of the native could not mix with that of the immigrant, and therefore the natives, who were in the minority, retired to a sphere in which they could conduct public affairs in the manner their culture prescribed.

Richard Hofstadter described the difference of ethos very well in *The Age of Reform:*

Out of the clash between the needs of the immigrants and the sentiments of the natives there emerged two thoroughly different systems of political ethics. . . . One, founded upon the indigenous Yankee-Protestant political traditions, and upon middle class life, assumed and demanded the constant, disinterested activity of the citizén in public affairs, argued that political

[7] Peter H. and Alice S. Rossi, "An Historical Perspective on Local Politics," paper delivered at the 1956 meeting of the American Sociological Association (mimeo).

[8] Joseph Rosenstein, "Small-Town Party Politics," unpublished dissertation, Department of Sociology, University of Chicago, 1950.

life ought to be run, to a greater degree than it was, in accordance with general principles and abstract laws apart from and superior to personal needs, and expressed a common feeling that government should be in good part an effort to moralize the lives of individuals while economic life should be intimately related to the stimulation and development of individual character. The other system, founded upon the European background of the immigrants, upon their unfamiliarity with independent political action, their familiarity with hierarchy and authority, and upon the urgent needs that so often grew out of their migration, took for granted that the political life of the individual would arise out of family needs, interpreted political and civic relations chiefly in terms of personal obligations, and placed strong personal loyalties above allegiance to abstract codes of law or morals.[9]

The Anglo-Saxon Protestant middle-class style of politics, with its emphasis upon the obligation of the individual to participate in public affairs and to seek the good of the community "as a whole" (which implies, among other things, the necessity of honesty, impartiality, and efficiency) was fundamentally incompatible with the immigrants' style of politics, which took no account of the community.

The native elite withdrew to the community service organizations because these constituted the only sphere in which their political style could prevail. The boards of these organizations were self-perpetuating; they could not be "crashed" by "outsiders." Because of the nature of their political ethos, Protestants and Jews have been in the vanguard of every fight for municipal reform. In Worcester, Massachusetts, for example, according to Robert Binstock:

> Yankees are the cultural, business, and social leaders—in short, "the first families of Worcester." They are not numerous enough to control the governmental apparatus of the city, yet by forming an alliance with the Scandinavians, they manage to place two representatives on the City Council. The influence of the Yankee within the city government is limited, but participation in a strong and active citizens association, the CEA, enables this group to enlarge its role in the political process.
> The Jews, more often than not, are political allies of the Yankees and Scandinavians. . . .[10]

Conflict as between one immigrant ethnic group and another has tended to be over "recognition"—the prestige that accrues to a nationality group when one of its members is elected to public office. Since

[9] Richard Hofstadter, *The Age of Reform* (New York: Alfred A. Knopf, 1955), p. 9.

[10] Robert H. Binstock, *A Report on Politics in Worcester, Mass.* (Cambridge, Mass.: Joint Center for Urban Studies, 1961, mimeo), part V, p. 2.

in the nature of the case there cannot be enough recognition to go around (if all were equally recognized, none would be recognized at all), the question of which groups are to get it must inevitably lead to conflict. The avidity of the "newer" ethnic groups to see their kind in office has been, and still is, of great importance, both as a motive force in the political system and because of certain incidental effects.

When one recalls the contempt with which "micks," "wops," and "polacks" were once—and to some extent still are—treated by some other Americans, no further explanation of the appeal of ethnic "recognition" is needed. But an additional reason is that ethnic politics, like sports, entertainment, and crime, provided a route of social mobility to people who were to a large extent excluded from power in business and industry. Mayor Daley of Chicago was born behind the stockyards. John E. Powers, the president of the Massachusetts Senate, began life as a clam digger.

One would expect that as the "newer" ethnic groups became assimilated to the middle class, they would become assimilated to the Anglo-Saxon Protestant political ethos as well, and that their interest in ethnic politics would decline accordingly. This seems to be happening, but at different rates among different groups. Jews, particularly those in the reform tradition, seem to acquire the Protestant political ethos very readily.[11] It is interesting that the Jews have not sought ethnic "recognition" in city politics to the extent that other groups have. It may be that they have never doubted their worth as a group, and therefore have not felt any need for public reassurance. More likely, however, their political ethos is such that a politics of ethnic appeal strikes them, as it does the Anglo-Saxon Protestant, as uninteresting and even immoral.

Other ethnic groups also seem to be taking on the middle-class political ethos, but to be doing it more slowly. Third-generation Poles, for example, usually show a decided preference for Polish candidates,

[11] Compare the findings of Edgar Litt: "Jewish Ethno-Religious Involvement and Political Liberalism," *Social Forces*, May 1961, pp. 328–332; "Ethnic Status and Political Perspectives," *Midwest Journal of Political Science*, August 1961, pp. 276–283; and "Status, Ethnicity, and Patterns of Jewish Voting Behavior in Baltimore," *Jewish Social Studies*, July 1960, pp. 159–164. Litt argues that the basis of Jewish identification with the Democratic party varies with socio-economic status: upper-class Jews are Democratic because they see the party as an instrument of "social justice" on national and international issues; lower-class Jews are Democratic because they see it as a source of material benefits and economic welfare. These findings are broadly consistent with our argument about political ethos.

and third-generation Italians usually prefer Italian candidates. Middle-class Irish Catholics who seem entirely to have shed the mentality that caused the immigrant to vote on the basis of personal loyalty to a ward politician are nevertheless rarely found in the ranks of the civic reformers; these are almost all Protestants and Jews.

Where the taste for ethnic recognition persists, it is for a special kind of recognition, however. The candidate must not be *too* Polish, *too* Italian, or *too* Irish in the old style. The following description of Jewish candidates in Worcester suggests the trend:

> Israel Katz, like Casdin, is a Jewish Democrat now serving his fourth term on the Worcester City Council. Although he is much more identifiably Jewish than Casdin, he gets little ethnic support at the polls; there is a lack of rapport between him and the Jewish voter. The voter apparently wants to transcend many features of his ethnic identification and therefore rejects candidates who fit the stereotype of the Jew too well. Casdin is an assimilated Jew in Ivy-League clothes; Katz, by contrast, is old world rather than new, clannish rather than civic-minded, and penny-pinching rather than liberal. Non-Jews call Katz a "character," Casdin a "leader." It is not too much to say that the Jews, like other minorities, want a flattering, not an unflattering, mirror held up to them.[12]

Apparently, nowadays, the nationality-minded voter prefers candidates who represent the ethnic group but at the same time display the attributes of the generally admired Anglo-Saxon model. The perfect candidate, then, is of Jewish, Polish, Italian, or Irish extraction and has the speech, dress, manner, and the public virtues—honesty, impartiality, and devotion to the public interest—of the upper-class Anglo-Saxon.

The cleavage between white and Negro is pervasive in city politics. Until World War II, few Northern cities had many Negroes. As we have already seen, the Negro population of most Northern cities now is growing at a very rapid rate, partly from natural increase and partly from migration from the rural South. The new arrivals go into the Negro slum, which almost everywhere is the oldest part of the central city, where housing has been swept by successive waves of low-status and low-income migrants. For many years restrictive covenants, written into deeds and prohibiting sale of property to Negroes, made it difficult or impossible for Negroes to buy in districts that were not already Negro; their districts therefore became more and more crowded. But after 1948, when the Supreme Court declared such

[12] Binstock, part II, pp. 33–34.

covenants to be unenforceable in the courts, the Negro community began to spread more rapidly.[13]

In many Northern cities, the question of where Negroes are to live lies behind almost every proposal for civic action. Will locating a major highway here prevent them from "invading" that white neighborhood? And where will those Negroes who are displaced by an urban renewal project resettle? If a school or a hospital is placed here or there, will it bring Negroes to the neighborhood? And if it does, will the neighborhood eventually "tip" and become all Negro?

Many whites have fled to the suburbs to get away from the Negroes. One reason why many suburbanites want to remain politically separate from the central city is that they think this will make it easier for them to resist "invasion" by Negroes.

In all this, upper-class Negroes exhibit much the same attitude as do whites. Everything that we have said of the reaction of whites to Negroes can also be said of the reaction of upper-class Negroes to lower-class ones.

Political Parties

The central cities are almost all heavily Democratic; the suburbs tend to be heavily Republican, although there are many exceptions, and their Republicanism is nowhere near as solid or stable as the Democracy of the central cities.

The Democratic ascendancy is so great in most central cities that cleavage along party lines within the cities is not of great practical importance. Party cleavage is important, however, in matters that involve both the central city and the area which lies outside of it. Table 4 shows how the biggest cities voted in the Presidential election of 1960.

About 60 percent of all cities (but fewer large ones) are nonpartisan, which means that candidates are not chosen in party primaries and are not identified by party on the ballot. In some places, there are purely local parties—the "blues" and the "yellows," so to speak—and in other places local politics is carried on without anything that could properly be called a party (it is "unorganized"). Some cities are nominally nonpartisan and actually partisan (Chicago is an example) and others are nominally partisan and actually nonpartisan in the sense of having no connection with the *national* parties (La Guardia, for

[13] *Shelley v. Kraemer,* 334 U.S. 1 (1948).

TABLE 4. Cities over 500,000 population° ranked by the Democratic percentage of their 1960 Presidential vote

Rank	City	Percent	Rank	City	Percent
1	Boston	74.7	9	Baltimore	63.9
2	Detroit	71.0	10	Chicago	63.6
3	Cleveland	70.9	11	New York	62.8
4	Philadelphia	68.1	12	Milwaukee	61.8
5	Pittsburgh	67.0	13	San Francisco	58.0
6	St. Louis	66.6	14	Cincinnati	50.4
7	New Orleans	64.9	15	Seattle	48.8
8	Buffalo	64.9			

° No data available on Dallas, Houston, Los Angeles, San Antonio, or San Diego. Residents of Washington, D.C., could not vote. The figures for Buffalo and New York City combine the vote for President Kennedy on both the Democratic and Liberal party lines.
Source: Richard M. Scammon, *American Votes 4* (Pittsburgh: University of Pittsburgh Press, 1962).

example, was a nominal Republican who ran on a Fusion ticket, and so was in this sense nonpartisan).

The most interesting thing about party, with respect to the present analysis, is that it is an *artificially-created* cleavage which cuts across all other cleavages and often supersedes them in importance: party "regularity" requires that the voter ignore all cleavages except the party one. The party cleavage *has* to cut across others because in the nature of things there are no general organizing principles under which all cleavages can be subsumed. The nearest thing to general organizing principles, perhaps, are "conservatism" and "liberalism." But the cleavages in the city do not fall logically into this or any other pattern; each side of each cleavage stands by itself and ought, in logic, to have its own party. The attachment to party, then, *must* cut across issues. If people were divided into fat men and lean (or Guelfs and Ghibellines, as in medieval Florence) and party feeling were then whipped up, the result would be not unlike the American political party. Indeed, in Salt Lake City the party division is said to have been formed in a way as arbitrary as this. The Mormon hierarchy, obliged to liquidate its church political party when it was admitted to the Union, is said to have told people on one side of the street to vote Republican and those on the other side to vote Democratic. Their descendants, some people insist, still vote the same way.

M. I. Ostrogorski wrote on the development of American parties:

The problems preoccupying public opinion being numerous and varied, it was necessary, instead of grouping the men in accordance with the issues, to adapt the issues to fixed groups of men. With this object confusion of the questions of the day was erected into a system; they were huddled together into "omnibus" programmes; they were put one on top of another; they were shuffled like a pack of cards, some being played at one time and some at another; at a pinch those which caused irreconcilable divergencies were made away with.[14]

This suggests something about the social function of cleavage in general. If cleavages run across each other (so to speak), they may serve to moderate conflict and to prevent "irreconcilable divergencies," because those who are enemies with respect to cleavage *a* are close allies with respect to cleavage *b* and indifferent (and therefore in a position to mediate) with respect to cleavage *c*. The "artificial" cleavage represented by party is especially functional in this respect because it cuts across *all* other cleavages. What Ostrogorski regarded as defects may therefore be great virtues.

Atlhough logically all of these cleavages—between the haves and have-nots, the suburbanites and the central city, the natives and the immigrants, and the major political parties—are separate and often cross-cutting, there is a tendency for them to coalesce into two opposed patterns. These patterns reflect two conceptions of the public interest that are widely held. The first, which derives from the middle-class ethos, favors what the municipal reform movement has always defined as "good government"—namely efficiency, impartiality, honesty, planning, strong executives, no favoritism, model legal codes, and strict enforcement of laws against gambling and vice. The other conception of the public interest (one never explicitly formulated as such, but one all the same) derives from the "immigrant ethos." This is the conception of those people who identify with the ward or neighborhood rather than the city "as a whole," who look to politicians for "help" and "favors," who regard gambling and vice as, at worst, necessary evils, and who are far less interested in the efficiency, impartiality, and honesty of local government than in its readiness to confer material benefits of one sort or another upon them. In the largest, most heterogeneous of our cities, these two mentalities stand forth as distinctly as did those which, in another context, caused Disraeli to write of "The Two Nations."

[14] M. I. Ostrogorski, *Democracy and the Organization of Political Parties* (New York, 1902), II, 618.

CHAPTER 4 · ATTACHMENTS

THE LIFE of the city is not all conflict and struggle; integrative forces are also at work. Some of these arise from the need that city dwellers have of each other in order to survive and prosper. Others arise from the extreme specialization of labor, and consequent complexity of market organization, that characterize the city. Businessmen require labor, raw materials, legal protection, transportation, utilities, a medium of exchange, and a source of capital. Similarly, politicians require votes, campaign funds, publicity, and the support of important groups in the community. Each actor's needs constrain him to moderate his demands on others; the businessman and the politician, for example, must cultivate good will, or, at any rate, must consider the costs in good will of what they want to do, and this necessity is—so far as it goes—an integrative force.

In order to get something done in the city, one must make bargains, accommodations, and concessions until the groups and individuals whose cooperation is needed are persuaded to extend it. To build a new housing project, for example, certain politicians and administrators must be induced to approve the plan, sources of capital must be shown that it is to their advantage to invest in it, neighborhood associations must be reassured, and newspapers and civic associations must be persuaded that it is in the public interest. The creation of a system of incentives that brings such diverse interests to cooperate is obviously integrative in its effect.

The integration of the city does not, however, result entirely from the kind of mutuality of interest that exists between a buyer and a seller, or among housing reformers, slum dwellers, investors, and politicians. To some extent, it is the consequence of a shared attachment to the city itself. The city is among other things a set of values, habits, sentiments, myths, and understandings which are (more or less) shared by the people who live in it, and the sharing of which constitutes (again, more or less) a social bond attaching the people of the city to one another and—if the bond is sufficiently strong (it may not be)

—making them feel themselves to be, and therefore to be in fact, a community.

How important consensus (etymologically, "to feel together") may be as an integrative element in the life of a particular city, or of cities in general, no one can say with assurance. The subject is one of the most difficult in social science. Perhaps the most useful approach that can be taken is to ask how the city is seen by its inhabitants and what kinds of attachments they have to it or to parts of it.

THE MEANING OF CITY LIFE

Urban sociologists (especially Georg Simmel, Robert Park, Louis Wirth, and Harvey Zorbaugh) have stressed disenchantment and alienation as accompaniments of city life. In an influential essay, Wirth defined a city as a "relatively large, dense, and permanent settlement of socially heterogeneous individuals."[1] Specialization, competition, and social disorganization, he said, are the inevitable outcomes of urbanization. He saw the large city as a hostile environment in which the associational ties of smaller, more homogeneous communities have been broken. Individuals who differ greatly in personal traits come to live together in the large city to perform specialized functions and to play distinct roles. They segregate themselves along ethnic, religious, or class lines, and city life perpetuates and exaggerates their heterogeneity. The social and psychological consequences of this are anonymity, impersonality, and disorganization. City life is lonely. Relationships are transitory, limited, and depersonalized. Men know each other by the roles they play, not by their characters as individuals. Primary groups—especially the family and the work group—are weakened or destroyed, and the consequence is the kind of restless wantlessness that Émile Durkheim termed "anomic." Whereas in the village or small town the directing forces of life are natural and spontaneous, arising from primary social groups, in the big city they are artificial and consciously created by formal organizations.

From this point of view politics, like other activities in the city, appears to be carried on by impersonal, formal organizations in which paid workers exercise specialized skills without involving the ordinary

---

[1] Louis Wirth, "Urbanism as a Way of Life," *American Journal of Sociology*, July 1938, reprinted in P. K. Hatt and A. J. Reiss, Jr., *Cities and Society* (Glencoe, Ill.: Free Press, 1951). For a good analysis of the sociological literature here under discussion, see Scott Greer, "Individual Participation in Mass Society," in Roland Young (ed.), *Approaches to the Study of Politics* (Evanston, Ill.: Northwestern University Press, 1958), pp. 329–342.

citizen deeply. The larger the city, the less likely the individual is to participate significantly in the political process. Indeed, if the city is a hostile place, the citizen will view politics with fear and distrust, feeling that it is one of the many forces over which he has no control.

Other sociologists have pointed out that the very features of urban life stressed by Wirth may—to the extent that they really exist, which is itself problematical—be regarded as advantages as well as, or perhaps rather than, disadvantages.[2] Urbanization, they say, enhances the opportunities of the individual. Specialization enables people to produce more and to enjoy higher levels of living. The anonymity and impersonality of city life—to the extent that they really exist—give the individual greater freedom to adopt a style of life he finds desirable. If the city means loneliness, *anomie*, and restlessness for some, it means civility, privacy, and urbanity for others.

The large city has been viewed by Robert Park and other sociologists as composed of a number of "natural areas" each with its distinctive social organization and ethos.[3] According to Park and the others who take this view, sub-communities within the city exist because they satisfy fundamental human needs. Ethnic, religious, and racial neighborhoods, for example, by affording a common style of life to those who live in them, help to maintain familiar social organization and to create a sense of community that offsets the tendency toward alienation and *anomie*. Some natural areas, those organized around Jewish or Chinese community institutions, for example, are more cohesive than others—Negro ones, for example. Ethnic and religious attachments are not the only basis for natural areas, however. The presence of a university may stimulate the formation of a sub-community of intellectuals and of persons who like to be near intellectuals.

The modern suburb, which is a kind of natural area, is one of the ways by which a prosperous society offers a choice among styles of life.[4] Suburbanites endeavor strenuously to maintain the "character" of their communities. This usually means excluding "undesirable" people

[2] For views contrasting with that of Wirth, see A. J. Reiss, Jr., "An Analysis of Urban Phenomena," in E. M. Fisher (ed.), *The Metropolis in Modern Life* (Garden City, N.Y.: Doubleday, 1955), pp. 41–51; and Robert C. Wood, "The New Metropolis," *American Political Science Review*, March 1958, pp. 108–122.

[3] Robert Park, *Human Communities* (Glencoe, Ill.: Free Press, 1952), and *Society* (Glencoe, Ill.: Free Press, 1954); Harvey Zorbaugh, *Gold Coast and the Slum* (Chicago: University of Chicago Press, 1928). This literature is discussed by Maurice Stein, *The Eclipse of Community* (Princeton, N.J.: Princeton University Press, 1960).

[4] See Robert C. Wood, *Suburbia* (Boston: Houghton Mifflin, 1958).

(Negroes, Jews, the poor, and people whose taste in architecture is not generally approved) or undesirable enterprises. Sometimes, however, it means *attracting* certain kinds of individuals, or certain enterprises. Some areas around New York—Fairfield, Westchester, and Rockland Counties, for example—have distinguished themselves by the income, occupations, or standing in art circles of the exurbanites they attract. Two suburbs of Chicago have offered gambling and vice to central-city residents in a manner not too different from the way in which these services were once provided by natural, segregated areas within the central city itself.

Attachment to such natural areas, both within and without the city, seems to be a generally significant fact. Many people think of themselves as residents of Hyde Park, Woodlawn, South Shore, or Rogers Park (sub-communities within Chicago) rather than of Chicago; of Silver Springs, Hollywood, Canoga Park, or Sherman Oaks, rather than of Los Angeles; of Shaker Heights or Cleveland Heights, rather than of Cleveland. The importance of these attachments varies a great deal from place to place and from person to person, but many studies have shown that it is usually present in some degree.

One important influence in creating and maintaining these neighborhood ties is the community press. Morris Janowitz concluded from a study of the influence of weekly neighborhood newspapers in Chicago that the papers both reflect and create a sense of community which is an important counterweight to the allegedly depersonalizing effect of the city.[5]

Some city planners think that the local community ought to be preserved as the basic structural component of the metropolis. Beginning with Clarence Perry, the "neighborhood unit" concept has often been put forward as a means of fostering the sense of community that planners—those of them who accept the concept—think indispensable to a wholesome style of life.[6] A neighborhood unit, as the planners

[5] See Morris Janowitz, *The Community Press in an Urban Setting* (Glencoe, Ill.: Free Press, 1952); Scott Greer and Ella Kube, "Urban Worlds: A Comparative Study of Four Los Angeles Areas," Laboratory in Urban Culture, Occidental College, 1955 (mimeo); and Scott Greer, "Urbanism Reconsidered: A Comparative Study of Local Areas in a Metropolis," *American Sociological Review*, February 1956, pp. 19–25.

[6] Clarence Perry, "The Neighborhood Unit: A Scheme of Arrangement for the Family-Life Community," *Regional Survey of New York and its Environs*, vol. VII (New York, 1929), pp. 22–140; and Perry, *Housing for the Machine Age* (New York: Russell Sage Foundation, 1949), chap. ix. A useful bibliography is that of James Dalier, *The Neighborhood Unit Plan: Its Spread and Acceptance* (New

conceive it, is physically relatively self-contained. The elementary school is its central institution, and this is placed so that all children can walk to it easily and without crossing major streets. In addition to the school, the neighborhood includes a church, a community meeting place, and a convenient, central shopping area. Some planners are skeptical of the neighborhood unit idea. Is a local attachment, they ask, really of such great moral and social significance? If "homogeneity" is the basis of the neighborhood, doesn't this mean that "heterogeneous" elements (e.g., racial or ethnic minorities) will be excluded? If a community can support only one church, for example, which church is it to be? In any case, they say, no neighborhood can be self-sufficient and none should want to be: the great advantage of living in a large city is that one can choose whatever it is that one wants—friends or groceries—from among a very wide range of possibilities.

COMMUNITY ATTACHMENTS AND POLITICS

Where a city is made up of distinct natural areas or sub-communities, its politics often reflects these attachments and intensifies them. Ward boundaries are usually consciously drawn to reflect the ethnic, religious, and class divisions within the city, and many wards are still highly homogeneous. Negro, Polish, Italian, and Jewish wards, "Gold Coast" wards, steelworkers' wards, university wards, and many other kinds still exist in the big cities. In such places, political organization and ethnic organization are closely related (Polish politicians work with Polish-American groups, Negro politicians with Negro ministers, and so on) and one is more or less created by the other.[7] As Oscar Handlin has observed, nationality-group politics has had an integrative effect; the ward organization made the immigrant aware for the first time that he was a Czech, a Pole, an Italian, or a Serbo-Croat. In part it did this by creating leadership; ward politics consisted largely of bargaining among the representatives of nationality groups, and the man who could create a sense of community identification and then turn it to his advantage was most likely to get ahead. Community identifications created in this way were integrative in themselves, of

York: Russell Sage Foundation, 1947). A major critique is that of Reginald Isaacs in two articles in the *Journal of Housing*, vol. V (1948): "Are Neighborhood Units Possible?" (pp. 177–180) and "The Neighborhood Unit Is an Instrument for Segregation" (pp. 215–219).

[7] Cf. William Foote Whyte, *Street Corner Society* (Chicago: University of Chicago Press, 1943).

course, but their main importance was that they produced wider identifications. Becoming aware that one was a Czech, a Pole, or an Italian was, as Handlin says, a first step toward becoming aware that one was an American.[8]

If neighborhood and ward identifications were integrative in these ways, they were also disintegrative in others, for ward politics tends to keep issues on a local rather than on a city-wide basis. When a city undertakes to reconstitute its political system by dropping ward in favor of at-large elections, the change is fundamental, not procedural; elected officials find that they must represent the city, not the ward, and voters find that neighborhood projects are likely to be shunted aside in favor of city-wide ones. Sometimes a problem arises because under the at-large system there is no way for purely local interests to reach the attention of the elected officials. When Kansas City, for example, changed from the ward system to one in which half the aldermen were elected at large (a change which coincided with election of a "reform" government), the new regime had to find some way of establishing contact with the neighborhoods. In lower-income neighborhoods this was not simply a matter of creating a channel of communication. Ways had to be found of giving the city government a neighborhood appeal—not, of course, the kind of appeal that had been exercised by the old ward leaders, who shared the ethnicity, religion, language, style of life, and interests of the residents—but a neighborhood appeal nevertheless.[9]

The political significance of the natural areas varies a great deal according to their kind. Some are tenement districts in which low-income migrants live, where family life is disrupted, church membership low, and social life limited to a few friends or to a "gang." In such areas, political preferences are unstable, people care little about the area or about the city as a whole, and they vote (and, more rarely, participate in politics in others ways) mainly when prompted to do so by organizations that offer material inducements or that appeal to particular, often personal loyalties.

[8] Oscar Handlin, The Uprooted (Boston: Little, Brown, 1951), chap. vii.

[9] An account of the measures taken is to be found in A. Theodore Brown, The Politics of Reform: Kansas City's Municipal Government, 1925–50 (Kansas City, 1958), especially chaps. vii and x. Reprinted in part in Edward C. Banfield (ed.), Urban Government (New York: Free Press of Glencoe, 1961), pp. 543–553. See also Joel Smith, William H. Form, and Gregory P. Stone, "Local Intimacy in a Middle-Sized City," American Journal of Sociology, November 1954, pp. 276–284.

Another type of natural area consists of small houses in which live semiskilled and clerical workers. In these areas, family activities are of the greatest importance, there is much "neighborliness," many people attend church regularly, and there is a sense of obligation to the "community" and to neighbors. Few people have much leisure, however, and the educational level is rather low. Membership in voluntary associations (other than churches and unions) is also low. Although the sense of community is fairly strong, few people participate in local affairs and few take much interest in the government of the larger city or have much confidence in their ability to influence it. Such areas tend to exert a stabilizing, "balance wheel" effect in city politics, but they seldom take a leading active role in it.

In a third type of natural area, where incomes and educational levels are high, neighborliness may not be very marked; this is especially the case where there are high-rise apartments. Membership in voluntary associations is high, however; both husbands and wives belong with varying degrees of enthusiasm to organizations having civic, educational, or fraternal purposes. Many people participate in civic projects and cultural affairs that transcend neighborhood lines, and the sense of obligation to the "community," by which is generally meant the city (or even the metropolitan area) "as a whole," is particularly strong.

The kinds of people recruited into the politics of a city depend to a large extent upon the interaction of two factors: the social structure of the sub-communities and the political structure of the city. The political structure will be discussed at length in Part II. Some political arrangements, it will be seen, give power and place to middle-class people whose sense of civic consciousness is strong, who have many city-wide ties through voluntary associations, and whose interest in purely local or neighborhood matters is small. Other political arrangements, by contrast, practically exclude such people and instead make it easy for neighborhood-minded people to acquire power.

VIEWS ABOUT THE ROLE OF GOVERNMENT

The nature of people's attachments to their city influences their conception of the nature of the public interest and thus also their view of the proper role of local government. Oliver Williams has supplied a typology by which to describe what citizens and officials in middle-sized cities expect of their city governments. Local government, he says, may be seen as: (a) the instrument of community growth, (b) the provider of life's amenities, (c) a "caretaker," or (d) the arbiter of conflicting interests.[10]

Those who regard the city government as the instrument of community growth assume that the most important ends to be served are population expansion, industrial development, commercial activities, net worth, and the like. Politics, in short, is intended to serve production. This view is common among industrialists, but is not confined to them; it is often also the view of city planners, local merchants, businessmen's clubs, bankers, and large property owners. A city dominated by this view will stand ready to enact zoning variations, reduce tax assessments, provide subsidies, develop industrial parks, install utilities, and do whatever else may be required to keep labor costs low and promote production.

Where the prevailing view is that the function of local government is to provide life's amenities, people will expect it to preserve some "way of life" which is valued and, in general, to safeguard and improve the advantages of the city as a place to live. Consumption will be stressed at the expense of production. Outsiders and transients will be excluded, the labor force kept low, neighborhoods defended by rigid zoning laws and building codes, open space jealously guarded, noise and smoke curtailed, and traffic routed around the city. The cost of such measures may be high, but they will be borne. Such communities are likely to consist largely of upper-middle-class families, including wealthy, elderly retired people and young couples who are anxious for the "right kind of town" for their children. Park Forest, Illinois, is an "amenities" community which has been extensively decribed.[11] Oliver Williams' own study (done with Charles Adrian) of four middle-sized Michigan cities offers another example, that of a city which, by absorb-

---

[10] Oliver Williams, "A Typology for Comparative Local Government," *Midwest Journal of Political Science*, May 1961, pp. 150–164. Williams' typology is somewhat akin to the distinction we made in Chapter 2 between the service function of government and its function in managing conflict. His distinctions, however, have been drawn for a different purpose from ours: they are for use in describing how the citizens and officials of middle-sized cities perceive the character of their local governments whereas ours are for use in describing the social functions of government no matter how it (government) is perceived by citizens or officials. Two of Williams' types ("instrument of community growth" and "provider of life's amenities") define city government as the producer of a special kind of service; another ("the arbiter of conflicting interests") defines it as an institution for managing conflict; the remaining type ("caretaker") defines it in terms of both functions.

[11] William B. Whyte, *The Organization Man* (Garden City, N.Y.: Doubleday, 1957).

ing its upper-class suburbs, brought amenity-seeking people into power.[12]

Where local government is seen as a caretaker, its functions are very limited. People are expected to work out their own problems and to pay on a fee-for-service basis for what they get. The market performs many functions which elsewhere are performed by local government. Keeping down the cost of government is an overriding consideration. Matters are passed on to higher levels of government (the county, state, or federal government), given over to private groups (a chamber of commerce or a fraternal order), or else ignored. We have already referred to such a community, "Springdale," New York, governed by a small clique of long-time residents who occupy strategic places—a lawyer, a newspaper publisher, a farm supply merchant.[13] In this community, even facilities that everyone wants—adequate roads, for example—are supplied parsimoniously. Nothing new is tried. The community is governed on behalf of its small merchants and property owners and often at the expense of the farmers who live outside its limits.

Finally, the role of government may be defined as that of an arbiter whose task is to manage conflict among competing interests and to find a lowest common denominator on the basis of which some settlement or *modus vivendi* can be worked out. An "arbiter" government may be similar to a "caretaker" one in being generally passive, but it cannot be simply a caretaker because the heterogeneity of the community gives rise to questions that cannot be evaded. Arbiter governments frequently exist in the larger cities, where diversity is great and a politician's power depends upon a broad coalition of supporters. Ethnic-based, patronage-fed, political machines usually provide "arbiter" government; the machine arbitrates internally among the ethnic groups on which it is based and externally among the interests that compete to influence public policies. Such organizations are not confined to large cities; Williams describes one in a middle-sized Michigan city.

Obviously the social and ecological structure of a city largely determines which view as to the proper role of government will prevail in it. If, for example, upper-income people live mostly in suburbs outside the

[12] Oliver P. Williams and Charles R. Adrian, *Four Cities: A Study in Comparative Policy Making* (Philadelphia: University of Pennsylvania Press, 1963).

[13] Arthur Vidich and Joseph Bensman, *Small Town in Mass Society* (Princeton, N.J.: Princeton University Press, 1958). For another example, see the account of Beloit, Wisconsin, in Warner E. Mills, Jr., and Harry R. Davis, *Small City Government* (New York: Random House, 1962).

city, the "amenities" and "good government" orientation that they would give the city is lacking. Because their influence is not felt, the central-city government may be dominated by machine politicians or, perhaps, by small merchants and property owners. If a city consists of a variety of natural areas all seeking to assert their identities, it is likely to be governed by politicians who regard the adjustment of such claims as the principal business of government.

Causality may run in the other direction as well: if the ecology of the city determines the style of its politics, so may the style of its politics determine its ecology. In other words, the kinds of people who live in the city, their distribution in natural or other areas, and the conceptions that they have of the public interest both affect and are affected by political circumstances. If, for example, the central city is dominated by a political machine, this may cause middle-class people to move to the suburbs and thus may prevent metropolitan organization and planning. Or, to give another example, a "caretaker" government put in office by small businessmen may prevent industry from locating in the city, with the consequence that the city is deprived of the leadership that the managers of the industry would give it.

THE ATTACHMENTS OF INFLUENTIALS

The perspectives toward the city of its most active and influential people are of course particularly important. Robert K. Merton has contributed to our understanding of these by describing, on the basis of a study of a New Jersey city that he calls Rovere, two types of influentials—the "local" and the "cosmopolitan"—who differ mainly in their orientation toward the city.[14] The local influential confines his interests mainly to the community; the Great Society hardly exists for him; he is parochial in the strict sense. The cosmopolitan influential, on the other hand, is oriented toward the larger world outside the city, especially toward the national and international scene. As Merton puts it, "He resides in Rovere but lives in the Great Society."

The locals, Merton finds, have mostly grown up in and with the town. Their influence rests upon an elaborate network of personal relations—on *whom* they know rather than *what* they know. They are particularly active in organizations that are designed especially for

---

[14] Robert K. Merton, "Patterns of Influence: Locals and Cosmopolitans," in *Social Theory and Social Structure*, rev. ed. (Glencoe, Ill.: Free Press, 1957), esp. p. 400. Reprinted in part in Banfield (ed.), *Urban Government*, pp. 390–400.

"making contacts," such as the Elks and the Rotary. The cosmopolitan, by contrast, has usually come to the city from another place. His influence is based upon knowledge or upon a reputation which has preceded him, not upon personal relations, and he tends to belong to professional societies and hobby clubs rather than to fraternal or "service" organizations. Not having to prove to the community that he is no longer a "boy," he is less concerned about personal relations than is the local.

In the present context, the most significant difference between local and cosmopolitan influentials is in the nature and degree of their attachment to the community. This difference, Merton says, is marked. Local influentials are great local patriots. He quotes one of them: "Rovere is the greatest town in the world. It has something that is nowhere else in the world, though I can't say quite what it is." The cosmopolitan is not economically and sentimentally rooted to the community in this way. He thinks that Rovere is a "pleasant enough town" but only one of many, and he is aware that he may advance his career by moving on to another.

Cosmopolitans generally rank higher than locals in income and education and they are more likely to be in professional or managerial occupational roles. However, both cosmopolitans and locals exist in all social classes, and their orientation toward the community seems to influence their attitudes on public questions irrespective of their class position. Thomas R. Dye classified a sample of Philadelphia suburbanites according to whether their orientation, as measured by their responses to certain test questions, was cosmopolitan or local; he then found that cosmopolitans were significantly more likely than locals to favor certain proposals regarding mass transit and metropolitan area government.[15]

It is apparent that the proportion of the two types of influentials in a city and their distribution among official and unofficial leadership roles will profoundly affect the style and content of the city's politics. Presumably locals will find themselves most at home in ward politics and will want the city to engage in "booster" activities. Clean city cam-

---

[15] Thomas R. Dye, "The Local-Cosmopolitan Dimension and the Study of Urban Politics," *Social Forces*, March 1963, pp. 239–246. Some supporting evidence can be found in Richard A. Watson and John H. Romani, "Metropolitan Government for Metropolitan Cleveland: An Analysis of the Voting Record," *Midwest Journal of Political Science*, November 1961, pp. 365–390; and Daniel Elazar, "Metro and the Voters: Nashville," *Planning, 1959: Journal of the American Society of Planning Officials*, pp. 69–76.

paigns, parade committees, and exhibition halls will be principal items on the civic agenda where they are dominant. Cosmopolitans will be more interested in city-wide, or better yet metropolitan-wide, political organization (although less interested in that than in state and national organization), and they will favor activities that are "professional" or that involve issues that are being discussed on the state and national scenes—e.g., the board of education, urban renewal, and human relations. Obviously, circumstances which affect the supply of the two types of influential will have important long-run effects on the political ethos and institution of the city. If, for example, suburbanization drains cosmopolitans from the central city or, again, if the explosive growth of a city prevents the production of locals (Los Angeles is a case in point), the attachment of the city's influentials to it, and therefore the character of its politics, may be altogether changed.

"LEARNING" A CITY'S POLITICAL CULTURE

The attachment people have to a city is in great part based on a set of common expectations about how others will behave in civic and political affairs. These common expectations might be called the city's "political culture" which, like culture generally, is "learned" by the members. A participant acquires a more or less stable set of beliefs about who runs things, how to get things done, whom to see, who wants what, and where "the bodies are buried."

This learning process contributes, as much as anything else, to the perpetuation of the distinctive features of a city's character. "Things are done differently here," even though the formal aspects of the situation—the system of government, the economic base, and the composition of the population—may be quite similar to many other cities. The process of learning consists in great part of *imputing* to certain people, organizations, ideas, or strategies those qualities which make them important to everyone involved in politics. In one city the word may be, "check it with X, the publisher"; in another city, one has to "touch base with A, B, and C," none of whom is connected with the local newspaper. In part, people are said to be powerful because at one time they made some "power play" which everyone agreed was successful or because they participated in some civic association which got a job done. After the initial success or the initial involvement, however, reputations tend to become cumulative: men are *expected* to be powerful or *expected* to play a certain civic role because they did so in the past. These learned expectations often induce the men to do more or less what is expected of them, and the imputation of power or the definition of the role is thereby strengthened. And thus the process continues. It is in this way that a more or less common vocabulary about a city's politics is created among those involved; it is this shared rhetoric, and the cumulative reputations which it both describes and maintains, that give to a city some of its unique flavor.

This is not to say that the important things about city politics are figments of the imagination of the people concerned—it is only to argue that politics takes place in a world compounded not only of hard facts (recognized material stakes in certain issues, unmistakable legal or economic powers and sanctions, and clear instances of influence being wielded) but also of cultural artifacts (learned responses, shared vocabularies, general expectations, and imputed reputations).

It is exceptionally difficult to disentangle what is learned as a result of bumping into hard facts and what is learned by a process of cultural transmission. Indeed, the whole problem of making accurate statements about power and influence is fundamentally a problem of separating the experienced from the anticipated. Some elements of a political culture can be mentioned, however.

A new participant in local politics quickly learns the appropriate forms of civic action. Depending on the circumstances, he may be told he must join the party and work his way up, or that he must join the University Club and get in with the right "crowd," or that he ought to start an organization with certain people on the letterhead. Trying to accomplish things by other strategies may be regarded as eccentric or doomed to failure, even though other strategies exist—such as organizing a neighborhood protest movement, building a radio or television following, or simply going to see the mayor and making a request.

Closely related to beliefs about appropriate strategies are expectations that define in a limited way the possibility of change. These expectations, which are often quite powerful, are expressed in such injunctions as "the mayor doesn't listen to anybody," "the politicians have things sewed up," "you can't put that through in this town," and so forth. For example, reformers are exceptionally active in New York City and only intermittently active in Chicago. Party posts are frequently contested in New York, almost never in Chicago. In part the explanation may be that New York has a long history of insurgency and political ferment, perhaps sustained by the memory of its early successes (the Fusion party and the Citizens' Union were powerful in 1901 and have periodically staged comebacks). Chicago, on the other hand, has few examples from which prospective reformers can draw a sense of optimism.

Finally, new groups in a city's political life may learn the appropriate forms and tactics of politics from their predecessors. For example, Negroes who come to power usually do so by ousting white party leaders or elective officials in their districts. But in the very act of winning, Negroes—and others in similar circumstances—learn from those they are supplanting how politicians behave in that particular city. Groups locked in combat with each other tend to acquire similar characteristics, as the sociologist Georg Simmel often noted, and thus conflict is an important way of learning a distinctive political culture.

The life of the city, then, is a continual balancing between forces that tend to tear the community apart in conflict and others that tend both to suppress conflict and to hold the community together in the face of it. Complementarity of interests is one integrative force. Others are shared attachments (especially to natural areas and to group leaders) and a sense of belonging to a city that has an identity of its own. The explicitly political elements in the life of the city—especially governments, parties, and interest groups, and the practices, informal as well as formal, which exist in connection with them—although only a part of the complicated mix of integrative and disintegrative forces, are of principal importance in a study of city politics. We will therefore turn our attention to these explicitly political elements (it will be convenient to call them the political "structure" of the city) in an effort to see how they affect—and are in turn affected by—the more or less balanced pressures of conflict and attachment.

PART II

THE STRUCTURE OF CITY POLITICS

CHAPTER 5 · THE CITY
IN THE FEDERAL SYSTEM

THE AMERICAN federal system does not grant any inherent right of local government. Article 10 of the Bill of Rights says: "The powers not delegated to the United States by the Constitution, nor prohibited by it to the States, are reserved to the States respectively, or to the people." Cities are not mentioned in the Constitution, and from a constitutional point of view they do not exist.

Having all the powers of government that are not possessed by the federal government, the states and the people (meaning, presumably, legislatures, electorates, or both) may exercise them through such organs as they please. In fact they exercise them through organs of three types:

1. Departments of state government, and state bureaus and commissions. These exist by provision of state constitutions or under state statutes, and they depend upon the state legislatures for their appropriations.

2. Quasi-corporations, which are involuntary territorial and political subdivisions of the states. These include counties, townships, the New England town, and special districts (e.g., school districts, sewage disposal districts, mosquito abatement districts, and so on). The quasi-corporation is an administrative arm of the state government, but it differs from others in that its heads may be elected from an electorate which is not that of the whole state. It is subject to the legislature in the same way that other parts of the state government are, however.

3. Municipal corporations, which are artificial persons created by the state and having a standing in the eyes of the law. These include cities, villages, and boroughs. The municipal corporation may be specially chartered, or it may be voluntarily organized under general acts of the state legislature. In these respects it is like a private corporation. It differs from a private corporation, however, in that it is chartered to serve public purposes only and its charter does not constitute a contract binding the state. The state can change the charter, or take it away altogether, without infringing anyone's rights. Private corpora-

tions are chartered only at the request of the people who are to constitute them; municipal corporations, on the other hand, may be forced upon the people of a locality by the legislature against their will.

CITIES AND STATES

Unlike the quasi-corporation, the municipal corporation is *both* an arm of the state and a body which serves needs which are unique to the locality. Much of what the city government does it does as an agent of the state; for example, a city policeman who enforces a state law does so as an agent of the state. But the city government also does things which are solely for the benefit of the city, and with respect to which the state has no policies; for example, a city council may make traffic regulations that are designed to meet purely local problems.

Even in the matters with respect to which it acts solely on behalf of the people of the locality, the municipal corporation is subject to the state. The charter given it by the state fixes the form of its organization, lists the powers that it may exercise, and prescribes the manner in which it may exercise them. The inferior legal position of the city was given its most sweeping statement in a decision of the United States Supreme Court (*Trenton v. New Jersey*, 262 US 182) written in 1923 by Mr. Justice Butler:

> The city is a political subdivision of the state, created as a convenient agency for the exercise of such of the governmental powers of the state as may be entrusted to it. . . . The state may withhold, grant, or withdraw powers and privileges as it sees fit. . . . In the absence of state constitutional provisions safeguarding it to them, municipalities have no inherent right of self-government which is beyond the legislative control of the state.

It is a well-established principle that grants of power by states to municipal corporations are to be interpreted very narrowly. The classic statement of this principle was made by a commentator on the law and is known as "Dillon's rule":

> It is a general and undisputed proposition of law that a municipal corporation possesses and can exercise the following powers, and no others: First, those granted in express words; second, those necessarily or fairly implied in or incident to the powers expressly granted; third, those essential to the accomplishment of the declared objects and purposes of the corporation—not simply convenient, but indispensable. Any fair, reasonable, substantial doubt concerning the existence of power is resolved by the courts against the corporation, and the power is denied.[1]

[1] John F. Dillon, *Commentaries on the Law of Municipal Corporations*, 5th ed. (Boston, 1911), I, 448.

This means that a city cannot operate a peanut stand at the city zoo without first getting the state legislature to pass an enabling law, unless, perchance, the city's charter or some previously enacted law unmistakably covers the sale of peanuts.

Some states have given their cities broad grants of power. This has not been the usual practice, however, and some city charters run to several hundred thousand words. A city may have a charter that applies to it exclusively or it may be blanketed with other cities in the same state, but in either case the charter consists of *all* acts dealing with the form and powers of cities, not merely the initial act of incorporation. Here, to illustrate the detail into which city charters often go, is an excerpt from Section 101 of the charter of Nashville, Tennessee:

> In the event any regular member of the Fire Department, above the rank of pipeman or ladderman, shall be temporarily absent from his duties without pay, because of illness or disability, the chief of the Fire Department, subject to the approval of the Mayor, shall designate any regular member of the Fire Department from a lower rank to perform the duties of such member during his absence, and the member so designated shall receive the rate of pay of the absent member during said member's absence and until he returns, or the position has been permanently filled under the general provisions of this Charter.

In those instances in which legislatures have given cities broad grants of power, the courts have later narrowed them down by interpretation. For example, although the constitution of New York has been amended to give New York City broad powers, the city recently found itself unable to require that milk sold in the city have the date stamped on the container. Although the home rule clause in the New York constitution gives all cities the "power to adopt and amend local laws not inconsistent with the Constitution and laws of the State relating to its property, affairs or government," the courts have regularly permitted the state legislature to pre-empt local autonomy on the grounds that such matters as apartment houses, sewers, local taxes, transit systems, and regulations governing plumbers are all of "state interest."[2]

Special act charters (those specially drawn for the cities named in

[2] Wallace S. Sayre and Herbert Kaufman, *Governing New York City* (New York: Russell Sage Foundation, 1960), pp. 585–586. See also, for a case study of the erosion of a general grant of power by the action of court interpretations, W. Bernard Richland, "Constitutional Home Rule in New York," *Columbia Law Review*, March 1954.

them) were once the general rule and are still the rule in New England and the Southern states. The Massachusetts legislature, for example, recently had the following bill before it:

H.1918. That Fall River be authorized to appropriate money for purchase of uniforms for the park police and watershed guards of said city.

There is nothing to stop the legislature from making the purchase of those uniforms *mandatory*. Not infrequently a legislature saddles cities with expenses for things that they do not want. St. Louis, for example, is required under Missouri law to appropriate whatever funds are requested by the city's police commissioner—who is appointed by the governor.

For more than a hundred years municipal reformers have fumed about such special acts. *General act* charters—that is, laws applying equally to all cities in the state, have been tried but found impractical: what fits a small city usually does not fit a large one. The usual practice now, in those states which have abandoned special acts, is to classify cities, usually according to size, and then pass general laws applicable to each class. Thus a legislature may pass one law applying to all cities of less than 10,000 population, another to all cities of from 10,000 to 25,000, and so on.

This has improved the situation somewhat from the standpoint of the cities, but the classification is often a thin disguise for special legislation. The Illinois legislature, for example, passes acts applicable to all cities of more than 500,000 population, although it is well aware that there is only one such city in the state, Chicago.

Optional charter laws are another device by which a city may be given a measure of autonomy. In such laws the legislature offers several different charters and allows the voters of a locality to select one. Massachusetts, for example, allows cities—except Boston, which gets special treatment—to adopt any one of five charter forms: Plan A (strong mayor and weak council); Plan B (weak mayor and strong council); Plan C (commission); Plan D (city manager); and Plan E (a modification of D).

Under either a special act or a general act charter, a city must go to the legislature whenever it wants to make a change in its form of organization or in its powers. Under a *home rule* charter, so called, this is unnecessary. A home rule city may amend its charter at its own initiative, usually by action of a majority of the voters, provided that in doing so it stays within certain limits laid down by state law.

Home rule is sometimes granted to cities by statute; in such cases the independence of the city is rather insubstantial, since any session of the legislature can put an end to it. About twenty states give cities home rule by constitutional provision. But even in these, cities do not have real autonomy. The courts have diluted most of these constitutional grants of power, and it is not too much to say that the position of the constitutional home rule cities is not greatly different from that of the others.

About two thirds of the cities of over 200,000 population have some form of home rule. It would be a great mistake to think of these cities as being really independent, however. The reins are short in most cases, and they may be pulled even shorter almost any time. Moreover, where a legislature no longer decides what the city may do, the courts decide instead. This is an important difference politically, of course, but it means that the cities are far from autonomous.

The position of the American city is to be contrasted with that of the European one. The American city can do *only* what the legislature expressly permits it to do.[3] The European city, by contrast, can do anything that it is *not* expressly forbidden to do. This is what American municipal reformers—especially the American Municipal Association—would like. But it is hard to believe that it would bring a final solution to the problem of city-state relations, or perhaps even any real change in the situation, for even under the European arrangement it would be possible for the legislature to pass a general law limiting the tax base of the cities rather stringently. By doing that, it would restore the substance of its control over them.

The problem seems to be inherently insoluble on any general and lasting basis. It is one that must be worked out by friction, and worked out anew every time it arises. What cities are to do or not do will in the last analysis always have to be decided on the basis of concrete political issues. The main question is whether these decisions are to be made by legislatures, courts, or so-called "experts in administration."[4]

Meanwhile politicians on both sides will continue to capitalize on city-state differences as an election issue. Two recent extreme proposals

[3] More precisely, only what the legislature expressly permits, what is necessarily or fairly implied by what it permits, or what is indispensable to its objects. What is expressly permitted may be stated in very general terms by the legislature; this is the case with respect to home rule cities.

[4] Chicago Home Rule Commission, *Chicago's Government* (Chicago: University of Chicago Press, 1954). Chaps. ix, x, xi, and xii treat of the general problem of home rule.

illustrate the rhetoric of the controversy. In 1959, the New York City Council adopted by a vote of 23 to 1 a resolution that a committee be appointed to study the possibility and legality of the city's seceding from New York State and constituting itself an independent, fifty-first state. If this half-serious proposal had been adopted, the city could have kept over two billion dollars a year in taxes which now go to Albany.[5] The other proposal, made two years later by the governor of Rhode Island, was that all city and town governments be abolished so that the state, by running everything from the capital, could "come out of the 19th century."[6]

Financial Supremacy of the State

The state has financial as well as constitutional supremacy. The cities have always relied mainly upon the property tax for their revenues. Other tax sources have been largely pre-empted by the states and by the federal government, leaving the cities—where the legislatures permit—such relatively undesirable tax sources as remain. Many states have established debt limits beyond which the cities cannot borrow, or cannot borrow without special permission from the legislature. Some cities are chronically at or near the limit.

In these circumstances the states have become indispensable sources of financial aid to the cities. The states collect revenue, much of it from city taxpayers, of course, and then give it back as grants-in-aid. As a rule, the city pays more in taxes than it gets in grants; from its point of view, it is being milked by the state government for the advantage of the rural and small-town areas. Miami, Florida, for example, in a recent year paid $47 million in state taxes and got back only $1.5 million in grants-in-aid. Most of the state's expenditures, of course, were made directly by state agencies, not given to the cities to spend; but, even so, the state collected 24 percent of its total taxes in Miami and made only 15.8 percent of its total expenditures there.

Such arrangements are not necessarily unjust, although mayors invariably claim that they are. The state, after all, carries on activities which benefit everyone and for which everyone ought therefore to pay. Big-city residents, for example, are protected by the state highway patrol when they take trips. Presumably even when they stay home they benefit from conservation, forestation, and fish and wildlife

[5] *New York Times*, April 8, 1959.
[6] Associated Press dispatch dated June 30, 1961.

projects and from the improvement of rural schools. There is really no more reason to say that each city should get back in grants or expenditures exactly what the state takes from it in taxes than to say that each state should get back exactly what the federal government takes from it in taxes. Nevertheless, there can be little doubt that the political power wielded by the hinterland in the state legislature—and for that matter in the Congress as well—is employed to benefit the hinterland at the city's expense.

Such grants-in-aid as a city gets from the state are likely to be limited to particular uses. Nashville, for example, is permitted to put only about a third of what it gets from the state into a general fund; the rest is all earmarked by the state—so much for the pension fund, so much for the park fund, so much for the school fund, so much for the bond retirement fund.

The charter of Los Angeles says that the city's tax rate (for purposes other than payment of pensions or bond interest and principal, and except for special district taxes) may not exceed $1.25 on each $100 of assessed valuation. Of the $1.25, the charter specifies that six cents shall be placed in the permanent improvement fund, seven in the library fund, and 13 in the recreation and park fund. This leaves not more than 99 cents for general purposes.

Underrepresentation of Cities in Legislatures

The ultimate power over the cities, then, is in the state—the electorate, the legislature, and the courts. This is a political fact of the greatest importance.

Historically, as we have already mentioned, rural and farm interests have dominated the legislatures, and even today an alliance of the rural hinterland and the suburbs controls them. As a general rule the cities have not been fairly represented in the legislatures. In the mid-1950's, Gordon Baker divided forty-eight states into five categories according to the degree their urban areas were underrepresented in the legislatures.[7] (In no state were they overrepresented.) He put eight states in the category of "severe" underrepresentation (Georgia, Florida, Maryland, Delaware, Connecticut, Rhode Island, New Jersey, and California); twenty-two in the category of "substantial" underrepre-

[7] Gordon E. Baker, *Rural versus Urban Political Power* (Garden City, N.Y.: Doubleday, 1955). See also W. C. Havard and L. P. Beth, *The Politics of Mis-Representation* (Baton Rouge, La.: Louisiana University Press, 1962).

sentation; and sixteen in the third and fourth categories of "moderate" underrepresentation. In only two states, Massachusetts and Wisconsin, were the urban areas correctly represented.

In the early 1960's, Los Angeles, with over five million population, had the same representation in the state senate as Alpine County, which had a few thousand. Dade County (Miami), Florida, with 495,000 population, had three representatives in the house; Glade County, with 2,199 population, had one. That meant that Glade County had seventy times as much representation per person as did Miami.

All such inequities were upset by an historic decision of the United States Supreme Court (Baker v. Carr, 369 US 186), which on March 26, 1962, declared in a Tennessee case that federal courts had the power to inquire into the constitutionality of state systems for distributing seats in state legislatures. The decision at once provoked a rash of suits demanding reapportionment (a new allocation of seats among political units) and redistricting (a redrawing of boundary lines for legislative districts). As of August 1962, federal and state courts had upset existing arrangements in more than a dozen states, four states had already accomplished token or provisional reapportionment, and most of the others appeared to be on their way toward doing so. How sweeping the changes will have to be no one can tell; the Supreme Court did not say how nearly equal in population the districts must be in order to meet the constitutional requirement for "equal protection of the laws," and it offered no guidelines that lower courts and legislatures could use in determining what is "fair." The Solicitor General of the United States, who had urged the Supreme Court to take the stand that it did, suggested that in one house of a legislature there ought to be representation directly proportional to population and that in the other there might be variation to allow for geographical and other factors, provided "that the departure from equal representation in proportion to the population is not too extreme."

In some states, especially in the South, reapportionment would shift power from rural to urban areas to an extent that would be profoundly important. When, for example, a vote in a "wool hat" county of Georgia ceased to be worth ninety-nine times one in Atlanta, the character of state politics and also, to a certain extent, of national politics was bound to be changed. It would be a mistake to suppose, however, that *all* large central cities will increase their representation in the legislatures by reapportionment, that their populations would be unanimously in favor of having more representation in them if they could get it, or that if the cities get more representation they will be better off because of it.

As to the first of these points, it is the suburbs, not the central cities, that now are the worst underrepresented in the legislatures. As Paul T. David and Ralph Eisenberg show in the accompanying Table 5, several large central cities used to be more underrepresented than were the suburbs, but now it is the other way around in most cases. Since the populations of the suburbs are expected to increase greatly in the next decade or two while those of the central cities are expected to remain the same or to decline, the central cities will have fewer rather than more representatives in the legislatures.

That city populations are by no means unanimous in wanting fair representation in legislatures can be shown on both *a priori* and empirical grounds. The influence of the out-of-city (upstate or downstate) vote on the affairs of the big city tends to be conservative; because the overrepresentation of the hinterland is in effect overrepresentation for them, conservatives within the city do not want it eliminated. This, perhaps, explains why a few years ago enough New York City voters— a minority, to be sure, but enough nevertheless—voted "No" to defeat a constitutional amendment which would have given the city more representation.

Not only conservatives in general but also special interests (whether conservative or not) within the large city may gain from the overrepresentation of the hinterland. The so-called "cow counties" of California, for example, are said to be in effect the "rotten boroughs" of certain Los Angeles interests. Legislators from these counties, having no stake themselves in the issues that matter most to the Los Angeles interests and demanding for their own constituents little more than roads, bridges, and other such local public works, make valuable—but inexpensive—allies.

That getting fair representation in the legislature may not help the city may be seen from the fact that some of the cities which get the worst treatment from their legislatures are among the least underrepresented. Boston is a case in point. State Senator John Powers has as much to say about its affairs as does Mayor John Collins. Indeed, except where a powerful local party organization exerts its discipline over state legislators elected from the big city (as in Chicago, for example), the legislators from the city may constitute the principal threat to the mayor's proposals. This appears to be the case in Minnesota, where a handful of Hennepin County (Minneapolis) legislators can defeat a proposal which has the backing of the mayor and city council of Minneapolis.

Frequently, the hinterland is blamed for the failure of legislation about which the city is itself divided. When, as often happens, the

TABLE 5. Relative value of the right to vote for representation in state legislatures for selected central cities and suburban counties, 1930 to 1960°

Central city and suburban counties	Relative values		
	1930	1950	1960
New York City	71	81	93
Nassau County	54	101	59
Rockland County	127	108	86
Suffolk County	79	100	47
Westchester County	88	109	95
Philadelphia	88	88	98
Bucks County	147	124	63
Chester County	131	113	92
Delaware County	67	67	55
Montgomery County	80	72	53
Boston	91	99	123
Essex County	106	110	110
Middlesex County	101	98	92
Norfolk County	119	100	83
Plymouth County	115	108	91
St. Louis	67	74	92
Jefferson County	99	79	62
St. Charles County	105	96	71
St. Louis County	38	71	45
Baltimore	51	62	83
Anne Arundel County	125	83	62
Baltimore County	55	36	26
Carroll County	154	175	197
Howard County	258	257	218

° Generally speaking, the relative values shown in this table are based on a scale in which *over*representation increases as the value exceeds 100 and *under*representation increases as the value falls below 100. More exactly, these values were determined for each house of the state legislature by dividing the state-wide average population per representative by the population per respresentative from each county. The values for each of the two houses were then averaged to give the figures presented in the table.

Source: Adapted from Paul T. David and Ralph Eisenberg, *Devaluation of the Urban and Suburban Vote* (Charlottesville: University of Virginia Press, 1961), pp. 12–13.

hinterland offers to support whatever the delegation from the city unanimously recommends, the delegation may not agree upon anything. What, then, is the hinterland to do? No matter what it does, it will be charged with interfering in the affairs of the city.

All this suggests that the nature of state-local relations cannot be inferred from apportionment statistics. Of more interest to the student of urban politics as an indicator of the forces at work is the character of the groups that turn to the state government for support. In many states, perhaps most of them, conservative, business-oriented, and suburban groups regard the state as their natural protector against a "liberal," big-city administration; in other states, however, labor, Negro, and other "liberal" groups regard the state as their ally. In Illinois and New York the state governments have generally been conservative strongholds. In Minnesota and California, on the other hand, they have generally been closely allied to "liberal" forces. The California legislature, in which urban areas have been severely underrepresented, has outlawed racial discrimination in both employment and housing and has provided generous old-age pensions and welfare plans; the city government in Los Angeles, on the other hand, has resisted "liberal" welfare and race relations measures.

The states whose administrations are most closely allied to the urban "liberal" groups tend to be the states whose major cities are nonpartisan. Detroit, Los Angeles, Minneapolis and St. Paul, for example, are all nonpartisan, and the state governments of Michigan, California, and Minnesota are normally conspicuously "liberal." In nonpartisan cities, for reasons we shall explain, business interests often get particularly sympathetic treatment. The state governments, chosen by partisan arrangements, are less dependent upon them and more dependent upon the electorates, which in recent years have been at least moderately Democratic and "liberal."

CITIES AND THE FEDERAL GOVERNMENT

A little more than half a century ago, Professor Frank J. Goodnow wrote in one of the first textbooks on city government that "as the city has no relations with the national government it is not necessary for our purpose that we make any study of the national administrative system."[8]

[8] Frank J. Goodnow, *City Government in the United States* (New York, 1904), p. 69.

This is still true, of course, from a legal-formal standpoint. Constitutionally the cities and the national government have no relations.

In Goodnow's time the legal form and the actual practice corresponded pretty well, although by no means perfectly. Now they are dramatically at odds. The federal government plays a leading role in city affairs. Indeed, some of the most important decisions respecting the future of our cities—those regarding urban renewal, for example —are being made in Washington. It is a sign of the times that the National Municipal Association favors creating a department of urban affairs and of a standing committee on urban affairs in each house of Congress.

The federal government is able to intervene because of its financial strength. The cities are prevented by the legislatures and by the unwillingness of their taxpayers to be taxed (cities almost never pass up a chance to get money from the federal government—that seems like "free" money) from raising enough revenue to do for themselves what they want done. The state governments are generally conservative; even when they are not, they may be unwilling to help because of partisan considerations. Therefore the federal government rides to the rescue. Of course, there are always many conditions attached to the acceptance of federal funds; municipal officials working with grants-in-aid therefore become in effect agents of the federal government as well as agents of the states.

The federal government is now in one way or another involved in an astonishing range of city activities: low-rent public housing, urban renewal, civil defense, sewage treatment construction programs, hospital grants, rivers and harbor improvements, National Guard armory construction, air pollution control, public health, the school lunch and school milk programs, library services, airport construction, highways, surplus property distribution, FBI training of local police officers, training for sanitary engineers, mental health, and public facility loans.[9]

[9] In the fiscal year 1961–62, various federal agencies planned to make commitments to cities totaling over 3.1 billion dollars, including:

$700 million for urban renewal projects
$1.4 billion for highways
$511 million for low-rent public housing
$75 million for airports
$150 million for public facility loans
$80 million for sewage treatment facilities
$190 million for hospitals

These totals exclude many other grant and loan programs, including federal insurance or purchase of home mortgages.

This trend toward the greater dependence of cities on the federal government continued without even a momentary check despite the determined efforts of the Republican administration in 1953–1960 to change it. President Eisenhower was keen on transferring from the federal government to the states activities that he thought were properly theirs. Speaking at a Governors' Conference in June 1957, he said that federal powers should be "checked, hedged about, and restrained" and he suggested creation of a committee of high federal and state officials to "designate functions which the states are ready and willing to assume and finance that are now financed wholly or in part by the federal government." The committee, he said, should look for revenue sources that could be turned over from the federal government to the states in order to enable them to carry the additional functions that they would assume under the reorganization.

The Joint Federal-State Action Committee was then appointed to carry all this into effect. It was composed of distinguished men, including three members of the cabinet, the director of the Bureau of the Budget, and ten governors. It had the full support of the President, an excellent staff, and the advantage of a vast amount of background research data. There were no party or factional disagreements within it. The President, his cabinet, and the committee all wanted action—not just another report. The committee worked for more than two years and found just two programs to recommend for transfer from federal to state hands. One was the federal grant program for vocational education and the other was federal grants for municipal waste treatment plants. These programs together amounted to about two percent of the federal grants for that year. To enable the states to finance these programs, the committee recommended a four percent credit against the federal tax on telephone calls. President Eisenhower recommended these modest measures to Congress, where they promptly died.[10]

No doubt there are many reasons for this dismal record. Probably one of the most important is that the agencies affected and the interest groups allied with them knew that the programs would not flourish in the climate that most state governments would provide. But another reason, and doubtless a very important one, is that the city governments were appalled at the prospect of having to work with and through state governments.

[10] See Morton Grodzins, "The Federal System," in President's Commission on National Goals, *Goals for Americans* (New York, 1960), pp. 265–284.

CHAPTER 6 · THE DISTRIBUTION
OF AUTHORITY WITHIN THE CITY

THE AMERICAN city is not governed by a single hierarchy of authority in which all lines are gathered together at the top in one set of hands.
On the contrary, from a purely formal standpoint, one can hardly say
that there is such a thing as a local government. There are a great many
of them. Or, more aptly, bits and pieces of many governments are
scattered around the local scene. To make any one of the governments
work, it is necessary for someone to gather up the bits and bring them
into a working relation with each other. For most important matters,
the activity of several of the local governments is needed, and therefore
governments, as well as bits of governments, must be brought into
proper relation with each other. All this gathering up and bringing
together of authority requires the generation and use of political influence. The politician is a kind of broker who arranges the terms on
which the possessors of the bits and pieces of power will act in relation
to one another. To understand how he works, it is necessary to look at
how authority is distributed.

Much of it is decentralized all the way to the voter. This occurs in
three ways:

1. *In elections.* The voter has the opportunity frequently—sometimes every year or every two, otherwise every four—to replace the
mayor, councilmen, and sometimes several other heads of the government. The mayor (if there is no mayor, the council) is usually elected
at large; thus the leading element of the city government is within
reach of the whole electorate. In many places, the council is elected
on a ward basis. From a formal standpoint, this decentralizes authority
even further, for there are then several (in Chicago fifty) different
electorates. There was a time when the voters of many cities could
recall their elected officials from office, but that can be done in very
few places today.

2. *In referenda on public expenditures, taxes, and other policy questions.* These represent the extension to city government of the principles
of the New England town meeting. Over half the state constitutions
prohibit cities from incurring debts or issuing bonds except with the

approval of a majority of the voters. In some cases, the voters also pass on tax proposals, or on whether or not liquor shall be sold. In some states, the legislature may refer questions to the people of the localities. In some cities, city officials may ask the voters for advisory opinions on certain questions. The use of the referendum is widespread; even in the largest cities, crucial matters—especially concerning capital expenditures—are put before the electorate, and in these cases the policy of the city officials necessarily hinges upon their expectations as to what the voters will do, or as to what they can be persuaded to do. In many cities, the voters have repeatedly turned down proposals to build new schools, to install modern waste disposal plants, to improve the police force, and so on. In Los Angeles, which is an extreme case, the strategy of political conflict is more often than not based upon the assumption that the crucial decision will be made not by the city council of Los Angeles, the board of supervisors of the county, or the legislature of the state, but by the voters in a referendum election. For example, the voters there decided by referendum not to have a public housing program.

This reliance on direct democracy in the conduct of the affairs of cities is a peculiarly American phenomenon. In London, for example, the voters are never asked to decide policy questions. It would be taken for granted on all sides that that is the job of the elected officials.

3. *In the possibility of taxpayers' suits.* The courts have in many states made it possible to bring suits against a local government in cases where one has no other standing than as a taxpayer. By initiating such a suit, a taxpayer may sometimes frustrate and may usually hamper and delay the actions of the local government. For example, a group of taxpayers brought suit in 1939 to enjoin the New York Board of Higher Education from employing Bertrand Russell to teach philosophy at City College. The suit was never decided in court, but it succeeded in its purpose because the adverse publicity caused the mayor to withdraw the invitation. In 1960 some business interests (Tiffany jewelers and the Plaza and Pierre hotels) brought suit to prevent New York City from using some $800,000 given to it to construct a sidewalk cafe in Central Park. In 1961 certain Democratic party leaders brought suit to block the efforts of Mayor Robert Wagner (who is also a Democrat) to create a charter revision commission.

A recent survey by the *Yale Law Journal* classified taxpayers' suits (in descending order of importance) as follows:

(1) challenges to the use of the eminent domain power in connec-

tion with slum clearance, housing, highways, airports, and other public works projects;

(2) attacks on the constitutionality of various methods of bond financing used by municipalities to circumvent limitations on indebtedness;

(3) cases questioning the granting of franchises or licenses which represent public approval of privately owned but publicly used facilities;

(4) efforts to withhold salary payments to civil servants who hold office in violation of statutory standards;

(5) challenges to sales or donations of the public domain to private parties;

(6) cases to achieve civil liberties objectives such as the prevention of expenditures for illegal methods of law enforcement or expenditures which would violate the separation of church and state;

(7) suits to reapportion election or judicial districts.

The editors commented:

Such litigation allows the courts, within the framework of traditional notions of "standing," to add to the controls over public officials inherent in the elective process the judicial scrutiny of the statutory and constitutional validity of their acts. Taxpayers' suits also extend the uniquely American concept of judicial review to legislative action by allowing minorities ineffective at the ballot box to invalidate statutes or ordinances on constitutional grounds. . . . Taxpayers' suits thus create an army of potential private attorneys-general acting on whatever private incentives may induce them to spend the time and money to bring a taxpayer's suit: . . . And since group financing of such litigation is not infrequent, taxpayers' suits also mobilize various voluntary associations seeking private, economic, or social objectives to further law enforcement and prevention of corruption in government.[1]

In Los Angeles, a well-known attorney has built his practice almost entirely out of taxpayers' suits; he helps citizens in their efforts to stop the government from taking their property for highways, housing developments, and countless other civic projects.

"THE CITY GOVERNMENT"

Turning now to what is commonly called "the city government" (but which is really only the most conspicuous of several governments within the city), we find that the principle of the separation of legislative from executive power is generally observed. When this country

[1] "Taxpayers' Suits, A Survey and a Summary," *Yale Law Journal*, April 1960, pp. 895–924.

was formed, cities were governed (to the extent that they were governed at all) by councils which had undivided control. This was, and still is, the British system. The separation of executive from legislative authority in American cities began about 1820 with the popular election of executives. Not only mayors but certain other officials became less and less the creatures of the councils. In New York City, for example, the charter of 1849 created separate city departments whose heads were popularly elected. A few years later (1853), the mayor was given authority to appoint department heads with the approval of the council. Apparently the reason for introducing the principle of the separation of powers into American local government was doctrinaire rather than practical: the separation of powers was a fashion of those days, one which the much-admired federal system had helped to spread.

The principle of the separation of powers was implemented very slowly, especially in the smaller cities. Throughout the nineteenth century, most cities had what is now called the "weak-mayor" council form of government. The council appointed the principal administrative officers, prepared the budget, and supervised the expenditures. The mayor presided over the council, recommended legislation, and exercised a veto. He and the council shared responsibility for the management of the city's affairs.

Beginning about 1850, there was a general movement toward dividing the authority of the council into smaller pieces. By the end of the century, about one third of the cities of over 25,000 population had bicameral councils. Of the twelve largest cities, six had them. (Philadelphia, for example, had 41 members in its select council and 149 in its common council.) Apparently people were becoming more distrustful of centralized authority and—what was not very different—the power of wealth. At any rate, as the size of the councils grew, the property interests of their members decreased. For example, in 1822, when the Boston council had 8 members in its upper house and 48 in its lower, all those in the upper house and all but 3 of those in the lower were property owners. In 1895, when there were 12 in the upper house and 75 in the lower, only 9 in the upper house and 16 in the lower were property owners. In 1822, the members of the lower house owned 200 of every 100,000 dollars worth of property in Boston; in 1895, they owned only 3 of every 100,000 dollars worth.[2]

---

[2] John A. Fairlie, *Essays in Municipal Administration* (New York: Macmillan, 1908), p. 135.

Around 1880, there was a general effort to strengthen the position of the mayors by increasing their appointive powers, as had been done in New York earlier. This of course was a movement *toward* centralization, but its impulse was also democratic. Strengthening the executive was a way to increase popular control, for the executive, being elected at large, was responsive to the will of the majority, and a strong executive could overcome a city council. The councils, in many places, were beginning to come under the control of political machines.

Where the mayor's authority exceeds that of the council, what is called the "strong-mayor" form of government exists. One cannot distinguish sharply between systems having a "weak" and a "strong" mayor, but in a general way the strong-mayor form resembles the national government. The mayor shares with the council responsibility for policy-making, but he alone has administrative responsibility. He appoints department heads without the approval of the council, makes up the budget, and usually his veto can be overridden only by a two-thirds vote of the council. He is the dominant force in the city government; the council must follow his lead.

Most cities of over 500,000 population now have something approximating the strong-mayor form of government, although the closeness of the approximation varies greatly from place to place. For example, although Chicago has a strong-mayor form of government, authority in city and county matters (most important problems involve both the city and the county) is shared among no less than 341 officials as follows:

53 city officials: Mayor, City Treasurer, City Clerk, 50 Aldermen

21 county officials: Assessor, Treasurer, Clerk, Coroner, State's Attorney, Sheriff, 15 County Commissioners

12 special officials: 9 Trustees of the Metropolitan Sanitary District, 3 members of the Zoning Board of Appeals

95 judges: County Judge, Probate Judge, 20 Circuit Court Judges, 36 Superior Court Judges, 37 Municipal Court Judges

160 party officials: 50 ward and 30 township committeemen for each of the two political parties

In Los Angeles, several departments of the city government control their own funds and are therefore largely independent of the mayor and council. These include the departments administering airports, the city employees retirement system, the harbor, the library, recreation and park facilities, water and power, and the fire and police pension systems. Minneapolis elects forty-nine officials. The mayor can appoint no one except his own secretary without approval of the council, and he can remove only his secretary, the superintendent of police, and the director of civil defense. The comptroller of New York City is elected and therefore not subject to control by the mayor. Normally he is a political opponent of the mayor's.

In the smaller cities—those of them that do not have the council-manager form of government—the division of authority is often even greater. Most of them are on the "weak" mayor side of the continuum.

The council-manager form, which from its inception in 1910 has been favored by municipal reform groups, carries the separation of powers a step further by placing all "administrative" authority in the hands of a professional manager who is hired by the elected council (which is the "policy-making" body) to serve at its pleasure. Under this plan, there is a mayor, but his duties are purely ceremonial. The manager does not take orders from the members of the council as individuals: he takes them only from the council as a collective body, and then only in matters that are "policy."

This means in effect, of course, that where the manager has the confidence and respect of the council he may run the city with little or no interference. But it means, also, that where the council is divided, he may not be able to venture beyond routine. Nearly half the cities of over 25,000 are under this plan, but Cincinnati, Dallas, San Antonio, and San Diego are the only cities over 500,000 having managers.[3]

One other form should be mentioned in passing, although it is of little importance. In a commission form of government the voters elect a small commission (usually five members) which exercises both executive and legislative functions. Each commissioner is the chief executive of one of the city departments, and the commission collectively makes policy. This is the system in St. Paul, Salt Lake City, and a few other places, but it is generally obsolete.

OTHER "CITY GOVERNMENTS"

Except perhaps in very small cities, the mayor and council—what is usually spoken of as "the city government"—constitute only one of several governments within the city. In most sizable cities and in many very small ones there are boards and commissions, councils, single

[3] For details, see below, pp. 168 ff.

officers, and special districts having little or no formal connection with the city government proper (i.e., the mayor and council).

During the nineteenth century, when reformers were anxious to keep certain city functions out of the hands of party machines, the practice was to create a large number of entirely independent boards and commissions—sometimes twenty or thirty. Most of these eventually became city departments under the mayor and council, but today many are still loosely tied, or not tied at all, to the city government proper. The distribution of authority in Manchester, New Hampshire, a city of 86,000, is typical of what exists in many small cities. Manchester has twenty-one boards and commissions that are loosely tied to the city government. The mayor appoints three by himself and nine subject to confirmation by the council, and the council appoints nine others by itself. The mayor has a veto which can be overridden by ten of the fourteen councilmen. The budget is made up not by the mayor but by the whole board of aldermen. There is an elected board of education, but it has practically no power. The head of the police department is appointed by a state commission, and the commissioner of charities is elected at large. There is a finance committee, appointed by the governor, which can veto any expenditure by the city but whose own decisions in turn can be vetoed by the mayor and council together. Municipal judges are appointed by the governor.

The New York City school system, a very large government indeed (it spends half a billion dollars a year to provide schooling for a million pupils), offered, prior to its reorganization in 1962, another example of the extreme division of authority. The nine members of the Board of Education were appointed by the mayor for seven-year terms (tradition virtually compelled him to appoint three Catholics, three Protestants, and three Jews and to appoint from names submitted to him by certain voluntary associations) and could not be removed by him except after hearings on formal charges. The board appointed the superintendent and ten assistant superintendents; these constituted the Board of Superintendents. The Board of Education, however, could not remove any of these officials except after hearings on formal charges; and although they were appointed for six-year terms they normally served for life. The superintendent, therefore, had little real control over his nominal subordinates. He cast one vote out of eleven in the Board of Superintendents and was, Wallace Sayre and Herbert Kaufman say, "simply the chairman of a committee." But this was not the end of the division of authority. The school system got its operating budget from the Board of Estimate, a wholly separate body in which borough presidents, most of whom are the creatures of party organizations, were in a majority. Moreover, the state education law placed many detailed restrictions on the operation of the school system. After some scandals in school construction in 1961, the state commissioner of education (an appointee of the Board of Regents, which is in turn chosen by the legislature) pointed out to the New York City Board of Education that although it was appointed by the mayor, he (the commissioner) had power to remove both board members and school superintendents for neglect of duty. The board, he said, had better improve itself, or else. "There was no doubt about it," one of the board members told a reporter later, "the Commissioner is our boss and he had us on the carpet."[4]

This division of authority might be thought sufficient to satisfy almost everyone. Yet, when the question arose of how to improve the organization of the school system so as to avoid a recurrence of the 1961 scandals, two members of the legislature's committee on school finance said what was needed was to "break the concentration of power" in the city education board by establishing "smaller, more responsive, and more workable borough-wide units."[5]

In many cities, most of the city's affairs are carried on by independent agencies the heads of which, although they may be appointed by the mayor, have longer tenure than he, an arrangement that usually deprives him of the opportunity to exercise influence by threatening not to reappoint.

Many such independent boards and commissions have power to make ordinances (essentially laws of local application) and to raise revenue by levying taxes or issuing bonds. For example, Sayre and Kaufman write:

The Sanitary Code is enacted by the New York City Board of Health, a body appointed by the Mayor and invested by state legislation and the charter with authority to adopt regulations on all matters of health and sanitation. . . . The regulations of the Board—that is, the Sanitary Code— have the effect of state or city legislation within the city; the Board is thus really a unifunctional legislative organ. The Board of Education and the Board of Hospitals are somewhat similar institutions.[6]

[4] *New York Times*, July 21, 1961.
[5] *Ibid.*, July 25, 1961.
[6] Wallace S. Sayre and Herbert Kaufman, *Governing New York City* (New York: Russell Sage Foundation, 1960), pp. 97–98.

Some independent boards have their own police forces. Until recently, for example, the Chicago Park District patrolled some streets which the Chicago police could not enter.

Still another kind of local government with financial autonomy— taxing power and usually power to issue bonds—is the *special district*. This is created by the state legislature and is an arm of the state government (more precisely, it is a quasi-corporation); it is therefore independent in a somewhat different sense from the boards and commissions (municipal corporations) mentioned above. Usually a special district administers only one function of government, such as schools, airports, housing, sewage disposal, rapid transit, recreation, or highway construction. Its boundaries may coincide with those of the city, or it may include several cities. Its officials are usually appointed either by officials of local governments or by local and state officials together. Some special districts, however, are run entirely by the state. Others are run by boards whose members, or some of them, are *ex officio*. Very rarely are the governing boards of special districts elected.

Because they are independent of other governments, of the voters, and to a large extent of the legislatures, special districts are a very important element of decentralization in urban governmental systems. They are in a position to do very much as they please, and it sometimes pleases them not to collaborate with the other city governments. Robert Moses of New York, who ran several such authorities, was a case in point.

Special districts exist for three main reasons. One is to avoid the debt limits that often hamper city governments. Another is to take the schools (or airport, or sewage plant, or whatever) "out of politics," meaning, of course, out of partisan politics. The third is to get the advantages of a centralized—and therefore in effect undemocratic— structure of authority; the idea is to put all authority over the matter in a single set of hands, and to prevent others, including the legislature and the electorate, from interfering. Naturally, this last reason is not advanced publicly, at least not without a fig leaf to cover it.

It must be clear by now that it is no exaggeration to say that a city (meaning now the area within the boundaries of a municipality) is governed not by one but by several governments. In most cases, there is no *formal* mechanism by which all of these governments can be brought together to coordinate their activities or to decide jointly on matters of general interest. In most sizable cities, collaboration among governments is essential to all important undertakings, but it must be arranged—if it can be arranged at all—informally, and therefore, usually, by means of a political process.

METROPOLITAN ORGANIZATION

If we define the city not as the area within the boundaries of a single municipality, but as the *whole of a contiguous area of compact settlement*—i.e., as a metropolitan area—then we are much further from having a single local government. There are now 212 metropolitan areas (as defined by the Census), and in none of them is there a government having general jurisdiction over the whole area. Most of the smaller metropolitan areas have within them about ten municipalities, one or two counties, and several special districts. The larger ones have hundreds of governments.

The nearest approaches to metropolitan area government are in Dade County (which includes Miami), Florida, and Davidson County (which includes Nashville), Tennessee. Dade County employs a manager and carries on many, but not all, functions of local government; its boundaries, however, are not coterminous with the metropolitan area. The Davidson County government, which will eventually carry on most local government functions, went into full operation in April 1963.

In a number of places there are planning commissions supported and controlled jointly by the cities and counties within a metropolitan area. Some of these planning bodies are expected to produce comprehensive plans for the development of their regions. If they were to do so, and if these plans had the force of law, they would be governments —indeed, supergovernments. Actually, these bodies nowhere have the authority to do more than recommend, and their recommendations are rarely taken very seriously. In principle, there is nothing to stop a state legislature from creating a metropolitan government which *will* have ample authority to make and carry out plans for the whole metropolis. Numerous proposals of this kind have been put forward, but none, for reasons to be discussed later, has made much headway.

Several metropolitan areas include parts of two or more states (the New York–New Jersey area is the outstanding case). In these cases, supergovernments could only be created by means of interstate compacts ratified by Congress.

Professor Charles Merriam once proposed that the great metropolitan areas break themselves off from their rural hinterlands and become states. This would be another way of creating metropolitan governments. But it is a most unlikely possibility, for the Constitution says that "no new State shall be formed or erected within the Jurisdiction of any other State; nor any State be formed by the Junction of two or more States, or parts of States, without the Consent of the Legislatures of the States concerned as well as of the Congress."

We have said that the politician is a kind of broker who works out the terms on which the many possessors of bits and pieces of legal authority can be brought to concert their action so as to produce a public policy. But this chapter should make it clear that some elements of this decentralization of authority—taxpayers' suits, for example—are largely or entirely beyond the reach of the politician. Further, as a rule more than one politician-broker is required to bring the possessors of power together, and this means that the politicians themselves must first come to terms with each other.[7]

[7] For a formalized account of how decentralization of authority is overcome in a political system, see Banfield, *Political Influence* (New York: Free Press of Glencoe, 1961), chap. xi.

CHAPTER 7 · ELECTORAL SYSTEMS

THE ARRANGEMENTS whereby a city's legislators (called council-men or aldermen in most cities and commissioners in a few) are chosen —especially the number and size of election districts (called wards in some cities) and the procedures by which votes are cast and counted —constitute what we will call its "electoral system." Around any such system there develops a set of strategies for the gaining of power. The strategists take account both of the "rules of the game" and each other's strategies, and there arises by mutual adjustment an equilibrium that becomes in time so familiar and taken for granted that the electoral system appears to be a purely technical, and therefore trivial, feature of the city's politics. But this is an illusion, for the electoral system pro-foundly affects the character of politics. It should not be surprising, then, that efforts to change fundamentally the distribution of power within a city are often directed toward changing the electoral system. And it should likewise not be surprising that the changes proposed are discussed by proponents and opponents as if they could be judged on purely technical grounds.

Both sides usually act as if "right" or "democratic" electoral rules could be arrived at by logical deduction from a set of clear, simple, and agreed-upon principles. In reality, there are very few principles that are of much use in settling such matters, and none at all that can be decisive. For example, the principle that all votes should count equally does not tell us whether we should have two, three, five, ten, or twenty districts, or perhaps none at all, and it does not tell us how to draw district lines. It affords no basis for choosing the right point on the spectrum between an electoral system in which each legislator represents a single voter and one in which one legislator represents all of the voters.

Similarly, to say that all districts should have the same number of voters does not help much. Districts having the same number of voters may be drawn in such a way that one political party is greatly disad-vantaged by having its voters concentrated in a few districts while the other party's voters are spread evenly through many districts. It is usually—perhaps always—impossible to draw district lines that will not favor one party against the other. But even if it were possible to draw lines that were "correct" with respect to the parties, these lines might be "incorrect" with respect to some or all of the many other cleavages within the community. Should district lines encompass or divide certain ethnic, racial, religious, neighborhood, and income groupings? By one method of districting we assure that a given group will be "represented" in the legislature, and by another we assure that it will not be, or that it will be under some handicap. Sometimes even the members of such a group cannot decide what rules are best for them. Negroes, for example, do not agree whether it is better to "give" Negroes a legislator by throwing all Negro voters into one district or, by splitting the Negro voters among several districts, to enable them to influence (but not to "have") a larger number of legislators.

In short, any electoral system confers advantages and disadvantages —sometimes some of both on the same persons. No system can possibly do perfect justice to all under all circumstances.

Let us consider first the number and size of election districts. Although the popular notion is that every alderman has a ward, actually, as Table 6 shows, 60 percent of all cities of over 10,000 population elect their councilmen at large and only 23 percent elect them solely from districts. The other 17 percent combine the at-large and district principles by electing some councilmen in one way and some in the other.

TABLE 6. Electoral systems by size of city, 1960

| | Percentage of cities under system | | |
	At-large	District	Combination
All cities over 10,000	60	23	17
Cities 100,000–250,000	65	15	20
Cities 250,000–500,000	70	10	20
Cities over 500,000	45	20	35

Source: *Municipal Yearbook, 1962*, p. 103.

Most cities elect five, seven, or nine councilmen, although a few large ones elect many more. Chicago elects fifty, Cleveland thirty-three, St. Louis twenty-nine, New York twenty-five, and Baltimore twenty-one. Some small cities have large councils, however, and some large cities have small ones. Stamford, Connecticut, has forty councilmen and Detroit has only nine. With very few exceptions, cities have unicameral legislatures. New York City is the most important of the exceptions; it divides the legislative powers between the City Council, having twenty-five members, and the Board of Estimate, having eight.

In about half the cities of over 5,000 population, councilmen are elected for four-year terms. Forty percent of the cities elect them for two-year terms, and ten percent of them for three-year terms.

Although in this chapter we shall speak mainly of councilmen, it should be remembered that the city elects other officials as well. Three fourths of all cities of over 5,000 population elect their mayors directly; in most of the others they are chosen by the city council or commission. Of the twenty-one cities of over 500,000 population, only three (Cincinnati, San Antonio, and, of course, Washington, D.C.) do not have directly elected mayors. Furthermore, half the cities of over 5,000 population elect city-wide officials in addition to the mayor: most commonly, a treasurer, clerk, assessor, or auditor. Of the twenty largest cities, only five (Boston, Cincinnati, Cleveland, Dallas, and San Antonio) do not elect executives in addition to the mayor. Finally, most large cities (although only about a third of all cities) elect their mayors for four-year terms; most of the others elect them for two-year terms.

In this chapter, we shall describe the district and at-large electoral systems and show the consequences that they seem to have for the distribution of power in the city and the manner in which the city is governed. The electoral system is, of course, only one among many factors affecting the politics of the city, and it is difficult—in fact, impossible—to isolate its effects from those of party structure, social cleavage, ethos, the organization of interest groups, and so on. In order to avoid some needless complications and to make the most significant comparisons we can, we discuss the electoral systems of large cities only. By focusing on cities with large and therefore heterogeneous populations, we can exhibit the consequences of the various types of electoral system more clearly.[1]

THE DISTRICT SYSTEM

As Table 7 shows, those large cities which have partisan elections tend also to have district rather than at-large systems. (Chicago is

[1] For another classification of big-city electoral systems, see Charles E. Gilbert and Christopher Clague, "Electoral Competition and Electoral Systems in Large Cities," *Journal of Politics*, vol. XXIV (1962), pp. 323–349.

only nominally nonpartisan and therefore belongs in the partisan group where it appears.) The connection between the partisan and district systems, as well as between the nonpartisan and at-large systems, is of considerable significance, for, as we shall see later, the connected elements tend in both cases to produce the same style of politics and to reinforce one another.

TABLE 7. Electoral systems in cities over 500,000 population,* 1960

	At-large	District	Combination
Partisan cities	Pittsburgh	Chicago Cleveland	Baltimore Buffalo New York New Orleans Philadelphia St. Louis
Nonpartisan cities	Boston Cincinnati Dallas** Detroit San Antonio San Diego** San Francisco Seattle	Los Angeles Milwaukee	Houston

* Excluding Washington, D.C.
** In Dallas and San Diego, councilmen are nominated by districts but run at large.

Source: *Municipal Yearbook,* 1961.

Among the large cities using the district system, the ratio of population to number of districts varies a great deal. Table 8 shows that New York, Philadelphia, and Los Angeles, for example, have what we shall call "large" (i.e., populous) districts, whereas St. Louis and Cleveland, for example, have "small" ones. The importance of such differences is great. On an *a priori* basis—that is, considering only what logically follows from the size of the district, all other factors being left out of account—one would expect that the smaller the district: (a) the wider the dispersal of power and therefore the harder to get councilmen to act in unison; (b) the greater the number of points of access through which the citizen could bring influence to bear upon the city government; (c) the better the representation of neighborhoods and of ethnically defined natural areas; (d) the easier for minorities to secure "recognition"; (e) the worse the representation of such city-wide interests as are not also neighborhood ones; (f) the greater the tendency for the council to proceed by a process of trading (Councilman A agreeing to support Councilman B's effort to get something for his district on condition that Councilman B do the same for him in return) and to do nothing when advantageous trades cannot be arranged; and (g) the more accessible the councilman and the greater his willingness to do favors for constituents.

TABLE 8. Average population of council districts in selected large cities

City	1960 population	Number of districts	Population per district (approx.)
New York	7,781,984	25°	311,000
Philadelphia	2,002,512	10°°	200,000
Los Angeles	2,612,704	15	161,000
Chicago	3,550,404	50	71,000
Baltimore	939,024	20°	47,000
Minneapolis	482,872	13	37,100
Milwaukee	741,324	20	37,200
St. Louis	750,026	28°	26,800
Cleveland	876,050	33	26,500

° In each of these three cities, there is one additional council member (a "Council President" usually) who runs at large.
°° In addition, seven councilmen are elected at large, making a total of seventeen.

To a considerable extent, these *a priori* propositions describe how things do in fact work in the large cities. For example, in Chicago, a city with a small-district system, aldermen are extremely responsive to local pressures; people wanting zoning variations, driveway permits, business licenses, and help in dealing with the police go to them as a matter of course.[2] District lines in Chicago are drawn to conform to neighborhood boundaries and to natural areas that are ethnically-defined, and the council is filled with men who are, in Robert K. Merton's term, "locals" whose influence depends upon a network of personal relations and whose orientation is parochial. A Chicago councilman represents his districts symbolically as well as directly; after he

[2] See Martin Meyerson and Edward C. Banfield, *Politics, Planning, and the Public Interest* (Glencoe, Ill.: Free Press, 1955), especially chap. iii.

has become rich and powerful, he continues to live in the neighborhood and to dress and talk as "one of the boys." Minority groups get "recognition" easily; there has been a Negro in the Chicago council since 1915 and now there are six. In Cleveland, another small-district city, a study of a sample of 410 eastside voters showed that more than half the heads of households had some contact with their councilmen; this was more than twice as many as had contact with other local officials.[3] Cleveland, incidentally, has nine Negroes in its council.

A small-district system often exists in conjunction with a machine. For present purposes, a "machine" may be defined as a party organization held together and motivated mainly by the exchange of personal favors for votes; thus it is based on the same principle as small-district politics. Indeed, small districts are, so to speak, the building blocks from which machines are normally constituted. Chicago and Cleveland are cases in point; in both cities party organization and council organization are based on the same geographic units. The operation of a machine, however, tends to produce some effects that are inconsistent with the *a priori* logic of the small-district system. As we will explain later, a "boss" may acquire enough informal power to compel the councilmen to do as he says; when this happens, the council may have to put city-wide matters before neighborhood ones.

Anyone who seeks to legislate for the city "as a whole" (whether for selfish or unselfish reasons) will object to the small-district plan. Typically, businessmen, upper-class civic leaders, and reformers oppose small districts. Such people are invariably placed at a disadvantage by them; this is true in part because they are minority groups, in part because the resources they command (social status, expertise, corporate wealth) are not effective in influencing small-district councilmen, and in part because they feel that a politics of personal influence and neighborhood interests is wrong and inefficient. They will favor large districts or, even better, at-large elections, in order to encourage councilmen to act on behalf of the city "as a whole" and because the wealth, publicity, and prestige they control will then be more effective.

When the size of the districts is increased, the nature of a city's politics changes markedly. In 1901, New York City, with 3.4 million inhabitants, had a board of aldermen of seventy-three members. Each alderman therefore represented only 47,000 people. This electoral

[3] Marvin B. Sussman and R. Clyde White, *Cleveland, Ohio: A Study of Social Life and Change* (Cleveland: Western Reserve University Press, 1959).

system was found by the leaders of the Democratic machine to be highly congenial to their style of politics. By 1949 a series of reforms had reduced the number of seats to twenty-five and meanwhile the population had risen to nearly eight million. Each alderman now represents about 315,000 persons. The nearly seven-fold increase that occurred in the size of the council districts in fifty years has had important consequences. Councilmen are now elected from districts far larger than the basic geographic unit of the party. (The basic party unit is the assembly district, but some of these are subdivided for party purposes into halves and even thirds; a typical district leader has about eighty thousand persons in his district.) The councilman is no longer the "errand boy" of some one party official; if there are several party leaders in his councilmanic district, he must try to please them all. This, of course, may increase his freedom of action; if there are, say, five party leaders, he can probably play them off against each other.

As the New York councilman's district grew in size, he became less accessible to his constituents, and they, in turn, became more heterogeneous. Few districts of 315,000 persons can comprise a "natural" neighborhood or be composed of a single ethnic group. Because of this size and diversity, there are more conflicts within a district than there used to be and it is harder for any one neighborhood or ethnic group to assert itself through its councilman: to him it is only one neighborhood or ethnic group among many. For this reason, it is harder than before for one locality to veto the projects of another; the councilman whose district includes both localities can arbitrate or do what he thinks best for the district "as a whole."

The entry into elective office of the "newer" ethnic groups has been slowed. Although New York City has over a million Negroes, only two Negroes are on the city council, and the first did not win his seat until 1938. Minority-party representation is also reduced. Although Republicans cast from one fourth to one third of the votes in city elections, from 1949 to 1961 there was never more than one Republican on the city council. (In this same period, Chicago has had as many as sixteen Republicans on its council.)

The exclusion of racial and minority-party representatives occurs partly because large districts are often easier to gerrymander than small ones. Given a certain population density, the smaller the district the harder it is to draw district lines so that a particular ethnic or party group will have no chance of winning office. This is best seen in Los

Angeles. There districts are large, population densities low, and re-districting occurs as frequently as every four years. Although about one voter in six is a Negro, there was no Negro on the council until 1963.

THE AT-LARGE SYSTEM

The significant feature of an at-large system is, of course, that it theoretically gives all councilmen the same constituency: the city. Supporters claim this as a great virtue of the system. Since a councilman must look to the city as a whole for votes, they say, he is obliged to take a city-wide view of things and to concern himself with important issues. At-large election, those who favor it say, eliminates the petty politics of favor-giving and of neighborhood and ethnic advantage and, by doing so, strikes a mortal blow at the machine. To these claims the opponent of the at-large system replies that neighborhood and ethnic-group representation ought not to be sacrificed, that voters cannot possibly know enough about the many at-large councilmanic candidates to choose them wisely, and that the high cost of at-large campaigns (high because they are city-wide) gives interest groups with large bankrolls too much influence in the council.

There seems to be a good deal of truth in these claims and counter-claims. The effect of at-large election is difficult to determine, however, since it is usually combined with nonpartisanship, and the effects of one feature are therefore usually indistinguishable from those of the other. (Among the large cities using the at-large system—Boston, Cincinnati, Dallas, Detroit, San Antonio, San Diego, San Francisco, Seattle, and Pittsburgh—all but the last are nonpartisan.)

There is, as we have suggested above, an affinity between the district type of organization and the machine style of politics. The at-large system does not invariably prevent the growth of a machine, however, as is shown by former Mayor David Lawrence's success in creating a machine in Pittsburgh.

The experience of Boston is of special interest because that city had a nine-member at-large council (1909–1924), then changed to a district system of twenty-two members (1924–1949), and then changed back to a nine-member at-large one in 1949, while all the time remaining nonpartisan.[4] In Boston, it appears, councilmen elected at large

---

[4] Banfield and Martha Derthick (eds.), A Report on Politics in Boston, 2 vols., mimeo (Cambridge, Mass.: Joint Center for Urban Studies, 1960), vol. I, part II, p. 20. It is possible that in the earlier period the elections were nonpartisan in name only.

do in fact take a larger view of city affairs than did the ward-based ones. For example, in 1958 the at-large council passed only twenty orders requesting street improvements in particular localities; but when election was on a district basis the council passed hundreds of such orders every year.

The at-large election system does not always entirely eliminate special constituencies, however. One or two of the Boston councilmen, for example, think of heavily Irish South Boston as "home base"; they do most of their case work there and get an especially heavy vote there. Another councilman has his "home base" in heavily Italian East Boston. Still others treat certain city-wide interest groups (city employees, for example) as their special constituencies. Despite these partial exceptions, it is generally true that councilmen elected at large are less responsive to the voters' wishes than ones elected on a district basis. As one of the Boston councilmen who was brought up under the old ward system explained, "I'm here at City Hall seven hours a day, five days a week. People come to me from all over the city. They know I'm available. But do you see any of the other Councillors around? You bet you don't. They're statesmen, not politicians."

As one would expect, in Boston the old ward system gave minority interests better representation than does the present at-large one. Among the 110 councilmen elected during the twenty-five years under the ward system there were (besides the Irish) 12 Jews, 9 Yankees, 4 Italians, and one Negro. Among the first 45 councilmen elected after the return to the at-large system the Irish and Italians made a clean sweep, electing 39 and 6 respectively.

To a large extent, the choice between an at-large and a district system turns on the conception that one has of the nature of the public interest. Those who think (as middle-class and upper-class people usually do) that the "city as a whole" has an interest which should be paramount will tend to favor the at-large system. On the other hand, those who think (as the lower class people generally do) that politics is a struggle for personal, neighborhood, or other special advantages will favor the district system.

In some cities, the at-large system (combined, of course, with non-partisanship and other related factors) seems to produce a city council that is powerless. This is most strikingly the case in Boston, where the council has no real function in city government. The council members have little knowledge of the details of city affairs; if they act at all, it can only be to obstruct the plans of the mayor. But this is risky, for the mayor not only has responsibility for and information about the government, but also can—if he is strong—build a city-wide constituency which a councilman would be foolish to challenge. A weak mayor can be almost paralyzed by a council which interferes with day-to-day administration; a strong mayor can virtually ignore the council, compelling it to talk in idle generalities. This may be why some Yankee Republicans prefer the at-large system in Boston even though it denies them representation. They may think it better to be left out of an impotent council than to be a minority in a strong one. They may also think it better to have a council that argues futilely about important matters, leaving decisions to the mayor and the bureaucracy, than to have one which exercises real power but only on neighborhood matters.

But in other cities which have a different ethos—cities which are less heavily lower-middle-class than Boston, or less Irish—at-large councils may behave differently and have more power because different kinds of politicians get elected to them. Boston may be a city in which, for demographic and historical reasons, "locals" who are well-suited to a ward-style politics are elected to an at-large council in which they find themselves unable to perform effectively the role expected of them. They flounder like fish out of water. In other cities—perhaps Detroit or Cincinnati—the council is composed more of "cosmopolitans" who are well-adapted to playing the role of at-large "statesmen" and who therefore can wield considerable influence.

PROPORTIONAL REPRESENTATION

A modification of the at-large system known as "proportional representation" (PR) was proposed by reformers in the first decade of the century and subsequently tried in about twenty-five cities (notably Cincinnati from 1924 to 1957 and New York from 1936 until 1949) and abandoned in all but one (Cambridge, Massachusetts).[5] Various kinds of proportional representation systems have been used in American cities; none has had any enduring popularity. The system that was used in Cincinnati and New York, called the "Hare system" after Thomas H. Hare, whose book (which appeared in London in 1859) first popularized the subject, is one important example. The candidates run at

[5] See Ralph A. Straetz, *PR Politics in Cincinnati* (New York: New York University Press, 1958), and Belle Zeller and Hugh A. Bone, "The Repeal of PR in New York City: Ten Years in Retrospect," *American Political Science Review*, December 1948, pp. 1127–1148.

large and each voter ranks them in accordance with his preferences, usually by marking "1," "2," "3," and so on after their names. To be elected, a candidate must receive a "quota." This is determined by dividing the total vote cast by the number of council seats to be filled plus one and adding one to the quotient. Ballots are then sorted according to first choices; any candidate with the quota or more is declared elected. His ballots in excess of those he needs to be elected are then distributed according to the second choices marked on them. If no one has enough first choices to be elected, the candidate with the least number of first choices is eliminated and his ballots distributed according to the second choices marked on them. This process continues until as many candidates are elected as there are seats to be filled. The continual redistribution of ballots according to voter preferences means that often fourth, fifth, or even sixth choices are counted.

The effect of PR was to increase the representation of minority parties and groups. In Cincinnati, it usually resulted in the election of one or two Negroes to the council. This, indeed, was one of the principal reasons why it was abandoned there; eventually, its opponents said, it would give the city a "Negro boss." In New York, PR gave the Republicans a sizable representation in a council that had hitherto been almost entirely Democratic, and it permitted over time the election of five members of the American Labor Party, two Liberals, and two Communists. The election of the Communists enabled its opponents to destroy it. In Worcester, Massachusetts, where it was tried from 1947 to 1960, PR produced a council in which two minority groups—Jews and Yankees—were represented. Its proponents (Republicans and Jewish Democrats) argued that going back to an ordinary plurality system would mean that Irish Catholics would elect all nine councilmen.

PR breaks down party control over nominations and permits mavericks who owe nothing to party leaders to win office. For this reason, the Republicans in New York, although they gained seats by it, did not exert themselves to prevent the Democrats, who of course opposed it strongly, from succeeding in their campaign for its abolition.

Other means besides PR have been devised to permit representation of a minority party in a large, one-party city. Philadelphia, for example, has seventeen city councilmen, ten of whom are elected from districts and the remaining seven at large. A voter may vote for only five at-large councilmen and a party may nominate only five at-large candidates. This means that two at-large seats are bound to be won by the minority party. New York City, as part of the charter reforms of 1961, adopted a variant of this procedure. Beginning in November, 1963, two councilmen were to be elected at large from each borough (in addition to the district councilmen) but each party would nominate and each voter vote for only one.

KINDS OF ELECTIONS

Local elections are usually held in two stages. In a partisan system, the first stage is a primary election at which the registered voters of each party choose candidates from among whatever persons offer themselves. In an "open" primary a qualified voter need not be a member of the party whose candidates he helps to choose (he cannot vote in the primaries of *both* parties, however); in a "closed" primary he must declare a preference for a party or else be a registered member of one, and of course he can vote only in his party's primary. The candidates chosen in the primaries face each other in a general election held a few months later.

In a nonpartisan system, the first stage is usually called a "preliminary" election. This election, in which all qualified voters may vote on all candidates who present themselves, eliminates all candidates beyond twice the number to be elected finally. If, for example, there are five candidates for mayor in the preliminary, three will be eliminated. The candidates who are not eliminated then face each other in a runoff election.

In both partisan and nonpartisan systems, candidates get their names on the ballots by taking some or all of three steps: filing a formal declaration of candidacy, presenting a petition signed by some prescribed minimum number of qualified voters, and depositing a sum of money as evidence of the seriousness of their candidacy.

In most cities, local elections are held in years, or at seasons of the year, when there are no state or national ones. This practice accords with the view of the reform movement that local government should be kept separate from the "irrelevant" concerns of state and nation. Local politicians often find it advantageous to them to have local elections insulated from the uncertainties of state and national ones, and it is safe to say that this is an additional reason for their being held at different times.

Usually the qualifications for voting in local elections are the same as those for voting in state and national ones (although cities in four states limit the suffrage on certain classes of expenditure issues to property owners).

Referendum questions (as distinguished from choice among candidates) may in most cities be presented to the voters at either primary (preliminary) or general (runoff) elections.

VOTER REGISTRATION

The method of voter registration is another aspect of an electoral system that may have large consequences for the politics of the city. Registration may be either temporary or permanent. If it is temporary, a voter must re-register periodically, sometimes for each election. If it is permanent, a voter once registered remains on the rolls until he changes residence or dies. The political difference between the two systems arises from the fact that participation in elections varies with socio-economic status and party affiliation. Generally in large cities, members of the dominant party (usually the Democratic) turn out for *local* elections in larger proportions than do members of the other party. In New York City, for example, there were 46 percent fewer registered Republicans in the 1957 mayoral election than there had been in the 1956 Presidential election year, but the drop among Democrats was only 20 percent. Now that New York has permanent registration (it was introduced in 1957), the registration the Republicans build up in Presidential years will remain on the rolls during the local election years. In effect, then, permanent registration reduces the burden on the parties' precinct organization. Since in New York, as in other large cities, the Republican organization is weaker than the Democratic, the Republicans benefit more from permanent registration.

Similarly, the introduction of voting machines in place of paper ballots—seemingly a minor technical innovation—often is a partisan issue. Generally speaking, reformers favor voting machines on the grounds that they are more accurate and less liable to fraudulent manipulation than paper ballots. Professional politicians, on the other hand, sometimes resist the introduction of these devices, in part because they *do* provide a more accurate count, but also in part because the machine often appears to the lower-income, poorly educated voter (who is usually the professional politician's major supporter) as a forbidding, complicated mechanism which may deter him from voting at all. In the long run, however, voting machines—because they almost always have a "party lever"—may make it easier for voters to vote the straight party ticket (something that usually is disadvantageous to the reformer).

Also professional politicians have found ways of "beating" the machines; in Chicago, where state law allows election judges to "assist" illiterate, blind, and disabled voters, Democratic election judges—there are no Republicans to serve as judges in some precincts—are happy to work the machines for illiterate voters who carry cards asking help in voting the straight Democratic ticket. On the whole, therefore, the costs and benefits to machine politicians and reformers may be in a rough balance.

CHAPTER 8 · THE CENTRALIZATION OF INFLUENCE

IN ORDER for anything to be done under public auspices, the elaborate decentralization of authority that we described in Chapter 6 must somehow be overcome or set aside. The widely diffused *right* to act must be replaced by a unified *ability* to act.[1] The many legally independent bodies—governments or fragments of government—whose collaboration is necessary for the accomplishment of a task must work as one. If, for example, the task is an urban renewal program, the various possessors of authority—say the mayor, the city council, the redevelopment authority, the legislature, the governor, and perhaps also the voters—must act concertedly. If any possessor of authority refuses to "go along" with the others, if they will not exercise their authority in the ways that are necessary, nothing can be done. For example, if the mayor will not collaborate with the redevelopment authority, there can be no renewal program, for he alone has authority to do certain things that must be done.

If all possessors of authority subscribe to a common purpose, this may conceivably be enough to bring about the necessary collaboration, each actor "voluntarily" exercising his authority as the common purpose requires. Such voluntary concerting of action is a very important element in most governmental action, but it is rarely sufficient to overcome the decentralization of authority in the city. In almost every situation there are some possessors of authority who either do not see the common purpose in the same way as the others or have some contrary purpose of their own. The mayor may withhold cooperation from the redevelopment authority because he thinks its plans unwise or because he thinks that they will hurt him politically. But even if he does not, some other possessor of authority—say the city council—probably

---

[1] We use "authority" to mean the *legal right* to act or to require others to act. We use "influence" to mean the *ability* to act, or to cause others to act in accordance with one's intention. (Authority, then, may or may not give rise to influence: i.e., the legal right to require action may or may not suffice to evoke it.) We use "power" to mean influence the basis of which is something other than authority (e.g. the promise of favors and the threat of injuries).

will. Therefore if the action of the various independent possessors of authority is to be concerted, mechanisms must exist which in one way or another render nugatory the decentralization of authority.

MECHANISMS OF CENTRALIZATION

In city government, this is accomplished mainly through the operation of these mechanisms:

1. Indifference and apathy
2. Deference
3. Party loyalty
4. Inducements, either specific or general
5. Salesmanship

Here is how the mechanisms work:

1. *Indifference and apathy.* Some people in effect give over their authority to others by failing to exercise it because they do not care what happens. A voter who fails to vote, for example, in effect gives his authority (vote) to those who do vote. An actor's indifference may extend to all of the affairs of the city (apathy) or only to those which he thinks do not affect him. Except for politicians and bureaucrats, few people have a very active interest in most city affairs. To the extent that there is indifference or apathy, the decentralization of authority is overcome and action is made easier.

2. *Deference.* Some possessors of authority may in effect lend it to others because they feel that they ought to do so. The members of a board of education, although disagreeing with the mayor, may feel that they ought to defer to his wishes; in such a case, the decentralization of authority to them is overcome by their action in deferring. This happens often. People see that the particular circumstances require more centralization than the law provides and they act accordingly. Of course, *pretended* deference may be used to avoid responsibility; "Let the mayor have his way" may be a way of saying "Let the mayor take the blame."

3. *Party loyalty.* Possessors of authority may abdicate the use of it because of loyalty to party. This is really a special case of the class just described; the possessor of authority, instead of giving it over to the one who wants to act, gives it over on a continuing basis to the party managers who dispense it as they see fit. Party "loyalty" thus transfers authority from many hands into few.

4. *Inducements.* A promise of reward (or threat of punishment) may induce the possessor of authority to exercise it in the way some-

one else demands, thus in effect turning the authority over to that someone else. This happens, for example, when a politician agrees to "take orders" from one who can assist his political career.

A *specific* inducement can be given to (or withheld from) a specific individual. A *general* one can be given only to all members of a given group; if one gets it, all must get it by the nature of the case. Jobs, favors, and bribes (but also intangibles like friendship) are specific inducements.[2] Generous welfare payments, able administration, and an attractive public personality are general inducements. The importance of the distinction is that specific inducements, where they can be used at all, are more dependable and effective in their operation. A politician who promises someone a particular job can count on his support because if the support is not forthcoming the job will not be either. But a politician who promises a whole class of people jobs cannot count on their support; each member of the class knows that even if he opposes the politician he will share in any benefits of a kind (full employment, for example) that must accrue, if they accrue at all, to the whole group.

It is useful to distinguish inducements that involve compromise of measures from ones that do not. A mayor who can induce councilmen to vote for his measure only by accepting certain crippling amendments that they want to make in it is in a very different position from one who can get their votes by giving inducements (such as patronage) that are unrelated to the measure. A particularly important way of generating inducements that do not involve the compromise of measures is "logrolling"—the arrangement by which A supports B's measure as a means of inducing B to support his.

5. *Salesmanship.* The possessor of authority may be induced by the arts of rhetoric or by the exercise of charm or charisma to put it at the service of another. A mayor who "sells" an independent board of education on doing what he wants done in effect overcomes the decentralization of authority. Robert Moses has described how Mayor Fiorello La Guardia used a familiar sales approach—the appeal to ethnic attachments—to help centralize the power that he needed to govern New York City:

It must be admitted that in exploiting racial and religious prejudices La Guardia could run circles around the bosses he despised and derided. When it came to raking ashes of Old World hates, warming ancient grudges,

2 See Chester I. Barnard, *The Functions of the Executive* (Cambridge, Mass.: Harvard University Press, 1938), chaps. vii and xi, and especially p. 142.

waving the bloody shirt, tuning the ear to ancestral voices, he could easily out-demagogue the demagogues. . . . He knew that the aim of the rabble-rousers is simply to shoo into office for entirely extraneous, illogical and even silly reasons the municipal officials who clean city streets, teach in schools, protect, house and keep healthy, strong and happy millions of people crowded together here.[3]

PATTERNS OF CENTRALIZATION

Most of these ways of overcoming the decentralization of authority are used in most cities most of the time. There are important differences among cities, however, both in the combination of methods that is used and in the amount of centralization that is achieved. In the rest of this chapter, we shall describe and compare the ways in which influence is centralized in the nation's three largest cities. The result, we think, will be a simple typology into which most other cities could reasonably well be fitted.

Extreme Centralization of Influence (Chicago)

Chicago is a city in which an extreme decentralization of authority has been overcome by an extreme centralization of power, the power being based mainly on specific inducements. The mayor of Chicago is a boss. That is to say, he is a broker in the business (so to speak) of buying and selling political power. He performs an entrepreneurial function by overcoming the decentralization of authority that prevents anything from being done, and in this his role is very like that of the real estate broker who assembles land for a large development by buying up parcels here and there. Much of what the political broker gathers up is on speculation: he does not know exactly how it will be used, but he is confident that someone will need a large block of power.

As a rule, the boss gets his initial stock of influence by virtue of holding a party or public office. He uses the authority of the office to acquire power, and then he uses the power to acquire more power and ultimately more authority. By "buying" bits of authority here and there from the many small "owners" (voters, for example) who received it from the constitution-makers or got it by being elected or appointed to office (strictly speaking, it is control over the use of authority, not authority itself, that he "buys"), the boss accumulates a "working capi-

[3] Robert Moses, *La Guardia: A Salute and a Memoir* (New York: Simon and Schuster, 1957), pp. 37–38.

tal" of influence. Those who "sell" it to him receive in return jobs, party preferment, police protection, other bits of influence, and other considerations of value. The boss, like any investor, has to invest his influence shrewdly if he is to maintain and increase it.

The Chicago city council, which has the authority to be a powerful check on the mayor, hardly exists as a real influence. All but three of the fifty members of the council in 1961 were Democrats, and Democrats hardly ever vote contrary to the mayor's wishes. He can use specific inducements, especially patronage and party preferment and the threat of "dumping" a rebel (removing his name from the ballot in the next election) to maintain strict discipline. Here is a newspaper's account—somewhat exaggerated perhaps, but certainly true in the main—of the way that discipline may be exercised:

Ald. Keane (31st) arrived 11 minutes late for a meeting Tuesday morning of the council committee on traffic and public safety, of which he is chairman. The committee had a sizeable agenda, 286 items in all to consider.

Ald. Keane took up the first item. For the record, he dictated to the committee secretary that Ald. A moved and Ald. B seconded its approval, and then, without calling for a vote, he declared the motion passed. Neither mover nor seconder had opened his mouth. He followed the same procedure on six more proposals, again without a word from the aldermen whose names appeared in the record. Then he put 107 items into one bundle for passage, and 172 more into another for rejection, again without a voice other than his own having been heard.

Having disposed of this mountain of details in exactly ten minutes, Ald. Keane walked out. The aldermen he had quoted so freely, without either their concurrence or their protest, sat around looking stupid.

Most likely they are.[4]

The mayor has a big block of votes in the legislature. Few Cook County Democrats would dare to go against him and many Cook County Republicans get patronage or other favors from him. (He expects these Republicans to vote with him only when they can get away with it, or only on something that is very important to him and not very important to them.) He controls indirectly the votes of many downstate Democratic legislators who are beholden to downstate bosses who must bargain with him. So strong is the mayor in the legislature that even when both houses are Republican a Republican governor must bargain with him. There are always some occasions when a Republican governor needs help from outside his party; when these

[4] *Chicago Tribune*, editorial, April 13, 1955.

occasions arise and the mayor sees fit to give the help, he gets something in return. A few years ago, a Republican governor wanted to increase the state police force. His bill was opposed by the county sheriffs association, and the legislature was about to turn it down. The mayor came to the rescue, and in return the governor gave the mayor a city sales tax. Thus the authority of the legislature over the city is mitigated or overcome by the influence of the "boss." There are times when the city (the mayor, that is) comes closer to running the state than the state to running the city.

Even the decentralization of authority to the voters is largely overcome in Chicago. Through his control of the party machinery, the mayor can usually get his proposals approved by the electorate. If an unpopular public expenditure is to be voted upon, he can have it put on the ballot at an election for minor offices when the vote is light and only the party regulars come out.

Having this influence, the mayor can use it to acquire more. Formally independent agencies like the Park District, the Board of Education, and the Housing Authority are well aware that without the mayor's help in the council and in the legislature and sometimes with the voters, they are helpless. So far as the law is concerned, there is nothing to stop them from crossing the mayor at every turn. But as a practical matter they are compelled to look to him for help and support and therefore to follow his lead.

In some matters and within certain limits, the mayor is a kind of informal metropolitan-area government. His influence in the legislature is so great that the suburbs, most of which want something from the central city or from the legislature, occasionally take their cues from him.

As all this suggests, the mayor of Chicago is rarely under the necessity of compromising his measures in order to "buy" support for them. Having an ample supply of other inducements, he can usually insist that they be adopted without crippling amendments.

Nor need he employ the arts of salesmanship. He does not try to make himself a "personality" (no machine politician would read the funny papers over TV, eat blintzes and pizzas on the sidewalk, or rush to fires in a fireman's uniform). For his purposes, the "organization" is a more effective way of accomplishing the end in view, i.e., the centralization of influence.

The importance of this high degree of informal centralization to the functioning of Chicago's government can perhaps best be seen from what happened when the centralization temporarily ceased to exist. In 1947, the Democratic party, beset with scandals, found it expedient to elect a "reform" mayor. Martin Kennelly, a businessman without political experience, took the nomination with the understanding that the party would not interfere in city affairs and he would not interfere in its affairs. In other words, there was to be no "boss"; the mayor's influence would depend entirely upon the authority of his office and such support as he might attract on other than party grounds and without the help of the party machinery.

The result was a weak and ineffective administration. The mayor did not have enough power to run the city; important matters were decided by default or else by an informal coalition of councilmen—the Big Boys, they were called—whose authority and party-based influence made them independent of the mayor. When a controversial public housing proposal came before the city, Mayor Kennelly stood by while the council, after much delay, compromised and curtailed the program in response to neighborhood pressures. There was no doubt, the housing officials thought, that under Boss Kelly, Kennelly's predecessor as mayor, the city would have got a better housing program and would have got it quicker.[5]

Halfway Centralization (New York)

New York is an example of a city in which the decentralization of authority, although less than in most other cities, is not much mitigated by a centralization of influence. Successive reforms have given the mayor more authority than he used to have and more than most mayors have. But at the same time his power—his ability to use means other than the legal right of his office in order to get others to do what he wants them to do—has declined, leaving his total influence (authority and power together) no greater than before, perhaps less. The city seems to have arrived at a halfway house where authority is not so decentralized as to give rise to an informal centralization of influence such as exists in Chicago and not centralized enough to allow of effective government on the basis of authority alone.

The charter adopted in 1937 under Mayor La Guardia radically redistributed and to a large degree centralized authority. Previously the mayor of New York had as often as not been the creature of party

[5] See Martin Meyerson and Edward C. Banfield, *Politics, Planning, and the Public Interest* (Glencoe, Ill.: Free Press, 1955), especially the difference between Kelly's and Kennelly's handling of race riots, pp. 128–129.

bosses whose names did not appear on the ballot. The charter reform gave him a large measure of control over the city bureaucracy and it reduced the opportunities for legislators to interfere with his administration. For the first time a mayor, once in office, could defy the party bosses. Under La Guardia, whose gifts as a salesman enabled him to supplement his authority greatly, the city appeared to have a strong government. After 1945, when the Little Flower had gone, it was evident that a less talented salesman could not govern the city in the form that the reformers intended.

The fact was that the 1937 charter had centralized authority enough to weaken the Democratic party machine but not enough to create an executive who could perform the functions that it had previously performed. Civil service reform, administrative reorganization, and reduction in the size and authority of the council had weakened the party machine critically. The mayor's enhanced authority was partially offset by that of a newly created Board of Estimate. This body, which consisted of the mayor, the comptroller, the president of the city council (all elected at large) and the presidents of the five boroughs, had the principal say in budget matters and therefore, for all practical purposes, in all matters. The reformers had weighted the votes of the board members so as to assure a majority to the ones elected at large. As it turned out, however, the Democratic party, although broken into five separate borough organizations and therefore without a leader who could force it to take a city-wide point of view, could always bring together the votes of the borough presidents and could usually pick up a vote or two among the at-large members to check the mayor. Under these circumstances, New York had the worst of both worlds: neither the mayor nor the party could govern, although each could check the other, and the party, moreover, was merely a coalition of sectional interests.

Another charter reform in 1961 increased somewhat the authority of the mayor and decreased somewhat that of the Board of Estimate, but did not change the structure of the situation fundamentally. In the middle of 1962, a *New York Times* writer pointed out that final approval of a $100,000,000 crosstown expressway project that had been discussed and debated for twenty years was being delayed because of the sensitivity of City Hall to the protests of two thousand families who would have to be relocated, and that plans for fluoridation of the city's water supply had been quietly pigeonholed after a stormy public hearing in 1957. The sensitivity of city officials to local dissatisfactions, the writer said, "seems to be increasing as the influence of local political organizations over the voters decreases."[6]

New York's "halfway" centralization of influence, the characteristic feature of which is a mayor who has much authority and little power, proved conducive to the growth of an institution which greatly extended the centralization of influence with respect to a certain class of matters, thus enabling the government to do some things even though it could not do others. This institution was Robert Moses. For many years he presided over and controlled a dozen special districts or authorities which were free of the usual controls exercised by the legislature and the voters and could in most cases finance themselves from revenue or from the sale of bonds. That one man held so many offices was of course a way of centralizing authority; from a formal standpoint there were a dozen different and independent bodies, but realistically there was only one, Moses. His influence did not arise entirely from the authority of his many offices, however. He was a boss—a nonparty boss—who maintained a huge stock of favors that could be exchanged for such bits and pieces of authority as he needed but did not have. Contractors and bankers were particularly beholden to him.

Moses was also a great salesman. He had the sharpest tongue in New York, something which assured him attention in the press, and he used the techniques of Madison Avenue with skill and enterprise. Rexford G. Tugwell has described his approach:

The first thing Moses does when the time is right to start something is to get it clearly in focus for everyone likely to be concerned. This means that while he has been doing his own casting about he has had studies made—often elaborate and costly ones—as to the feasibility of the project, its best structure and method, and its permanent value. When he goes to his bankers and begins to ask for authorization from the appropriate bodies, he is ready with the kind of publicity which it seems churlish to oppose.

The Moses pamphlet is really formidable. A file of them shows such similarity that clearly a most effective model has been evolved and has been followed faithfully. It can be understood at a sharp glance. Pictorial charts and superb photographs are accompanied by descriptive sentences that are little more than captions. Predictions are unequivocal; concise references are made to time and costs. And usually they run in series. As the work progresses, its various stages are followed. One can see the project take shape and become operational on the schedule that was originally laid out.

[6] Charles G. Bennett, "Politics and Protests," *New York Times,* July 9, 1962, p. 16.

The impact of this reporting is tremendous. It creates confidence, it builds pride. As a result, when another project is proposed, the original doubts are bound to be less than they would otherwise have been. In New York, anything Moses wants to do is presumed to be worth doing. The faint voices of objectors are carried away on the wind of his propaganda.[7]

Finally, Moses commanded a great deal of deference because he made himself a model of an absolutely honest, tireless, devoted, and hugely effective civil servant. People "went along" with his proposals partly because the hurricane force of his accomplishments overwhelmed them. To take Bagehot out of context, Moses was "a charmed spectacle which imposes on the many, and guides their fancies as it wills."

Extreme Decentralization (Los Angeles)

Many cities have neither the considerable formal centralization of New York or the even more considerable informal centralization of Chicago. In nonpartisan cities, for example, there are no bosses, and mayors have few if any specific inducements that they can offer in return for support. And yet the decentralization of authority in these cities is often extreme. How in these cities are the voters, councilmen, state legislators, independent boards and commissions brought to act together?

Los Angeles presents a problem of this sort. The mayor shares the executive authority with a separately elected city attorney and a controller. Of the twenty-eight city departments, nineteen are run by independent boards and commissions whose members, although appointed by the mayor, are removable by him only under unusual circumstances. When in 1961 Sam Yorty defeated incumbent Mayor Norris Poulson, some key commissioners refused to resign until Yorty made a major public issue of the matter. The fifteen councilmen owe nothing to the mayor or to each other, and are therefore under no discipline. Not being elected at the same time, they do not represent the point of view, or mood, of the electorate at a particular time. There are no stable voting blocs in the council. In many matters, decentralization of authority extends all the way to the voters. In recent years, they have decided by referendum to permit higher buildings, to give pensions to firemen and policemen, and to give the Dodgers a baseball stadium, but not to have public housing.

[7] Rexford G. Tugwell, "The Moses Effect," in Banfield (ed.), *Urban Government* (New York: Free Press of Glencoe, 1961), p. 467.

As to how this decentralization of authority is overcome in the absence of the party control, several answers may be given: (1) To a large extent it is *not* overcome; many things are not done because it is impossible to secure the collaboration of all those whose collaboration is needed. (2) When overcome at all, it is overcome on an *ad hoc* basis; the mayor, for example, must consider anew with each issue how to get the eight votes he needs in council. (3) Widespread indifference and apathy among voters mitigates the effect of the decentralization of authority to them. (4) The mass communications media are fairly effective in overcoming by salesmanship such decentralization of authority to the voters as remains; causes with strong newspaper support and with big budgets for TV advertising are usually approved at the polls. (5) The devices of salesmanship are extensively used; it was in Los Angeles that the mayor scolded Khrushchev to his face in public while Khrushchev was the city's guest (a stunt like this would not have been resorted to by Mayor Daley of Chicago, whose machine makes salesmanship unnecessary). (6) Measures are frequently compromised so as to "give something to everybody" in order to get them accepted.

PART III

POLITICAL FORMS AND STYLES

CHAPTER 9 · THE MACHINE

A POLITICAL "machine" is a party organization that depends crucially upon inducements that are both *specific* and *material*.[1] As we explained in the last chapter, a specific (as opposed to general) inducement is one that can be offered to one person while being withheld from others. A *material* inducement is money or some other physical "thing" to which value attaches. *Nonmaterial* inducements include especially the satisfactions of having power or prestige, doing good, the "fun of the game," the sense of enlarged participation in events and a pleasant environment. A machine, like any formal organization, offers a mixture of these various kinds of inducements in order to get people to do what it requires. But it is distinguished from other types of organization by the very heavy emphasis it places upon specific, material inducements and the consequent completeness and reliability of its control over behavior, which, of course, account for the name "machine."

Business organizations are machines in that they rely largely upon specific, material incentives (such as salaries) to secure dependable, close control over their employees. A political machine is a business organization in a particular field of business—getting votes and winning elections. As a Chicago machine boss once said of the machine in that city, it is "just like any sales organization trying to sell its product." Or as Lord Bryce put it in his famous work, "The source of power and the cohesive force is the desire for office and office as a *means of gain*."[2]

---

[1] For the organization theory employed here, the reader is again referred to the work of Chester I. Barnard, especially *The Functions of the Executive* (Cambridge, Mass.: Harvard University Press, 1938), chaps. vi, vii, and ix, and *Organization and Management* (Cambridge, Mass.: Harvard University Press, 1948), chap. v.

[2] James Bryce, *The American Commonwealth* (London and New York, 1889), II, 111 (italics added). Martin Meyerson and Banfield quote a Chicago machine leader: "What I look for in a prospective captain is a young person—man or woman—who is interested in getting some material return out of his political activity. I much prefer this type to the type that is enthused about the party cause or all hot on a particular issue. Enthusiasm for causes is short-lived, but the necessity of making a living is permanent." Meyerson and Banfield, *Politics, Planning, and the Public Interest* (Glencoe, Ill.: Free Press, 1955), pp. 70–71.

The machine, therefore, is apolitical: it is interested only in making and distributing income—mainly money—to those who run it and work for it. Political principle is foreign to it, and represents a danger and a threat to it. As D. W. Brogan has remarked, "The true character of the machine is its political indifferentism. . . . It exists for itself."[3]

In the next section of this chapter we shall describe the machine in what might be called its classical form. Actually no big city today has a city-wide machine that is like the model (Chicago, Philadelphia, Pittsburgh, Albany, and Gary are some of the nearest approximations, but even they do not resemble it closely in all respects), and the party organization of most cities today is far from machine-like. One reason why we devote a chapter to the machine is its historical importance: between the Civil War and the New Deal, every big city had a machine at one time or another, and one cannot understand the present without knowing something about what went before. Another reason is its analytical importance: every kind of party organization employs inducements, and an extreme case of one kind—namely, almost exclusive reliance on specific, material ones—illumines the logic of the other kinds.

The model is by no means without present-day application, however. In many cities, large and small, there are elements of party organization that are surviving fragments of old machines or that are at any rate machine-like. In parts at least of every old city of the northeast, politics is organized on a machine basis. Tammany has been weakened and perhaps destroyed in Manhattan, but Democratic machines are still powerful in the Bronx and in Brooklyn. A revitalized machine plays an important part in Philadelphia. The Trenton Democratic Club flourishes in many parts of Baltimore. The Crump organization no longer exists in Memphis and James Curley has no successor in Boston, but some sections—particularly the Negro ones—of both cities have small-scale, ward-size "bosses" who behave very much like the famous bosses of old.

THE STRUCTURE OF THE MACHINE

The existence of the machine depends upon its ability to control votes. This control becomes possible when people place little or no value on their votes, or, more precisely, when they place a lower value

---

[3] D. W. Brogan, *An Introduction to American Politics* (London: Hamish Hamilton, 1954), p. 123.

on their votes than they do on the things which the machine can offer them in exchange for them. The voter who is indifferent to issues, principles, or candidates puts little or no value on his vote and can be induced relatively easily (or cheaply) to put it at the machine's disposal.

The votes most crucial to the machine are those cast in *primary* elections, for it is in primaries that party officials like precinct captains and district leaders are chosen. Fortunately for the machine, primaries are the easiest elections to control. Most voters place less value on their primary vote than on their general election vote; there seems to be less at stake in the primary. Moreover, in the primary the machine does not ask them to forsake their normal party allegiances, which are often deep-rooted. The turnout of voters is also much lower in primaries, and the votes which must be controlled are therefore fewer. For example, although the 1953 New York mayoralty primary was bitterly contested, only about one fourth of the registered Democrats cast ballots.

Sometimes a machine gets the votes of people who are intensely interested in elections. It does this by asking them for their votes only on such offices—the minor ones at the bottom of the ticket—as are *not* of interest to them. The minor offices are the ones essential to control of the party machinery, and this, of course, is half the battle in the short run and the whole of it in the long run.

Even though the precinct captain asks for something that is almost worthless to the voter, he must offer something in return. What he offers is usually a personal, nonmaterial incentive, "friendship." A Chicago captain explained, "I never take leaflets or mention issues or conduct rallies in my precinct. After all, this is a question of personal friendship between me and my neighbors."[4]

Much has been made of the "favors"—turkeys at Thanksgiving, hods of coal at Christmas, and so on—with which the machine in effect buys votes. Such material inducements are indeed given in some instances. The voter, however, is the one contributor to the machine's system of activity who is usually given nonmaterial inducements, especially "friendship." The reason for this is, of course, that people will exchange their votes for "friendship" more readily than for cash or other material benefits; and the machine cannot afford to pay cash for many of the votes it needs.

[4] Quoted in Meyerson and Banfield, p. 72.

Many voters, indeed, seem to have valued the turkeys and hods of coal mainly as tokens of friendship, and, accordingly, of the humanity and goodness of the "organization" and its "boss." Jane Addams, the settlement house worker, explained this long ago: "On the whole, the gifts and favors are taken quite simply as an evidence of genuine loving kindness. The alderman is really elected because he is a good friend and neighbor. He is corrupt, of course, but he is not elected because he is corrupt, but rather in spite of it. His standard suits his constituents. He exemplifies and exaggerates the popular type of a good man. He has attained what his constituents secretly long for."[5]

Working-class people, especially immigrants unfamiliar with American ways and institutions, have always been the mainstay of the machine. To use the terminology of the politician, the "delivery" wards are also the "river" wards, and they are a long way in both social and geographic distance from the "newspaper" wards. A delivery ward, of course, is one whose vote can be "delivered" by the machine, and a newspaper ward is one in which voters take the newspapers' recommendations seriously. The delivery wards are river wards because the oldest, and hence poorest and most run-down, parts of the city are those that lie along the river near the warehouses and the railroad yards. Almost without exception, the lower the average income and the fewer the average years of schooling in a ward, the more dependable the ward's allegiance to the machine. As one moves out from the river and the railroad yards first into lower-middle-class districts, then into middle-class ones, and finally (usually in the suburbs beyond the city proper) into upper-middle-class territory, fewer and fewer precincts are manned and the ties to the machine become fewer and weaker until they cease to exist.

The job of a precinct captain is to get out the vote for his party's slate and to keep at home the vote for the other party's. He usually has about 400 to 600 voters to keep track of; this keeps him busy one or two evenings a week ordinarily and full-time for a few days before elections. His superiors rate his performance according to how reliable—i.e., predictable—party voting is in his precinct.

The precinct captain is chosen by and works under the direction of a ward leader, usually an alderman or elected party official. The leader has under him thirty to forty precinct captains (the size of wards is extremely variable and some precincts are not manned). It is up to

[5] Jane Addams, *Democracy and Social Ethics* (New York, 1902), p. 254.

him to recruit and manage this force and to keep it happy—he is the district sales manager. He also dispenses the larger items of patronage, favors, and protection to those who have earned them. One or two evenings a week he is available to all comers in his office. People come to him to inquire about welfare payments, to get their relatives into public institutions, to get something done about neighborhood nuisances (the garbage has not been collected from an alley or a policeman is needed at a school crossing), and to make complaints about the police or other city departments. Some, but not all, ward leaders sell illicit privileges such as protection for gambling, prostitution, and after-hours liquor sales. The ward leader is one of his party's high command in the city; he is consulted, more or less, in the choice of candidates and on matters of city policy that affect his ward.

A *good* precinct captain or ward leader has very little time for home life; he spends his evenings visiting his neighbors, doing chores at ward headquarters, traveling to and from city hall on errands, and talking politics. To get the services of men with the ability and energy that the jobs require, the machine must offer precinct captains and ward leaders substantial inducements. Captains are often "payrollers," that is, they have appointive public jobs that they could not get or keep if it were not for the party. Some have "no show" jobs: they are carried on the public payroll without being required to show up for work. A larger number have "show" jobs and work like other employees —some more conscientiously than most—but their absence on election day and on other special occasions when the party needs them are overlooked. Some precinct captains look forward to running for office or to rising in the party hierarchy. The hope that the party will in due course run them for alderman keeps these captains at work.

Although ward leaders are sometimes payrollers, they more often have elective offices, such as that of alderman, which give them salaries without taking their time from politics. In addition, they almost always have some sideline which enables them to use their political connections to supplement their incomes. The alderman may be an insurance broker, for example, with an "inside track" at City Hall (insurance is all the same price, so why not give the business to one of the boys?). Or he may be a lawyer whose firm gets lucrative cases because clients think it is "good to be on the safe side." "Honest graft" of this kind shades imperceptibly into outright bribery, of course, and the ward leader, if he wants to, can always find some way to take money for misusing his office.

As a rule, however, there is not enough "gravy" to go around, especially among precinct captains. One consequence of this is that able people who can earn a living in less strenuous ways will not work for the machine. Or, to put the same thing another way, the machine is more likely to attract as workers those who, like Negroes, first-generation immigrants, and women, are at some disadvantage in the labor market. Many Irish, once the mainstay of the precinct, have, so to speak, been priced out of the market by the increase of their opportunities in other lines.

Another consequence of a shortage of "gravy" is that the ward and precinct workers are selected from among those people who will respond to nonmaterial inducements. Having a place where one can go to play cards and talk to "the boys" is the main inducement holding some ward organizations together. There is little doubt, however, that the substitution of nonmaterial for material inducements is not only an effect of the weakening of the machine but a cause of it as well: the fewer the material rewards, the less able and energetic the precinct and ward leaders, and the fewer the votes delivered on election day.

These conditions are dynamic elements in the internal life of the machine. Its relative attractiveness to young and aspiring representatives of the most recently arrived, lower-status ethnic groups means that the "old line" leaders who control it are continually challenged by men who are abler, more energetic, and more strenuously "on the make." Many of the "old line" leaders are receiving nonmaterial rather than material benefits for the most part and are therefore not easily disciplined. If they spend their time in the clubhouse when they should be canvassing the voters, there is not much the boss can do about it, for the comforts of the clubhouse are about all that the organization can offer them. To replace these clubhouse types with energetic, ambitious youngsters would be easy if—but only if—the boss were willing to accept the threat to his own position that their entry into the organization could represent.

The machine is run by a coalition of a few of the more powerful ward or district leaders or by a boss (himself a ward or district leader) who, through his control of patronage or by means of other material inducements, is able to exercise control over the others. In a survey of twenty bosses published thirty years ago, Professor Harold Zink found that only two had ever been mayors. In recent years, the situation has changed. Chicago's recent bosses (Cermak, Kelly, and Daley) were mayors, and so was Pittsburgh's (Lawrence). The reason for the change is perhaps to be found in the greatly increased authority of the mayor's office. Today's mayor has authority—especially over the police, the budget, and contracts and purchasing—which enables him to check, and ultimately to displace, any competing party leader. In general, having the authority of the mayor's office is today a necessary (but not a sufficient) condition of being the party leader in the city. That is, if the mayor is not the party leader there often *is* no party leader. This, of course, greatly affects the machine's internal life: it means that the boss must be a person who is reputable enough, and otherwise qualified, to face the electorate. The modern boss cannot run the city anonymously from a smoke-filled room, and this in itself has pervasive effects on the character of the machine.

EXTERNAL FORCES MAKING FOR CHANGE

The main reason for the decline and near disappearance of the city-wide machine was—and is—the growing unwillingness of voters to accept the inducements that it offered. The petty favors and "friendship" of the precinct captains declined in value as immigrants were assimilated, public welfare programs were vastly extended, and *per capita* incomes rose steadily and sharply in war and postwar prosperity. To the voter who in case of need could turn to a professional social worker and receive as a matter of course unemployment compensation, aid to dependent children, old-age assistance, and all the rest, the precinct captain's hod of coal was a joke.

Only those who are least competent to cope with the conditions of modern life, those who are culturally or personally incapacitated in one way or another, still value and seek the "favors" of the machine. They are, of course, the poorest of the poor, especially Negro slum dwellers, rooming-house drifters, criminals, and near criminals. Nowadays there is little that the machine can do for such people except to give them information about where to go and whom to see in the city bureaucracy and (what is probably more important, despite its illusory character) to give them the feeling that they have a friend and protector. The ward leader cannot arrange to have welfare payments made to someone not entitled to them; he can, however, tell a needy person who *is* entitled to payments how to apply for them. In doing so, he may, of course, manage to leave the impression that if he had not made a telephone call and used his "influence" as a "friend" the payments would never have been made. Even his opportunities to serve the voter by giving information (and thus to lay the basis for a later claim upon him) diminish, however, as the giving of information and other functions which are the politicians' special stock in trade are transferred to the executive departments. As Mayor Clark of Philadelphia remarked, "When the word gets around that you can't get things done by favor anymore, there tends to be a sort of channeling of complaints and desires to get things done away from the legislative branch and into the executive branch."[6]

"Friendship" is also harder to give. One reason is television. The precinct captain who visits in the evening interrupts a television program and must either stay and watch in silence or else excuse himself quickly and move on. Another reason is the changing ethnic character of the inner city. When, for example, a white neighborhood is "invaded" by Negroes, the white precinct captain cannot, or will not, form friendships among them as easily as he does among whites. He may even be afraid to enter a tenement of Negroes after dark. In time he will be replaced by a Negro captain, but meanwhile the organization suffers.

While the value to the voter of what the machine offers has declined, the value to him of what he has to give—his vote—has increased. This has happened because of the changing class character of the electorate. Except in the inner parts of the larger central cities, the proportion of middle-class people is greater than it was. Machine-style politics has rarely worked in predominantly middle-class districts. People who have, or pretend to have, opinions on political questions will not give away their votes or exchange them for petty favors. Middle-class people do not want the precinct captain's "friendship" or the ward leader's help. It is easy for them to be virtuous in these matters: they don't have to worry about getting into the county hospital or out of the county jail. And they generally resent his efforts at persuasion. They think of themselves as well informed, able to make up their own minds, independent. Being qualified to pass upon public questions follows from their education status, they think, and therefore exhibiting the qualifications is a matter of pride. Whether justified or not, these claims to political competence make it hard for the precinct captain to exercise influence. Recently a Chicago captain told of calling on a voter

[6] Chicago Home Rule Commission, *Modernizing a City Government* (Chicago: University of Chicago Press, 1954), p. 47.

one Sunday afternoon and finding him with three newspapers spread out on the floor and the TV set on. "What can you tell me that I don't already know?" the voter asked.

The assimilation of lower-class people into the middle class has, of course, entailed their assimilation to the political ethos of the Anglo-Saxon-Protestant elite, the central idea of which is that politics should be based on public rather than on private motives and, accordingly, should stress the virtues of honesty, impartiality, and efficiency.

Wherever the middle class is dominant, this ethos prevails and fixes the character of the political system. If, as seems likely, the middle class will in the very long run assimilate the lower class entirely, the final extinction of the machine is probably guaranteed.

Meanwhile, there remain enclaves that are heavily lower-class in all of the central cities and many of the older suburbs. In these, machine-style politics is as popular as ever. It does not flourish as of old, however, because of restraints and impediments imposed by the middle class, which constitutes the majority in the metropolitan area if not in the city proper, controls the legislatures, and has a virtual monopoly on federal office, both elective and appointive.

Some machines, however, are managing to adjust to the changing circumstances and to substitute, little by little as necessary, one kind of inducement for another so that they gradually become less machine-like. The Chicago machine is one which has survived by "reforming" itself piecemeal. The dynamics of its adaptation are worth examining briefly.

The central city of Chicago is overwhelmingly Democratic, but the outlying wards are moderately or strongly Republican. If the "country towns" (actually suburbs which lie in Cook County) are included, Cook County is marginally but not "solidly" Democratic. If a boss were concerned only with the central city, the old style of machine politics would work well enough. In fact, however, he must try to carry the county and the state for the party. Their loss would deprive him of patronage, expose him to hostile acts by a Republican state's attorney, sheriff, governor, and state legislature, and weaken his power in the councils of the party. He must therefore appeal as well as he can to the independent and Republican voters who live in the outlying wards and suburbs. To do this, he must minimize, or at least render inconspicuous, his use of patronage and payoffs, and he must exert himself to find "blue ribbon" candidates for important offices and "professional" administrators for important departments and to inaugurate civic projects that will suit the "good government" voter without costing very much. In effect, he must take political resources away from those central-city wards where the machine is strong and give them to the independent voters in the "newspaper" wards and in the independent suburbs, thereby, of course, creating disaffection among his machine lieutenants. Every step taken in the direction of appeasing the independent voter is, of course, a step toward destruction of the machine.

The civic projects that Mayor Daley inaugurated in Chicago—street cleaning, street lighting, road building, a new airport, and a convention hall, for example—were shrewdly chosen. They were highly visible; they benefited the county as well as the city; for the most part they were noncontroversial; they did not require much increase in taxes; and they created many moderately paying jobs that politicians could dispense as patronage. The mayor's program conspicuously neglected the goals of militant Negroes, demands for the enforcement of the building code, and (until there was a dramatic exposé) complaints about police inefficiency and corruption. These things were all controversial, and, perhaps most important, would have no immediate, visible result; either they would benefit those central-city voters whose loyalty could be counted upon anyway or else (as in the case of police reform) they threatened to hurt the machine in a vital spot.

Other big-city machines have not adapted as successfully. The Pendergast machine in Kansas City was destroyed. Carmine DeSapio's efforts to refurbish the "image" of Tammany Hall in Manhattan not only failed but actually seemed to incite reformers to attack more energetically. Why is it that most machines did not adapt and survive as the Chicago machine has?

One reason is that the bosses have been too greedy for money. Tom Pendergast, for example, gambled heavily at the race tracks and thereby placed himself in a position where, even if he wanted to, he could not afford to cut the "take." Daley, by contrast, has not enriched himself. The satisfactions he gets from politics are apparently of an entirely different sort, and this has enabled him to use greedy lieutenants without exciting their envy and to gain personally in prestige, power, and whatever other such values he seeks by making reforms.

Some machines failed to adapt because their leaders waited too long before making reforms. The leader who makes a reform only under duress is not likely to be able to salvage the situation by making it on his own terms. This is what happened in New York. Carmine DeSapio

tried in the early 1950's to remodel Tammany Hall but the power of
the machine had by then withered away to such an extent that he
could not make the kinds of changes in the situation that would have
saved the organization.

In a word, the machines failed because bosses lacked statesmanship.
Colonel Jacob Arvey, who persuaded Mayor Kelly to step down and
the ward leaders to endure the eight-year Kennelly drought of reform,
and Mayor Daley, who then took the initiative in reform, are exceptions to the general rule. The "accident" of their presence in Chicago
probably accounts more than anything else for the strength of the party
there. James Finnegan, who brought Philadelphia's regular Democratic
organization into temporary alliance with the "blue blood" reformers,
Joseph S. Clark and Richardson Dilworth, seems to have been another
such statesman. In Philadelphia, as in Chicago, the machine suffered
temporarily by reform. By 1960, however, the reformers were fast
fading from the scene.

SOME EVALUATIVE CONSIDERATIONS

It goes without saying that a system of government based upon
specific, material inducements is wholly at odds with that conception
of democracy which says that decisions ought to be made on the basis
of reasonable discussion about what the common good requires. Machine government is, essentially, a system of organized bribery.[7]

The destruction of machines would therefore be good if it did no
more than to permit government on the basis of appropriate motives,
that is, public-regarding ones. In fact, it has other highly desirable
consequences—especially greater honesty, impartiality, and (in routine
matters) efficiency. This last gain deserves special emphasis because it
is one that the machine (or its boss) cannot, in the nature of the case,
adopt at its own initiative. A boss who, like Mayor Daley of Chicago,
has with great effort centralized, to an extreme degree, political influence cannot be expected to turn around and delegate to subordinates
that influence so that city government can be carried on expeditiously
and without obtaining the mayor's (i.e., the boss's) approval on all
matters, however trivial.

Great as the advantages of reform are, they are at least partly offset

---

[7] Early in this chapter we said that all business organizations are machines. This
does not imply that they also are systems of bribery. Bribery is payment for not
doing what one's duty requires. The citizen always has a duty to act on public
rather than private grounds. A citizen who exchanges his vote for private benefit
violates his duty, whereas a consumer, who is under no such obligation, does not.

by certain disadvantages. Because these disadvantages are less obvious than the advantages, we will focus our attention upon them. In doing so we do not, of course, imply any derogation of the values sought by reformers.

The machine served certain latent social functions, functions which no one intended but which presumably would have had to be served by another means if not by that one. This has been remarked by Robert Merton, David Riesman, and other sociologists. According to Merton, it humanized and personalized assistance to the needy; afforded businesses, including illicit ones, privileges that they needed in order to survive; provided a route of social mobility for persons to whom other routes were closed; and was an antidote to the constitutional dispersal of authority.[8]

The last item on this list is of particular interest here. As we showed in the last chapter, the decentralization of authority in the city must be overcome in one way or another if public undertakings are to be carried forward. A system of specific, material inducements (i.e., a machine) is not, we explained, the only way of bringing about a centralization of influence; in principle, measures to weaken the machine may be accompanied by other measures to centralize influence. In fact, however, this never seems to happen; if any substitute at all is provided for the power of the boss, it is a partial one. La Guardia's reforms in New York, Clark and Dilworth's in Philadelphia, and Daley's in Chicago, although strengthening administrative authority, nevertheless weakened the influence of the city government as a whole. Because of this weakening of the city government, the reform of the machine, although increasing efficiency in routine matters, may at the same time have decreased it in those more important matters which call for the exercise of political power.

The Chicago police scandals of 1960 are a case in point. Mayor Daley's excessive regard for the opinion of the "good government" forces restrained him from taking measures which might have prevented these scandals. He had inherited a civil service system which in effect put control of the police department in the hands of its senior officers (neither he nor the commissioner could fire a policeman), and —again to avoid the charge of "playing politics"—he did not ask the legislature for authority to reorganize the department.

[8] Robert K. Merton, *Social Theory and Social Structure* (Glencoe, Ill.: Free Press, 1957), pp. 71–81.

The machine provided the politician with a base of influence deriving from its control of lower-income voters. As this base shrinks, he becomes more dependent on other sources of influence—especially newspapers, civic associations, labor unions, business groups, and churches. "Nonpolitical" (really nonparty) lines of access to the city administration are substituted for "political" ones. Campaign funds come not from salary kickbacks and the sale of favors, but from rich men and from companies doing business with the city. Department heads and other administrators who are able to command the support of professional associations and civic groups become indispensable to the mayor and are therefore harder for him to control. Whereas the spoils of office formerly went to "the boys" in the delivery wards in the form of jobs and favors, they now go in the form of urban renewal projects, street cleaning, and better police protection to newspaper wards. Better police protection in white neighborhoods means greater police harassment in Negro ones. Appointment of white experts means non-appointment of Negro politicians.

Even though in the abstract one may prefer a government that gets its influence from reasonable discussion about the common good rather than from giving jobs, favors, and "friendship," even though in the abstract he may prefer government by middle-class to government by lower-class standards, and even though in the abstract he may prefer the rule of professional administrators to that of politicians, he may nevertheless favor the machine in some particular concrete situation. The choice is never between the machine and some ideal alternative. If there is any choice at all—and in some instances there may not be— it is between it and some real—and therefore imperfect—alternative. It is at least conceivable that in some of the large central cities the political indifferentism of the machine may be preferable to any likely alternative.[9]

[9] For argument along these lines with reference to Chicago and New York, see Banfield, *Political Influence* (New York: Free Press of Glencoe, 1961), pp. 260–262.

CHAPTER 10 · FACTIONS
AND FACTIONAL ALLIANCES

IN MANY cities elections are won by organizations, or alliances of organizations, other than well-defined, well-disciplined, city-wide parties. We will call all such organizations "factions." In some cities factions exist as subordinate parts of city-wide parties: in effect, these are parties within parties. In other cities an alliance of factions *is* the party: apart from the alliance, the party has only a nominal existence. In still other cities factional politics entirely takes the place of party politics: city-wide parties do not have even a nominal existence and elections are fought by factions or alliances of factions.[1]

KINDS OF FACTIONS

We shall distinguish four analytical types of factions according to the nature of the inducements by which support is secured from voters and others. These are: the "machine of less than city-wide scope," the "personal following," the "interest grouping," and the "political club."

The Machine

The machine has already been described. As we have pointed out, many cities which do not have city-wide machines nevertheless have neighborhood or district ones. These are often important and quite distinct components of city-wide parties. For example, in Nashville a one-precinct machine is run by a colorful Negro restaurant owner and bootlegger, "Good Jelly" Jones.[2] In Boston's ninth ward, a Negro druggist, Balcolm S. Taylor, runs a small machine that he inherited from his brother, Silas "Shag" Taylor. In Baltimore, James H. (Jack) Pollack is "boss" of the fourth and fifth districts in the old-lower-income Jewish areas.[3] Remnants of the Hague organization are still found in Jersey

---

[1] Throughout this paragraph we refer to local elections only. Parties exist locally to fight state and national elections even in cities which, so far as local elections are concerned, are entirely nonpartisan.

[2] David Halberstam, " 'Good Jelly's' Last Stand," *Reporter*, Jan. 19, 1961.

[3] Harvey Wheeler, "Yesterday's Robin Hood: The Rise and Fall of Baltimore's Trenton Democratic Club," *American Quarterly*, Winter 1955, pp. 332–344. See also J. Anthony Lukas, "Boss Pollack: He Can't Be There But He Is," *Reporter*, July 19, 1962, pp. 35–36.

City. The "Old Regulars" of the Choctaw Club of New Orleans have from time to time functioned as a machine, one of the few in Southern cities.[4]

The Personal Following

A politician has a "personal following" to the extent that people will vote for him and otherwise support him because of an attachment they feel to him as a person, or as a "house," and not from regard for his political principles, loyalty to the party he represents, or in expectation of material rewards. These considerations may be present, but they are not the basis of the politician's hold on his followers; they would vote for him anyway.

Very often the attachment arises from long personal association. The politician draws his following from the neighborhood in which he grew up. The members of his family, including in-laws, the gang with which he ran as a boy, his schoolfellows, the members of his sandlot baseball team—these are the nucleus of his following. If he maintains his ties with the old neighborhood and manages by "personality," charm, and charisma to extend his circle, he may in time accumulate several hundred "friends" who will not only vote for him themselves but even ask their relatives and friends to do so too.

Not infrequently the politician is viewed by a "natural area" (a neighborhood constituted by ethnic or other such attachments) as "its boy." In this case, the voter's loyalty is really to the area, but the politician is its symbol and representative. Sometimes a family establishes a name for dealing in a particular kind of political product: the attachment here is to the "house."

The politician with a following may be hard to distinguish from the machine politician. Like the machine politician, he does "favors" for "friends." His favors, however, are valued less for themselves than as tokens of the feeling that he has for the follower. The test of this is, of course, that a competing politician who offers larger favors but lacks the same personal relation is unable to entice the follower away.

So long as he is able to maintain a sufficiently warm personal relationship, the politician with a following does not require a stock of favors, patronage, or other such inducements. For this reason he can survive under conditions which would destroy the machine politician. The following, however, is usually small by the standard of what is

[4] V. O. Key, Jr., *Southern Politics* (New York: Alfred A. Knopf, 1951), pp. 397–398.

needed to win a city-wide election, and beyond a point it is not susceptible to expansion. This is so because of limitations inherent in the nature of the attachment. A machine can, in principle, expand almost indefinitely; as long as there are people willing to be hired and wherewithal to hire them, it can grow. But the following is in a very different situation. It can expand only as far as the basis of the attachment extends. If this is "old neighborhood and family friends," the following cannot grow beyond that small circle. If it is "ethnic natural area," it cannot expand beyond that. If it is "personality, charm, and charisma," it cannot extend beyond those who are attracted to the individual. Few politicians have been able to create large, city-wide followings. James Michael Curley of Boston was one and Fiorello La Guardia of New York City was another. Both relied mainly on charm and charisma, the one basis for a personal attachment that extends beyond a small, relatively intimate circle.

A following, unless it is built on the exceptional charm that can capture a mass audience, is necessarily a faction of slow growth. It cannot be manufactured overnight or brought into being synthetically. Therefore followings seldom characterize the politics of places that have been recently settled or of those where the social composition of "old neighborhoods" has changed fundamentally.[5]

The politician with a following and the machine politician are natural enemies. The politician with a following is, from the standpoint of the machine, a disruptive force. He cannot be disciplined in the normal way because his ultimate political strength is not dependent upon the favors, patronage, and other inducements the machine has to give. Moreover, the fundamental logic of his position is such that he is likely to come into headlong collision with the machine; for the force of his appeal depends upon creating a conspicuous contrast between himself as a personality and all else—namely the machine. Fighting the Martin Lomasney machine gave Curley an opportunity to establish the dominance of his personality in Boston just as fighting both Tammany and the Republicans gave La Guardia an opportunity to establish the dominance of *his* in New York.

[5] The concept of personal followings in city politics has certain obvious parallels to the "personal factions" and "friends and neighbors effect" described by V. O. Key, Jr., in his account of Southern state politics. Key suggests that personal support is "transferable," at least within reasonable limits, and that a local "friends and neighbors effect" can sometimes be extended beyond the original area. Since hardly any studies of this sort have been done using urban election returns, we are unable to pursue this subject here. *Ibid.*, esp. pp. 37–41, 69–75, 108, 168–179.

A politician who gets power by winning a city-wide following is almost certain to try to destroy an existing machine rather than to take control of it. This is what Curley and La Guardia did; and it is hard to imagine that any man who can win elections by the charm of his personality will see anything to be gained from the limiting business of maintaining an organization—limiting because the chief executive of an organization cannot be a *prima donna*. If he should succeed in maintaining the organization, there would always be a danger that someone would take it away from him and use it against him. So long as he relies upon his personal appeal to the voters, he runs no risk of that; the appeal is his and his alone.

The Interest Grouping

In the "interest grouping" the cohesive force is not specific material inducements, as in a machine, or personal attachment to a politician, as in a following, but rather concern for some shared interest. The interest may be narrow and group-serving, such as the wages and working conditions of city employees, or general and community-regarding, such as "good government." The interest grouping may (but of course does not always) cohere around a particular politician who represents and symbolizes it. In this case it resembles a following, and one is tempted to employ the term "interest group following" in contrast to "*personal* following." The defining characteristic of an interest grouping, however, is its attachment to an interest rather than to a person, and the politician who fails to represent the interest soon finds himself without followers; so it seems best to reserve the word "following" for attachments to persons either as personalities or as symbols.

The interest groupings under discussion here are, it should be noted, integral and functioning parts of political parties. Although they may sometimes be concretely indistinguishable from what are usually called "interest groups" (i.e., groups which seek to influence office-holders), they differ in being an element of the party, the organization that selects candidates, carries on campaign propaganda, gets out the vote, and in general does what it can to win elections.

It is probably safe to say that the less structured the party organization, the larger is the number of interest groupings that exist within it. A party which has a high degree of formal organization with a chain of command, strict discipline, and a clear-cut division of authority does not present a hospitable or encouraging environment for the growth of interest groupings. Only by subordinating the group interest to the party interest as defined by the leaders at the top of the party hierarchy can the group make itself acceptable, and if it does this it will not long continue as an interest grouping.

Even in a disciplined party, however, there are interest groupings, although ones that are usually highly informal. In the Chicago Democratic organization run by Mayor Daley, for example, there is an element which in some sense "represents" the AFL building trades unions, another which in some sense "represents" organized crime, and others which "represent" certain neighborhood and ethnic interests. It is unlikely, however, that in a tightly controlled organization like Daley's any interest grouping—the building trades unions, for example—would be formally or explicitly recognized and given special rights or standing.

On the other hand, where parties are loose coalitions rather than well-defined hierarchies, interest groupings may be formally organized. There may, for example, be a labor committee within the party which is explicitly declared to exist for the purpose of making labor's influence felt. In nonpartisan cities, where the law prevents the national parties from participating in local elections, the local parties—the organizations which select candidates and carry on election campaigns—may consist mainly or entirely of such interest groupings. And these factions need not be purely vote-getting in nature; they may be voluntary associations and business firms which exist for other purposes than to win elections.

The Club

The "club" is an element of the party that is held together simply by the satisfactions people find in being members of it, especially the satisfactions that arise from solidarity with the other members of the club and with it as an entity.

Political machines, when they collapse, often break into factions, and clubs are a common form that the factionalism takes. Tammany Hall—the Democratic party of New York County (Manhattan)—was a machine during the period of its greatest strength when it was led by Charles F. Murphy. Even then, however, its basic component was the neighborhood or district club.[6] These clubs were centers for the

[6] See Roy V. Peel, *The Political Clubs of New York City* (New York: G. P. Putnam's Sons, 1935).

distribution of patronage and other specific, material inducements and they offered some secondary attractions such as the opportunity to rub elbows with "important" figures and to relax in a congenial atmosphere. After many waves of reform had washed away the patronage and other material benefits, many clubs offered nothing but sociability. By 1960, few club members were payrollers. Tammany, at least at the bottom of its hierarchy, had ceased to be a machine and had become instead an alliance of clubs.

Efficient precinct work is much harder to obtain when one controls, not a worker's job and income, but only his access to a social club. The individual does not respond as readily to discipline. Furthermore, attempts to discipline him are likely to be disruptive of organization. "Firing" a captain from his post, Tammany leaders found, often created resentment and uncertainty among the members of his club. In the circumstances there was nothing to do but put up with workers whose only interest was in the club, and therefore Tammany suffered many defeats in the 1950's and 1960's at the hands of reform organizations whose members were imbued with missionary zeal.[7]

Mixed Cases

It should be understood that the distinctions that have been made among these four kinds of faction (machine, following, interest grouping, and club) are analytical rather than concrete. Concretely, a faction may be both a machine and a following; this would be the case if some voters were attached to the politician by specific material inducements and others by his charm or if all were attached to him in both ways at once. A faction may even be a machine, a following, and an interest grouping; this would be the case if the voters were also held together by a shared interest. Such mixed cases are common. In general, however, one type of attachment is dominant enough to make the classification of the cases under one head or another fairly easy. From the standpoint of the professional politician, the acid test is whether the vote can be delivered. From the standpoint of a politician who has a following, it is whether the voter can be counted on in the absence of any inducement except personal regard. The vote of an interest grouping can both be delivered *and* counted on, but only when the interest will be served thereby.

[7] See James Q. Wilson, *The Amateur Democrat: Club Politics in Three Cities* (Chicago: University of Chicago Press, 1962), chap. x.

FACTIONAL ALLIANCES

In many cities the main task of election politics is to create a working coalition among the diverse elements—machines, followings, interest groupings, and clubs, and mixtures of some or all—which can influence or control votes. Sometimes this entails bringing harmony and discipline into a confusion of factions which, although warring against each other, nevertheless acknowledge that they have some obligation to a larger entity, the party. Sometimes, however, it is to create, *de novo* or almost so, a working coalition among elements which have nothing in common except the desire for success at the polls.

Something more than a mere coalition of factions is required for success at the polls, however. In association with these elements of organization—machines, followings, interest groupings, and clubs—there must be individuals who have the special skills and resources needed to influence those voters (usually a large proportion of the electorate) who are not attached to the organizations and are largely beyond their reach. Public relations men, lawyers, and other professionals with a knack for campaign strategy, and donors who will put up money for television and other advertising media must be brought into the coalition. If the resources or skills of these persons are very great, or if the factions are evenly divided, or if the circumstances make organization relatively unimportant, such individuals may play leading and even dominating parts in the campaign. Even so, the chief beneficiaries of a victory are likely to be the organizations.

Kansas City presents an example of one kind of factional politics. As described by Kenneth E. Gray in 1959, politics there was a struggle within and between two coalitions.[8] One, which may be called "regular Democratic" (although Kansas City is nominally nonpartisan) consisted of several personal followings and several machines. Jim Pendergast had a following which he inherited from his uncle, Tom Pendergast, the boss of the old "goats" machine; Alex Presta, an ex-convict, had a machine in the Italian slum; Henry McKessick had one in the Negro slum; William Sermon, the county Democratic leader, inherited a following from his brother, Roger; the Nordberg-Gallagher machine—or perhaps following—consisted of remnants of the old anti-Pendergast machine. The inability of these factions to work together

[8] Kenneth E. Gray, *A Report on Politics in Kansas City, Mo.* (Cambridge, Mass.: Joint Center for Urban Studies, 1959, mimeo).

led to six consecutive victories for the opposing coalition. This was called the Citizens' Association and consisted of a diverse collection of elements: independent (anti-machine) Democrats, an AFL-CIO interest grouping, a Negro editor with a following, the Republican party organization, the Republican *Kansas City Star*, and some reform-minded civic associations.

In 1959, the regular Democratic factions finally managed to create a working coalition. At the same time the Citizens' Association lost some of its cohesion—some said because of the illness of the editor of the *Star*, others because many independent Democrats were confident that the bad old days of civic corruption were gone forever. The reform administration was voted out of office, and City Manager L. P. Cookingham at once left the city.

It is not clear why the machines and followings in places like Kansas City do not coalesce into a single city-wide machine, as in Chicago. The Kelly-Arvey machine in Chicago broke into factions when Kelly retired, but the factions were soon united under the firm control of Richard J. Daley. One reason why this is rare may be that politicians outside a city (in the Kansas City case, county ones) use patronage to keep the factions divided in order to prevent the city leaders from challenging them.[9]

In St. Louis, factional politics seems to result from the structure of government. The two principal factions are the "mayor's office group" and the aldermen, ward committeemen, and county officials.[10] The mayor, the comptroller, and the president of the board of aldermen are elected at large, and lack patronage. All three men tend to be chosen from among the candidates put forward by the newspapers and the good-government groups. The aldermen, on the other hand, are elected from small districts, and in most cases are dominated by the party leaders (ward committeemen), as are the county officials who, although elected by the city (St. Louis is not part of any county), do not come within the city charter. These officials—the sheriff, collector of revenue, license collector, and recorder of deeds, among others—have about seven hundred patronage jobs at their disposal. Members

[9] The county plays a crucial role in the politics of Cincinnati also. The Hamilton County Republican organization can help or hinder the city party in its contests with the good-government charterite group.

[10] Robert H. Salisbury, "St. Louis Politics: Relationships Among Interests, Parties, and Governmental Structure," *Western Political Quarterly*, June 1960, pp. 498–507, and Kenneth E. Gray, *A Report on Politics in St. Louis* (Cambridge, Mass.: Joint Center for Urban Studies, 1961, mimeo).

of the board of education, elected on still a different basis, also have favors to give and therefore an independent power base. Thus, it seems to be the multiplicity of jurisdictions and constituencies that produces the factional splits; if St. Louis had fewer elected officials and if all were elected by the same constituency, the Democratic party would probably soon be unified.

As matters stand, no one faction has enough resources to dominate any of the others, but each has enough to maintain its independence. Usually each faction needs support from the other; aldermen, for example, need the financial and newspaper support that the mayor commands, and he in turn needs help from the precinct workers in the "delivery" wards that are controlled by the aldermen and the county leaders. Sometimes, as when the mayor must demonstrate his independence or when the "county" leaders decide to "punish" an opponent, the factions run separate slates in the primaries. In 1957, good-government groups proposed adoption of a new city charter that would have increased the power of the mayor and of the city-wide forces around him and would have decreased both the authority and the size of the board of aldermen. Naturally, the aldermanic and county groups opposed the measure, and it was defeated.[11]

Kansas City and St. Louis are examples of factional politics within a partisan electoral system. But factionalism is even more characteristic of truly nonpartisan cities. There are a good many cities—Boston and Nashville are examples—where nonpartisanship keeps the parties weak and divided but does not eliminate them altogether, as it does in Detroit and Los Angeles. In Boston, there are about as many factions as politicians and since the city political system yields practically no patronage or power, all are fated to remain undernourished and small. Nashville is also divided into factions, but there the mayor controls enough patronage and city services to be able—at least until very recently—to dominate the Davidson County Democratic Executive Committee.[12]

There seem, therefore, to be at least three sets of circumstances that may produce a politics of factionalism: (a) politicians outside the city may use their resources to create divisions within it; (b) the formal structure of government may offer incentives to factional competition;

[11] See Robert H. Salisbury, "The Dynamics of Reform: Charter Politics in St. Louis," *Midwest Journal of Political Science*, August 1961, pp. 260–275.
[12] Mayor Ben West suffered a setback in the spring of 1962 when the voters, acting against his recommendation, consolidated the city and county governments.

and (c) the distribution of political resources (money, followings, etc.) within the city may be such that no faction can acquire enough resources to dominate the others. In principle, this last case might occur in a city where the total of such resources is very large. In fact, however, it seems to occur mainly where, as under nonpartisanship, resources are exceedingly few.

CHAPTER 11 · REFORM

EVER SINCE the Civil War the reformer has been a conspicuous figure in the larger cities. He has rarely been elected to office and, when elected, he has even more rarely survived for a second term. He has been ridiculed by professional politicians; "goo-goo," the professional calls him, in derision of his creed: "good government." Nevertheless, he has exerted a profound influence on the structure of government and a somewhat lesser one on the character of its personnel and the content of its policy. Although out of power, he has somehow succeeded to a large extent in making city government over. And he has made it over in accordance with an ideal fundamentally at odds with its long-standing tradition. Viewed in the widest perspective, the struggle between the reformer and the professional politician has been, and is, between two fundamentally opposed conceptions.

From the Rev. Charles H. Parkhurst, who in 1892 donned checked black and white trousers in order to penetrate New York's saloons and brothels on behalf of the City Vigilance League, to the scholarly young women in toreador pants who now do battle with the remains of Tammany Hall, reform has exhibited a variety of types and forms. Almost all reformers, however, have had a basic point of view in common, and, despite differences in style and tactics, they have generally agreed about what ought to be done. Some of the measures most characteristic of their point of view and most important in themselves —nonpartisanship, the council-manager form, and master planning— will be discussed in the three chapters following this one.

THE REFORM IDEAL

From its beginnings to the present, the municipal reform movement has had the goals of eliminating corruption, increasing efficiency, and making local government in some sense more democratic. The relative emphasis that reformers have placed upon these goals has of course varied with the person, the place, and the time; but reform has always and everywhere stood for some combination of the three.

These goals are parts of the larger whole that we have described as the Anglo-Saxon Protestant middle-class ethos—a view of the world which sees politics as a means of moralizing life and which attaches great importance to the individual's obligation to "serve" the public. As we pointed out in Chapter 3, the Yankee elite which ran the Northern cities throughout most of the last century had this ethos in a very marked degree. When in the post-Civil War period the elite was displaced from control of local government by businessmen and manufacturers who were after street railway and other utility franchises, by machines, and by the immigrant vote, it withdrew to a sphere—the community service organization—in which it could carry on public service activities in its own way. Municipal reform was one such activity. Many of the early municipal reformers were Mugwumps—independents, usually Republican, who protested the transfer of power from the old public-serving elite to the new self-serving tycoons (they were portrayed as birds whose "mugs" were on one side of a fence and whose "wumps" were on the other.[1] The Mugwumps and their allies became a permanent opposition to the interest-serving style of local government that replaced the traditional public-serving one. Although, of course, particular candidates and practices were the immediate objects of their attack, what they really wanted was to restore to government its former character. It was not simply a change of regime that the reform movement was after; it was a change of constitution. It was not a difference of degree, but one of kind.

The reformers assumed that there existed an interest ("the public interest") that pertained to the city "as a whole" and that should always prevail over competing, partial (and usually private) interests.[2] Local government entailed simply the businesslike management of essential public services. The task of discovering the content of the public interest was therefore a technical rather than a political one. What was necessary was to put affairs entirely in the hands of the

[1] For an account of the social forces at work in reform locally and nationally, see Richard Hofstadter, *The Age of Reform* (New York: Alfred A. Knopf, 1955), especially chap. iv. See also Lorin Peterson, *The Day of the Mugwump* (New York: Random House, 1961); Frank Mann Steward, *A Half Century of Municipal Reform: The History of the National Municipal League* (Berkeley: University of California Press, 1950); and T. R. Mason, *Reform Politics in Boston*, unpublished dissertation, Department of Government, Harvard University, March 1963.

[2] To this generalized account there are, of course, exceptions. See, for example, John R. Commons, *Proportional Representation* (New York, 1896). Professor Commons challenged the most basic assumption of the reformers—that partial interests should be excluded from consideration—but he and his book had little influence.

few who were "best qualified," persons whose training, experience, natural ability, and devotion to public service equipped them best to manage the public business. The best qualified men would decide "policy" and leave its execution ("administration") to professionals ("experts") who would work under the direction of an executive (mayor or manager) in whom authority over administration would be highly centralized. Interference in the management of public affairs, especially attempts to assert private or other partial interests against the public interest, would not be tolerated.

The style of local government toward which the reform ideal tends may be seen in some cities where it has been nearly realized in practice. An example is Winnetka, a suburb of Chicago the residents of which are almost all upper-middle-class Anglo-Saxon Protestants.[3] Winnetkans are in fundamental agreement on the kind of local government they want: it must provide excellent schools, parks, libraries and other community services and it must provide them with businesslike efficiency and perfect honesty. Politics, in the sense of a competitive struggle for office or for private advantage, does not exist. No one offers himself as a candidate for office. Instead the civic associations agree upon a slate of those "best qualified to serve" which the voters ratify as a matter of course. Members of the city council leave "administration" entirely in the hands of the city manager.

That the Winnetka style of local government reflects the middle-class ethos and is not a mere historical accident may be seen from the fact that the same style exists in other, similarly constituted communities. For example, Scarsdale, New York, although about a thousand miles distant from Winnetka, follows the same practice of "tapping" those "best qualified to serve."[4]

THE PROGRAM OF REFORM

This general view of the reformers implied a variety of objectives and particular measures:

(a) Putting the electorate in the position to assert its will despite professional politicians. The favorite measures were nomination by petition, the initiative, recall, and referendum.

---

[3] Our account of Winnetka is based upon D. G. Monroe and H. Wilson in F. C. Mosher *et al.*, *City Manager Government in Seven Cities* (Chicago: Public Administration Service, 1940); and Samuel K. Gove in Lois M. Pelekoudas, *Assembly on Illinois Local Government*, Institute of Government and Public Affairs, University of Illinois, May 1961.

[4] See the story by Merrill Folsom in the *New York Times*, Nov. 13, 1959, p. 31.

(b) Simplifying the voter's task (the short ballot), improving his information (the municipal research bureau), and exhorting him to do his civic duty (citizens' associations). Between 1871 and 1885, citizens' associations were formed in most large and many middle-sized cities, especially in the East. Municipal research bureaus were created soon afterward.

(c) Checking the tide of immigration. In Boston, for example, many leaders of reform were leaders of the Immigration Restriction League.[5]

(d) Separating the "business" of city government from state and national politics (home rule, nonpartisanship, and the holding of local elections at times when there were no state and national ones), weakening the power of neighborhood and other partial interests (at-large elections and reduction in the size of councils), and strengthening the executive (longer terms for mayors, subordination of departments and commissions to them, and extension of the merit system).

These measures were brought together in a "municipal program" in 1900 by the National Municipal League, an organization that had been created a few years before by representatives of fifteen citizens' associations.[6] In 1916 the League published a "second municipal program" which modified some of the earlier measures slightly and added some new ones, notably the council-manager form and city planning. These recommendations the League published in the form of a Model City Charter. This, in several successive editions, has been the orthodox text of the municipal reform movement ever since.

The "municipal program" and the subsequent Model City Charter left to local option the questions of whether to have proportional representation and direct legislation through the initiative and the referendum. PR did not logically belong with the other items in the reform package; it was, after all, a procedure for obtaining a representation (albeit a "correct" one) of competing interests, not for finding the interest "of the whole." Those reformers who accepted it did so, presumably, because they thought that if government in the interest of the whole were out of the question, the next best thing was a system that would give them—the "good government" minority—representation as an interest. Charles Francis Adams favored PR because it would

[5] Barbara M. Solomon, *Ancestors and Immigrants* (Cambridge, Mass.: Harvard University Press, 1956), pp. 104 ff.

[6] Frank Goodnow, who made much of the separation of "legislative" and "administrative" functions, was a member of the committee which drafted the "municipal program." For his views, see especially his *Municipal Problems* (New York, 1897). For the history of the League, see Steward, *Half Century.*

enable men like himself to occupy public office as a matter of right and without political struggle.[7]

To the reformers who devised them, the measures of the first municipal program all seemed obvious expedients for coping with the great evil of the day, boss-rule corruption. It was not from the struggle against bosses and boodlers that the reform program got its logic, however. It got that from the middle-class political ethos, and the logic would have been the same if bosses and boodlers had never existed. Indeed, it was in relatively small, middle-class cities, where indeed those persons had never existed, that reform measures were most popular. Many such cities adopted the Model City Charter in its entirety almost at once. Most of the large cities adopted some parts of it, but none ever adopted the program as a whole.

ORGANIZATIONAL STRATEGIES[8]

Reform organization has varied from place to place and time to time, but in general has taken, and takes today, one or more of the following five forms:

1. *Citizens' associations and research bureaus.* These are extraparty committees of public-spirited citizens who, usually with the help of paid research directors and staffs, scrutinize local government structure, programs, and expenditures, and recommend changes and reforms. As a rule, these organizations do not endorse candidates, participate in election campaigns (except perhaps by providing "factual" information), or take sides in controversial policy questions. The New York Citizens' Budget Commission, the Chicago Civic Federation, the Detroit Citizens' League, the Seattle Municipal League, and the Boston Municipal Research Bureau are examples. The League of Women Voters is a national organization of this general character.

The confidence of many reformers in the local associations and bureaus has declined as it has become more and more apparent that

---

[7] Adams is quoted in Commons, *Proportional Representation*, p. 209. That the eminent man, once in office, would have to bargain and compromise with other men elected by other bodies of voters was a defect, of course, but one that it was practically necessary to accept. Commons, however, thought some city problems required political rather than business management (although not by national parties), and he believed that compromise was necessary and desirable in politics (pp. 177 ff).

[8] This section is based on James Q. Wilson, "Politics and Reform in American Cities," in Ivan Hinderaker (ed.), *American Government Annual, 1962–63* (New York: Holt, Rinehart & Winston, 1962), pp. 41–50.

"objective" information about expenditures and administrative procedures is of little or no interest to most voters. They are supported mainly by reformers whose interest is more in the "business efficiency" than in the "democracy" of local government. In the main, they make their effect not by "informing" the electorate directly but by "feeding" the newspapers information the publication of which, although it will not affect the vote significantly, nevertheless embarrasses politicians and department heads who are sensitive about "public relations" and the "image" being presented of them and their administration.

2. *Candidate appraisal committees.* These exist outside the political parties on a permanent or *ad hoc* basis to recommend, or to evaluate, candidates. In some nonpartisan cities, formal or informal slate-making associations put forward "good government" candidates. In cities where the regular parties are so strong that there is no possibility of electing third-party or independent candidates, appraisal committees confine themselves to evaluating the qualifications of the party nominees. Committees which merely evaluate candidates are composed of "less important" people than those which select them (there is not enough at stake in mere evaluation to occupy "top" men). The actual work is often done by staff men who assemble and publish essential biographical information, divide the candidates into categories—"endorsed," "preferred," "qualified," and "unqualified"—and, sometimes, rank them in order of qualification. The Citizens' Union of New York is an appraisal committee as well as a research bureau.

3. *Independent local parties.* Reformers have on occasion organized independent parties in the hope of taking office or, at least, of influencing an election. Reform parties, however—even those that have been reasonably successful at the polls—do not last very long. The reason is that, like all formal organizations, they can endure only by offering a continuing and sufficient stream of inducements to those (for example, voters and party workers) whose cooperation they require. This they find it impossible to do. They have no specific, material inducements to offer, and even if they did they would be prevented by their principles from offering them. They must, therefore, rely on nonmaterial inducements, especially the satisfaction of doing one's duty as a citizen. Unfortunately, this appeals to relatively few people, and ordinarily even to them only so long as their indignation at some recent outrage to civic decency stays hot.

New York's experience with reform parties is illustrative. The City

Fusion Party has been the principal vehicle for the election of three of the four reform mayors New York has had in this century (Seth Low, 1901, John Purroy Mitchel, 1913, and Fiorello La Guardia, 1933). But in each instance its success depended upon an alliance with the Republicans, and when victory was won the alliance always collapsed and the Fusion Party was always unable to sustain itself apart. The Liberal Party of New York affords an interesting contrast. Formed in 1944 when certain labor leaders broke away from the left-wing American Labor Party, it has since had considerable success at the polls and shows every sign of enduring. It is not, however, a reform party in the sense of one motivated and held together by reform ideals. It is, rather, the political arm of the International Ladies' Garment Workers' Union, and it endures because it serves the interests of this financially powerful and professionally led organization. If its maintenance depended mainly upon the idealism of part-time reformers, it would doubtless have ceased to exist long ago.[9]

4. *"Blue ribbon" leadership factions.* Party leaders, acting sometimes out of "good government" principles and sometimes out of shrewd regard for what will maintain the party as a going concern, now and then nominate candidates who are conspicuously identified with "good government." A "blue ribbon" candidate is a throwback to the Mugwump ideal: he is a man of unassailable integrity, high professional competence, and complete devotion to the public service. He is likely to be "old family" and wealthy or to be a business success and wealthy, to have a record of "statesmanlike" participation in public affairs (perhaps as chairman of a nonpartisan inquiry), and to be a loyal party member without having had too close a personal identification with the local machine or with professional politicians. Richardson Dilworth and Joseph S. Clark were "blue ribbon" candidates of the Democratic machine in Philadelphia and Martin H. Kennelly was a "blue ribbon" candidate of the Democratic machine in Chicago. Once elected, a "blue ribbon" candidate may introduce many reforms and in general run the city on "good government" lines. However, he cannot (at least not without losing his blue ribbon!) take control of the party

[9] Other examples of independent good-government parties are the City Charter Committee in Cincinnati, the Citizens' Association in Kansas City, the San Francisco Volunteers for Better Government, the San Antonio Good Government League, the Phoenix Charter Government Committee, the Minneapolis Citizens Organized for Responsible Government, the Independent Voters of Illinois (Chicago), and the Cambridge (Mass.) Civic Association.

machine, and when he leaves office the machine, having been made lean and hungry by the rigors of reform, is likely to restore itself to something at least approaching its old vigor and prosperity in a surprisingly short time. This, at least, was the experience in Philadelphia and Chicago.[10]

5. *Intraparty reform clubs.* These are units of the regular (usually Democratic) party organization that are dominated by reformers. The reformer enters the party at the ward or district level and uses its normal procedures and techniques to capture positions in the lower levels of its hierarchy in the expectation of using them to influence the party leadership and eventually to gain control of the party. Intraparty reformers associated with the New York Committee for Democratic Voters have succeeded in overthrowing the Tammany leader, Carmine DeSapio. Others under the aegis of the California Democratic Council are trying to lead the party in that state.

Because the intraparty reform movement is indicative of changes that are occurring in the structure of big-city politics and in the reform mentality, we shall examine the most important instance of it—the club movement in Manhattan.

INTRAPARTY REFORM IN MANHATTAN

The Manhattan reformers are mostly young (under forty) professional people of middle-class origins.[11] Many are recent arrivals in the city, and about two thirds are single, separated, or divorced. Over half are Jewish, and less than ten percent Catholic. Among the club officers, there is a high proportion of male, married, Jewish lawyers. Practically all the Manhattan reformers are "liberals" of the left (in some cases, of the extreme left). Adlai Stevenson's candidacy for the Presidency brought many of them into politics, and he has been the idol of the movement ever since.

The Manhattan reformers are keenly anxious to make the Democratic party—and through it ultimately the nation and the world—democratic. They are the heirs of the Populist strain of the older reform movement.

---

[10] On both cities, see Wilson, "Politics and Reform," pp. 44–46, and on Philadelphia, see James Reichley, *The Art of Government* (New York: Fund for the Republic, 1959).

[11] Wilson, *The Amateur Democrat,* (Chicago: University of Chicago Press, 1962) pp. 13–15. The reform movements in California and Chicago are also described in this book, on which this section is based.

The important difference between them and their predecessors is that they are trying to reach their objective by first capturing and reforming the party machinery. Several circumstances account for this difference. The most important, perhaps, is the success of three or four generations of writers and teachers in making it plain that power in this country can only be had by influencing votes and that in the long run this can only be done by painstaking attention to the mechanics of party organization. In short, the indispensability of good precinct work had entered into the common knowledge of the middle class via the textbook.

This entailed certain consequences for the kinds of people who would become active and successful reformers. One was that they had to be young. It is impossible to win control of an election district merely by writing a check and allowing one's name to be used on a letterhead. One can do it only by working strenuously; one must master the esoteric art of drawing up an election petition, induce hundreds or thousands of strangers to sign it, speak on street corners, and trudge to the tops of tenements to get out the vote. Prosperous, prestigious, middle-aged businessmen concerned about their coronaries will not do these things. The intraparty reformer, accordingly, is young, at the beginning of his professional career, and relatively free of family and other responsibilities.

He is also highly motivated. Earlier generations of reformers were also highly motivated, of course; the difference is that today's reformer sees more connection than they did between local politics and the matters that are most "interesting" ideologically. He sees more clearly than they did that the roots of national political power are in local party organization. And the extension in recent years of city government to spheres—especially race relations, housing, and planning—that are ideologically important has enhanced its intrinsic interest for him. Consequently, "cosmopolitans" (to employ a concept of Robert K. Merton's that was introduced earlier) are now more attracted to *municipal* reform than they formerly were.

That young "liberals" want power in local politics would count for little, however, if changes had not occurred within the parties (in the Manhattan case, the Democratic party) to make the parties more receptive to them. The most striking of these changes is one that we have already discussed—the progressive inability of the parties to offer their workers material rewards. This inability enabled the ideologically motivated reformers to price themselves into the market, so to speak. Because reformers were willing to work hard for nonmaterial rewards, they outdid the old-line party workers. Another change occurred in the mentality of the electorate and was reflected in party organization. The same writings and teachings that persuaded reformers to seek power from within the parties dramatized machines and bosses as arch-villains in the political folklore of the growing middle class. Professional politicians found that the cry of "bossism" would stir the electorate when nothing else would. Consequently, the professionals, while still regarding the reformers within the party as an evil, recognized that the reform slogans were necessary—necessary for both offensive and defensive purposes.

Another circumstance that facilitated the rise of the Manhattan reformer was his marginal standing. A person who has attributes of two or more competing political groups (for example, La Guardia, a Protestant of Italian extraction whose mother was Jewish) is always in a favorable position when votes must be drawn from all of the competing groups. The Manhattan reformers have this advantage. That they display in marked degree the middle-class ethos (having in many cases assimilated it at Ivy League colleges) not only accounts for their presence in the reform movement but also makes them acceptable to "good government"-minded voters. That their parents, or grandparents, were immigrants and therefore near the bottom of the status heap makes them acceptable (or at any rate more acceptable than they would be if they came from a long line of "blue-nosed" Presbyterians or Episcopalians) to the bulk of the working class.

The Manhattan reformers are not, however, able to overcome entirely the handicap of being middle-class, and this, indeed, is one of the principal obstacles they face. In Manhattan, as in all large central cities, middle-class people live in relatively few parts of the city, often in parts that are surrounded by lower-class areas or slums. In these middle-class districts most voters are Republican. This is no handicap to the reformers in their fights for control of the Democratic party within the district, since these fights are settled by primary elections in which only Democrats can vote. But when, having captured the Democratic party in the middle-class districts, the reformers seek to extend their influence, they come up against the hard fact that the vast majority of Democrats live in districts—Negro Harlem, Puerto Rican East Harlem, the Jewish Lower East Side, and others—where there is not much middle class and therefore no support for reform and reformers.

They encounter the same obstacle when they try to influence an election for mayor. Then members of all parties can vote, and usually the Democratic reform-controlled districts lose overwhelmingly to the Republicans. In the November 1961 election, for example, the reform-backed Democratic candidate, Robert F. Wagner, got strong support from lower-class districts (whose leaders—regular Democrats—had fought him in the primary) and little or no support from the middle-class districts (whose leaders—reform Democrats—had backed him in the primary). Although the reformers had helped him get the nomination in the primary, the regulars helped him win the election. The reformers, therefore, could not expect him to be their man.

What substantive program the Manhattan reformers would offer if they came to power is not at all clear. Their attention has so far been almost entirely absorbed in the struggle to take possession of the party machinery. It is entirely possible, of course, that if they succeeded in this the exigencies of maintaining the machinery would divert them from their present ideological purposes and make them in some degree like their anathema, the party professional.

THE SIGNIFICANCE OF REFORM

When one tries to evaluate the significance of the municipal reform movement over the years, he is struck by a series of anomalies. The first is that although reformers have lost most of their battles for power, they have in the main won their war for the adoption of particular measures of structural and other change. To be sure, none of the larger cities has adopted the whole reform program. Nevertheless, there are few if any large cities which have not adopted important parts of it, and city government today is in general fairly close to the structural ideal presented by the reformers.

A second anomaly is that although reform has won its war, victory has not yielded the fruits for which the reformers fought. It is true that machines, bosses, and boodlers are almost everywhere things of the past, that the mayors of the larger cities are apparently all honest and reasonably capable, and that the day-to-day management of city services is generally in the hands of professionals who are chosen for merit. These improvements, however, although they occurred after the adoption of reforms, were probably seldom caused by them. Certainly reform did not cause good government in the small middle-class cities where it was most popular. In the large cities, the reform measures did not in themselves change matters fundamentally. Mayor Hague found the commission form of government more a help than a hindrance to boss rule in Jersey City, and Boss Pendergast found the council-manager form wholly satisfactory for his purposes in Kansas City.

Nonpartisanship, the strengthening of the chief executive (whether mayor or manager), and the merit system and other reforms did not, as the reformers expected they would, eliminate corruption and inefficiency. As this is written, nonpartisan Boston is shaken by charges of corruption in the construction of a public garage and several major highways, in building inspection, in the sale of tax-delinquent properties, in the awarding of contracts, and in the enforcement of the law against gamblers. New York City at the same time is uncovering corruption and inefficiency in school construction, the certification of weights and measures, and building inspection. In Philadelphia, the reform administration is being embarrassed by corruption in the awarding of contracts.

Insofar as reform has put a stop to the use of jobs and favors to influence votes, it has made local government more democratic. But the net improvement may be considerably less than at first appears; for the system introduced by reform, to the extent that it influences voters by means other than rational argument about the common good, is itself undemocratic. If reform has merely substituted influence by "brand name" and "charm" for influence by "favors" and "friendship" (and we do not assert that it has), it may be hard to claim any net gain.

Moreover, the effectiveness as well as the democratic character of local government must enter into the reckoning. If reform has tended to make city governments weaker by destroying the informal centralizing influence of party without at the same time producing a compensating reduction in the decentralization of authority, the loss of "efficiency in the large" may more than offset any gain in "efficiency in the small."

There is, however, a third anomaly. Although reform measures have not produced the effects that the reformers have anticipated (and have indeed often produced opposite ones), those desired effects are being produced by other causes. City government is vastly more honest, efficient, and democratic than it was a generation or two ago. The measures for which the reformers fought are not the cause of this. Rather, we think, those measures and the improvements that have occurred are both effects of a common cause: the steady diffusion in our culture of the political ideal of the Anglo-Saxon Protestant middle-class political ethos.

CHAPTER 12 · NONPARTISANSHIP

BY THE MOST inclusive definition (which is also the usual one), a nonpartisan system of elections is one in which no candidate is identified on the ballot by party affiliation. Sixty-one percent of cities of over 5,000 population are nonpartisan in this sense. These include both large and small cities; nonpartisanship has very little connection with size of city. It does have a connection with the council-manager plan and with at-large election, however. Of the 1,756 council-manager cities (almost all of which have at-large elections), 84 percent are nonpartisan. By contrast, only 44 percent of mayor-council cities (most of which have district elections or a combination of district and at-large elections) are nonpartisan. The basis of this connection is easy to see; nonpartisanship, the council-manager plan, and at-large election are all expressions of the reform ideal and of the middle-class political ethos.

Some of the cities in which party affiliations do not appear on the ballots are far from being nonpartisan in any other respect. Chicago is an example. In aldermanic elections the names of the parties do not appear on the ballots; nevertheless, it is practically impossible to be elected to the city council except as a candidate of one of the major parties. As a wit remarked, the council is composed of 47 nonpartisan Democrats and three nonpartisan Republicans. In this chapter we will not be discussing cities like Chicago which are nonpartisan only in the sense that party affiliations are not printed on the ballot.

The other cities—those that are nonpartisan in some additional sense—fall into one or another of three types:[1]

1. Those in which the Democratic and Republican parties play limited and occasionally behind-the-scenes roles in local elections. In these cities, the general opinion is that the Democratic and Republican parties ought not to "interfere" either in the selection of candidates or in the conduct of election campaigns. The parties defer to this view

[1] Cf. Charles R. Adrian, "A Typology of Nonpartisan Elections," *Western Political Quarterly*, June 1959, pp. 449–458.

to some extent: they do not (as in cities like Chicago) play leading or dominant parts, but neither are they entirely absent from the scene. Denver, Seattle, Cincinnati, Kansas City, and some California cities are of this type.

2. Those in which the Democratic and Republican parties play no part at all but in which other formal organizations *do* play a part. These other organizations may come into being to fight a single campaign or they may exist from campaign to campaign. They may have no purpose except to put their candidates into office or they may be civic associations which have a variety of other purposes. Frequently they are coalitions of organizations organized and led by newspapers or business firms. Some cities of this type have "purely local parties," i.e., organizations which not only elect candidates but exercise some control over what they do in office afterward; others have "slate-making associations," i.e., organizations which do no more than select and endorse candidates. Cities in which local elections are dominated by formal organizations other than the Democratic and Republican parties include San Francisco, Detroit, Dallas, Fort Worth, Flint (Michigan), and Cambridge (Massachusetts).

3. Those in which the Democratic and Republican parties play no part and in which there are no purely local parties or slate-making associations. In cities of this type, candidates select themselves and either create their own supporting organization or get along without one. This is the most common type of nonpartisanship in very small cities, and it seems safe to say that the smaller the city the more its politics will be one based on friendship and acquaintance rather than on formal organization. There are some big cities, however, which are closer to this type of nonpartisanship than to any of the others. Boston and Los Angeles are examples.

In what follows we shall call cities, like Chicago, which are nonpartisan in no other respect than in not printing the names of parties on their ballots, "nominally nonpartisan." This will enable us to reserve the word "nonpartisan" for cities that are such in some additional respect, that is, which fall into the three types just described.

Unfortunately it is impossible to say what proportion of cities is nominally nonpartisan or what proportion of those that are nonpartisan (in the sense we have just now given the word) belong to each of the three types. So far as we know, all data-gathering organizations lump together indiscriminately all cities which do not put party affiliations on their ballots. The *Muncipal Yearbook,* for example, describes Chicago as "nonpartisan."

THE RATIONALE OF NONPARTISANSHIP

The nonpartisan ballot was one of the several reforms put forward at the turn of the century to curb the machines and put city government on an honest and businesslike basis. The only proper function of city government, many reformers believed, was to provide certain necessary public services and facilities and to provide them as cheaply as possible. In this view, there was no need or justification for politics. The reformers believed that it was the introduction into local public affairs of considerations of party interest and party advantage that led to machines, bosses, corruption, and waste. The reason American cities were the "worst in Christendom," Andrew D. White, the first president of Cornell University, wrote in 1890, was that they were governed on the "evil theory" that "the city is a political body."

> My fundamental contention is that the city is a corporation; that as a city it has nothing whatever to do with general political interests. . . . The questions in a city are not political questions. They have reference to the laying out of streets [and such matters]. The work of a city being the creation and control of the city property, it should logically be managed as a piece of property by those who have created it, who have a title to it, or a real substantial part in it [and not by] a crowd of illiterate peasants, freshly raked in from the Irish bogs, or Bohemian mines, or Italian robber nests. . . .[2]

Reformers who were progressives—for example, Brand Whitlock, the novelist who became the first nonpartisan mayor of Toledo—thought nonpartisanship, by freeing the people from the shackles which the machines and bosses had fastened upon them, would give the democratic impulse a chance to express itself. The National Municipal League, which was founded in 1894, urged the nonpartisan ballot then and urges it now. Richard S. Childs, one of its founders and leaders, thought that nonpartisanship and a short ballot in combination would, by enabling voters to choose between men rather than parties, make for better-informed choices.

Not all reformers shared this enthusiasm for nonpartisanship. Nathan

[2] Andrew D. White, *The Forum,* December 1890. Part of the article is reprinted, along with other materials on nonpartisanship, in Banfield (ed.), *Urban Government* (New York: Free Press of Glencoe, 1961), pp. 209–237 (the quotation is on p. 213).

Matthews, Jr., one of the last Yankees to serve as mayor of Boston (1891–1895), wrote in his valedictory to the board of aldermen that although nonpartisanship seemed a plausible reform, it might have a harmful result overlooked by its advocates, namely, dividing the people in cities along class and social, rather than party, lines. "As a city is a political institution, the people in the end will divide into parties; and it would seem extremely doubtful whether the present system, however illogical its foundation be, does not in fact produce better results, at least in large cities, than if the voters were divided into groups separated by property, social, or religious bounds."[3]

Boston did not heed this advice. In 1909 it became the first large city to adopt nonpartisanship. Soon afterward, the California legislature made nonpartisan election of almost all local officials mandatory. By 1929, more than half of 282 American cities included in a survey had nonpartisan elections. Two states, Minnesota and Nebraska, elected (and still elect) state legislators on nonpartisan ballots.[4]

Nonpartisanship is a characteristic expression of what we have called the middle-class Anglo-Saxon Protestant political ethos. The principle of nonpartisanship is consistent with, and indeed logically implies, the view that politics, rather than being a struggle among partial and private interests, is (or at any rate ought to be) a disinterested effort to discover what is best for the community "as a whole." Parties, hardly less than pressure groups, represent the interest of "parts" against that of "the whole." For the same reason that the citizen ought to take a public-regarding rather than a private-regarding view of candidates and issues, he ought to take a public-regarding rather than a *party*-regarding one. And for the same reason that officials should be elected at large, so that they will represent the city "as a whole," they should be elected without regard to party.

The connection between ethos and institutional form is suggested by Table 9. Those regions in which Progressivism and Populism were strongest during the early years of this century are the ones with the highest proportion of nonpartisan cities. As Richard Hofstadter has

[3] Nathan Matthews, Jr., *The City Government of Boston* (Boston, 1895), pp. 177–178. The last chapter of this book is a brilliant review of most of the reforms then under consideration in municipal affairs. Although Matthews favored "conservative experiment" with measures intended to strengthen the executive, improve the civil service, and limit the ward system, he was keenly aware of, and emphatically opposed to, the antipolitical bias of many of his fellow reformers.

[4] These details are from Eugene C. Lee, *The Politics of Nonpartisanship* (Berkeley: University of California Press, 1960), pp. 22–27.

shown, Progressivism was a political expression of the Anglo-Saxon Protestant ethos.[5] Where Progressives scored their greatest victories (for example, in California and Wisconsin) they left, as a political legacy, nonpartisan cities.

TABLE 9. U.S. regions ranked by proportion of nonpartisan cities, 1960

Region	Number of cities 25,000 and over	Percent nonpartisan
Plains	49	98.0
West	68	95.6
Mountain	12	83.3
South	96	75.0
Border	34	73.5
New England	71	62.0
Great Lakes	101	54.5
Middle Atlantic	97	23.7

Source: Calculated from the *Municipal Yearbook, 1960.*

NONPARTISANSHIP IN ACTION

There has been little research on the consequences of nonpartisanship for urban politics. One reason for this is that it is difficult to isolate nonpartisanship from associated factors, such as at-large election. Another is that a political system, or an aspect of one, must be judged not simply by the quality of the decisions that it produces with respect to certain of the service functions of a city government (although even that would be extremely difficult) but rather by the quality of the decisions that it produces with respect to the whole range of functions that the government serves, i.e., the political as well as the service ones. To find even two cities that are alike in all relevant respects except that one is nonpartisan and the other is not is obviously out of the question. But even if such cities could be found, it would be hard to measure the value of some gain in the performance of certain service functions against that of some loss in the performance of certain of the political ones.

What is known about the effects of nonpartisanship pertains to the way in which elections are conducted and to the kinds of people who

[5] Richard Hofstadter, *The Age of Reform* (New York: Alfred A. Knopf, 1955), introduction and chap. iv.

are elected, and only indirectly to the quality of the decisions that are reached. It can be summarized under four headings: politicians, voters, parties, and public policy.

1. The Politician under Nonpartisanship

Nonpartisanship divides politicians into two separate groups—those who run for nonpartisan (usually city) office and those who run for partisan (usually county, state, or national) office.[6] Members of one group rarely switch over to the other, and when they do they even more rarely switch back. In part this is because voters are reluctant to vote for a candidate who may be using the nonpartisan office as a stepping stone to a partisan one. When the president of the Massachusetts senate ran for mayor of Boston, he felt it necessary to assure the voters that if elected he would never again run for partisan office. Occasionally someone does rise from a nonpartisan office to be governor or senator, but this is rare. (Frank Murphy, who was mayor of Detroit, became governor and then United States senator. But Edward J. Jeffries, Jr., the greatest vote-getter in Detroit's history, came in last in a field of four when he ran for governor.) In California, where nonpartisanship is widespread, partisan politics is the main route to important state office. No mayor of either Los Angeles or San Francisco has in recent years been able to climb the other, taller political ladder.[7]

That nonpartisan politicians rarely rise to high office is not necessarily a consequence of the separation of the nonpartisan from the partisan political world, of course. As we explained in an earlier chapter, anyone who is closely identified with a city, especially a large one, is under a handicap in a statewide election.

The politician who moves from nonpartisan to partisan politics must usually assume that he is taking a one-way trip, and this of course has consequences for the recruitment of partisan politicians. That the recruitment of nonpartisan ones is also affected by the separation between the two systems is even clearer. Nonpartisan candidates are,

[6] See Charles R. Adrian, "Some General Characteristics of Nonpartisan Elections," American Political Science Review, September 1952, pp. 766–776.

[7] On the other hand, Eugene C. Lee found that of the 162 state officials in office in California in 1960, 13 had once been nonpartisan mayors and 41 had held some nonpartisan local office. It need not be inferred, however, that in these cases the nonpartisan offices were stepping stones to the partisan ones; the state officials may conceivably have advanced in spite of rather than because of these earlier associations. Lee, Politics of Nonpartisanship, pp. 107–110.

as we have said, chosen by purely local parties, by civic associations, by *ad hoc* groups of one kind or another, and by themselves. Because they will not be identified to the voters by Republican or Democratic party affiliation, they must try to be identified in other ways. This leads them to seek publicity of a kind that will make their names familiar to the voter, and to try to secure organizational endorsements. The readers of newspapers and the members of civic associations, labor unions, women's clubs, and the like often rely heavily upon an "approved slate" in choosing among the party-less—and for most voters, meaningless—names on the ballot.

Newspapers are particularly important to the election of candidates in nonpartisan cities—especially the larger ones—and the nonpartisan system is therefore understandably dear to the newspapers. ("You can't tell the players without a scorecard," a newspaperman remarked happily, "and we sell the scorecards.")

These recruitment and endorsement practices tend to give an advantage to certain kinds of candidates. The "typical" nonpartisan councilman has been described by two California studies as a registered Republican (but one not active in partisan affairs) 45 to 50 years old who is in a professional, managerial, or sales occupation and lives in the "better part of town." He is likely to be a Protestant, a Mason, a member of the Chamber of Commerce and of a veteran's group, to have lived in the city for a long time, and to be without previous experience in politics, having "made his mark" in the community chest, the Red Cross, or some other civic or welfare organization.[8]

This pattern is general enough to cause some Democrats and labor leaders to oppose nonpartisanship. The pattern is by no means universal, however. In Boston, as we have seen, most councilmen are Irish Catholic Democrats, and the others are Italians. Yankee Republicans are conspicuous by their absence.

In some overwhelmingly Republican communities, nonpartisanship permits a few Democrats to win offices that Democrats could not win in partisan contests.[9] These are probably Democrats who are con-

---

[8] *Ibid.*, p. 50, and Robert J. Huckshorn, "Spotlight on City Councilmen," *BGR Observer* (Los Angeles: University of California Bureau of Governmental Research), November 1957. Lee's data are for 38 councilmen in six middle-sized cities; Huckshorn's are for 283 councilmen and mayors in Los Angeles County's fifty-three cities.

[9] Oliver P. Williams and Charles R. Adrian, "The Insulation of Local Politics Under the Nonpartisan Ballot," *American Political Science Review*, December 1959, p. 1063.

sidered "respectable" in everything except their peculiar party affiliation; nonpartisanship renders that unimportant.

Nonpartisanship, especially when combined with at-large election, appears to favor incumbent councilmen. Charles Gilbert and Christopher Clague calculated, for each of twenty-three of the largest cities, "incumbency ratios" for several councilmanic elections.[10] These showed the frequency with which incumbents ran for re-election and the frequency with which those who ran were re-elected. They found that, in two partisan cities (Chicago and Pittsburgh) that have machines, incumbent councilmen did significantly better than in nonpartisan cities. However, incumbent councilmen in all other partisan cities (where party organization is normally not as strong as in Chicago and Pittsburgh) were not re-elected as often as incumbents in nonpartisan cities. Incumbent mayors fared about the same in both systems. (Perhaps mayors are more vulnerable than councilmen because their higher political visibility makes them natural targets when voters have accumulated grievances.) Former mayors who had been deposed by the electorate, Gilbert and Clague found, were much more likely to run again in nonpartisan than in partisan cities. Presumably this difference reflects both the special value in a nonpartisan system of having a name that is known to the voters and the special difficulty in a partisan system of getting the party's nomination.

Minority-group candidates are disadvantaged by nonpartisanship. Negroes, Mexican-Americans, and Puerto Ricans are rarely put forward and endorsed by newspapers and prestigious civic organizations. Nor do they ordinarily get the kind of public attention that would make their names well known. If a Negro is known politically to the public at all, it is likely to be only on account of his race But in a partisan system, being a member of a minority group may be a positive advantage. The party runs a "ticket" or "slate" which it "balances" with candidates who represent the elements within the party in due proportion to their voting strength. A minority-group member "adds strength to the ticket" because his being on it causes members of his group to vote for it without causing other persons who are indifferent to, or mildly hostile to, his group to vote against it. In some nonpartisan elections, to be sure, a "slate" is made up and endorsed by a local party

[10] Charles E. Gilbert and Christopher Clague, "Electoral Competition and Electoral Systems in Large Cities," *Journal of Politics,* vol. XXIV (1962), pp. 338–347.

or party-like organization. Although the slate-makers may try to balance it, their effort is likely to be futile for lack of one indispensable element—party loyalty. The voter who is presented with a slate by an organization to which he feels no special loyalty and which cannot discipline him—an organization which may even be opposed to "regularity" on grounds of principle—will pick and choose among candidates to suit his taste. In highly partisan Chicago, Negroes on the Democratic ticket do as well in white wards as in Negro ones. But in nonpartisan Detroit and Los Angeles, Negroes often fare badly in white areas.[11]

The disadvantaged groups are not necessarily low-status ones, of course. If Boston were a partisan city, the Democratic party would find it advantageous to nominate a Yankee or two to balance an otherwise Irish and Italian ticket.

2. The Voter under Nonpartisanship

If nonpartisanship works as we have said, one would expect the vote for successful nonpartisan candidates to correlate to some extent with that for Republicans in partisan contests. There is evidence that it does. In three Michigan cities, Oliver Williams and Charles Adrian found a fairly high correlation between the Republican vote for governor (a partisan office) and the vote for the winning nonpartisan slate of local officials.[12] The correlation was not high enough, however, to suggest that the voters regarded the winning local slate as an adjunct to the Republican party. The more intense the competition for local office and the more sharply drawn the issues, the higher was the correlation.

A nonpartisan system tends to reduce the turnout of Democrats. This helps to explain why many cities which are heavily Democratic in state and national elections (Detroit is an outstanding example) elect mayors and councilmen who are very conservative. In California (and perhaps also in Michigan) the decline in voter turnout between a national (partisan) and a local (nonpartisan) election is greatest in Democratic and least in Republican precincts.[13] By contrast the decline in turnout between national and local elections in such partisan cities as New York and Chicago is generally greatest among Republican

[11] See James Q. Wilson, Negro Politics: The Search for Leadership (Glencoe, Ill.: Free Press, 1960), pp. 41–44.

[12] Williams and Adrian, "Insulation of Local Politics," pp. 1056–1058.

[13] Lee, Politics of Nonpartisanship, pp. 139–140; Williams and Adrian, "Insulation of Local Politics," pp. 1059–1061.

voters. Democratic voters are less likely than Republicans to vote when the familiar party labels do not appear on the ballot and when a local Democratic organization does not prod them to the polls. Moreover, when they do vote in nonpartisan contests, Democrats often favor candidates who are ideologically closer to the Republicans. As David Greenstone observes about Detroit,

> Defenders of nonpartisan government argue that it helps separate local from state and national issues which are fought out between the parties. This is certainly what happens in Detroit. Many white union members, particularly Poles and native Southerners, are loyal Democrats who support the party's domestic programs. But these same voters are also homeowners laboring under Detroit's heavy property taxes who are concerned about maintaining the economic level and white racial character of their neighborhoods. They are not friends of the Negroes. If city elections were partisan, they would probably vote Democratic and therefore for liberal candidates. But in nonpartisan elections, they are free to desert the liberal alliance to support conservative, pro-white candidates like Mayor Cobo, without repudiating the Democratic Party.[14]

It would be interesting to know how voters would behave if they knew whether their nonpartisan candidates were Republicans or Democrats. In Denver, where a poll was made to find out, the conclusion was reached that it made no difference whether they knew or not.[15] It is doubtful whether this settles the matter, however. Regardless of what people may tell interviewers, their votes may be affected when a party label is actually put on a ballot. California's "cross-filed" primaries, in which Republican office-seekers were permitted to file in Democratic primaries and vice versa, used to be, in effect, nonpartisan; for in each primary Republicans and Democrats ran on one ballot without party labels. When, in 1954, the law was changed to require party identifications after candidates' names on the ballots, the effect was striking—it became practically impossible for a Republican to win a Democratic primary or for a Democrat to win a Republican one.[16]

Because nonpartisanship seems to favor candidates who live in "the better parts of town" and because it usually is combined with at-large

---

[14] David Greenstone, *A Report on the Politics of Detroit* (Cambridge, Mass.: Joint Center for Urban Studies, 1961, mimeo), pp. II–7, II–8.

[15] G. W. Pearson, "Prediction in a Non-partisan Election," *Public Opinion Quarterly*, Spring 1948, p. 115.

[16] See Robert J. Pitchell, "The Electoral System and Voting Behavior: The Case of California's Cross-Filing," *Western Political Quarterly*, vol. XII (1959), pp. 459–484.

election, one would expect that in a nonpartisan city there would normally be a good many sections where no local elective official resides. Generally speaking, this seems to be the case. In Berkeley, California, for example, six sevenths of the city officials live on the fashionable "hill" although more than half the population of the city lives in the lower-income south and west districts.[17] There is no way of knowing what effect this has on the relation between voters and officials, or on the views that officials have of city problems. It would be surprising, however, if the effect were not to reduce somewhat both the effectiveness with which the voter is represented and—what may perhaps be more important—his confidence that he is being effectively represented.

Generally speaking, the only contact between the voter and the nonpartisan official is through the ballot box. There is no party headquarters, no precinct organization, and no ward office to provide a basis for informal contact at the neighborhood level. If a constituent meets his representative, the meeting is likely to take place in a city hall office downtown; often the official leaves relations with constituents to a secretary. In Boston (where nonpartisanship is combined, as it usually is, with at-large election), voters seldom turn to city councilmen for assistance; they go instead to the state representative, who is elected from a small district on a partisan ballot.

3. The Political Parties under Nonpartisanship

In California, the Democrats have a three-to-two lead in registrations, but the Republicans have a three-to-two lead in the number of local elective offices held. In Los Angeles County, two thirds of all city councilmen were registered Republicans when Eugene Lee was making a study of nonpartisanship. Indeed, in California, the larger the city the greater the Republican predominance; 80 percent of the mayors and 68 percent of the city councilmen in the twenty-six nonpartisan cities of over 50,000 population were Republicans. Only Los Angeles, San Francisco, and two other large cities had a majority of Democratic councilmen. Perhaps the best evidence that nonpartisanship helps the Republicans is that Democrats usually oppose it. In California, two polls showed that most Republican county chairmen favored retaining it in local elections and most Democratic chairmen did not.[18] These results must be interpreted cautiously, however. That

---

[17] Lee, Politics of Nonpartisanship, p. 54.
[18] Lee, Politics of Nonpartisanship, pp. 56 and 110–111.

a mayor is a registered Republican may imply nothing whatever about his behavior in local matters. Furthermore, Republican chairmen may favor nonpartisanship not because of party advantage but because their class and ethnic characteristics dispose them to accept the ethos it implies. Besides, California may be unique. In Boston, it is highly unlikely that a known Republican could be elected mayor, and the Democrats are well pleased with the system.

The extent to which organizations (either purely local parties or slate-making associations) are created to choose candidates and fight election campaigns varies a great deal from place to place. The larger the city, the more need—and the more opportunity—to create such organizations, to finance them liberally, and (if one is a candidate) to get their endorsements. It might be expected that large cities would have local parties rather than slate-making associations. Some do: examples are the Cincinnati Charter Committee and the Kansas City Citizens' Association. But others do not: in Detroit and Los Angeles, for example, *ad hoc* coalitions of interests are formed every four years to fight a single election.

In Los Angeles, the selection of a candidate to represent the important downtown business and commercial interests is made after a series of meetings in which are brought together the spokesmen of the metropolitan press, the larger manufacturing and utility companies, and the banks, department stores, and other leading interests. The *Los Angeles Times* has often taken the lead in arranging such meetings. Campaign funds are raised almost entirely from corporate gifts and from personal gifts by executives of large corporations. A public relations firm is hired to conduct the campaign. It is given a budget, told in a general way what issues are important, and left to manage the campaign as it thinks best.

Small cities, and large ones with district systems for choosing councilmen, may have no slate-making activity at all. In these, the candidate conducts his own campaign with such volunteer help as he can muster. Here is an account of such a campaign in Minneapolis:

Mrs. Deach is a woman of about fifty, with a warm and gregarious personality. Highly articulate, she is charming and socially at ease. Induced to run for office by a professor of political science at the University of Minnesota who was active in various reform groups, she began to organize her campaign early in March. He helped manage an intensive and highly individualized campaign. Mrs. Deach established a personal organization of about 200 women and men which included a precinct captain for each precinct and block workers under each captain. For the primary alone, each house was canvassed twice; brochures, post-cards, and throw-away cards were thoroughly distributed, as were yard and window signs, letters, and sample ballots. She held coffee hours every day at various homes in the neighborhood in an attempt to engage the support of the women in the electorate. Appeals were slanted towards stimulating a political and communal consciousness and a feminist assertiveness in women constitutents, but a large cadre of men workers was established to counteract the male prejudice to her feminine candidacy. She elicited the support of various religious leaders in the community and several of them sent out circulars endorsing Mrs. Deach. Recognizing the importance of publicity by name, Mrs. Deach originated a slogan which she emphasized throughout her campaign and printed on each piece of literature, proclaiming, "Reach for Deach." Mrs. Deach had more issue content in her campaign than most candidates, but, nevertheless, the issues were broad and vague. She campaigned to the housewives on revising the liquor patrol laws and on the establishment of public housing, for example. . . .

One factor worthy of note was Mrs. Deach's detachment from party or group affiliations. She contested a ward which was largely labor and Democratic, even though she herself was an avowed Republican with a slightly anti-labor prejudice. Nevertheless, she stated that she supported organized labor, in her brochures stressing that she would be an alderman who would "represent the wishes of all the people and not of any one special interest group." She never once mentioned her party affiliation or business support in her public appearances.[19]

It is sometimes said that nonpartisanship weakens the national political parties. By reducing their opportunities to train and test their workers in campaigns and by depriving them of local offices and patronage, it is said to cut off their local roots. This assertion, of course, cannot be either proved or disproved (the Democratic party is strong in California and Michigan even though Los Angeles and Detroit are nonpartisan, but they might be stronger still if those cities were partisan). The assertion, however, is highly plausible. And if nonpartisanship does cut the local roots of the parties, its effect is important, for in large sections of the United States local roots are the only ones that the parties have. The Democratic party in Gary, Indiana, for example, is organized around the distribution of power in Gary, not in the United States or even in Indiana. If Gary issues are withdrawn from party politics, party organization there is likely to fall to pieces.

[19] Charlotte Frank, "Nonpartisanship in Minneapolis," unpublished M.A. thesis, Department of Political Science, University of Chicago, 1958.

It must be remembered, however, that in Detroit, Los Angeles, Minneapolis, Cincinnati and other such cities the alternative to non-partisanship is not a powerful, patronage-fed machine. In all probability the parties would be weak in those cities anyway, because they could not offer the kinds of inducements to which voters and potential party workers would respond.

4. The Character of Government under Nonpartisanship

Discussion of the effect of nonpartisanship upon the content of policy and the character of a city government must be based upon the distinctions among kinds of nonpartisan systems. The most important distinction, perhaps, is one we made above between cities where purely local parties or slate-making associations choose candidates and finance campaigns and others where candidates select themselves and create their own, largely informal organizations. Cities with purely local parties or slate-making associations tend to produce governments that (in the typology by Oliver Williams that we introduced in Chapter 4) are "instruments of community growth." They are "business-oriented," honest, efficient (that being a way of keeping taxes down); they are conservative in spending for welfare, and aggressive in efforts to "create a good business climate." In the smaller, residential cities where candidates make personal appeals to voters, nonpartisanship is not so business-oriented. These cities tend to fit into Williams' "caretaker" type.

An even more general hypothesis may be offered, as follows. Officials in nonpartisan cities are elected on the basis, not of party affiliations or party loyalties, but of whatever sources of power or symbols of legitimacy may be dominant in the community; and their policies tend to express the interests and values associated with those symbols. In a large industrial city like Detroit, nonpartisan policy expresses big-business culture. In a small, resident-owned manufacturing city like Beloit, Wisconsin, it expresses "old family" culture.[20] In Boston, again, it expresses Irish-Catholic culture.

[20] In Beloit, which is strongly Republican by tradition, nonpartisan elections are sometimes spirited and sometimes routine, according to Warner E. Mills and Harry R. Davis, Small City Government (New York: Random House, 1962), p. 6. "Campaigns are personality contests, rarely turning on overt or important issues," they report. "Incumbents have a decided advantage over challengers. Usually only 30 to 35 percent of the eligible electorate will turn out. The prosperous and middle-class wards show consistently greater participation than others." They put Beloit in Williams' "caretaker" category.

Despite such important differences, nonpartisanship tends in general to be identified with "good government," i.e., government that is honest, efficient, and impartial. To a large extent, of course, this "good government" character may be its cause rather than its effect; cities that are not at all amenable to "good government" do not adopt the nonpartisan form and those that are most amenable to it adopt the form most often. However the causal relation may run, Minneapolis, Milwaukee, Detroit, Los Angeles, and Oakland are all notable for "good government," and some of those cities were not known for it before nonpartisanship (along with other reforms, to be sure) was introduced.

To put the matter somewhat differently, cities in which a "good government"-minded middle class is dominant tend to be nonpartisan and, as we have shown, in such cities nonpartisanship tends to strengthen and reinforce this control not only by putting in office people who think it wrong to trade favors for votes but by rendering such trades unnecessary—indeed even dangerous—to the officeholder.

There is, as we have shown, empirical evidence to support these observations. Some additional observations can be made on *a priori* grounds by examining the logic of the nonpartisan system.

First, it seems clear on *a priori* grounds that corrupt or incompetent persons are eliminated from nonpartisan systems more readily than from partisan ones. In a partisan system, getting rid of such persons is likely to "be bad for the party." In a nonpartisan one, by contrast, no institution has any stake in protecting them; therefore their elimination puts no strain upon the system.

Second, the logic of nonpartisanship (except perhaps in those large cities where business interests and newspapers perform a function similar to that of the party) tends to dispose candidates to avoid controversial questions and therefore, in the nature of the case, important issues. Because the situation requires them to try to appeal to the whole electorate (and not to the faithful of one party plus a few voters who may be detached from the other), candidates will utter bland generalities and try to differentiate themselves on the basis of "personality," a tactic which is likely to bring them to "mud-slinging."[21]

Third, a city council elected on a nonpartisan basis is not likely to

[21] The logic is that of a multiparty rather than a two-party system. On this see Anthony Downs, *An Economic Theory of Democracy* (New York: Harper, 1957), chap. viii.

develop a stable governing majority (unless, again, some slate-making association functions in the manner of a party). Having no obligation to a party with a "past to honor and a future to protect,"[22] each councilman will decide on an *ad hoc* basis how to vote. Accordingly, there will be no "collective responsibility" of the council. Nor, for the same reason, will there be a minority with an organizational commitment to criticism.

Fourth, the nonpartisan council will feel no special loyalty to the mayor and will not be under his discipline. Its political fortunes will not depend upon his. Indeed, if the voters are dissatisfied, it is he, the most visible target, who will probably be hit. Knowing this, the councilmen will tend to take the voters' side against the mayor in order to profit politically from his unpopularity.

FIGHTING THE NONPARTISAN ELITES

When there is a sufficiently high level of voter discontent, all of the forces—businessmen, unions, newspapers, civic associations, and prominent men—that play such an important part in nonpartisan politics can be defeated. In 1961, this happened in both Detroit and Los Angeles, when the two incumbent mayors, both backed by almost every group of any consequence, were defeated by political "outsiders," neither of whom was well known before the campaign.

In both cities, the nonpartisan "elites" lost apparently because of an accumulation of voter grievances artfully emphasized by the winning candidates. Negroes were angry at what they took to be police harassment and brutality. Large numbers of workers were unemployed owing to layoffs in the auto industry and the cancellation of government contracts. Numerous neighborhood groups were upset at various civic programs—such as urban renewal projects, trash collection arrangements, harbor oil leases, and the construction of a new baseball stadium—that seemed to be the work of "downtown interests" which ignored local community sentiments. As a result, although the incumbent mayors had the unanimous support of the metropolitan newspapers, they were generally opposed by the local neighborhood press. The winning candidates made good use of television to familiarize the voters with their names and faces and on these programs they often went out of their way to attack business and newspaper groups, characterizing them as hostile, even sinister downtown forces.

[22] Adrian, "Some General Characteristics of Nonpartisan Elections," p. 775.

Interestingly enough, the fate of the nonpartisan city councilmen who ran for re-election in these same mayoralty elections was strikingly different as between the two cities. In Detroit, where the council is chosen at large, three of the nine incumbents were defeated, with "liberals" generally replacing "conservatives." In Los Angeles, where the councilmen are elected from districts, no incumbent was defeated or even seriously challenged. It may be that the at-large nonpartisan system produces such a low level of identification between voter and councilman and so few neighborhood ties that in a period of general unrest the voters rely on ideological distinctions in order to express their discontent. When the councilmen are chosen from districts, neighborhood ties are stronger, the councilman is identified with local sentiments and interests, and he can retain voter confidence in a period of general discontent because he can dissociate himself from the mayor and the other "downtown forces" to whom the voters impute responsibility for undesirable conditions.

CHAPTER 13 · THE COUNCIL-MANAGER FORM

MORE THAN 41,500,000 Americans live in communities governed by a complex collaboration between an elected council and a professional administrator. In the typical council-manager city, a small council (five, seven, or nine members), elected at large on a nonpartisan ballot, sets policies, adopts ordinances, votes appropriations, and appoints a chief executive officer, called a city manager, to serve "at its pleasure." A mayor, elected by the council from among its members, performs ceremonial duties. The manager carries out the policies of the council and supervises the conduct of the city's affairs.

DEVELOPMENT OF THE PLAN

The council-manager plan was recommended in 1911 by the National Short Ballot Organization, of which the president was Woodrow Wilson and the secretary and prime mover was the advertising-man-turned-reformer, Richard S. Childs.[1] It was not until 1914, however, that a sizable city, Dayton, Ohio, put the plan into operation. Soon afterward, the National Municipal League recommended it for all cities, and a national movement was underway.

A total of 1,756 places in all but three states (Indiana, Hawaii, and Louisiana) had the plan as of January 1, 1961. Of these, 1,110 were cities of 5,000 or more within the continental United States. Their distribution by size is shown in Table 10.

The plan boomed after the Second World War, with about seventy-five cities a year adopting it for a fifteen-year period. However, its spread seems to have lost momentum except in very small places. Of the sixteen cities of more than 250,000 population which have the plan, all but one adopted it before 1933; that one (San Antonio, Texas) adopted it in 1952. Of the thirty-nine cities of 100,000 to 250,000 population which have it, seventeen adopted it before 1933 and only five after 1952. From 1958 to 1961, it was adopted by only two cities

[1] See Richard S. Childs, *Civic Victories* (New York: Harper, 1952).

of more than 100,000, by only four of between 50,000 and 100,000, and by only twenty of between 25,000 and 50,000.[2]

TABLE 10. Council-manager cities distributed by population groups, 1961

Population group	Total number of cities in group	Cities with council-manager plan	
		Number	Percent
5,000–10,000	1,292	360	27.9
10,000–25,000	1,033	393	38.2
25,000–50,000	406	207	51.0
50,000–100,000	192	95	49.5
100,000–250,000	80	39	48.8
250,000–500,000	30	12	40.0
Over 500,000	21	4	19.0
Totals	3,054	1,110	28.2

Source: See footnote 2, below.

Many council-manager cities are upper-class or middle-class in character; few if any are predominantly lower-class. In the Chicago area, for example, a ranking of seventy-four suburban cities according to median value of homes (a rough indicator of social class) showed that eighteen of the twenty cities with the highest home values had the plan, whereas none of the thirty-one cities with the lowest home values had it.[3] Its popularity with people of the upper and middle classes explains its popularity in small communities, which are more likely to consist predominantly of those classes than are large ones.

[2] All data from International City Managers' Association, *Recent Council-Manager Developments and Directory of Council-Manager Cities* (Chicago: International City Managers' Association, 1961). The four cities of over 500,000 having the plan are Dallas, San Antonio, San Diego, and Cincinnati; the twelve of from 250,000 to 500,000 having it are Kansas City, Phoenix, Oakland, Fort Worth, Long Beach, Oklahoma City, Rochester, Toledo, Norfolk, Miami, Dayton, and Wichita. The number of large cities having the plan has increased in the last ten years, but not because large cities have adopted it; rather, because cities having it have grown.

[3] Edgar L. Sherbenou, "Class, Participation, and the Council-Manager Plan," *Public Administration Review*, Summer 1961, pp. 131–135. See also Leo F. Schnore and Robert R. Alford, "Forms of Government and Socioeconomic Characteristics of Suburbs," *Administrative Science Quarterly*, June 1963, pp. 1–17. Schnore and Alford show that, for 300 suburbs, in 25 large metropolitan areas, communities with the council-manager form of government are, compared to those with the mayor-council or commission form, likely to have a smaller proportion of nonwhites, foreign-born, and persons over 65 years of age; to have a larger proportion of persons in white-collar occupations with a high school education or better; and to be growing more rapidly in population.

The basis of these preferences may be best understood by looking at the rationale of the plan. The intention of its inventors was to make local government a more responsive and effective instrument of the popular will. Decentralization of authority had been carried so far, they thought, that it was often impossible to do the things that most people wanted done. The remedy was to put all authority in matters of policy in the hands of a small elected council and all authority in matters of administration in the hands of a single, expert administrator, who would be employed by the council and would work under its general direction and control.[4] This, as we pointed out in the last two chapters, was a characteristic expression of the "good government" point of view—that of the middle-class and upper-class people who believed that the interest of the community "as a whole" should be determined in disinterested ways and then be carried into effect expeditiously and efficiently by technicians. This point of view was at odds with that of the lower class, which preferred favors, "friendship," and "recognition" to the public-serving and self-denying virtues of efficiency, honesty, and impartiality.

Many early promoters and supporters of the plan were enthusiastic about it for a reason other than the one its inventors had in mind: they thought it would make local government cheaper and lead to lower taxes. The reformers' idea that local government should be run in a businesslike way was entirely congenial to the tax-minded. When in 1930 the plan was under consideration in Dallas, a newspaper asked: "Why not run Dallas itself on a *business* schedule by *business* methods under *businessmen*? . . . The city manager plan is after all only a *business* management plan. . . . The city manager is the executive of a corporation under a board of directors. Dallas is the corporation. It is as simple as that. Vote for it" (italics added).[5]

Many supporters of the plan wanted not only tax savings but also the satisfaction of putting political handicaps in the way of the "great

---

[4] Don K. Price, "The Promotion of the City Manager Plan," *Public Opinion Quarterly*, Winter 1941, pp. 563–578.

[5] Harold Stone, Don K. Price, and Kathryn Stone, *City Manager Government in the United States* (Chicago: Public Administration Service, 1940), p. 27. Nathan Matthews, Jr., the Yankee mayor of Boston, exposed the fallacious business-municipality analogy in 1895, in his *The City Government of Boston* (Boston, 1895), pp. 179–181, but the argument dies hard. On October 17, 1961, the *St. Petersburg Times* could still editorialize on the advantages of turning the "business of city government" over to a manager because "there is nothing political about drainage, sewers, street lights, police and fire protection, and so on."

unwashed" on the other side of the railroad tracks. Making local government "businesslike" meant "getting rid of politics," which, in turn, meant curtailing the representation of low-status minorities. In its early years, the plan appealed to a good many people as a convenient means of putting the Catholics, the Irish, the Italians, the labor unions, and all other "underdogs" in their places. When Jackson, Michigan, accepted the plan in 1938, for example, the new council first celebrated with a reception in the Masonic Temple and then replaced most of the Catholic city employees with Protestants.[6]

It was, and is, standard practice for a campaign for the introduction of the plan to begin with a few business and club leaders who then enlist the support of the newspaper and of the leading civic associations. Labor unions and minority group organizations are usually not represented on such sponsoring groups, or else are represented only nominally. As a rule, unions and professional politicians oppose the introduction of the plan. The vote in favor of it is almost always high in high-income neighborhoods and the vote against it is almost always high in low-income ones. Adoption of the plan represents a victory for those who favor the Anglo-Saxon Protestant middle-class ideal. Compare, for example, Richard S. Childs' approving account of what happened in Dayton, Ohio, with the account we gave in the last chapter of the way things are done in Winnetka, Illinois. "Politics," Childs says, "went out of the window when Dayton's first city manager blew in and, after a single splutter, the local wings of the political parties ceased to function in municipal elections, either visibly or covertly. A self-renewing group of responsible and respected citizens finds and sponsors candidates. . . ."[7]

There is, of course, no reason why the council-manager idea could not be made part of a ward-based, partisan system as well as of an at-large, nonpartisan one. The Republican and Democratic parties could contest for control of the council, and the winning party could make policy which the manager would have to carry out. Something of this sort exists in a good many places (16 percent of council-manager cities have partisan elections, the largest being Rochester, N.Y.), but

[6] Stone, Price, and Stone, *City Manager Government in Nine Cities* (Chicago: Public Administration Service, 1940), pp. 221–223. Evidence of similar biases on the part of those who supported the plan in its early years is to be found in many of the case studies in this volume and in its companion volume, F. C. Mosher *et al., City Manager Government in Seven Cities* (Chicago: Public Administration Service, 1940).

[7] Childs, *Civic Victories*, p. 148.

the International City Managers' Association lists nonpartisanship and at-large election as among the "main features" of the council-manager plan. Probably the unwillingness of the "good government" forces to combine the council-manager plan with partisan, ward-based elections reflects its commitment to the underlying logic of the Anglo-Saxon Protestant middle-class ideal. Harold Stone, Don K. Price, and Kathryn Stone certainly gave this impression in their 1940 evaluation of the council-manager plan when they said that "real changes in municipal policy were rarely brought about by competition among self-interested groups or political groups" but instead were made "by leaders of the community as a whole, acting out of public spirit on the proposals of a trained administrator."[8] To these considerations may be added one of a somewhat different kind: the personal and class interest of the reformers. Nonpartisan, at-large elections were more likely than partisan, ward-based ones to put them and their kind into office.

To revert to Oliver Williams' typology of cities which we presented in Chapter 4, it seems likely that the council-manager system is well suited only to communities dominated by a view of the public interest which stresses community growth or the providing of amenities. There is often too much conflict in an "arbiter" city for the manager to survive for long; in a "caretaker" city, a manager is likely to be regarded as an unnecessary luxury. If there is a manager at all in those two kinds of cities, he is likely to be a "local amateur"—a home-grown boy with a personal following and little formal training—rather than a career professional.

In its present-day version, the doctrine of the city manager movement, as enunciated by the International City Managers' Association (I.C.M.A.) and the National Municipal League, combines the values sought by the plan's inventors (to make easier the effectuation of the popular will) with that sought by its later promoters and supporters (to economize). The plan, according to a recent I.C.M.A. publication, is a

far-reaching attempt to solve the apparent conflict between democracy and efficiency. Democracy is preserved in the popular election of a small council, on a short ballot which does not overtax the attention which citizens usually bestow on government. Efficiency is achievable by the employment of a manager professionally trained for the technical job of administration. The danger of bureaucracy irresponsible and unresponsive to the will of the

[8] Stone, Price, and Stone, *City Manager Government in the United States* (Chicago: Public Administration Service, 1940), p. 236.

community is met by giving the council complete control of the manager's tenure of office.[9]

THE COLLABORATION BETWEEN COUNCIL AND MANAGER

The orthodoxy of the city manager movement defines the proper division of labor between the council and the manager very simply. Policies, it says, shall be determined by the council, and administration shall be vested in the manager. This does not mean that the manager may not participate in the making of policy. "The city manager as a community leader," the I.C.M.A. Code of Ethics says, "submits policy proposals to the council. . . ." He may also (another I.C.M.A. publication says) "sell" a policy to the people of his city, but only *after* the council has decided upon it; then he "joins" with the council in selling it "as an administrative duty." He must not, the Code of Ethics warns, come in public conflict with the council on controversial issues. "To preserve his integrity as a professional administrator" he resists encroachments on his authority and deals with the council as a unit rather than with its individual members.

These principles are incorporated into most council-manager charters. Usually the charter gives the manager the following duties: (1) to see that laws and ordinances are enforced; (2) to appoint, supervise, and remove department heads and subordinate employees and to exercise control over departments; (3) to make such recommendations to the council as seem to him desirable; (4) to advise the council about the city's financial condition and needs; (5) to prepare the annual budget; (6) to prepare whatever reports the council may request; and (7) to keep the public informed.

How far the actual practice of councils and managers conforms to the rules laid down in the Code of Ethics and in the city charters is debatable. Critics of the plan say that managers tend to dominate their councils and "run" their cities highhandedly and also that they tend to be conservative, unenterprising, and devoted to routine. The critics may be biased, of course, and in any case they cannot possibly have the information that would be needed for safe generalization. The 1,756 council-manager plans in operation are enough, certainly, to insure a good deal of diversity—and no one has yet studied a significant sample of them systematically.

[9] International City Managers' Association, *Recent Council-Manager Developments*, p. 2.

Nevertheless, some general observations may be made, partly on the basis of such sketchy and impressionistic data as exist and partly on the basis of inferences from the logic of the plan. In general, we think, city managers have tried hard to stay within the role assigned to them and to avoid usurping the council's functions or becoming political figures. At least two circumstances have inclined them in this direction.

First, many of them have been selected from among people who by training and temperament are more used to dealing with things than with people. The first city managers were mostly engineers, and although the background of today's managers is diverse, the typical manager's mentality is probably still a good deal closer to that of the engineer than to that of the politician.[10] There are many exceptions, of course, some of them very conspicuous ones, but the impression is unavoidable that managers as a class are better at assembling and interpreting technical data, analyzing the logic of a problem, and applying rules to particular cases than they are at "sensing" the complications of a human situation or at manipulating people, either in face-to-face contacts or through the media of communications. (It is, after all, his technical skills, his objectivity, and his affinity for rules and logic that are the manager's special stock in trade and reason for being.)

Second, the very existence of an authoritative definition of his role tends to keep the manager within it. Whether or not he regards managing cities as his life's work, he knows that it is a profession and that what is "right" and "wrong" both for him and for the council is to be found in the professional Code of Ethics and in the "common law" that has grown up around it. If he regards city managing as a career and hopes to move up the ladder to larger cities, he knows that he must conform to the code of the profession.

This is not to say that a manager does not step over the invisible lines between "submitting proposals" and "making policy," between "exercising leadership" and "engaging in politics." There is considerable evidence that he is on the line most of the time and that he steps over it frequently. And he probably steps over it more frequently when he thinks his future will be determined mainly by the reputation he enjoys

[10] Stone, Price, and Stone found that of forty-eight managers hired from 1918 to 1937, thirty-nine had been to college and of these all but three were engineers. The I.C.M.A. does not at present recommend any particular educational background. In 1960, according to the I.C.M.A., 67 percent of the managers appointed were (or had been) managers in other cities, assistant managers, or administrative assistants to managers.

among other city managers rather than by his standing in the community that he happens to be serving. Gladys Kammerer and her associates note that the "outside professional"—the trained manager brought in from outside the city—is more likely to take controversial positions, look forward to promotion to bigger and more "interesting" cities, and thus have a shorter tenure than the "local amateur" who acquired his position because of his personal following rather than his expertise. Furthermore, however the manager may conduct himself publicly, in the nature of the case it is almost inevitable that he will be the major source of policy proposals in the city government.[11]

Two features of the situation tend to push the manager willy-nilly into a powerful and sometimes political role. One is his virtual monopoly of technical and other detailed information. The councilmen are part-time amateurs whereas he is a full-time professional. Moreover, he sits at the center of things, where all communication lines converge. In the nature of the case, then, the councilmen must depend on him for their information. Whether he likes it or not, this gives him a large measure of control over them. The other factor in the situation is that it is normally "good politics" for councilmen to maneuver the manager into taking, or seeming to take, responsibility for risky or controversial measures. Being elected at large on a nonpartisan ballot, they are much more likely to be turned out of office by a vote *against* them than by one *for* their opponents. Their strategy, consequently, is to avoid "rocking the boat." If the boat *must* be rocked, they want the public to think that the city manager's hand is on the tiller. If all goes well, they can take credit later with the electorate. If not, they can blame him and perhaps even make "political capital" by firing him.[12]

[11] See Gladys M. Kammerer, *et al.*, *City Managers in Politics: An Analysis of Manager Tenure and Termination*, University of Florida Monographs: Social Sciences, no. 13 (Winter 1962), pp. 59–66. Charles R. Adrian found in a study of three middle-sized (50,000 to 80,000 population) cities in Michigan which had had managers for at least twenty-five years that although the managers avoided acting as policy innovators in public, all were in fact the principal sources of policy and the effective leaders of their governments. On thirty issues, they exerted leadership in half; interest groups exercised leadership in ten, and the mayor and council in only nine. Councilmen played leading parts as sources of opposition in fifteen of twenty-two issues. See Adrian's "Leadership and Decision-making in Manager Cities, A Study of Three Communities," *Public Administration Review*, Summer 1958, pp. 208–213.

See also Jeptha J. Carrell, "The Role of the City Manager: A Survey Report," *Public Management*, April 1962, pp. 74–78.

[12] Gladys M. Kammerer, *Florida City Managers, Profile and Tenure*, University of Florida Public Administration Clearing Service, Studies in Public Administration, no. 22 (1961), pp. 32–34.

It is not simply the at-large, nonpartisan features of the system that give councilmen these incentives, however; the defining feature of the plan—employment by the council of an administrator to serve at its pleasure—is a contributing factor. That a manager exists and can by the "rules of the game" be used as a decoy practically assures that competent players of the game will so use him. That this political side of his role is not countenanced in the orthodoxy of the profession does not mean that it is not functional to—perhaps even indispensable to—the successful working of the plan.

Probably the functional requirements of the plan, and not the "good government" ideology behind it, account for the political aspects of the manager's role. This is inferable at any rate from the evolution that has occurred in the definition of the role. When city managers first met as an organization in 1914, they criticized the ineffectiveness of councils and favored an "active" rather than "passive" role for themselves. Later they distinguished "policy" from "politics" in order to justify their participation in policy. When the Code of Ethics was revised in 1952, even the explicit repudiation of politics was dropped out.[13]

An experienced manager knows perfectly well that his council will use him for its political purposes if it can. For the sake of good relations with the council, he is usually willing to be accommodating and to play its game—up to a point. As a rule, he stops short of getting into a position that would jeopardize his job or his professional standing. Sometimes, however, through a mistake of judgment or through wanting to accomplish something of importance, he goes beyond the point of safety and takes responsibility for something that, according to the orthodoxy, should be in the council's sphere. This, when it succeeds—but only then—is called "providing leadership."

The fencing that commonly occurs between council and manager is suggested very well by Warner Mills and Harry Davis in their account of relations between the Beloit, Wisconsin, council and City Manager Telfer who had been employed by it for more than twenty years.

While Telfer believes it is a manager's duty to carry out the will of his council, he knows from long experience that city councils do not always

[13] This is remarked upon by Kammerer, *Florida City Managers*, p. 24. Leonard D. White, writing in 1927, found the "failure" of the council "one of the most startling weaknesses" of the plan. He thought the trouble was that when the flush of enthusiasm that accompanied adoption of the plan passed, the "old crowd" took control of the council; it was "politician government," not the absence of it, that gave the council's trumpet that uncertain sound. See White's *The City Manager* (Chicago: University of Chicago Press, 1927).

know their own will. This is most likely to occur with a problem whose political dimension is not clear. In such a case councilmen may either ignore the issue in the hope that it will go away, or offer some informal authorization for action to avoid going officially on record. Telfer knows that a nod of the head from a key councilman, or an oblique remark in informal conversation, may (or may not!) be as significant a cue to action as a formal resolution. As manager he is left with the dilemma whether or not to make a decision on the matter himself, and if he does so, what that decision is to be.[14]

A TYPOLOGY OF COUNCIL-MANAGER RELATIONS

Within this general framework, there is a good deal of variety in the structure of council-manager relations. The key variable in the situation seems to be the amount and kind of cleavage in the city. This tends to shape relations into five principal patterns:

Type 1: In a city where there is little or no conflict—and hence no important issues—the manager is likely to occupy a position of considerable strength. He is in full charge of routine matters, and almost every matter is routine. Small communities with prosperous, homogeneous populations most often fit this type. This is the political role—if it can be called political—in which managers are probably most happy. Winnetka, the wealthy suburb of Chicago whose politics was described in the last chapter, is a rather extreme case of this sort. Winnetkans are fundamentally at one with regard to local questions; and they want the manager to have a free hand to conduct the city's business as efficiently as possible. In the forty-six years of the plan to 1961, Winnetka had only three managers, one of whom was the incumbent in 1961.[15]

Type 2: Where there is an approximately even division between factions, a manager who is a strong personality may dominate the situation by playing one side against the other and, when it suits him, by ignoring both. The situation is likely to be unstable, however. When one faction comes into the ascendancy, it will make getting rid of the strong manager its first order of business.[16]

In Cambridge, Massachusetts, for example, there is an approximately equal division of voting strength between the upper middle class

[14] Warner E. Mills, Jr., and Harry R. Davis, *Small City Government* (New York: Random House, 1962), p. 32.

[15] In Florida, according to Gladys Kammerer (*Florida City Managers*, p. 30), small, stable communities dominated by a clique that exercises monopolistic power for a long period of time are one of the two principal types of council-manager city.

[16] In Florida cities where factional control is unstable, the displacement of one faction by the other usually means the dismissal of the city manager. *Ibid.,* p. 31.

(largely Yankee and Jewish and oriented toward Harvard and M.I.T.) and the lower middle class (largely Irish and Italian Catholics, and hostile to the universities). Between 1900 and 1940, the city government was in the hands of "old style" professional politicians whose appeal was mainly to the lower middle class. Then, in a wave of reform, a nonpartisan council-manager plan was adopted along with a proportional representation system of election which usually guaranteed both "East Cambridge" (the Catholic area) and "Brattle Street" (the university area) roughly equal strength on the council. The first city manager, John Atkinson, was a successful businessman who had the confidence of Brattle Street. He was determined to lead the city without regard to factional politics, and for ten years did so. He was scornful of council politics, and especially of the unwillingness of councilmen to take positions that might offend people. He went over the heads of the councilmen in an effort to lead the city personally. On occasion he even attacked councilmen in public. He kept his job, however, because the councilmen could not agree upon a successor.[17] Finally an issue arose on which Brattle Street would not support him. A temporary coalition between the Brattle Street and the East Cambridge councilmen dismissed him.

Type 3: An approximately equal division between factions may also result in a stalemate. If the manager sees that nothing of importance can be done without antagonizing one side or the other, he may conclude that it is best not to attempt very much. He is likely to occupy himself wtih routine tasks, to be patient and noncommittal in dealing with factional leaders, and to avoid identifying himself closely with any issue or personality. If he is able to "represent" both factions symbolically, as for example through ethnic and other personal attributes, he is particularly fortunate.

Cambridge again provides an example. It replaced Atkinson with a manager of the third type, John Curry, who unlike Atkinson depends upon his salary for a living. Curry was a coalition choice, elected by the full council without dissent. He likes to emphasize that Cambridge has a *council*-manager form of government, not a manager-council one, and that he is the *servant* of the *whole* council. He handles routine matters without interference, and leaves it to the mayor (with whom

[17] See Frank C. Abbot, "The Cambridge City Manager," in Harold Stein (ed.), *Public Administration and Policy Development: A Case Book* (New York: Harcourt, Brace, 1952), for a lengthy account of one of the fights between Atkinson and the council.

he is on very close personal terms) to take the initiative on policy matters in the council and before the public. Ambitious, and therefore controversial, undertakings are rarely attempted. Some say the fault is Curry's: "He ought to be more of a leader." Others think that he from behind the scenes and the mayor from in front lead the city very adroitly, and that little is undertaken because both men are very conservative. Still others think that Curry and the mayor are simply responding realistically to political facts: the Cambridge electorate is split down the middle on almost everything, and a manager who pressed hard for action would only get himself fired. Even Curry's prudence might not have kept him from being fired if he did not have the advantage of being politically marginal. Being an Irish-Catholic helps him in East Cambridge. Having a Ph.D. in philology helps him in Brattle Street.

A manager who chooses to be the servant rather than the master of a council that is equally divided between factions may, if he is less adroit or less fortunate in his attributes than Curry, have to put up with interference from the leaders of the competing factions. This situation is also likely to be unstable; where a manager lets factional leaders participate in management, the city's affairs are likely soon to be in a mess, and the council—and thereafter the manager—are likely to be replaced before very long.

Type 4: In a city which is divided by cleavage, a manager may occupy a secure and powerful position if he is the instrument of a stable majority, or of a faction which has the balance of power. A manager who has the confidence of a stable majority (or ruling group) may have great freedom of action. Not infrequently he becomes the informal leader of the majority. Where an alliance of "good government"-minded citizens and business-minded merchants supports a citizens' association which elects a majority of the council, a manager may tacitly accept the association's direction in major matters in return for the protection and freedom that it affords him. As a rule, he is in no danger of having to accept its interference in minor matters, for the "good government" leaders of such associations are as much imbued as he is with the doctrine that a manager should take orders only from councilmen and from them only as a body.

The Citizens' Association of Kansas City, although representing a minority, maintained in office a very powerful manager, L. P. Cookingham, for nineteen years until in 1959 the various factions of the Democratic Party formed a coalition and reform was defeated at the polls. In Oakland, California, Wayne E. Thompson has had striking success in carrying "good government" principles into effect in a city which has a large lower class (Oakland is nearly one fourth Negro). Thompson's base of support includes the *Oakland Tribune*, Kaiser Industries, and other powerful, civic-minded interests.

Type 5: Where there is considerable conflict but not a stable majority or a factional stalemate, a manager must put together a working majority on each issue by persuading the individual councilman to "go along" with him. In these circumstances, he is not likely to attempt very much, and his tenure is likely to be brief. Several of the situations that have been described tend to develop into, or break down into, this one, and it is therefore probably one of the most common. If in Oakland, for example, there should develop a serious split within the business elite which now supports the manager, or if the indifference of the large lower-class minority should turn into active hostility, Manager Thompson would have to deal with a council of "individuals." No matter how skillful his handling of the councilmen, he could not accomplish as much as he does when he acts on behalf of a stable ruling group.[18]

GROWTH AND CHANGE: THE CASE OF SAN DIEGO

As a city grows in size and heterogeneity and as it is confronted with problems requiring more comprehensive measures for their solution, it is likely that the structure of conflict—and therefore the nature of the council-manager system—will change. In the normal course of its growth, a city may therefore be expected to move from one to another of the types described above.

San Diego is a case in point. In 1932, when it installed the council-manager plan, it was a fast-growing, heterogeneous port city of 160,000.[19] It had never had corrupt or machine politics, and no organization or clique had ever been strong enough to govern it. Elections were nonpartisan free-for-alls long before nonpartisanship was for-

---

[18] When the commissioners of the new metropolitan government of Dade County, Florida (containing Miami), before dismissing the manager, O. W. Campbell, complained that he failed to provide adequate leadership, he contended that he could not "carry the ball" without assistance from a strongly organized good-government group of business and professional persons. Edward Sofen, *A Report on Politics in Greater Miami* (Cambridge, Mass.: Joint Center for Urban Studies, 1961, mimeo).

[19] Stone, Price, and Stone, *City Manager Government in Nine Cities*, pp. 135–206.

mally introduced; city employees were probably the most influential group in the city's affairs. In the first three years of manager government, the council was divided into approximately equal factions reflecting a fundamental cleavage within the electorate. The manager felt harassed because he could get no agreement on policy from the council ("No councilman can say publicly in San Diego that he proposes to permit illegal business like gambling and prostitution, and no councilman could be re-elected if the whole city took him seriously in an effort to eliminate it altogether")[20] and because the leaders of the factions continually interfered. The situation was of the kind we described as Type 3.

Mismanagement contained the seeds of its own destruction. A Civic Affairs Conference was organized by a Ford dealer (who was trying to obtain a Ford building for the San Diego exposition and was ashamed of the city government with which his company had to deal), by the scion of an old Virginia family who ran a bond company, and by the headmistress of a progressive school. The Conference elected as a majority of the council "substantial business and professional men completely independent of any interest or pressure group."[21] The majority was stable, and employed a manager who, his critics said, always proposed what he knew would please it. City employees ceased to be an important force in city affairs. The situation was now Type 4.

For some years all went well. The manager's office was conducted in an exemplary way and taxes were kept at a minimum. Politics never intruded into the manager's office and seldom into the council chamber; to the casual eye, it might seem that the city had no politics. Actually, of course, important and controversial decisions were being made, but they were being made behind the scenes by leaders of the business community who exercised a controlling influence over both the council and the manager. Decisions were being made apolitically, without public controversy and without regard to elections or to the legal-formal decision-making institutions.

Suddenly, in 1961, there was an eruption of popular discontent which, with other causes, led to the dismissal of Manager George Bean, a man highly regarded in his profession. He had proposed measures to improve the use of parking meters—the installation of meters on certain business streets, an increase in the meter charge, and more

[20] *Ibid.*, p. 165.
[21] *Ibid.*, p. 174.

stringent enforcement. The council, with only one dissenting vote, approved his plans and he then carried them into effect. The public was furious. Several civic groups at once circulated initiative petitions to secure repeal of the ordinance. When the council refused to put the question on the ballot, a petition was circulated for recall of the mayor. Twenty-five thousand persons signed it. This was not enough to remove the mayor, but it was more than enough to convince the council that the ordinance needed modification. The popular protest did not end there, however. In the next election, three anti-administration candidates for council (two of whom ran against incumbents) were elected. In part, the vote was directed against City Manager Bean. Many people felt that he was too inflexible. In the fall of 1961, the new council dismissed him.

Between 1932 and 1960 the population of San Diego had increased from 160,000 to 573,224. The city had perhaps become too big for informal decision-making procedures. Commenting on the uproar over the parking meters, David Greenstone wrote in a report on politics in San Diego that "the voters' action may well have been a chaotic and disorganized appeal from the area of informal decision-making to the area of formal government."[22] If this was indeed the case, the stable base which had supported managers since the organization of the Civic Affairs Conference had been dissolved by the rising tide of voter interest, and unless a new, differently constituted base could be constructed—something that seemed unlikely in 1962—Bean's successor would have to come to terms with each councilman on each issue. In short, San Diego's situation was apparently of the kind described as Type 5.

THE PLAN AND THE LARGE CITY

As we noted earlier in this chapter, most of the large cities that have adopted the plan did so, as San Diego did, when they were considerably smaller. Very few large cities have adopted it in recent years. The question arises, therefore, why not?

The larger the city, generally speaking, the more is at stake politi-

---

[22] This part of the case study is based upon David Greenstone, *A Report on Politics in San Diego* (Cambridge, Mass.: Joint Center for Urban Studies, 1962, mimeo). Bean came from (and returned to) Peoria, Illinois. For an account of his earlier troubles there, see John Bartlow Martin, "The Town That Reformed," *Saturday Evening Post*, Oct. 1, 1955, reprinted in Banfield (ed.), *Urban Government* (New York: Free Press of Glencoe, 1961), pp. 276–284.

cally, and consequently the greater the effort that professional politicians will put forth to avoid being displaced.[23] This is certainly a factor that generally tends to prevent adoption of the plan in a large city. But this obviously does not account for those large cities that have adopted it.

The large cities that have adopted it (again generally speaking) are, or were when they adopted it, ones that the professionals could not control. They fall into two main classes: (1) "old" cities, like Cincinnati, which are (or, more likely, were when the plan was adopted) dominated politically by a small, reform-minded elite, and (2) "young" ones, like San Diego, which have never had a tradition of party organization and whose electorate consists largely of people who are recent arrivals and therefore do not have long-standing attachments to neighborhoods, to political personalities or "houses," and to political clubs and other associations which support local party organization, which is the indispensable environment for professionalism in politics.

Another, somewhat overlapping, cause has also been at work. The council-manager plan, as we have said, appeals to the upper classes more than to the lower. Many small cities, but few very large ones, are (or have been) dominated by the upper classes. So far as this factor is involved, then, it is not the size of the city *per se* which has made the difference; rather it is the empirical correlation between large size and the relative number and political power of the lower class. In other words, large cities have not adopted it for essentially the same reason that small lower-class ones have not.

If this view is correct, it may be inferred that as cities which were under upper-class control when they adopted the plan grow out of that control (as San Diego seems to have done), the plan, or at least a strictly orthodox version of it, will become unworkable. To govern a very large, heterogeneous city whose lower class is not content to leave government to the upper-class elite, the plan must be adapted so that it will give the lower-class voter what he wants, or at least will not rub him the wrong way too often and too hard. Among the modifications that might make the plan more acceptable and more workable in

[23] There are some notable exceptions to this rule, of course. Boss Pendergast supported the reform charter of 1925 in Kansas City, probably because he saw in it a way to eliminate a rival Democratic faction and because he thought his chances of controlling a majority of the council were good. In fact, for the first fifteen years of city manager government, the manager and the boss got along very well together.

cities (whether large or small) having a politically significant lower class are the following: partisan rather than nonpartisan elections, election of some councilmen on a ward rather than an at-large basis, appointment of managers whose ethnic and other personal attributes enable the lower class to identify with them and to feel "recognized" by these appointments,[24] and appointment of managers who are temperamentally capable of recognizing the reality (if not the justification) of a politics of personal and group interests.

Such modifications are, of course, at odds with the underlying ideological premises of the city manager movement, and therefore it is not likely that the movement will ever favor them in principle. Some prominent exponents of the plan deny that there is anything to be said for them on grounds of expediency; they say that the chief benefit of the plan—competent and impartial administration—will in the long run prove politically popular; racial minorities and low-income people will eventually realize (they say) that competent and impartial administration means in practice, among other things, fair employment practices in police, fire, and other city departments and nondiscriminatory treatment in municipal courts. When the members of the minority groups and of the lower class become aware of these advantages in the council-manager plan, they will (the exponents of the plan believe) become its firm supporters.[25]

The large cities are nevertheless coming to a form of government that is in fact, if not in name, a close relative of the plan. The pressure of middle-class opinion and the intricacy of the tasks that the governments of large cities now perform tend to put professional administrators into positions of great authority and independence. In very large cities like New York, Chicago, and Philadelphia, mayors have at their right hands "city administrators" who, under their general direction, manage the "housekeeping" functions of the city government very much in the manner of a city manager. In these cities there are also dozens of department heads with domains far larger than those of most city managers and with at least as much freedom of action within their domains. Moreover, it should not be assumed that because a mayor

[24] Inspection of the names of the city managers (the list is given in International City Managers' Association, *Recent Council-Manager Developments*) shows that very few—probably less than three percent—are obviously of "foreign" origin.

[25] Wayne E. Thompson, city manager of Oakland, California, and president of the International City Managers' Association, has argued this in conversations with the authors.

reaches his office by politics he is not qualified for "top level" administration. The larger the enterprise over which an administrator presides, the less his need for technical skills and the greater his need for political ones. It is therefore not unreasonable to suppose that in the largest cities professional politicians may make better managers than would professional administrators. It seems safe to say, at any rate, that neither Mayor Wagner of New York nor Mayor Daley of Chicago would provoke their people into a fury over parking meters.

A mayor who is neither a professional politician nor a professional administrator may (but does not necessarily, of course) represent the worst of both worlds. In this connection, it is interesting that in the summer of 1961 Mayor Richardson Dilworth of Philadelphia, who is not a professional politician, was stoned when he made a speech announcing his intention to levy a substantial charge for parking in the neighborhood.

In his report on San Diego, Greenstone suggests that if that city had had a partisan system, a party-led majority of the council would have heeded the one councilman who said that in his ward (the one most affected) the proposed meter changes were highly unpopular.

THE PLAN EVALUATED

Most of what we said in evaluation of nonpartisanship and of "good government" and reform applies to the council-manager plan as well. If honesty, impartiality, and efficiency—efficiency "in the small"—are the criteria, council-manager cities have with few exceptions been conspicuously well governed. To be sure, they would probably have been well governed under a mayor-council plan; it is because a city wants good government that it gets the council-manager plan in the first place. Nevertheless, although there is no way of proving it, we suspect that the council-manager plan has been a cause as well as an effect of "good government," and that most of the cities that have it are, by these criteria, better governed than they otherwise would have been.

The expectation that the plan would reduce the cost of local government has been sadly disappointed. Generally, taxes have gone up, not down, after its adoption. The reasons for this, its supporters assert, are twofold: (1) citizens now have greater confidence in the integrity of their government and are therefore willing to entrust more money to it, and (2) the centralization of authority now permits the government to undertake larger tasks. These hypotheses are plausible, perhaps, but before one can place confidence in them it is necessary to establish the existence of the situation they are supposed to explain. This is almost impossible. That costs have gone up after the adoption does not mean that they have gone up *because* of it.[26] So far as we know, no one has shown that as between *similarly situated* cities (in respect to size, per capita income, and so on) some of which adopted the council-manager plan and others of which did not, expenditures (or for that matter the effectiveness of the government or public confidence in its integrity) rose faster in the council-manager cities. And even if this could be shown, it would not necessarily mean very much, for one would not know how much of the increased expenditure represented waste and inefficiency and how much the efficient provision of a higher level of service demanded by the public.

Our analysis of council-manager relations has left us with the impression that however great the achievements of the plan in providing government that is honest, impartial, and efficient "in the small," it is not clear that it has always accomplished what its inventors mainly intended—namely by centralizing authority to make local government an effective instrument for carrying out the popular will. In those cities where a coalition of "good government" and business interests provides a stable base, the plan has indeed been effective "in the large" as well as "in the small." There are many such cases, but they are by no means universal and, as we have shown, under most other circumstances a manager and council are not likely to deal boldly with a city's larger problems. And although such coalitions may represent the popular will in small, upper-class suburbs, they are less likely to do so in the larger, more heterogeneous cities.

[26] Sherbenou (cited in our note 3, above) found that among the Chicago suburbs average per capita city expenditures and property taxes were higher in council-manager cities; municipal debt was higher among nonmanager cities. As he acknowledged, these data do not necessarily mean more than that prosperous people tend to live in council-manager suburbs. Sherbenou, p. 134.

CHAPTER 14 · MASTER PLANNING

EVERY large and almost every small city has a "planning" agency which employs professionally trained "planners."[1] In most cities there are other agencies that also do planning (an urban renewal authority, for example, usually has a planning division). These other agencies, and the official planning agencies as well, employ professionals—especially enigneers, economists, statisticians, and administrators—who apply techniques similar to, or even the same as, those applied by planners. Moreover, five different, although closely related, activities are commonly called planning (they are called this whether carried on in planning agencies or elsewhere and whether by planners or by other professionals). These are: (1) the preparation and administration of zoning ordinances and subdivision regulations, (2) fact-gathering with regard to land use, population movements, housing conditions, transportation and similar matters, (3) the design of particular facilities or the making of plans for dealing with special land-use problems ("project planning"), (4) the preparation of a capital expenditures budget, and (5) the preparation of a master plan (also called a "comprehensive," "general," or "development" plan).

Until the Second World War the typical large-city planning agency was mainly—and often almost exclusively—occupied with zoning and subdivision regulation; even today planning is practically synonymous with zoning in many small cities, especially new suburbs. We pass over it here despite its importance in the budgets of most planning agencies. About the politics of planning in the sense of fact-gathering nothing need be said: fact-gathering as such is rarely controversial. The politics of project planning is, of course, discussable only in terms of the politics

[1] We have put "planning" and "planner" in inverted commas to acknowledge that their meaning is somewhat problematical. In a sense, all city agencies plan: i.e., coordinate their activities and take account of the future. In this chapter, we use "planning" and "planner" to mean agencies and personnel that are relatively specialized for the performance of these functions.

In 1961, of 1,311 cities of over 10,000 population reporting, 1,226 had official planning agencies. All cities of over 100,000 population had them. *Municipal Yearbook, 1962.*

of particular subject matters such as housing, downtown redevelopment, or transportaion. The politics of planning in the sense of capital budgeting, although both important (despite the fact that few cities engage in capital budgeting) and discussable, is peripheral to what most people think of as city planning.[2]

That leaves master planning. This is almost always done (where it is done at all) by the planning agency, not by any of the other agencies (such as the urban renewal authority) that also do planning. Therefore this chapter is about the politics of one of the several activities that may be carried on by a city planning agency. It does not deal with any of the many other activities within a city government that might also reasonably be called planning.

THE IDEA OF MASTER PLANNING

People who work in planning agencies generally take a rather pragmatic view of their subject. The object of planning, they are apt to assume, is to avoid obvious mistakes, like putting a new school building in the path of a projected highway. People who write about or teach planning ("theorists," we shall call them) do not as a rule find this common-sense or "piecemeal" approach satisfying. The theorists contend that the only true planning is master planning. Zoning, fact-gathering, project planning, and capital budgeting, although they may be highly desirable in themselves, are at best preliminaries to master planning or adjuncts to it.[3]

A master plan is a set of maps and policy statements that describe in general terms the present intention of the authorities respecting actions they may take over the long run and that may affect the physi-

[2] Studies of the politics of project planning include Martin Meyerson and Banfield, *Politics, Planning, and the Public Interest* (Glencoe, Ill.: Free Press, 1955); Roscoe C. Martin *et al.*, *Decisions in Syracuse* (Bloomington, Ind.: Indiana University Press, 1961), chap. iii; and Robert J. Mowitz and Deil S. Wright, *Profile of a Metropolis, A Case Book* (Detroit: Wayne State University Press, 1962). For a case study dealing in part with the politics of capital budgeting, see W. H. Brown, Jr., and C. E. Gilbert, *Planning Municipal Investment: A Case Study of Philadelphia* (Philadelphia: University of Pennsylvania Press, 1961).

[3] For example, T. J. Kent, a prominent planner and teacher of planning, believes that the preparation and use of a general [master] plan is the "primary" responsibility of the planning profession. See "The Urban General Plan," (Berkeley: University of California, Dept. of City and Regional Planning, April 1962, multilith), p. 2. For a lawyer's discussion of the meaning of the master plan, see Charles M. Haar, "The Master Plan: An Impermanent Constitution," *Law and Contemporary Problems*, Summer 1953, pp. 353–418. The standard work on the subject is Edward M. Bassett, *The Master Plan* (New York: Russell Sage Foundation, 1938).

cal development of the city. In particular, the master plan shows the presently intended future location of working and living areas, of community facilities, and of circulation (transportation) elements. The master plan itself is not legally binding on anyone; but certain plans based upon it are—especially the official map and the detailed zoning ordinance. To the planner, the importance of the master plan is that it coordinates in space and over time those activities which affect the physical character of the city and which the city government can influence or control. To the planner, then, a plan made without reference to a master plan is a contradiction in terms. One cannot, for example, have a "transportation plan" in the proper sense of the term except by taking into account the interrelations among, say, transportation, housing, port development, and the location of industry—in short, without making a master plan or else using one that has already been made.

This conception of planning as the coordination of long-range land-use decisions underlay the Standard City Planning Enabling Act, which was prepared in the 1920's by a nine-man committee of leaders of the planning movement and approved by the then Secretary of Commerce, Herbert Hoover. The Act, which has been adopted verbatim or in substance in most states, defined the purpose of the master plan as follows:

. . . guiding and accomplishing a co-ordinated, adjusted, and harmonious development of the municipality and its environs which will, in accordance with present and future needs, best promote health, safety, morals, order, convenience, prosperity, and general welfare, as well as efficiency and economy in the process of development; including, among other things, adequate provision for traffic, the promotion of safety from fire and other dangers, adequate provision for light and air, the promotion of good civic design and arrangement, wise and efficient expenditure of public funds, and the adequate provision of public utilities and other public requirements.

The expectation of the planning theorists was that when a planning agency was created it would make the preparation of a master plan its first order of business. Frequently, indeed, planning agencies were directed by law to do so. In fact, however, only two or three cities made a serious effort to produce a master plan before the Second World War. Almost everywhere the budgets of planning agencies allowed for little more than the making and administration of zoning ordinances. In a few cities, documents called master plans were indeed produced, but most of these were mere compilations of data which contained no recommendations. Where recommendations were made, they were not made by the process of comprehensive coordination which is the defining characteristic of master planning.

The story of master planning in Detroit, a nonpartisan city long known for its good government, is revealing.[4] Under a charter adopted in 1918, a nine-member planning commission was appointed by the mayor to prepare a comprehensive plan for city development. Business was booming, however, and therefore there was resistance to any interference from a planning agency. The commission's budget was kept so small that it had hardly any staff; and except for arterial roads and the location of public buildings it had little effect upon the city's development. In 1940, Detroit adopted a zoning ordinance; *afterwards* the planning commission began work on a master plan. By this time, however, there was little vacant land left in the ctiy, an exodus of population and industry was underway, and the principal task of planning seemed to be the elimination of slums and blight and the conservation of deteriorating neighborhoods. The size of the commission's professional staff grew rapidly, but basic land-use decisions were usually the outcome of conflict (albeit of conflict in which the planners exercised considerable influence), not of technical planning procedures. As Robert J. Mowitz and Deil S. Wright have remarked, "there were no technical or scientific criteria by which decisions on land use could be made and the conflict thereby avoided."

The experience of other cities was not very different. "The record of the 1930's and 1940's speaks for itself," T. J. Kent has written. "Piecemeal plans and detailed zoning ordinances that were unrelated to even the sketchiest framework of a general plan were the familiar products of the time."[5] In those cities where master plans (so-called) were produced, mayors, councils, and operating officials filed them and forgot them. With few exceptions the plans were what Norton E. Long has called them: "civic New Year's resolutions."[6] Probably not a single city in the United States was significantly influenced before the end of the Second World War by a master plan even roughly resembling the ideal held forth by the planning movement.[7]

---

[4] This paragraph is based on Mowitz and Wright, *Profile of a Metropolis,* chap. iii.

[5] Kent, "Urban General Plan," p. 62.

[6] Norton E. Long, *The Polity* (Chicago: Rand McNally, 1962), p. 192.

[7] New York, Chicago, and many other cities were much influenced by city beautification schemes put forward early in the century. Although sometimes called

After the war, master planning received powerful impetus and support from the federal government. Under the Housing and Redevelopment Act of 1949 the government encouraged the cities to undertake vast new projects that would require planning, and it agreed to pay much of the costs of this planning. Housing and redevelopment suddenly became as important as zoning in the budgets of many planning agencies. In 1954 the Housing and Redevelopment Act was amended to require that a city applying for assistance produce a "workable program" and, as soon as feasible, a "comprehensive [master] plan." At the same time federal grants were offered to small cities for participation in metropolitan or regional planning programs. Five years later the act was amended again, this time to provide assistance for making, or for bringing up to date, a comprehensive plan as well as for project planning, zoning, and certain other related activities.[8] Meanwhile the federal highway program (under Title 23 *U.S. Code*, para. 307) offered grants to states for planning purposes. By 1961 cities could get federal assistance for planning (and construction of) airports, sewage systems, highways and other transportation, recreation and open-space facilities, and hospitals.[9]

One reason for the federal insistence upon planning by the cities was the fear that without it much money would be wasted. Federal administrators believed that strong local planning agencies would make their own supervisory task more manageable. There was also pressure for planning from conservatives (the legislation in question was passed during the Eisenhower administration, it should be remembered) who

master plans, these schemes were far from being comprehensive treatment of the main matters affecting city development. For an account of an ambitious and much-publicized attempt at master planning that resulted in "a compendium of hundreds of suggestions," see Guthrie S. Birkhead in Martin *et al.*, *Decisions in Syracuse*, chap. iii.

[8] Sec. 701(d) of the Housing Act of 1954 said that comprehensive planning includes the following "to the extent directly related to urban needs": "(1) preparation, as a guide for long-range development, of general physical plans with respect to the pattern and intensity of land use and the provision of public facilities, together with long-range fiscal plans for such development; (2) programming of capital improvements based on a determination of relative urgency, together with definitive financing plans for the improvements to be constructed in the earlier years of the program; (3) coordination of all related plans of the departments or subdivisions of the government concerned; (4) intergovernmental coordination of all related planned activities among the State and local governmental agencies concerned; and (5) preparation of regulatory and administrative measures in support of the foregoing."

[9] For a complete listing, see U.S. Department of Commerce, Area Redevelopment Administration, *Handbook of Federal Aids to Communities* (June 1961).

thought that local planning commissions, which in most cities had always been closely allied with real estate and other business interests, would afford some kind of a check on the liberals who (as it seemed to the conservatives) dominated the housing and urban renewal programs.

This is not to say that planning was forced upon the cities against their will. After the Second World War the general level of local government spending rose very rapidly, and technical and managerial personnel of many kinds were added to city governments. The increase in planning personnel was a part of this general increase. But it was also true that a city which wanted to share in the federal *largesse*— and which city did not?—had to be able to show that it had made, or was in the process of making, a master plan. And a city with an outstanding reputation in Washington for planning was likely, other things being equal, to be treated with special generosity.

Whether for one reason or another, most cities prepared documents called master plans. The *Municipal Yearbook, 1962* (the first *Yearbook*, incidentally, to give any information on master plans) showed that of 126 cities of more than 100,000 population only two were without a master plan, completed or in preparation (twelve others failed to report). Most of the planning was done in 1960 and 1961 by personnel who had little or no experience of master planning, and many of the plans, of course, were hastily contrived to satisfy the minimum requirements of the federal agencies. "Ninety day wonders," these plans were called by some of the planners who made them.

THE CASE OF MASTER PLANNING IN ST. PAUL

The making of one land-use plan (the principal component of a master plan) has been described in detail by Alan Altshuler.[10] Wanting to study plan-making at its best, he chose St. Paul (and Minneapolis, where he observed planning other than master planning) because a committee of planning and urban government specialists advised him that political and other conditions in these cities were highly conducive to good planning. In short, there was (and is) reason to believe that master planning in St. Paul would be much better than average.

---

[10] Alan Altshuler, *The Process of Planning in Two American Cities*, unpublished dissertation, Department of Political Science, University of Chicago, 1961. The account above is based on chap. iii. The authors wish to thank Mr. Carl R. Dale, the former member of the St. Paul planning staff whose activities are described in this account, for reviewing this case history.

Master planning began in St. Paul in 1957 when the city's housing and redevelopment agency, acting under pressure from the Federal Housing and Home Finance Agency, contracted with the city's planning board to make a plan. The plan was to be made in two years and was to cost $88,000. The planning board employed a recent graduate of a planning school to make the plan. He had never taken a course or read a book on how to make one (there were no courses or books on *how* to make city plans, only on the "theory" of such plans), and his only assistant was a draftsman. Within a year, however, he was to produce a preliminary land-use plan, the principal component of a master plan.

Looking over over the land-use plans that had been prepared in other cities, the young planner decided that he could do as well as the average in two or three weeks. Even the best of the plans, he found, were hardly more than inventories of land use. Most seemed to have been made from a common pattern.

He began by making a land-use inventory. This was a compilation of facts already available in city offices and in fire insurance company atlases. (To gather new material systematically was out of the question: there was neither time nor money for that.) Then he drove around St. Paul to get the feel of the streets and to note any particularly striking problems. He made no survey of social conditions, nor did he consult with civic associations or interest groups. The master planners in other cities had not gone into such things; besides, as it seemed to him, organized groups represented just *parts* of the community, whereas his task was to determine the goals of the community *as a whole*.

The facts about land use required interpretation. The planner supplied interpretation with regard to those matters that seemed important to him. These included the probable effect of population movements on business prospects, but did not include racial tension or the shortage of housing for low-income families. These "social problems" gave the planner concern, but he understood that the board would not allow him to say anything about them in the plan—they were "too controversial"— and besides, he realized he could do little about them.

The planner doubted whether St. Paul should spend tens of millions of dollars to prepare sites in order to compete with its suburbs for new industry. This, he thought, was a decision that the political authorities should make. His superiors, however, told him that politicians expect planners to know the answers and to issue calls to action. He should make simple and straightforward recommendations, avoiding ifs, ands, and buts. Omit "academic reveries," they told him.

When he came to predict future land-use requirements, the planner found he had practically nothing to go on. He had only his current data and data from one other point in time, 1934, when a scattering of facts had been collected by WPA workers. Depending upon which of twelve statistical methods he used, his estimate of population twenty years hence ranged from 382,000 to 600,000. His predictions about future industrial demand for land were even shakier. The trouble was not simply that he lacked time and money to gather facts: it was that the future—even less than twenty years hence—was highly unpredictable.

A master plan, the planner believed, should be based on some general goal, the content of which would be elaborated in ever-greater detail. What was St. Paul's most general goal? It was, he decided, "to make life more pleasant and investment more secure." From this he derived eight "general objectives" (e.g., "evolution of St. Paul as a better place to work and live") and then from these objectives seven "basic land-use principles" (e.g., residential areas should maintain desirable densities and, above all, be "livable"). From these principles he then spelled out ten pages of "policy statements"; these constituted a checklist of things that administrators should take into account (e.g., "the location of industrial sites should be one of the key considerations in developing a major street plan"). Finally, at the lowest level of generality, he sets forth numerous "standards" (e.g., no residence should be more than half a mile from a neighborhood playground). Most of the standards had been published by national organizations such as the National Recreation Association; the planner revised the national standards to bring them into accord with what he thought reasonable for St. Paul. In all of this, he did what competent planners normally do.

At the end of the year the planner turned his plan over to the planning director for review. By coincidence, a study of the central business district done under other auspices which was published at this time provoked bitter complaints from merchants and newspaper editors who felt that the tone of the study was too gloomy; there was no word of praise or support from any quarter. Noting this, the planning director edited the plan to give less emphasis to "problems" and more to "opportunities." Not many of the planner's recommendations were at all controversial, but the planning director softened some of the few that were. Here and there he changed predictions to make them more optimistic.

The revised plan was then sent to the planning board, which consisted of prominent business and civic leaders. The board discussed only a fourteen-page summary of the plan. It "toned down" a few recommendations and deleted one for more public housing. The board members had no political experience and did not intend to fight for the plan once they had approved it. Presumably the changes they made reflected their personal tastes, not political forces.

Finally in October 1959 the board sent the plan to the city council, which made it public. The newspapers reported it, but no one seemed to be much interested. The council did not schedule hearings on it and no councilman commented on it publicly. No civic association took a position on it. The planners concluded somewhat ruefully that the politicians and civic leaders had not bothered to read it. There was, after all, little reason why they should, since its real purpose was to satisfy the federal requirements, not to assist in the making of fundamental decisions.

Before discounting this description on the grounds that St. Paul is only one city and that presumably elsewhere, or even in St. Paul at some future time, master planning may more closely approach the theoretical ideal, the reader should remember that: (a) One of the main limitations on planning in St. Paul was the necessity of relying on a relatively inexperienced planner; this limitation operates in most cities and can at best be only gradually overcome by the accumulation of knowledge and the training of professionals. (b) Another limitation was lack of any well-defined and ordered goals upon which the planner could base his plan; this limitation also applies elsewhere: no large city has, or is likely ever to have, such goals. (c) A third limitation was the inability to predict demographic and other changes; useful prediction is generally impossible with respect to the more important aspects of the development of any city in a dynamic society. (d) Still another limitation was the concern of the planning director for the repute of "planning" in general and of his agency in particular; this also is a normal feature of such situations. (e) Lastly, lack of support and interest on the part of politicians, press, and public rendered the plan of no importance; the same would have happened in almost any city, and, unless the other limitations that have been mentioned are somehow transcended, it is hard to see how this one can be transcended.

Practical people with real interests at stake will never take seriously a master plan made as the St. Paul one was made.

THE PLANNING AGENCY'S PLACE IN THE
GOVERNMENTAL STRUCTURE

Although little or no real master planning has ever been done in this country, the planning theorists have always sought to fit the planning function into the structure of local government on the assumption that the ideal—master planning—would some day be realized. Accordingly they have tried to put the planning agency in the position of having as its client the officeholder (or institution) conceived to have the ultimate power in matters affecting land use and, more generally, city development. There has been much difference of opinion, however, as to which officeholder (or institution) this might be (or, as the question was sometimes put, *ought* to be). Six very different organizational arrangements, each based on a different assumption as to where the power lies (or ought to lie) and therefore as to who ought to be the client of the planning agency, are to be found.

1. The Semi-independent Planning Commission

The earliest and most widespread view, and the one that represents the most consistent application of the premises of the planning movement, asserts that the planning body itself ought to possess great independent power, which is to say that it ought to be its own client. Because the task of planning is to form and assert a comprehensive, internally consistent view of the public interest, a legislature, the principle of which of course is to represent special interests, is inherently unsuitable for plan-making. The elected executive is hardly more so, for his tenure is usually brief and he is rarely in a position to ignore the pressures of special interests. What is needed, then, is a body of disinterested statesmen who have long tenure and who are beyond the reach of political influences. This was the ideal which the Standard City Planning Enabling Act tried to approximate:

The members of the commission should feel secure in their tenure of office so long as they perform their functions faithfully and retain the confidence of the community. Conceivably, however, a situation might arise where a mayor might wish to remove members of the commission because they had recommended something that was not in harmony with his political desires. The members of the commission should be protected from such a situation by specifying removal for cause only and requiring the mayor to file a statement of his reasons.

Many semi-independent planning commissions are authorized by law to prepare and publish master plans and to pass upon all proposed public works and zoning changes. In a few instances their decisions can be overridden only by a two-thirds or three-quarters vote of the city council. The effect of these arrangements has almost always been to render the planning agency ineffective. Those who could win elections —i.e., "politicians"—have never had any trouble finding ways to bypass independent planning commissions when they wanted to, as they usually have.[11]

The semi-independent planning commission has been most thoroughly tried in New York City. There a planning commission was established in 1938 to be, in the words of Rexford G. Tugwell, one of its first chairmen, a "fourth power."[12] The commission had six members appointed for eight-year overlapping terms and one career civil servant *ex officio*. It was required by law to make a master plan and was put in charge of zoning and the capital budget. Protected from political interference (the mayor could not remove the commissioners and the Board of Estimate could override them only by a three-fourths vote), the commission had all the powers that the leaders of the planning movement wanted for it. Despite the amplitude of these powers —or perhaps because of it—the commission accomplished very little. It did not make a master plan.[13] It was twenty years securing adoption of a new zoning ordinance, and the ordinance it finally prepared was

[11] See the discussion by Robert A. Walker, *The Planning Function in Urban Government*, 2nd ed., (Chicago: University of Chicago Press, 1950), chap. v.

[12] Tugwell's paper, "The Fourth Power," although delivered while he was chairman of the New York City Planning Commission, dealt in general terms with the problem of institutionalizing the planning function and did not mention New York. It appeared in *Planning and Civic Comment*, part II, April-June 1939. Tugwell wrote later that he "thought rather poorly of legislatures"; they were "swayed by motives we distrusted and which ran against the general interest." *The Place of Planning in Society* (San Juan, P.R.: Puerto Rico Planning Board, 1954), p. 10. The great advantage of the New York City Planning Commission, in his eyes, was that it was "removed as completely from what is ordinarily called politics as is humanly possible—as much, for instance, as is the judiciary." The most significant feature of its activity was "implementing, for once, of a general interest rather than of special interests." But as matters turned out, "as it came closer and closer to representing the true central interest of the people of New York there was less and less available understanding and support from citizens." "Implementing the General Interest," *Public Administration Review*, Autumn 1940, pp. 37, 33, 43.

[13] In 1962 the commission was devoting nearly half of its $1,647,475 annual budget to the making of a "comprehensive" plan. This, according to James Felt, its chairman, is "a new kind of city planning program which focuses on the key issues of housing, employment and transportation, gives a searching look at major development alternatives and makes use of basic data on citizen needs and aspirations." *New York Times*, June 11, 1962, p. 1.

far from being the rationally arrived-at instrument the planning move-ment contemplated.[14] Its control of the capital budget was hardly more than nominal. As Sayre and Kaufman say, the commission, instead of planning, spent "its main energies in studious preparation for the eventual exercise of its powers and in protective preservation of its formal charter assignments."[15]

In some cities, semi-independent planning agencies have had con-siderably better success. In Philadelphia, for example, the planning commission had some real effect on the capital budget during the re-form administrations of Mayors Clark and Dilworth, and during the Republican one that preceded them. In 1960, it issued a master plan that was five years in the making. The plan was widely praised, but some observers believed that it was cast in such general terms that it could not be of much use to future decision-makers if—what could not be taken for granted, of course—they chose to consult it.

2. Planning as a Staff Aid to the Executive

Concluding that semi-independent planning commissions were bound to be ineffective, some supporters of planning decided that it should take the mayor as its client. Planning, Robert A. Walker wrote in 1941, is "essentially a research function" and therefore should be placed under the executive. (The council, he said, also needs research assistance; the reason for putting the planning agency under the mayor rather than the council is that the agency has other functions in addi-tion to the essential one of research, especially implementation of poli-cies and coordination of departmental planning.)[16]

This was the principle adopted in Chicago when in 1957 the mayor, acting on recommendations made by the Public Administration Service, created a city planning department responsible directly to him to re-place a large semi-independent commission. The new planning de-partment would take the mayor's decisions, be they broadly or nar-rowly political, as its premises. The semi-independent commission,

---

[14] For a detailed account of the manner in which the new zoning ordinance was made, see Frances Fox Piven, "Research in Formation of City Planning Policy," unpublished dissertation, Department of Political Science, University of Chicago, 1962.

[15] Wallace S. Sayre and Herbert Kaufman, Governing New York City (New York: Russell Sage Foundation, 1960), p. 372.

[16] Walker, Planning Function, p. 175.

reduced in size, was retained as an advisory body or (as some said) a "sounding board" for the mayor and his subordinates.[17]

In a few instances, the client of the planning agency is an executive other than the mayor. In Boston, for example, the agency was absorbed into the Redevelopment Authority which, strictly speaking, is a state and not a city agency.

Those who believe that the planning body ought to be a staff aid to the executive usually justify their view on the ground that otherwise the agency is almost sure to be ineffective. The executive, they point out, is always in a position to bypass the planning agency if he wants to; therefore the best hope of giving the agency influence is to make it his trusted instrument. Against this view others argue that subordination of the planning agency to the executive deprives it of its main reason for being, which is to frame and assert a comprehensive and objective—and of course nonpolitical—view of the public interest. From this point of view, the planning agency which takes as its main premises decisions made on political or other nonprofessional grounds by the executive ceases to be a "planning" agency at all.

3. Planning as a Staff Aid to the City Council

The client of the planning agency is sometimes the city council. T. J. Kent, an elected member of the Berkeley, California, council as well as a planner and a teacher of planning, advocates this arrangement on the ground that ultimately it is the council that decides the most important matters and ought therefore to have a plan—*the* plan for the city—which it has thought out and adopted.[18]

This theory applies, of course, only to cities where councils do in fact make important decisions. These are likely to be council-manager cities, but as we have explained in another chapter, even in council-manager cities councils are often rubber stamps. Moreover, even where they have real power, other conditions must also be met if planning with them as clients is to amount to anything. A council (or at least a stable majority of it) must be able to agree on fundamentals, and councilmen must be free enough from the pressures of constitutents so that generally (not always, of course) they can abide by the tentative commitments set forth in the plan.[19]

---

[17] See Banfield, *Political Influence* (New York: Free Press of Glencoe, 1961), pp. 215–216.

[18] Kent, "Urban General Plan," p. 101.

[19] In Berkeley (a council-manager city), Kent says, some of the most important

4. Planning as Community Decision-making

Some planning agencies take "the public at large" as their client and endeavor to supply it with information and technical guidance and to involve it as much as possible in the plan-making process. When a new planning director took up his duties in Haverhill, Massachusetts, in 1962, he explained that "the secret of planning and development success rests with the community-wide involvement of people of all areas and at all community levels." He hoped, he said, to "involve on an active basis every resident of the city."[20] Such hopes are always disappointed, of course; planning with the public as client means, in practice, planning with the activists of civic organizations, interest groups, and neighborhood associations as clients. Most planning agencies, however, although regarding some part of the city government as the primary client, do regard the public as a secondary or incidental client. "The common element in practically all public planning in the United States," Walker says, "has been the use of published reports and direct recourse to the public in an attempt to shape attitudes on public policy."[21]

5. Planning for "Potential Groups"

Planners sometimes define their function as that of representing certain interests which otherwise would be unrepresented or, at least, underrepresented. Usually, for example, there is no organized group to demand that the city be made more beautiful or that the rapid-transit rider be favored over the automobilist. Generations yet unborn, although having a conspicuous interest in many of the questions currently being decided, are, for an obvious reason, unorganized. Some planning agencies conceive their task to be largely that of righting the balance of representation in favor of such interests. Such agencies have as their clients what David B. Truman calls "potential groups."[22]

---

policies and proposals contained in the general plan were ignored by the council for several years after its adoption in 1955, and the plan was amended in several important respects. Nevertheless, he says, it has "slowly but surely enabled the council to face up to the implications of its most important and most controversial policies and proposals." Ibid., p. 178.

[20] Boston Sunday Globe, Dec. 9, 1962, p. 42.

[21] Walker, Planning Function, p. 366. For a good example, that of Syracuse, see Birkhead (cited in our note 7, above).

[22] David B. Truman, The Governmental Process (New York: Alfred A. Knopf, 1955), pp. 34–35 and 510–524.

6. Metropolitan and Regional Planning

The logic of planning leads to an ever-wider view of the area to be planned. Planning that is less than city-wide obviously cannot be truly comprehensive. But neither can planning that is merely city-wide, for some of the factors which affect the city fundamentally can only be managed on a metropolitan, or more-than-metropolitan (regional), basis. There being no true metropolitan (or regional) governments, master planning for a supra-city area must have some kind of coalition of local governments as its client. In 1960, planning was being done in this way in at least fifty places.[23] There were a number of joint city-county planning agencies; in some places several local governments, including a central city and a county, jointly supported a staff of professionals which was making a land-use survey and preparing certain phases (e.g., highway location) of what presumably would eventually be a master plan. Most of this activity was largely "educational" in purpose; the planners thought their first task was to persuade the public of the necessity of dealing "comprehensively" with problems that are (or are alleged to be) metropolitan or regional in character.

The Northeastern Illinois Metropolitan Area Planning Commission came into being through the efforts of a civic association, the Metropolitan Housing and Planning Council, which in 1955 recommended establishment by the legislature of an agency to prepare comprehensive plans for the area, to determine its optimum rate of economic growth, and to pass upon all capital expenditures proposed by local governments and by such state agencies as might be made subject to it. The Metropolitan Housing and Planning Council recommended that the new planning body be empowered to tax property for its support. A bill to create the Metropolitan Area Planning Commission was backed by the *Chicago Tribune* and "good government" forces in general, and was quickly passed. However, the legislature gave the commission practically no authority: it could accept voluntary contributions from local governments and it could make recommendations which these governments might accept or reject as they liked, and that was all it could do. After a few trial years it would have to go before the electorate for funds. At the end of 1961, the commission had done a

---

[23] Frank McChesney, "Trends and Prospects in Regional Planning," *Municipal Yearbook, 1961*, pp. 265–270. One third of the fifty programs involved three or fewer governmental units, and another third involved a dozen or more. Three regional bodies represented more than a hundred units each.

good deal of fact-gathering and had given advice to more than forty local governments that were without professional planning personnel of their own; most of this advice had to do with local rather than metropolitan problems. Whether the commission would ever do more than this depended largely on the attitude of the mayor of Chicago and his administration. This, according to Gilbert Y. Steiner, was "friendly but distant." The commission, he wrote, "has not had any real effect on the city's planning program or planning decisions, and there certainly is no disposition to surrender any of Chicago's planning autonomy to the metropolitan agency. The city's political leadership is generally indifferent to the existence of the metropolitan planning commission."[24]

The Chicago experience seems to be typical. "All regional planning," the *Municipal Yearbook* of 1961 said, "has the weaknesses and strengths of confederation. It is almost always advisory. It is subject to termination, succession, and apathy. Its principal tools must be education, influence, and leadership."

THE ADJUSTMENT OF PLANNING TO POLITICS

In recent years the planning movement has lost much of its former confidence in the feasibility, and perhaps also the desirability, of master planning. Many planners recognize that both the rate of change in cities and the logical structure of the problem of coordination limit very sharply the possibilities of master planning under even the most auspicious circumstances. As a leader of the planning profession observed in an address to his fellows, "the extent of our comprehension must limit the comprehensiveness of our planning."[25]

Planners are also becoming increasingly aware that the decentralization of authority and power that is so characteristic of American local government is radically incompatible with the ideal of master planning; they see that no matter how many planners are employed or how planning agencies are fitted into the structure of government, the political system continues to work mainly by bargaining and compromise, not by "implementing the general interest," and that the main decisions in a master plan must (as Mowitz and Wright said those in

---

[24] Gilbert Y. Steiner, "Administrative Reorganization in Chicago," *Illinois Government*, Leaflet no. 11, Institute of Government and Public Affairs, University of Illinois, Urbana, Sept. 1961.

[25] John T. Howard, "The Planner in a Democratic Society: A Credo," *Journal of the American Institute of Planners*, Summer 1955, p. 64. On the complexity of the formal problem of coordinating a set of decisions, see Michael Polanyi, *The Logic of Liberty* (Chicago: University of Chicago Press, 1951), pp. 170–179.

the Detroit one did) "reveal the power distribution in the community at that particular time."[26] Planners are becoming aware that the master plan must be a collection of bargains and compromises. This does not necessarily leave planning without any valid rationale, however. Even if it is politically, and perhaps also logically, impossible to make all of the most important decisions respecting land use in a city or a metropolitan area as a single system (i.e., every decision being taken in the light of every other), it may be entirely possible, both politically and logically, to make some smaller number of decisions within some limited sphere (for example, urban renewal) as a single system. Certainly in a particular city, circumstances, political or other, may favor coordination in some matters and not others. In general, "planning in the small" may be feasible even if "planning in the large" is not. Planners are not yet agreed as to what the central task of planning is if it is not master planning; both their practice and their theory, however, show adaptation to the reality of the American political system.

This adaptation, of course, means among other things that planning for limited objectives—project planning or planning within one agency —will proliferate and thereby make over-all or master planning even more difficult. Planning, which once was thought of as the means to coordinate all aspects of city development, has now made such coordination all the more difficult, as the following quotation from the mayor of Minneapolis suggests:

We have, as every large city has, a great need for coordinated planning. We have, in fact, quite good planning. We have one of the nation's best housing and redevelopment authorities. It is doing a magnificent job. We have a good city planning commission. It is doing a lot of imaginative work in re-designing a master plan for the city. We have a capital long-range improvements committee which is concerned with public works; it is a special committee that includes a number of private citizens appointed by the city council. Then we have the on-going responsibility of the city engineer's office for the actual construction of maintenance and rehabilitation projects. On top of all this we have the highway department streaking through with its new freeways and expressways. Also we have a seven-county body known as the Twin Cities Metropolitan Planning Commission which is doing studies in depth on traffic flow, water supply, and all the basic problems of the seven-county area.[27]

[26] Mowitz and Wright, *Profile of a Metropolis* (cited in our note 2, above), p. 135.

[27] Arthur Naftalin, mayor of Minneapolis, in *The City*, a leaflet published by the Center for the Study of Democratic Institutions (Santa Barbara, 1962), p. 42.

PART IV

SOME POLITICAL ROLES

CHAPTER 15 · CITY EMPLOYEES

CITY EMPLOYEES—there were 1,733,961 of them in 1961—play three distinct political roles. Some are party workers or participate in other ways as "individuals" in politics broadly or narrowly defined. Some are members of employees' associations or labor unions which function as pressure groups. And some are administrators who make decisions which are in some sense political. (Still others—probably a large majority of all—play no political roles at all.)

THE EMPLOYEE AS A POLITICALLY INTERESTED INDIVIDUAL

In theory, most employees of most sizable cities hold their jobs on merit and not as a reward for service to a political party or personality. As Table 11 shows, 62 percent of all cities over 10,000 population which replied to a *Municipal Yearbook* survey had some degree of formal civil service in 1961, and 28 percent had substantially all of their employees covered. (If the 604 cities—most of them small—which did not reply had done so, the percentage of communities without civil service would probably be substantially larger.) Under a "civil service" (or "merit") system, a semiautonomous lay board recruits and examines potential employees, certifies them for employment, and hears grievance and dismissal appeals. The purpose of the system is, of course, both to insure that competent employees are chosen and to prevent parties, or political figures, from offering patronage as a means of gaining votes or other political advantage.

It would be a mistake, however, to conclude either that all civil service employees are indeed appointed solely on the basis of merit or that their position as civil servants actually prevents them from playing active parts in party and other political matters. There are many devices by which the intention of the civil service system is more or less frustrated in some cities. Appointments may be made on a "temporary" basis in order to evade the operation of the law, the "temporary" appointment then being renewed indefinitely. Lists of eligibles may be canceled, and new examinations ordered. Or a civil service commission may be starved for funds or "packed" with party followers to prevent it from making more than a perfunctory examination of potential employees.

TABLE 11. Civil-service cities distributed by population groups, 1961

Population group	Number of cities reporting	Percentage of cities with:		
		Substantially all employees under civil service	At least some employees under civil service	No civil service
All cities over 10,000	1,158	28	62	38
10,000–25,000	618	18	48	52
25,000–50,000	289	35	70	30
50,000–100,000	136	46	85	15
100,000–250,000	66	39	82	18
250,000–500,000	28	53	93	7
Over 500,000	21	52	100	0

Note: The last two columns add horizontally to 100 percent.

Source: *Municipal Yearbook, 1962,* p. 191.

There is no way of knowing how widespread and important such evasions may be. In at least a few of the largest cities—Chicago, for example—there are undoubtedly thousands of jobs which although nominally under civil service (according to the *Municipal Yearbook* for 1962, *all* Chicago employees except those employed by public utilities are under civil service) are in fact dispensed as political patronage. Most of these are "temporary" jobs, many for unskilled laborers, and they are given as "favors" to persons who are expected to do no more in return than "show appreciation" by voting the "right" way and by seeing to it that close relatives do so as well. A relatively few jobs at a higher level—building inspector, budget analyst, or clerk, for example—go to deserving party workers and are, in effect, payment for service to the party. The holders of these "patronage" jobs are precinct captains and other cogs in the party machinery. Although they may be nominally under civil service, they know that if they fail to perform their tasks for the party satisfactorily or if the "sponsor" whose "endorsement" they have loses favor with the party bosses, ways will be found to dismiss or demote them.

Although politically distributed jobs are probably not numerous enough in any city to significantly affect the outcome of an election directly, the better-paying patronage jobs—even when few in number —are crucial to the maintenance of the party organization in some districts, and patronage may therefore have a very significant indirect effect on voting behavior and party organization.

However important may be the evasions of the civil service system in particular cases, it is clear that in general the effect of the system everywhere has been to make it increasingly difficult for the parties to maintain effective discipline over their workers by giving and with-holding jobs. Nowadays it is not always possible even by skillful "finagling" to reward a party worker appropriately; moreover, in those cases where finagling works and the appointment is made, there is a high probability that the fortunate party worker, having come under the protection of civil service regulations, will cease to work for the party. In short, even if the party gets him appointed, it may not be able to use his appointment as a means of getting political services from him.

Although the proportion of small cities without a civil service system is high (see Table 11), it does not follow that the employee of the small city is more likely than that of the large to owe a debt of political service to the appointing authority. In some small cities, to be sure, a good many appointments *are* political, although not necessarily parti-sanly so. Probably the more common practice among small cities with-out a civil service system is a rather informal but at the same time highly nonpolitical personnel system.

Some city employees are forbidden by law or by administrative regulation to hold party offices. Where such rules exist, evasions are common. For example, in Philadelphia, where a city employee may not be a ward committeeman, the common practice is for the party post to be held by the wife.

In some cities, limitations on employees' political activity are far-reaching. When the manager of Skokie, a suburb of Chicago which adopted the council-manager plan in 1957, undertook to prepare the city's 250 employees (many of whom were active and frank political partisans) for service in a nonpartisan system, he issued a directive which specified in considerable detail what would and what would not be permitted. His checklist, which was published in the magazine of the International City Managers' Association, and which is reproduced in our Table 12, is representative of the theory, if not the practice, of those cities where the "good government" ideal prevails.[1]

EMPLOYEES AS AN INTEREST GROUP

Since the employee has a bread-and-butter stake in city government, it is not surprising to find that he is one of the important pressures on it. Collectively, city employees are often the *most* important.

In small towns as well as large, unorganized employees are usually a political force to be reckoned with. In Massachusetts, for example, the traditional town meeting was replaced by the "limited" town meeting (200 triannually elected "town meeting members" have the floor and the franchise; other citizens watch from the gallery) primarily because self-interested town employees packed the meetings, but even under the new system the employee makes his influence felt.[2]

Employees also exert influence through unions and professional associations, some of which are affiliated with international unions. The American Federation of State, County, and Municipal Employees

---

[1] Bernard L. Marsh, "Regulating Political Activity of Employees," *Public Management*, October 1960, p. 229.

[2] In a study of Plymouth, Massachusetts, in preparation at Harvard University, George Von der Muhle tells, as follows, what happens when the finance committee made its recommendation regarding the salary of the Dog Officer (everything from here on, including the bracketed material, is Von der Muhle's):

A voice calls out from the gallery:

"I'm watching!"

"What do you mean, Louie?" [This from the floor amidst much whispering and craning of necks.]

"I'm watching how you fellows vote!"

[Here the Moderator intervenes with, "Do you have something to say, Mr. Capella?"]

"You bet I do, Mr. Moderator. I'm just telling those fellows down there I'm going to watch them real close when they vote. This Finance Committee, they say I don't need a raise. They said the same thing last year. $2,142! How long do you think I'm going to work for the Town for money like that? I got people to take care of, same as everyone else."

[From somewhere toward the center of the floor a representative calls out: "It's a part-time job."]

"Sure, it's part-time all right. Let me tell you how part-time it is. Last Saturday night about 3 a.m. a fellow called up on the phone. He said, 'There's a dog been run over on 3 near Manomet. Just over the hill. You'd better go get him, I don't think he's quite dead.' So I had to get up at 3 a.m. and put my coat on—it was freezing cold out—and go get the dog. I bet it was close to zero. How many of you fellows have jobs that make you get up at 3 a.m. in freezing weather just because somebody calls up? ["What about the Fire Department?" several voices inquire, but the interruption is ignored.] That's what part-time means—you never know when your time's your own. Well, all I can say is, if any of you fellows don't have dog tags for your dog, you'd better look real sharp how you vote. I'm going to pay a little visit to those of you who don't think I need that extra $100 I asked for—you can see it right there in the Warrant—and you'll find out whether I'm earning my salary or not!"

TABLE 12. Regulation of political activities by Village of Skokie employees

Type of activity	Partisan elections	Nonpartisan elections	On village time	On employee's time
		Whether permitted or not		
Membership in a political party, club, or organization	Yes	—	No	Yes
Officer or committee chairman for a political party or organization	No	—	No	No
Attendance at political rallies or meetings, as spectator only°	Yes	Yes	No	Yes
Speak at political meetings, make endorsements or appear on behalf of any candidate or proposal	No	Yes	No	Yes
Circulate petitions, distribute printed matter or badges, or sell tickets for any candidate or party	No	No	No	No
Sign a petition	Yes	Yes	Yes	Yes
Solicit or accept money from any person for any political purpose	No	No	No	No
Serve as precinct captain or party worker for any political organization	No	No	No	No
Assist in getting voters to polls on election day	No	No	No	No
Act as poll watcher for a political party	No	—	No	No
Make contributions to political party or organization	No	No	No	No
Be a candidate for public office°°	Yes	—	No	Yes
Use or threaten to use influence of position to coerce or persuade vote	No	No	No	No
Participate in nonpartisan voter registration campaigns	—	Yes	No	Yes
Participate in partisan voter registration campaigns	Yes	—	No	Yes
Be a delegate to a political convention	No	No	No	No
Cast a vote	Yes	Yes	Yes	Yes

° Not permitted in uniform.
°° Must take leave of absence during campaign and term of office.

(AFSCME), the International Association of Firefighters (IAFF), and the American Federation of Teachers, all three of which are AFL-CIO unions, have affiliates in most of the major cities. In many cities there are also local unions that have been organized to represent workers in particular agencies; examples are the Transport Workers Union in New York City and Local 18 of the International Brotherhood of Electrical Workers in Los Angeles. Some city employees belong to associations which, although not labor unions in a strict sense, are very similar to them and function, like them, as pressure groups in local politics. These associations include the Fraternal Order of Police, the Uniformed Firemen's Association, the National Educational Association, and others.

The unions and other employee associations exist mainly in the larger cities. Of the 51 cities of over 250,000 population in 1961, all but two had employee organizations that were affiliated with a national body. On the other hand, of the 1,439 cities of from 10,000 to 50,000 population, 335, or 23 percent, had no employee organization affiliated with a national one.

There are twenty-four professional organizations of ranking city employees, including airport executives, fire chiefs, librarians, park executives, finance officers, traffic engineers, housing and redevelopment officials, police chiefs, and so on.

The long-standing practice of employee organizations (as well as other interest groups) has been to reward their friends and punish their enemies at the polls. In Los Angeles, for example, water department employees, acting as members of Local 18 of the International Brotherhood of Electrical Workers, constituted a powerful force until the election of a "reform" mayor in 1938.[3] In New York City, policemen and firemen have often worked openly for a favored candidate—at least as late as the 1949 mayoralty election when a former policeman and district attorney, William O'Dwyer, won office. From 1938 to 1949, Michael Quill, head of the Transport Workers Union (which represented employees on the city subway system), was a New York city councilman.

In recent years, employee unions have ceased to function as adjuncts of the party machinery. Several causes have been at work. The party organizations have become weaker, and their favor therefore less

[3] Richard Baisden, "Labor Unions in Los Angeles Politics," unpublished dissertation, Department of Political Science, University of Chicago, 1958.

valuable. Public opinion is such that the unions find it advantageous to be "above politics." And, finally, the position of the unions is now so secure in many places that they have little to gain and something to lose by close identification with any party or candidates. In New York and Los Angeles, for example, career officials who belong to the unions and associations have captured all but the highest offices in most city departments.

The employees' unions and associations are mainly concerned with "bread and butter" matters—pay and promotion policies, job security, pension systems, and grievance procedures. Frequently, however, they endeavor to influence the choice of the leading administrative officials. Their preference, as a rule, is for "career" as against "political" administrators. One of their main goals is to secure control of the personnel system. Beyond that, they want to make the bureaucracy as nearly independent and self-directing as possible. As Professors Sayre and Kaufman explain, they have three strategic aims in their search for autonomy: (1) to establish a taboo against "political interference" or interference by "special interests"—a taboo under cover of which they would be free from the supervision of a mayor, department head, city council, or any other "outsider"; (2) to achieve a maixmum and assured role in policy formation in order to protect their group values and settled traditions against the enthusiasms and whims of "amateurs" and "innovators"; and (3) to control the procedures under which their members monopolize the formulation of, or modification of, the procedures under which their members work, so there will be as little disturbance of work routines as possible. These being their goals and strategies, the leaders of the cities' bureaucracies are, as Sayre and Kaufman observe, a conservative force in the cities' politics.[4]

The autonomy of the city bureaucracy often entails advantages, such as the relative absence of corruption, favoritism, and malfeasance. These evils are reduced, not because bureaucrats are inherently more virtuous than politicians, but because such evils are a source of uncertainty and instability in the bureaucracy itself. The fixed rules which replace patronage and favoritism are a source of stable expectations and are valued by employees for that reason. It is not uncommon to hear patronage appointees speak with enthusiasm of the advent of civil service regulations, for the change means security for them—assuming they can meet the job requirements. The advantages to the employee of certainty may, of course, be disadvantages to the political official frustrated by the bureaucracy's resistance to change. Reasserting political control over city agencies may not require the reinstitution of corrupt practices, but the logic of the problem is similar.

The characteristic attitude of the organized employees was exhibited by the president of the New York City local of the American Federation of Teachers when he told the national convention of the union that Parent-Teacher Associations and similar civic groups should not meddle so much in education. "The PTA and other lay groups certainly have the right to consult with us," he told the convention, "but they should remember that we're the experts."[5]

The political weight of organized city employees in a particular city depends largely upon the nature of that city's political structure, and especially upon the degree to which influence is centralized. Where party organization is strong, the city administration is in a relatively good position to resist the demands of the organized employees (or, for that matter, any other pressure group). On the other hand, where party organization is weak or altogether absent, the political weight of the organized employees is relatively large and may be decisive. In many small nonpartisan cities, especially ones which elect their councils on the at-large system, organized city employees—and above all firemen, policemen, and teachers—may be the only, and at any rate by far the largest, city-wide organizations. In such cities, the organized city employees, along with the newspapers (another city-wide force), may play decisive roles at election time.

The contrasting position of the employee as between a city where power is centralized and one where it is not may be seen in the examples of Chicago and Los Angeles.

The mayor of Chicago, depending as he does upon the Democratic machine for his power, can afford to risk the displeasure of the city employees. The allegiance of many of the key employees has already been purchased by the machine and therefore need not be purchased again through the personnel office. In Chicago, accordingly, employee organizations are relatively weak. The teachers, for example, although they influence decisions taken by the board of education, do not participate in the elective process because the mayor and his party dominate that process.

[5] New York Times, Aug. 24, 1962.

In Los Angeles, by contrast, organized employees find it easier to organize and to exert pressure. Authority is highly decentralized and party organization is altogether lacking. In these circumstances, the power of an organized pressure group is magnified, and therefore the incentive to organize is increased. The All-City Employees Association of Los Angeles claims to represent nearly 30,000 workers, and there are many other associations representing special classes of employees, like teachers. In the average Los Angeles election district there are about 175,000 people, of whom only about 25,000 to 30,000 vote in councilmanic elections. Thus the members of the All-City Employees' Association, who are well disciplined and fairly evenly spread among election districts, and who respond energetically to the directions of their leadership, are a preponderant force, especially when they combine, as they sometimes do, with police, fire, and teachers' organizations to obtain wage and pension benefits. To the mayor, who is elected at large, the organized employees are a somewhat less formidable force than to the councilmen, and when the employees fail to get what they want, it is often because he vetoes a measure approved by the council.

In New York City, the weakness of the office of mayor and the dispersal of authority within the Board of Estimate (which we described in an earlier chapter as an intermediate case between Chicago and Los Angeles) encourage the vigorous assertions of employees' interests. Associations of teachers, policemen, firemen, transit workers, and sanitation workers represent numbers which have great political significance, Sayre and Kaufman say, "while the social workers, lawyers, engineers, accountants, and other relatively small groups depend for influence upon their professional unity and their strategic roles in the administration of public agencies."[6] Employee work stoppages and protests are not uncommon, and some city teachers have gone on strike. When the police commissioner forbade policemen to hold after-hours jobs ("moonlighting"), they demonstrated against his ruling, first by failing to write tickets for minor offenses and then, when they were rebuked for that, by writing tickets for the most trivial and technical offenses.

Not uncommonly, municipal employees in various cities succeed in appealing their cases from the elected mayor and council to the voters. In both Boston and Detroit, for example, the voters reduced the fireman's work week from 63 to 54 hours, even though in each instance the

[6] Sayre and Kaufman, *Governing New York City*, p. 74.

mayor insisted that the firemen were eating and sleeping for a good part of their 63-hour duty and should not have the reduction. In Boston, a city which at the time was hardly able to pay its bills, the voters also approved pay increases which the city officials had disapproved. In part the success of the employees in such referenda is to be accounted for by the advantage that disciplined organization gives them; they are, on these occasions, political machines.

THE EMPLOYEE AS POLITICAL ADMINISTRATOR

At the top of the hierarchy in a sizable city are a score or more of appointed officials whose role is in large part political in the broad sense if not the narrow (partisan) sense. These include the superintendent of schools, the urban renewal director, the city planner, the water works manager, the fire chief, the police chief, and so on. In some cities most or all of such officials think of themselves and are thought of by others as professional or career administrators; they are often technically trained, have risen to their top positions by administrative rather than political achievements and connections, and, sometimes, may even have civil service tenure. In other cities, especially the large ones, many or most department and commission heads are "political appointments": they are chosen less for their technical or professional knowledge and experience (although they may have some of that too) than for their ability to "attract support" to the city administration and to share the mayor's political burdens. The campaign manager for New York's Mayor Robert F. Wagner in 1961 was the fire commissioner.

Whether he is a "career" man or a "political appointee," the department head must of necessity make decisions that are political in the broad sense. This is because all decisions on controversial matters require more or less subjective judgments about values and probabilities. For example, there are political as well as technical aspects to a fire chief's decision to order one kind of equipment rather than another, or to deploy it in one part of the city or another. Similarly, the manager of the water works makes a political decision when he asks for recommendations for or against fluoridation, expansion of the system, or a change in the method of payment for water. Being a career man under civil service relieves the administrator of the necessity of participating in party politics, but it does not relieve him of the necessity of making decisions which are politically significant.

Both kinds of political administrators—the career man no less than the political appointee—may be active and autonomous forces in the city's politics. Whether under civil service or not, the head of a city department is likely to have more resemblance to Max Weber's ideal-type politician than to his ideal-type bureaucrat: instead of applying rules "without regard to persons" (the defining characteristic of the bureaucrat, according to Weber), he fights to alter the distribution of power (the defining activity of the politician).[7]

One reason why the top bureaucrats in American cities are (by European standards) so "unbureaucratic" is that practically all decision-making in American cities is highly political in character. So long as interest groups and the public generally can participate intimately in the making of decisions regarding, say, the purchase of fire equipment, the fire chief's role cannot be simply that of a technician; it must include finding the terms on which the conflicting opinions and interests can be reconciled or compromised; that is, it must be political.[8] Furthermore, in a governmental system in which all interests participate competitively in the making of decisions, the department itself is very likely to become a competitor along with the others. The head of the department, therefore, may be at the same time in effect a lobbyist on behalf of the department and a mediator or arbiter who decides the terms on which the issue is to be settled.

Even in strong-mayor cities, the mayor's ability to appoint and remove his chief subordinates and to give them directions is hedged about with legal restrictions, the purpose of which is to prevent the mayor from giving direction that is political in the narrow sense ("playing politics") but which of necessity also prevents him from giving direction that is political in the broad sense ("providing leadership"). For example, Philadelphia's reform charter, adopted in 1951, created a

---

[7] Max Weber, *Theory of Economic and Social Organization*, trans. A.M. Henderson and Talcott Parsons (Glencoe, Ill.: Free Press, 1947), pp. 329–341. See also Robert Merton, "Bureaucratic Structure and Personality," *Social Theory and Social Structure*, 2nd ed. (Glencoe, Ill.: Free Press, 1957), pp. 195–206; and Karl Mannheim, *Ideology and Utopia* (New York: Harcourt, Brace, 1936), pp. 105 ff. A statistical profile of the social origin, education, career patterns, and attitudes of 1,725 American municipal officials is given in the appendix to the report of the Municipal Manpower Commission, *Governmental Manpower for Tomorrow's Cities* (New York: McGraw-Hill, 1962), pp. 127–166. Sayre and Kaufman give an excellent account of the political role of the administrator in *Governing New York City*, chap. viii.

[8] For a case in point, see Warner E. Mills, Jr., and Harry R. Davis, *Government* (New York: Random House, 1962), chap. vi.

civil service commission of three persons who were appointed by the mayor from a list of nine names submitted by the heads of certain voluntary associations. The commissioners then appointed a personnel director who had complete charge of personnel matters for the city government. The city's finance director was selected by the mayor from a list of three names submitted by the president of the Philadelphia Clearinghouse Association, the president of the Philadelphia Association of Certified Public Accountants, and the dean of the Wharton School of Finance at the University of Pennsylvania. The first mayor under the reform charter, Joseph S. Clark, Jr., a Democrat, had to choose his finance director from a list of two Republicans and one Democrat who had the political disadvantage of being a "carpetbagger" (i.e., not a native Philadelphian).[9] From a formal standpoint, the mayor was free to dismiss all but one of his chief subordinates at will (this one could appeal his dismissal to the Civil Service Commission), but in fact, of course, it would be extremely awkward for him to do so; and since he would have little freedom of choice in the selection of a successor he would have an additional incentive to put up with an incumbent if he possibly could.

Even when a mayor can appoint and remove an official at will, he may not be able to give him directions in policy matters. In New York, when Mayor Wagner said something about sending police patrols into housing projects, he received a polite but firm reminder from his subordinate, the police commissioner, that he, the mayor, had nothing to say in the matter. "Needless to say," the police commissioner wrote him, "I, as Police Commissioner, having sole responsibility under the law for the disposition of the police force, will go on making my determinations according to professional police judgment and with reference to the best interests of the citizens as a whole."[10]

Not infrequently it is "good politics" for a mayor to make a conspicuous display of appointing a subordinate who is known to be entirely nonpolitical and, indeed, unresponsive to direction. In making such an appointment a mayor may publicly tie his own hands in order to persuade the public that matters are going to be decided on wholly nonpolitical grounds and that the activity in question is therefore worthy and sound and a credit to the administration.

Such officials are valuable to politicians not only because they sym-

[9] Chicago Home Rule Commission, *Modernizing a City Government* (Chicago, 1954), pp. 352 and 358.
[10] *New York Times*, Oct. 25, 1961.

bolize good-government values, but also—and much more practically—because they are crucial in negotiating settlements with or obtaining consent from other levels of government which are staffed by their professional colleagues. This factor has come to be of greater importance in recent years with the expansion of state and federal programs of subsidies to cities. Urban renewal and redevelopment and public housing all depend on federal funds and hence on federal consent. In the complicated and protracted proceedings necessary to fulfill all requirements of the law, the confidence one bureaucrat has in another whose professional reputation he knows can be an important factor. As a result, cities often compete for the services of planners and engineers known to be held in high regard by other levels of government.

Robert A. Dahl reports how urban renewal in New Haven, Connecticut, was facilitated because the city appointed Ralph Taylor as head of its redevelopment agency. Taylor, who was brought in from outside the city, had a high professional standing among planners and housers in the country and was respected by bureaucrats in the federal agencies which had to pass on renewal projects.[11] Another New Haven redeveloper, Edward Logue, gained such a reputation that he was lured to Boston at a great salary increase in order to lend his prestige to the stalemated Boston renewal program.

Cities, and agencies within a single city, vary in the extent to which career administrators wield real power. Administrators who fight for policy goals rather than simply apply general rules are likely to be persons who, for any number of reasons, are rewarded for playing (in the broad sense) politics. A city planner, engineer, doctor, accountant, or purchasing agent who is a member of and oriented toward an outside professional group which sets standards and defines "proper" conduct may value his standing in these circles sufficiently to challenge local elective officials even at the risk of his job. His future, he feels, depends more on the good will of his colleagues outside the administration than on the opinion of his superiors within it. Or the official may value the purposes of his agency more than the monetary rewards he gets from it. He may be, for example, a social worker committed to helping juvenile delinquents at all costs—inside the agency if possible, but outside it if necessary.

Further, cities where the formal government is expected to be a

[11] Robert A. Dahl, *Who Governs?* (New Haven: Yale University P[...] pp. 129–130.

source of innovation are likely to have influential administrators. A city committed to community growth and led by an elective official whose standing with the voters depends on his ability to catch their attention with civic projects (rather than, by contrast, with personal favors or party regularity) is likely to be a city with a stake in change and thus a stake in a bureaucracy which can initiate and implement change. Where the city is expected only to be an arbiter of competing interests or a caretaker of essential services and where the politician has bases of strength which do not depend on change or projects, the city administration, in such fields as planning and redevelopment, is likely to be small and compliant.

Urban renewal provides illustrations of these cases. In Chicago, renewal projects are often initiated and planned by nongovernmental organizations, usually institutions (such as hospitals, universities, or business firms) having a material stake in the outcome of the plan and willing to relieve the city administration of planning responsibilities. The city agencies most concerned with urban renewal are typically small and ineffectual. The mayor does not feel the need for his own innovating bureaucracy. The city is too complex and heterogeneous, with a multiplicity of conflicting interests, to make it politically desirable to innovate, and the mayor's power is such that innovation is politically unnecessary.

In Boston, on the other hand, the mayor has a personal, rather than an organizational, following, and he was elected in a campaign to "revitalize" the city. The Boston Redevelopment Authority quickly became one of the largest city agencies, under the leadership of men who were both highly professional and strong-willed. It became the source of surveys, plans, and goals. It, rather than any particular private organization, was known as the "sponsor" of urban renewal, and the mayor, of course, became closely identified with the fortunes of the agency.

In any city the question arises: where does the administrator get the answers to questions that are essentially political? Since he does not go before the electorate, the criterion most familiar to the out-and-out politician—will it gain or lose me votes?—is denied to him. And yet in the nature of the case he must have political criteria.

He may get the answers from other officials who, like the mayor, are elected, or who, like the city manager, are appointed but get political direction from an elected body. The extent to which the administrator turns to these others for political direction depends largely upon two factors: the freedom that the law gives him to make decisions independently of them and their ability to remove him.

In the usual case, one or both of these factors operate to give the administrator a considerable degree of independence. That he has independence is no guarantee that he will use it, of course; he may turn to the mayor or manager for political guidance even if he does not have to. In general, however, the greater the administrator's autonomy the more likely he is, on occasion at least, to take a political path that has not been marked out for him from above.

If the administrator does not get political criteria from his elected "superiors," where does he get them? He usually supposes, of course, that he gets them (in the words we quoted from the police commissioner of New York) from "professional judgment" about the "best interests of the citizens as a whole." But this is a delusion, for there are almost as many views of the best interests of the citizens as a whole as there are citizens, and therefore the question—how to choose among these views—is left unanswered.

Language like the police commissioner's usually concerns or conceals one (or both) of two sources of criteria.

One source is the maintenance or enhancement needs of the bureaucracy for which the administrator speaks. The administrator decides matters in a way that will not be disruptive of the morale or prestige of his agency. The agency has certain traditions and collectively defined standards which cannot be transgressed without "causing trouble" of some kind—for example, creating disaffection among leadership elements within the organization, endangering its relations with interest groups upon which it relies for support, damaging its "public relations," or reducing its appropriations. If, for example, the police captains of New York are strongly of the opinion that assigning men to housing projects will discredit the force because of the utter impossibility of coping with the situation in them, the commissioner may be under very heavy pressure to assert his independence of the mayor. If he were to accede to the mayor's wishes, his own subordinates might become so disaffected as to make it impossible for him to maintain his authority over them in other, more important matters.

The other source of criteria is the consensus of the profession as interpreted by its authoritative organs and personalities. In planning a public housing program for Chicago, for example, the executive director of the Chicago Housing Authority (Miss Elizabeth Wood) in effect appealed over the heads of the appointed board, which had the legal responsibility for making policy, and over the head of the mayor, who had *de facto* control of the situation. From her identification with the "national housing movement" (and perhaps also from an even more abstract entity, "the liberal position") she got a set of goals and standards which were entirely different in character from those that were supplied either by the "policy-making" officials who appointed her or by the maintenance and enhancement needs of her organization.[12]

An administrator, by claiming that the grounds of his decisions are "purely professional," may be able to resist the claims of those interest groups which, for one reason or another, it is convenient for him to resist, as well as the directions of his political superiors.[13] It is possible, therefore, for a bureaucracy which establishes its "highly professional" character to liberate itself from any will except its own. In a small city dominated by business interests, for example, a bureaucracy may ignore the local power structure and adhere to standards which are either "good professional practice" or "acceptable to the bureau," or both. In Haverhill, Massachusetts, a nonpartisan, council-manager city of about 46,000, the mayor recently suggested that shoppers be permitted to cross the city's main street at any and all points "as an aid to downtown business." The police chief took issue with the mayor. The city should avail itself of the provisions of a new state jaywalking law, he said, "so that Haverhill will be uniform with the rest of the state." The law, he said, "will be studied by the police on a recommendation by the traffic commission and the findings will be given to the city manager for approval by the council."[14] In this case it was clear that the elected official and the bureaucrat represented competing conceptions of the public interest.

---

[12] See Martin Meyerson and Banfield, *Politics, Planning, and the Public Interest* (Glencoe, Ill.: Free Press, 1955), chap. x. A city planner's decisions may often be no less technical than a city attorney's. But a mayor who is in a position to replace the planner at will nevertheless sets aside technical considerations in favor of political ones. See, for example, the account of Mayor Daley of Chicago and his planning department in Banfield, *Political Influence* (New York: Free Press of Glencoe, 1961), pp. 252 and 302.

[13] The elected politician sometimes uses the independence of the bureaucrat as a shield to protect himself against unwelcome pressures. Mayor Wagner, for example, seems to have arranged for publication of the police commissioner's letter, quoted above, in order to relieve himself of pressure to send policemen into housing projects.

[14] *Boston Globe*, Aug. 26, 1962.

The relationship between bureaucrats and politicians is not simply a product of situational constraints and the distribution of power, however. There are, in addition, problems which arise out of the differing styles of the two groups. This is clearest in cities where the politicians have risen to power from lower-class origins, often without the benefit of college education, and where they want (and need) to remain in contact with their lower-class constituencies. Their rhetoric, patterns of thought, and style of life are often vastly different from those of the bureaucrats. A city planner, say, with a postgraduate degree, an intellectual orientation, and a deep commitment to some specific goals may find it difficult to deal with politicians. And to the politicians, the attributes of the bureaucrat imply a difference in status which they resent or at least find uncomfortable.[15]

[15] This point is made in Meyerson and Banfield, pp. 263–264.

CHAPTER 16 · VOTERS

OVER almost every scene of political activity in the city there hovers as Unseen Presence. At intervals of two or four years it materializes for long enough to mark a ballot or pull the lever of a voting machine, thus deciding who is to be mayor, councilman, judge, and all the rest, and, often, whether a new school is to be built, the water supply fluoridated, or the firemen given a pay raise. At other times, the Presence, although out of sight, is seldom out of mind. To the professional politicians who run the city government, the voter is the ultimate reality. To please him, or at least to avoid displeasing him, is the goal of much of their endeavors.

THE LOCAL ELECTORATE

Because local elections are usually held at times when there are no state or national ones, and for other reasons as well, a considerably different body of voters turns out for local than for state and national elections and a still different body of voters turns out for local primary (or preliminary) elections than for local general (or run-off) ones.[1] As Table 13 shows, in the large cities the turnout of voters in a local general election is usually about 15 to 20 percent less than in a Presidential election. (New Orleans is an exception because in the one-party South the turnout in a Presidential election, the result of which is normally a foregone conclusion with respect to the state's electoral vote, is very low.)

These differences in turnout are enough to make the electorate which votes on local matters very different from the one which votes on state and national matters. Size is not the most important difference between these electorates, however. The voter may view local elections very

---

[1] The known correlates of voter turnout are summarized in Robert E. Lane, *Political Life* (Glencoe, Ill.: Free Press, 1959) pp. 45–62. A careful analysis of participation in *local* politics by class is found in Robert A. Dahl, *Who Governs?* (New Haven: Yale University Press, 1961), pp. 276–301. See also Eugene C. Lee's evidence that various "good government" reforms (e.g., nonpartisanship) reduce voter turnout in local elections (in *Municipal Yearbook*, 1963).

TABLE 13. Average turnout in mayoralty and Presidential elections in large cities, 1948–1952

City	Mayoralty	Presi-dential	City	Mayoralty	Presi-dential
Chicago	51.5%	71.3%	New Orleans	40.5%	38.6%
Pittsburgh	50.5	61.3	Minneapolis	37.0	63.8
Philadelphia	49.8	63.5	Denver	36.7	66.1
Buffalo	49.1	64.2	Cleveland	34.8	53.0
Cincinnati	49.0	61.2	Detroit	33.8	58.0
Boston	47.0	62.6	Baltimore	31.5	46.2
San Francisco	46.3	60.6	Los Angeles	31.3	58.7
New York	42.3	57.7	St. Louis	30.4	59.2
Indianapolis	41.4	63.1	Kansas City	29.9	59.2

Note: Turnout is here measured as the percentage of all persons of 21 years of age or over who vote in general elections. The figure for the Presidential elections is the average of the 1948 and 1952 turnouts; that for the mayoralty elections is an average of the same period.

Source: Charles E. Gilbert, Swarthmore College, unpublished data made available to the authors.

differently from state and national ones. He brings to the state and national elections some general ideology and some identifications with institutions (particularly parties) and political symbols of one kind or another. None of these have much of any application to local elections as a rule. In about 60 percent of the cities, local elections are non-partisan. Even where they are partisan, the words "Republican" and "Democratic" do not necessarily mean the same thing in local as in state and national politics. Sometimes, indeed, their meanings are (so far as they have any application to the local situation) reversed. That the Democratic party is more "liberal" than the Republican in national affairs does not prevent it from being more "conservative" or even "reactionary" in the local affairs of some cities. In some places, then, a voter may with consistency—indeed *must* if he is to be consistent—vote for a different party in state and national elections than in local ones. The Republican or Democratic vote in a mayoralty election cannot always be taken as indicative of the same voters' behavior in state and national elections.

THE PATTERNING OF THE VOTE

The principal question to be answered by an account of voting behavior is: How and why does the electorate differentiate itself into voting blocs? One wants to discover a "pattern" in the voting—to find out what kinds of people voted one way and what kinds another. In effect, one wants to discover on what few principles (for example, party membership, race, or class) voters can be most usefully classified, the purpose of the classification being, of course, to "explain" why they voted as they did or—what amounts to the same thing—to predict how they will vote in some future election. In this chapter, we shall describe the patterning that normally appears in local elections, and we shall then discuss some of the classificatory, or explanatory, principles in terms of which the patterning may be analyzed.

There is, of course, no logical necessity for there to be any patterning in a set of voting returns. Conceivably every voter could be actuated by purely idiosyncratic motives, in which case no "explanation" would account for a bloc of even two votes. In this event, one would not expect to find significant correlations between the way the voters cast their votes and any characteristics (such as, for example, conservative point of view, low income, or white skin) that they had in common.

But in fact there are apparently always some correlations—some patterning—in a vote. In any election, the "same kind of people" (somehow defined) tend to vote the same way. Moreover, the pattern that appears in one local election tends to be repeated in all others so long as the electorate is essentially the same (i.e., barring large differences in turnout or changes in the composition of the population). In other words, the wards that are furthest apart in their vote on one issue tend to be furthest apart on all issues and in all elections.

We have tested this proposition against election returns selected more or less at random from several cities where votes are tabulated by wards. In Cleveland, for example, on eight issues voted on at two separate elections in November 1959 and November 1960 the correlation between the votes by ward on any two issues was very high.[2] A similar pattern was found in Kansas City[3] and Detroit.[4] In short, if one knows how the wards of a city will divide on one issue, one can

[2] Computed using Kendall's *tau*, corrected for ties. The rank-order correlation ranged from +0.75 to +0.87. Essentially the same consistency appears if one includes in the correlation all the Cleveland suburbs in Cuyahoga County.

[3] In three referenda elections held at different times in Kansas City, ten of the eleven wards above the median on one vote were above the median on the other two as well.

[4] In three referenda elections held at different times in Detroit, nine of the eleven wards above the median on one issue were above the median on the two others as well.

usually predict fairly well how they will divide on others. This of course does not prove that certain classes of voters are voting the same way for the same reasons, nor does it in any sense "explain" people's votes; it only suggests the possibility that common causes are at work.

Furthermore, there is a good deal of similarity in the patterning of local election results from city to city. For example, no matter in what city they live, people with certain characteristics tend to favor the introduction of the city manager plan and—although there is no reason why the two should be connected—the fluoridation of public water supplies as well.

THE INFLUENCE OF PARTY

The explanation of patterning that comes to mind first is party. People vote the same way (according to this explanation) because they share a set of principles, loyalties, and sentiments associated with a party, or because they are subject to discipline from a party machine, or for both reasons.

Membership in a party generally signifies very little when it comes to voting in local elections. This is especially true where one party has tight control of the government; in such cities many voters think that it may possibly be to their advantage to be registered as a member of the dominant party, but this does not prevent them from voting against it. In New York, for example (according to Sayre and Kaufman), party membership is "nominal and, at bottom, ephemeral" and "only loosely related to voting behavior."[5]

Identification with a party, as distinguished from membership in it, is a much more important factor. Even though he does not belong to it, a voter may regularly vote for its candidates because he favors what it "stands for." This attachment of course need not be ideological. What the party stands for in local elections often has little relation to what it stands for in state and national ones, and moreover in local elections (even more than in state and national ones) the party as such seldom has any concrete program or platform. What it stands for is usually a certain aura of association that has grown up over the years around a few leading personalities. Thus the voter feels that one party has more of "my kind of people" than the other.

To some extent the voter is influenced by party discipline or party

[5] Wallace S. Sayre and Herbert Kaufman, *Governing New York City* (New York: Russell Sage Foundation, 1960), p. 129.

incentives. Studies in Detroit and in Gary, Indiana, suggest that under highly favorable circumstances precinct workers may increase a party's vote by 5 or 10 percent in state and national elections and by 8 to 14 percent in local elections and in primaries.[6] Such studies, of course, cannot take account of the long-run effect of party workers (even if they all "sat on their hands" in a particular election, the vote might reflect the cumulative effect of their efforts on previous occasions).

By one means or another, the parties do seem to have an influence on voting behavior in many cities. The extent of this influence is most strongly suggested by the fact that voters discriminate very little among party-endorsed candidates in local contests. In Chicago, for example, a Negro candidate will get only 1 or 2 percent more votes than his white running mates in the Negro wards, and only 4 or 5 percent less votes than they in most of the white wards. In nonpartisan Detroit, on the other hand, a Negro candidate will get almost four times as many votes in the Negro wards as any of his white running mates will get and he will get only about one fourth as many votes as they in the white middle-class wards. It must be understood, however, that the greater discrimination by voters among candidates of different ethnic groups in nonpartisan cities may be the result of nothing more than the absence of a party label on the ballot or a party lever on the voting machine. This is borne out by the fact that *partisan* elections in Detroit (for county and state offices) produce as high a percentage of straight-ticket voting as can be found in Chicago.[7] Nonetheless, we suspect that parties as *organizations* (rather than merely as labels) do have some influence on voting in *partisan* contests. In Boston, for example, where party organization is much weaker than in Chicago or Detroit,

---

[6] Unfortunately the Detroit study and some of the Gary studies dealt with Presidential rather than local elections. The elaborate and ingenious methodology —pioneered in Gary—cannot be easily summarized, but, generally speaking, it involves relating the activity of precinct workers to that portion of a precinct's vote which cannot be "explained" in a multiple regression equation by demographic factors—rent, homeownership, and ethnicity in the case of Gary; religion, occupation, race, and education in Detroit. For the Detroit study, see Daniel Katz and Samuel J. Eldersveld, "The Impact of Local Party Activity upon the Electorate," *Public Opinion Quarterly*, Spring 1961, pp. 1–24. The Gary studies are reported in Phillips Cutright and Peter H. Rossi, "Grass Roots Politicians and the Vote," *American Sociological Review*, April 1958, pp. 171–179; Cutright and Rossi, "Party Organization in Primary Elections," *American Journal of Sociology*, November 1958, pp. 262–269; and Rossi and Cutright, "The Impact of Party Organization in an Industrial Setting," in Morris Janowitz (ed.), *Community Political Systems* (New York: Free Press of Glencoe, 1961), pp. 81–116.

[7] For details of the Chicago-Detroit comparison, see James Q. Wilson, *Negro Politics* (Glencoe, Ill.: Free Press, 1960), pp. 39–47.

ticket-splitting in partisan state elections is very high and (as Table 14 below will indicate) tends to follow ethnic lines.

SOCIO-ECONOMIC AND ETHNIC STATUS

As is well known, there is generally a correlation between the party voted for and the income, education, religion, and ethnic origin of the voter. Sample surveys and election studies focused on state and national contests have amply demonstrated that, for example, lower-income Negroes or Catholics with little schooling are far more likely to vote Democratic than upper-income, college-educated, Anglo-Saxon Protestants.[8] We have no reason to believe that these findings do not hold generally true in partisan city elections as well.

Differences in income, education, and ethnicity are all closely associated with differences in social class. Sometimes, of course, class is *defined* in terms of income and education. But even if it is defined in terms of position in a deference hierarchy or participation in a subculture (i.e., the sharing of certain standards of taste and certain modes of behavior), it is usually closely related to the characteristics listed.

The relationship between class and political attitudes seems to vary somewhat with the size of the city. V. O. Key, Jr., finds, for example, that "blue collar" and "white collar" workers differ most in their attitudes toward certain policy issues in large metropolitan areas and differ least in smaller cities (with populations between ten and fifty thousand).[9] In almost every case, blue-collar (i.e., working-class) attitudes became more similar to white-collar (middle-class) attitudes in the smaller communities. Two other researchers found that laborers in small Michigan cities were less likely to vote Democratic than were laborers in large cities.[10] A study of Elmira, New York, suggested that workers there showed "less political solidarity and more political am-

[8] Studies of class, ethnicity, and voting include the following: Bernard Berelson, *et al., Voting* (Chicago: University of Chicago Press, 1954); Angus Campbell *et al., The American Voter* (New York: John Wiley & Sons, 1960); V. O. Key, Jr., *Public Opinion and American Democracy* (New York: Alfred A. Knopf, 1961); Seymour M. Lipset *et al.*, "The Psychology of Voting: An Analysis of Political Behavior," in Gardner Lindsey (ed.), *Handbook of Social Psychology* (Cambridge, Mass.: Addison-Wesley, 1954), II, 1124–1175; Samuel Lubell, *The Future of American Politics* (New York: Doubleday Anchor Books, 1956); Paul F. Lazarsfeld *et al., The People's Choice* (New York: Duell, Sloan & Pearce, 1944); Angus Campbell *et al., The Voter Decides* (Evanston, Ill.: Row, Peterson, 1954).

[9] Key, *Public Opinion and American Democracy*, pp. 116–118.

[10] Nicholas A. Masters and Deil S. Wright, "Trends and Variations in the Two-Party Vote: The Case of Michigan," *American Political Science Review*, December 1958, pp. 1078–1090, esp. p. 1088.

bivalence" than workers generally, in part because the community norms were favorable to middle-class business groups and thus reinforced middle-class attitudes and weakened working-class attitudes.[11]

All of these characteristics tend to be empirically associated: for example, the voters with low incomes tend also to have little education, to include a high proportion of foreign-born and nonwhites, and to vote for Democratic candidates. One would like to "factor out" the causal significance of each separate element in this mixture, so as to be able to say, for example, "If education, ethnic origin, and party affiliation are all held constant and if income is varied, the effect on the vote will be thus and so"; but this is often very difficult.

The importance in voting behavior of ethnic identifications varies a good deal with the ethnic and class status of the voter. Usually it is impossible to disentangle this influence from others, like party affiliation, but occasionally a situation arises in which some light is shed on the subject. For example, from the data in Table 14 one can make a rough assessment of the importance which ethnic attachments had to the Boston electorate in 1962. The table shows how certain ethnically different precincts chose among ethnically different candidates in the state and national elections. It would be easy to "over-interpret" these figures; for one thing, although the parties are notoriously weak in Boston, party loyalty rather than ethnic loyalty accounts for some of the differences; moreover, one cannot be certain that voters did not vote *against* ethnic groups rather than *for* them (some of the lower-class Irish, for example, may have voted for Kelly, not because he was Irish but because his opponent was a Negro). Nevertheless, the figures show, we think, that in the absence of strong party organization, ethnic attachments may be of considerable importance, especially among lower-class voters. For example, the lower-income Italian precinct, deserting the Democratic party, voted more heavily for the Italian Republican running for governor that did the middle-income Italian precinct; this comports with our general hypothesis that as voters rise in socioeconomic status they attach less value to ethnic considerations, which are part of the immigrant political ethos.

The size and concentration of a particular ethnic group (or, for that matter, of certain social classes) in a city seems to affect voting turnout. This is often called the "bandwagon effect." Where, for example, Italians, Negroes, Poles, or laborers are a sizable percentage of the total

[11] Berelson *et al.*, *Voting*, pp. 56–57.

population and where they live in close proximity to one another, turn-out is greater than when they are fewer in number or less concentrated.[12]

TABLE 14. Voting in selected "ethnic" precincts in Boston, 1962

Candidate's ethnic and party identification	Percentage division of vote in five precincts composed predominantly of:				
	Middle-class Italians	Lower-class Italians	Middle-class Yankees	Lower-class Irish	Lower-class Negroes
FOR U.S. SENATOR					
Irish Democrat (Kennedy)	77	74	28	87	76
Yankee Republican (Lodge)	23	26	72	13	24
FOR GOVERNOR					
Yankee Democrat (Peabody)	47	32	36	81	52
Italian Republican (Volpe)	53	68	64	19	48
FOR STATE AT-TORNEY-GENERAL					
Irish Democrat (Kelly)	56	63	17	85	11
Negro Republican (Brooke)	44	37	83	15	89

The large city, by concentrating the population, provides a necessary (but not sufficient) condition for ethnic political activity. The various nationality and racial groups are sufficiently large that they believe they have some reasonable chance of affecting the outcome of elections; there are enough members of the group to feel a sense of group solidarity and to support their own political leaders and institutions; and they are sufficiently set apart from other groups to stimulate a sense of competition and even conflict.

POLITICAL ALIENATION

Voters are sometimes classified according to the way they "relate" themselves to the political scene. Those who feel that politics is meaningless and that they are powerless, and who exhibit symptoms of withdrawal, are "politically alienated." "A large proportion of the elec-

[12] Herbert Tingsten, *Political Behavior* (London: P. S. King, 1937), pp. 126–127; Lane, *Political Life*, p. 262; James K. Pollock, *Voting Behavior: A Case Study* (Ann Arbor: University of Michigan Press, 1941), p. 12.

torate," Murray B. Levin concluded after a study of the 1959 Boston mayoralty election, "feels politically powerless because it believes that the community is controlled by a small group of powerful and selfish individuals who use public office for personal gain. Many voters assume that this power elite is irresponsible and unaffected by the outcome of elections. Those who embrace this view feel that voting is meaningless because they see the candidates as undesirable and the electoral process as a sham."[13]

Alienation has been described in several cities. In Detroit, a sociologist found that more than half of his respondents believed they could do nothing to improve the way the city was run and another third believed they could do no more than vote.[14] In two upstate New York communities where school bond elections were held, a considerable number of voters felt powerless, hostile toward those who (they thought) wielded power in the community, and critical of public education. These alienated voters tended not to vote or, if they did vote, to vote "No."[15] In other places, opponents of fluoridation have been found to display "feelings of political inefficacy" and to believe themselves threatened by a powerful "they."[16] In Nashville, alienation was found to have contributed to the defeat of a proposal for metropolitan reorganization.[17]

In order to evaluate such findings, one must look at the way alienation is defined by the researchers and at the kinds of evidence brought

[13] Murray B. Levin, *The Alienated Voter* (New York: Holt, Rinehart & Winston, 1960), p. 458. See also Levin and Murray Eden, "Political Strategy for the Alienated Voter," *Public Opinion Quarterly,* Spring 1962, pp. 47–63, and Levin (with George Blackwood), *The Compleat Politician* (Indianapolis: Bobbs-Merrill, 1962). The meaning and value of Levin's arguments are considerably reduced by the fact that he does not describe his samples, show that they are representative of the electorate, or present his data tabulated by party, class, religion, ethnicity, and so forth.

[14] Arthur Kornhauser, *Attitudes of People Toward Detroit* (Detroit: Wayne State University Press, 1952), p. 28.

[15] Wayne E. Thompson and John E. Horton, "Political Alienation as a Force in Political Action," *Social Forces,* March 1960, pp. 190–195; and Horton and Thompson, "Powerlessness and Political Negativism: A Study of Defeated Referendums," *American Journal of Sociology,* March 1962, pp. 485–493.

[16] See William A. Gamson, "The Fluoridation Dialogue: Is It An Ideological Conflict?" *Public Opinion Quarterly,* Winter 1961, pp. 526–537; and Arnold Simmel, "A Signpost for Research on Fluoridation Conflicts: The Concept of Relative Deprivation," *Journal of Social Issues,* vol. XVII (1961), pp. 26–36.

[17] E. L. McDill and J. C. Ridley, "Status, Anomia, Political Alienation and Political Participation," *American Journal of Sociology,* September 1962, pp. 205–213.

forward to establish its existence. Do feelings of "meaninglessness" and "powerlessness" necessarily go together? If not, is the individual who feels that politics is meaningless alienated in the same sense as the one who feels that he is powerless? What kinds of behavior are to be taken as evidence of what the individual feels? If, for example, he tells an interviewer that he voted for a particular candidate because that candidate seemed "the lesser of two evils," is this evidence that he feels politics is meaningless?[18]

The difficulties in defining alienation operationally are well illustrated by the study of the vote on metropolitan consolidation in Nashville. In this study an alienated voter was defined as one who agreed with more of the following statements than did the median of the respondents:

1. The government of a big city like Nashville doesn't take much interest in a person's neighborhood.

2. The government of a big city like Nashville is too costly to the average taxpayer.

3. The average person can't get any satisfaction out of talking to the officials of a big city government like Nashville.

4. The government of a big city like Nashville is controlled too much by machine politics.

5. The average person doesn't have much to say about the running of a big city like Nashville.[19]

In our judgment it would be possible for an entirely reasonable and perhaps well-informed voter to agree emphatically with all of those statements. If this is so, it cannot be assumed that those who rate high on the scale have a distorted view of reality—"a *Weltanschauung* of being mastered by threatening forces"—and therefore one cannot predict how they will behave. The individual who has a distorted view (arising, perhaps, from "rootlessness" and "normlessness") toward all social and political reality will doubtless feel hostile and powerless toward Nashville *and he will so no matter what the reality of the situation may be.* Having diffuse feelings of hostility and "political inefficacy," he will discharge them against any convenient object. But an individual who believes on reasonable grounds (although perhaps mistakenly) that he is powerless in Nashville will doubtless behave dif-

[18] Cf. Levin, *The Alienated Voter,* p. 37.
[19] McDill and Ridley, p. 208.

ferently when he has, or thinks he has, reason to suppose that the situation has changed. For purposes of predicting behavior, it is therefore crucial to distinguish voters whose withdrawal is reasonable from ones whose withdrawal is not.

If alienation is to refer to generalized and diffuse feelings of hostility and inefficacy (as distinguished from "rational distrust"), clearly it cannot be measured on a scale like that quoted above. This is so because reasonable men—even those who have the same information—often differ fundamentally on general political questions. Any set of general statements about Nashville with which no reasonable (i.e., nonalienated) voters agreed would not be agreed to by many non-reasonable (i.e., alienated) ones either.

Voters who are alienated (in the significant sense) can be identified by the use of projective and other personality tests. Studies of their number and behavior would certainly be of great interest. Nevertheless, it would be easy to exaggerate the significance of the concept of alienation for the explanation of most voting behavior. Even if *all* voters were found to be alienated, one could not necessarily predict the outcome of an election. About all that one can predict is that alienated voters will tend: (a) to refrain from voting, (b) to vote *against* rather than *for* something or somebody, and (c) to vote against "bosses," "machines," "the power structure," and "professional politicians." It follows that in many interesting cases—for example, a contest between two "professionals"—the fact of alienation cannot afford any basis for prediction.

It is also possible, of course, that an alienated voter may, in return for favors received from a precinct captain, vote *for* rather than *against* the machine, the boss, and the professional. Possibly many lower-class voters have always been alienated and have only recently, because of the decay of machines and the absence of the incentives the machines offered, begun to express their alienation at the polls.

ETHOS AND VOTING BEHAVIOR

Throughout this book we have maintained that two fundamentally opposed conceptions of politics are to be found in the cities. One, which was Anglo-Saxon Protestant in its origins but has been accepted by the middle class in general (and particularly by many Jews), is essentially public-regarding; the other, which had its origins in the lower-class immigrant culture, is essentially private-regarding.[20] We have not asserted that every citizen has one ethos or the other, or that those who have an ethos have it in clear-cut and consistent form, or that those who have an ethos always behave in a manner consistent with it. We are not, therefore, in the position of having to show that all voters, or even that most voters, are decidedly public-regarding or decidedly private-regarding. Nevertheless, if the difference of ethos is as widespread and marked as we think, it should certainly show up in at least some voting behavior, and it might even be of general importance as an explanatory principle.

The hypotheses that might be derived from our discussion of ethos are primarily these: (1) that in all social classes the proportion of voters who are decidedly public-regarding is higher among Protestants than among other ethnic groups; (2) that in all social classes the proportion who are decidedly private-regarding is higher among those ethnic groups (e.g., Poles) whose conception of politics is, in the relevant respects, most opposed to the Protestant one; (3) that people in the upper-middle and upper classes are more public-regarding than those in the lower-middle class; (4) that people who are decidedly public-regarding or decidedly private-regarding on one matter tend to be so on all matters; and (5) that decidedly public-regarding and decidedly private-regarding voters tend to be further apart on all matters, including those which have no public-private dimension, than are other voters.

These hypotheses can be tested by first measuring the degree of the voters' public- (or private-) regardingness and then correlating this with his vote. The measure of public- (or private-) regardingness can be made in either of two ways. One may use interviews or attitude-scaling techniques to measure public-regardingness in the same way

[20] See especially our Chapter 3. Explanations for the Jewish political ethos have been suggested in Lawrence H. Fuchs, *The Political Behavior of American Jews* (Glencoe, Ill.: Free Press, 1956), and Werner Cohn, "The Politics of American Jews," in Marshall Sklare (ed.), *The Jews* (Glencoe, Ill.: Free Press, 1958), pp. 614–626. With class (i.e., the income of the family head) held constant, significant differences appear in the attitudes of Protestants and Catholics in attitudes toward business, the value of work, labor unions, and standards of public morality. Jews seem more likely to be similar to Protestants than to Catholics. See Gerhard Lenski, *The Religious Factor* (Garden City, N.Y.: Doubleday, 1961), pp. 82–102, 148–153; Oscar Glantz, "Protestant and Catholic Voting Behavior in a Metropolitan Area," *Public Opinion Quarterly*, Spring 1959, pp. 73–82; Albert S. Mayer and Harry Sharp, "Religious Preference and Worldly Success," *American Sociological Review*, April 1962, pp. 218–227.

that one may use them to measure alienation. Or, alternatively, one may classify as public-regarding all voters who on some occasion voted for an expenditure which they knew would yield them no private benefit but which would cost them something in taxes or otherwise. For example, all property owners of middle or more than middle income who vote to provide a hospital facility for the indigent, the costs of which are to be assessed against the voters, are public-regarding.

Having measured the public- (or private-) regardingness of the voter, it is not necessary, in order to test the hypotheses, to be able to say with respect to each issue or candidate whether a vote for or against is public-regarding or the contrary. It is only necessary to show that those voters who were identified as decidedly public- or decidedly private-regarding tended to vote the same way. However, with respect to some issues (and perhaps even some candidates) it should in some cases be possible to say how the public- (or private-) regarding voter ought to vote, or, more precisely, how the public-regarding voter ought *not* to vote. A voter may have many reasons, both public- and private-regarding, to vote against a hospital for the indigent, for example, but if he is a person of middle or upper income he can have (for all practical purposes) no reason that is not public-regarding to vote *for* it.

One would expect public-regarding voters to favor proposals for metropolitan reorganization, regional planning, fluoridation of water supplies, city manager government, and the like. The rhetoric by which such proposals are usually justified is largely, if not entirely, in terms of "public interest" and, whatever the merits of the proposals, a voter would not normally be prompted by private interest to vote for them whereas he might well be prompted by private interest to vote against them.

Such evidence as we have been able to collect tends to support these hypotheses. In Cook County, Illinois, elections in 1957–1958, Chicago's upper-income residential suburbs heavily favored an expenditure to expand the county hospital, whereas the lower-income (but nevertheless property-owning) suburbs heavily opposed it. Since the hospital was used by indigents and the expansion of it would be paid for out of the property tax, only public-regardingness could explain a favorable vote from a high-income property owner. Such a vote suggests that public-regardingess ought in general to be found positively correlated with high income and negatively correlated with low income when the rate of homeownership (and thus liability to property taxes) is held constant. In fact, allowing for certain exceptions, most of which tend to confirm our general hypothesis, this seems to be the case.[21]

In Cleveland, favorable voting on expenditures for a county hospital in November 1959 was *negatively* correlated with the rate of homeownership in each of the city's thirty-three wards.[22] The higher the proportion of property owners (and thus of property-tax payers) in a ward, the lower the vote for the hospital. (See Figure 2.) Two deviations from this pattern are important, however. First, the three wards circled in Figure 2 were much more favorable to the measure than their rate of homeownership would have predicted; we suggest that this is because those three wards were also the highest in median home value. Second, wards which were two thirds or more Negro were much more favorable to the expenditure than were those other wards (most of which were heavily Polish Catholic) with the same level of homeownership. For all wards—although much less so for Negro and upper-income wards—higher rates of homeownership apparently produce greater sensitivity to costs and thus greater opposition to public expenditures. This is in accord with our hypothesis.

Nevertheless, public-regarding conceptions of the general interest are not a simple reflex of tax consciousness, as can be shown by using data in which the rate of homeownership is held constant. This is possible by using figures from Flint, Michigan, a city which—like others in the state—restricts voting on expenditure items to property owners and their spouses. Here, the higher the average home value in a precinct the larger the percentage of voters who favor public expenditures, including ones which will benefit the owners of less expensive homes

[21] On one issue—bonuses for veterans of the Korean War—the upper-income suburbs were most opposed, whereas the lower-income ones were least opposed. We feel that in this case also the upper-income people voted on public-regarding and the lower-income ones on private-regarding grounds. The bonus was to be paid by the state, i.e., not from the property tax; a lower-income property owner would therefore not expect to pay much toward it. Upper-income voters, in short, seem to have a conception of the public interest which attaches a high value to certain institutional benefits for disadvantaged people or for the community "as a whole," while attaching a negative value to measures such as the veterans' bonus which can be regarded as "give-aways" to "organized special interests."

[22] Although voter turnout in the hospital bond election was not high, the same set of relationships described above held in all other bond issues, including ones voted on in the November 1960 Presidential election when turnout was very high.

FIGURE 2. Relation between percentage voting "yes" on proposition to provide increased county hospital facilities (November 1959) and percentage of dwelling units owner-occupied in the 33 wards of Cleveland

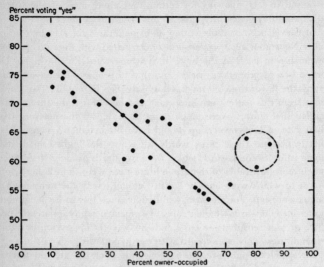

Note: Wards circled are those with the highest median home value.
Source of housing data: U.S. Census of Housing, 1960.

mainly and will be paid for disproportionately by the owners of the more expensive ones. This relationship is shown in a scatter diagram in Figure 3. Here, too, the Negro precincts (circled in the figure) tend to be deviants—voting more favorably for public expenditures than other precincts of comparable home value.

Voting returns from Cuyahoga County (outside Cleveland) tend to confirm and amplify these findings. Support for public expenditures comes generally from wealthy residential suburbs, suburbs where most voters are renters rather than homeowners, and suburbs where there is a substantial middle-class Jewish population. Opposition to these expenditures is found among industrial and working-class suburbs where there is a large proportion of homeowners of modest means. Data such as these test the public-regardingness of upper-income groups which have little or nothing to gain and something to lose by a public expenditure (the issues reported above were almost all of this

FIGURE 3. Relation between percentage voting "yes" on proposition to provide additional flood control facilities (November 1960) and median value of owner-occupied dwelling units in the precincts of Flint, Michigan

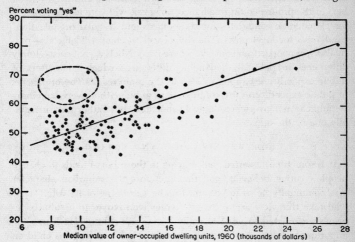

Note: Precincts circled are 90 percent or more Negro. Only property owners and their spouses could vote.

Source of housing data: U.S. Census of Housing, 1960.

kind), but the data do not test the public-regardingness of the lowest-income group, which often has much to gain and little to lose by a public expenditure.[23] Our hypothesis is that this low-income group will prove to be private-regarding when put to the test; we have not as yet found a situation in which it has been put to the test, however.

That the voting alliances which support public expenditures are composed of groups with differing conceptions of the public interest is suggested by the fact that the alliance collapses in elections for public officials. The upper-income group will (as in St. Louis and in Kansas

[23] It may be argued that the willingness of upper-income people to support public expenditures signifies only that the value of the dollar is less to them, i.e., that they buy more "charity" for the same reason that they buy more steaks and more Cadillacs. This is undoubtedly a factor. But the lower marginal utility of the dollar to the wealthy does not explain their vote against *some* expenditures (e.g., the Korean veterans' bonus mentioned above); in some instances upper-income voters have opposed expenditures which would benefit them while at the same time supporting others (e.g., public housing) which could not possibly benefit them.

City, where we have examined election returns) vote overwhelmingly for Republican candidates for partisan state offices and "good government" candidates for local offices. The lower-income and Negro members of the pro-expenditure alliance, however, will vote just as strongly for Democratic candidates for state offices and "regular organization" candidates for local posts. The differences in choice of officials—particularly in nonpartisan contests, where party labels do not exist—imply differences in political motivation, differences which on matters of public expenditure happen to lead to the same result. The opponents of public expenditures, by contrast, tend to be neither overwhelmingly Republican nor overwhelmingly Democratic, but rather only marginally one or the other.

SUBURBANIZATION AND VOTING

It is sometimes asserted that moving to the suburbs tends to change people's voting behavior, and that therefore the suburban character of a community helps to account for the patterning of its vote. Those who take this view argue that the voter who moves to a suburb becomes assimilated to what is really a new sub-culture. He learns the importance of "keeping up property values," of harassing his children into being "high achievers" in school, of joining and participating. In the same way, he learns a new style of politics, identifies with a set of political symbols, and acquires a new (Republican) party affiliation.

Although the evidence is fragmentary, it does not bear this theory out. National party affiliation is seldom changed by a move to the suburbs. Probably one reason why the data do not support the theory is that the theory erroneously identifies "suburb" with "middle-class suburb." In fact, as we have explained, there are industrial as well as residential suburbs, old and decaying ones as well as new and burgeoning ones, and blue-collar as well as white-collar ones. Some suburbs have a considerable Negro component; some are largely Jewish or Catholic.[24] It cannot be assumed, therefore, that the people who move to the suburbs—certainly not that those who move to any given suburb —are entering a social *milieu* that is significantly different from the one they left. Indeed, it seems likely that, in general, people select suburbs in such a way as to avoid any very sharp break with the style of life and, especially, the "kind of people" that they are accustomed to. Predominantly Republican suburbs probably attract Republicans

[24] See the discussion of this in the leading book on suburban politics, Robert C. Wood, *Suburbia* (Boston: Houghton Mifflin, 1959), pp. 114–121.

and predominantly Democratic suburbs probably attract Democrats.

Charles Edson found that in the suburbs of St. Louis County, there was little evidence of ticket-switching among persons who had moved in. Most poeple continued to vote as they had always voted; thus, class and family background continued to be the most important factors with which partisanship could be correlated.[25] Robert C. Wood found that the suburbs of Boston differed greatly in voting trends from 1940 to 1954. Suburbs which were becoming more Democratic had been Democratic from the beginning; those which were becoming more strongly Republican had always been Republican. As lower-income families displaced upper-income families from suburbs close to the central city, these suburbs changed from Republican to Democratic. No suburb changed in the other direction. This is to be expected, for it is unlikely that upper-income families would move into lower-income suburbs.[26]

Four suburban counties outside New York City—Nassau, Rockland, Suffolk, and Westchester—appear to be becoming more Democratic with almost every election.[27] They are being inundated with new arrivals from the city who show little sign of succumbing to the Republicanism of the older residents. David Wallace, in a study of Westport (Connecticut), one of New York's wealthiest and most distant suburbs, found that almost everybody continued to vote for the same party as their parents even though most of them had moved to Westport only since World War II.[28] Indeed, the only changes were, by and large, changes favoring the Democrats rather than the Republicans, particularly among white Protestants and Jews. These new arrivals had more education than the older residents and included a higher proportion of Jews. Presumably suburbs of comparable income levels which have not attracted Jewish residents would show changes which were less favorable to the Democrats.

When all of the necessary qualifications are made, the hypothesis that suburbanization has an effect on voting patterns is highly plausible, however. Where it does in fact involve the movement of lower middle-class people into middle-class communities, a fundamental change is probably produced in the political ethos of the newcomers.

25 Charles Edson, "The Suburban Vote," senior honor's thesis, Harvard University, June 1956. Quoted in Wood, *Suburbia*, pp. 144–145.

26 Wood, *Suburbia*, pp. 146–149.

27 See Ralph A. Straetz and Frank J. Munger, *New York Politics* (New York: University Press, 1960), pp. 41–45.

28 David Wallace, "Shifts in One Suburb's Voting Patterns," *Public Opinion Quarterly*, Fall 1962, pp. 486–487.

Even where suburbanization does not involve this kind of upward mobility, it may have important political effects. When people of the middle or upper-middle class are in such an overwhelming majority as to constitute the only "kind of people" in the community, their political ideal is likely to be expressed in a relatively pure form, as it is, for example, in Winnetka, the upper-middle-class suburb of Chicago described in Chapter 11.

Robert C. Wood has argued at length that middle-class suburbia produces, or reinforces, a pattern of community attachments and political attitudes different from that in the central city.[29] The pattern Wood describes is strikingly like the middle-class political ethos in its principled concern for the community as a whole, its insistence upon the importance of honesty, efficiency, and impartiality in the conduct of public affairs, its dislike of party politics and of all "artificial" cleavages, and its acceptance of an obligation to participate in community affairs and to "serve" the public. Opportunities exist for expressing this same ethos in the big city, of course: a young lawyer can serve the community by leading a reform movement against the "bosses" and a businessman can serve it by promoting an urban renewal project to restore the downtown buisness district. In the big city, however, the middle-class ideal is in competition with other views and usually the others—the "system"—will prevail. In middle-class suburbia, there is no "system," unless the middle-class ideal itself be counted as one, and accordingly one can do the "right thing" with less effort, with greater chance of success, and—perhaps most important—with less risk of hurting one's business or professional career.

This is not to say that middle-class suburban politics is issueless. Suburbanites often display an active, even an intense, concern. But their concern is usually about matters which do not involve reference to national party affiliations. The local tax rate, the curriculum of the schools, zoning and subdivision regulations—matters like these can be discussed and fought over by people who are essentially like-minded and who divide into camps solely on the merits of the issue as they see it. The problem that beset the big-city reformer—that many of his natural allies cannot support him because they belong to the other national party—rarely arises in middle-class suburbs.

[29] Wood, *Suburbia*, chaps. iv, v, and vi, esp. pp. 153–185.

CHAPTER 17 · POWER STRUCTURE AND CIVIC LEADERSHIP

THE AMERICAN CITY is not run by its politicians and bureaucrats alone. They have the help—often the hindrance as well—of a vast array of formal and informal associations and of individuals who, although occupying no office and having no authority, nevertheless play important and sometimes leading parts in the making of public decisions. In this chapter we shall discuss the nature of this informal "power structure," offer some reasons why it is characteristic of American but not of other cities, and focus attention on such unofficial activities as are in some sense community-serving in intention ("civic leadership") and on the formal organizations ("civic associations") which are the vehicle of much of the activity. In later chapters we shall look closely at other sectors of the power structure—businessmen, organized labor, and the press.

POWER STRUCTURE

The term "power structure" was popularized by a sociologist, Floyd Hunter, who found in a study of "Regional City" (Atlanta, Georgia) that about forty "power leaders," most of them businessmen, "set the line on policy" in city affairs while an "understructure" of about several hundred persons, including the principal elected and appointed city officials, merely carried out the policies decided upon by the very few at the top of the power pyramid. "The structure," Hunter wrote, "is that of a dominant policy-making group using the machinery of government as a bureaucracy for the attainment of certain goals coordinate with the interests of the policy-making group."[1]

Later investigators, using other research methods and studying cities that were doubtless very different from Atlanta, found power structures which, if they deserved to be called that at all, were entirely unlike that described by Hunter. In New Haven, for example, Robert A. Dahl found a highly pluralistic system, characterized by "stubborn and per-

[1] Floyd Hunter, *Community Power Structure* (Chapel Hill: University of North Carolina Press, 1953), p. 102.

vasive ambiguity," in which both leaders and led, drawn from many strata of the community and occupying diverse roles, both led and were led, and in which it was necessary to distinguish "direct" influence (possessed by relatively few) from "indirect" (possessed by a great many).[2] In Chicago, one of the present authors found that the heads of the Democratic party machine had ample power to decide almost any matter. For various reasons they preferred to "ratify" proposals put before them by affected interests, when the interests agreed among themselves, rather than to initiate proposals themselves. When the affected interests disagreed among themselves, the elected officials followed the strategy of delaying a decision as long as possible while at the same time encouraging those concerned to put pressure upon them. From the amount and nature—especially the "representativeness"—of this pressure they found cues by which to form an estimate of how the matter was viewed by the public at large. The elected official, according to this account, "feels that it is his duty to do what 'a broad cross-section of the community' wants"; efforts to influence him help him sense what the community wants.[3]

Despite such very important differences from city to city—differences that may be explainable largely but not entirely in terms of methodology[4]—one thing is common to all: persons not elected to

[2] Robert A. Dahl, Who Governs? (New Haven: Yale University Press, 1962). The quoted phrase is on p. 102.

[3] Banfield, Political Influence (New York: Free Press of Glencoe, 1961), p. 287. For critical discussions of many other studies of influence and power, see Nelson W. Polsby, "Power in Middletown: Fact and Value in Community Research," Canadian Journal of Economics and Political Science, November 1960, pp. 592–603.

[4] The method of Hunter and others is to ask presumably well-informed people ("judges") to rank according to relative "power" the "top leaders" of the city. Those nominated are then asked about their activities, associations, and friendships. The patterns thus revealed—"sociometric choices"—are assumed to describe "who really runs things" in the city. The method of Dahl, Banfield, and others is to discover who initiates, modifies, or blocks action on controversial matters. Attributions of power or influence, as distinguished from evidence of its exercise in concrete cases, are not relied upon. For discussion of the methodological question, see, in addition to the books already cited in this chapter, Herbert Kaufman and Victor A. Jones, "The Mystery of Power," Public Administration Review, Summer 1954, pp. 205–212; Nelson W. Polsby, "How to Study Community Power; the Pluralist Alternative," Journal of Politics, vol. XXII (1960), pp. 474–484; Polsby, "Three Problems in the Analysis of Community Power," American Sociological Review, December 1959, pp. 796–803; Raymond E. Wolfinger, "Reputation and Reality in the Study of Community Power," American Sociological Review, October 1960, pp. 636–644; Peter H. Rossi, "Community Decision-Making," Administrative Science Quarterly, June 1956, pp. 415–554; and Rossi, "Power and Community Structure," Midwest Journal of Political Science, November 1960, pp. 390–401; Howard J. Ehrlich, "The Reputational Approach to the Study of Community

office play very considerable parts in the making of many important decisions. The differences among cities in this regard (especially if Atlanta be left out of account) are more in degree than in kind. Public affairs in New Haven and Chicago, although not "run" by tiny, informal "power elites," are nevertheless much influenced by persons who occupy no official position.

Those who exercise power unofficially (we will call such people "influentials") do so for ends that range from self-serving or business-serving to group-serving or community-serving. A group of business-men, for example, may urge an urban renewal project upon the city for no other purpose than to make money. Or again such a group may urge a project out of concern for the welfare of some part of the city's population ("the better class of people") or from concern for the welfare of the city as a whole ("restoring the central city will be good for everybody"). Almost always motives in such matters are extremely mixed. The Urban League may be supported by some contributors who do so for purely business reasons, by others who think "the community needs it," and by still others whose motives are of both sorts. Distinc-tions along these lines, despite the impossibility of applying them unambiguously in many concrete cases, are indispensable in a dis-cussion of influence in the city. We shall distinguish exercises of influences that are "business-serving" from those that are "public-serving." Civic activity and civic leadership, as we shall use the terms, consist only of exercises of influence that are largely, or mainly, public-serving. Thus, insofar as a banker member of a housing improvement association seeks to serve the interests of his bank he is an "interest group representative" and insofar as he seeks to serve the interests (as he sees them) of the whole public, or of some considerable sector of it, he is a "civic leader."

AMERICAN POLITICAL CULTURE
AND PRIVATE INFLUENCE

The active participation of private parties in the conduct of public business, whether as interest group representatives or as civic leaders, is a peculiarly American phenomenon. In many other free countries, it

Power," *American Sociological Review*, December 1961, pp. 926–927; William V. D'Antonio and Eugene C. Erickson, "The Reputational Technique as a Measure of Community Power: An Evaluation Based on Comparative and Longitudinal Studies," *American Sociological Review*, June 1962, pp. 362–376.

is taken for granted that public affairs are to be managed solely by those who have been elected or appointed to office; no others may participate in the management of them, although they may, of course, make their views known and, when an election is held, give or withhold consent. In London, for example, there is not even a chamber of commerce or a taxpayers' association, and no businessman would dream of "giving leadership" to a local council from behind the scenes. If he wanted to take part in local government he would stand for election, and if he won a seat he would regard himself as the representative of a public, not of the "business community."[5]

The presence of the influential on the American civic scene is to be accounted for on several grounds. The most important of these, perhaps, is the decentralization of authority that is so characteristic of the American political system. In Europe, the formally constituted authorities have ample power to carry out whatever schemes they may decide upon. In our country, by contrast, authority is almost always fragmented. Accordingly, the businessman (or anyone else) finds it easy to "get in on the act." Because he can check the public official, he can also bargain with him; as it is usually expressed, the official "needs his cooperation." Businessmen are active in American civic affairs, then, because the nature of the political system encourages them to get and use influence.

Another reason for the influential's presence in civic affairs is that the community (or at least some sections of it) often has more respect for his judgment and integrity than for those of the politician or bureaucrat. Rightly or wrongly, local politicians and bureaucrats are seldom held in very high regard; the politician is often considered an "opportunist" at best and the bureaucrat is usually thought to lack enterprise and imagination. As the mayor of Minneapolis recently explained,

It is apparent that we have not yet evolved in America an understandable and acceptable role or status for the politician. The rewards of our economy and of our society are attached to other pursuits, notably to the professions and to business generally. "Success" is still identified with the amassing of wealth and the acquiring of economic "position." To some extent we now

[5] See Delbert C. Miller's two articles: "Industry and Community Power Structure: A Comparative Study of an American and an English City," *American Sociological Review*, February 1958, pp. 9–14, and "Decision-Making Cliques in Community Power Structure: A Comparative Study of an American and an English City," *American Journal of Sociology*, November 1958, pp. 299–310.

attach status to the leaders of the clergy and in higher education, but for the politician status is variable and uncertain. We do not have a tradition that regards the role of the civil servant or of the public official as involving a form of "calling" or dedicated service, such as religious or educational leadership.[6]

Since it is success in other than public service pursuits, especially business, that distinguishes the man of great capacity in our culture, it is not surprising that when a city wants assurance that its affairs are being managed efficiently it often turns to a businessman for "expert" opinion. In some cities politicians almost routinely exhibit to the electorate some "seal of approval" given by business and other civic leaders.[7] In others (Boston, for example) there are formal arrangements by which lay bodies are given powers to make continuing investigations of the conduct of city affairs.

The influential is often valued as much for his status attributes as for his judgment. One of the functions of much civic activity is to give some people an opportunity to "rub elbows" with others and by so doing to demonstrate that they and the institutions and causes they represent are worthy and statusful. Businessmen "keep score" on one another's prestige, and on the prestige of one another's firm, by noting who serves on the board of this or that civic association. For them and for others, sitting at the head table with "important" people may be a very rewarding experience.

The influential also serves a symbolic function in civic affairs. One who presides on public occasions must "represent" something to which the whole community aspires or gives allegiance. In England this is always the person closest to the throne. Lord So-and-So is the chairman of the committee to raise funds for the new hospital because in some mysterious way he partakes of the charisma attaching to royalty. Americans have to select their human symbols on a different basis, and often they select one who partakes of the charisma attaching to wealth. This need not mean that Americans are more materialistic than the British—only that it is much harder for Americans to symbolize what they have in common. According to Peter B. Clark, the businessman civic leader symbolizes a complex of widely held values, not only wealth but also achievement, efficiency, respectability, soundness,

---

[6] Arthur Naftalin, in *The City*, a pamphlet published by the Center for the Study of Democratic Institutions (Santa Barbara, Calif., 1952), p. 34.

[7] See Banfield, *Political Influence*, p. 276 ff.

public-spiritedness, and the qualities that make for local growth and expansion.[8]

Still another reason for the influential's role is that he shares with the general public the view that he owes the community a debt of service. He may not make any payments on this debt; indeed, he may even serve himself at the expense of the public. Nevertheless, he agrees in principle that he is under a moral obligation to "serve." This is an idea which businessmen in many other cultures, even the British, would find quixotic and which is seldom entertained even by members of "old" and "noble" families.

Finally, businessmen and other influentials are encouraged to participate in civic affairs because they and their fellow citizens think that they ought to help promote the economic growth and prosperity of the city. For generations Americans have been making money from the rise in land values and the increase in commercial and industrial activity that have accompanied urban expansion; even those people who have not owned land or had other direct economic interest in growth have enjoyed a psychic income from living in cities that are "going somewhere." Americans, in short, are natural-born civic boosters, and the more influential they are the more powerfully they are expected to boost.

THE VARIETY OF CIVIC AUTHORITY

Peter B. Clark divided the universe of civic activity in Chicago into five subject matter fields which differ in personnel, style of operation, and significance for public policy.[9] Although based on one very large city, Clark's findings are, we think, reasonably representative of a pattern that exists in most large and (in abbreviated form) many small ones. His five fields of civic activity are these:

1. *Race relations and inter-faith activities.* The welfare of the Negro, and to a lesser extent of the Jew and the Catholic as well, is the special concern of one set of civic leaders. The leaders in this field are not the most influential, wealthy, or prestigious ones. They tend to be Jewish and Catholic businessmen or lawyers or else to be second-level corpora-

[8] Peter B. Clark, "Civic Leadership: The Symbols of Legitimacy," paper delivered before the annual meeting of the American Political Science Association, New York City, September 1960.

[9] Peter B. Clark, "The Chicago Big Businessman as a Civic Leader," unpublished dissertation, Department of Political Science, University of Chicago, 1959. See also Wallace S. Sayre and Herbert Kaufman, *Governing New York City* (New York: Russell Sage Foundation, 1960), pp. 76–80 and chap. xiii.

tion executives assigned to race-relations work by their companies. Much of their activity is behind the scenes. Civic associations in this field issue press releases on what are for them particularly important issues; for the most part, however, they work through private discussions with employers, politicians, and others whose cooperation is wanted. Big businessmen tend to steer clear of this field because they consider it controversial.

2. *Good-government activities.* In Chicago there are three principal associations in this field. One of them analyzes the records of local candidates for election and makes recommendations to the voters; another sponsors panel discussions of city and metropolitan problems and proposes new policies and changes in the structure of government; and the third keeps track of criminal activities and the operation of law enforcement agencies. Most of the civic leaders in this field are Protestants who have a religious, or quasi-religious, concern for "improving public morality"—a motive, incidentally, that is not conspicuous in the other fields of civic activity. Their tactic is to carry on "a constant but low-keyed harassment of politicians through the newspapers"; the effect of this, if any, is by its very nature hard to identify. Partly for this reason, perhaps, the most influential, wealthy, and prestigious civic leaders find the good-government field "uninteresting" when it is not "too controversial."

3. *Welfare and fund-raising activities.* Chicago raises about $250,-000,000 a year by public subscription for charitable purposes. Organizing the various "drives" to collect money and giving general policy direction to the welfare professionals who spend it are what civic leaders in this field do. These leaders are of two general types: men of great wealth who contribute generously and representatives of the large corporations which put up most of the money in practically all "drives." Corporations take turns assigning their executives to service on civic fund-raising committees. Being on such a committee is, both for a wealthy family and for a corporation, a way of meeting a "civic responsibility" and of carrying on "good public relations." Civic leaders in this field do not, however, have much influence in public affairs by virtue of these activities.

4. *Cultural, university, and hospital work.* Those at the very pinnacle of civic prestige—people who have great inherited wealth or who are the heads of large corporations—are the trustees and officers of universities, hospitals, and art and other museums. These institu-

tions have big real estate holdings in the city and are in many other ways sensitive to political and other changes; therefore their trustees are frequently called upon to exercise influence on their behalf.

5. *Business promotion, construction, and planning activities.* Decisions affecting the growth and prosperity of the central city, and above all of the downtown business section, particularly decisions about urban renewal, expressway routes, port development, airport improvement, and the location of major public buildings, are a field of civic activity in which bankers, real estate men, and department store owners and other businessmen are prominent. There are, of course, always differences of interest and opinion among those who are concerned with these matters. To a large extent, therefore, civic activity in this field consists of efforts by civic leaders to reach agreement among themselves with regard to the recommendations that are to be made to the public authorities and, when agreement cannot be reached, of competitive efforts by the various factions of civic leaders to get their plans accepted and those of their opponents rejected or delayed.

Clark found that most Chicago civic leaders usually confine most of their civic activity to one or another of these fields, and that they are poorly informed about the fields in which they are not actually involved. The preoccupation of the wealthiest "old families" and of the heads of the largest corporations with cultural, university, and hospital work tends to make them unavailable for participation in the other fields of civic activity and therefore to leave civic leadership in these other fields to persons in the second rank of wealth and prestige.

THE CIVIC ASSOCIATION

Much (but by no means all) civic activity takes place through the medium of voluntary associations—"the characteristic social unit of the modern city," as Oscar Handlin has called them.[10] Few cities are too small to have at least one or two associations devoted to the cause of civic welfare, and in the larger cities there are scores or even hundreds. Not many associations take the whole range of city affairs as their domain; most are highly specialized, confining themselves to some sector of one of the subject matter fields listed above. Some have long histories, large memberships, and big budgets, and others are no

---

[10] In Lloyd Rodwin (ed.), *The Future Metropolis* (New York: George Braziller, 1961), p. 22.

more than names on a letterhead. Some are ceaselessly active in governmental affairs; others are active only intermittently.[11]

A civic association is held together largely, or even entirely, by general, nonmaterial (intangible) inducements, especially the opportunity to enjoy mutual association and to serve the community.[12] Having no specific, material inducements to offer, the association cannot put its members under a strict discipline; it may entice or persuade them but it cannot order them, and it must always be on the lookout for "program material" that will attract their interest and create enthusiasm for the organization and its purposes. What Wallace Sayre and Herbert Kaufman say of New York City civic associations—that they are "run by relatively small inner cores of activists"—may be said also of the associations in other cities.[13] Even the activists, though they often spend much of their time on association drives, have no vital personal stake in them (no one entrusts his vital interests to an organization he cannot control). The nonactivists' connection is often entirely nominal.

The "voluntary" character of the civic association greatly influences its choice of activities—those it does not engage in as well as those it does. For one thing, it is constantly under the necessity of convincing its members that they are accomplishing something worthwhile through it. But it must do this without touching anything controversial; even though a large majority of its membership approves its stand in a controversial matter, it risks losing the support of the minority who do not. Usually it deals with this dilemma in one or both of two ways: it gives the members prestige, publicity, and other such satisfactions in lieu of a sense of accomplishment, and it substitutes evidence of accomplishment of means for evidence of accomplishment of ends. The Philadelphia Housing Association, for example, cannot show accomplishment in terms of its ultimate end, the improvement of housing,

[11] The variety of nongovernmental groups in New York is well described by Sayre and Kaufman, *Governing New York City*, pp. 76–80.

[12] Peter B. Clark and James Q. Wilson, in their "Incentive Systems: A Theory of Organization," *Administrative Science Quarterly*, September 1961, pp. 129–166, distinguish three types of voluntary association: the *material*, which exists primarily to get tangible benefits for its members (e.g., a taxpayers' association); the *purposive*, which exists primarily to get intangible or ideological benefits (e.g., the National Association for the Advancement of Colored People); and the *solidary*, which exists primarily to afford the members the satisfactions of mutual association (e.g., B'nai B'rith). Their analysis of the significance of these differences in incentive systems for the role and strategy of associations in civic affairs is drawn upon in what follows.

[13] Sayre and Kaufman, *Governing New York City*, p. 481.

but it can show that it is doing many things that presumably further that end. Thus, according to a recent issuance,

the Association undertakes research and data analysis in fields of concern; sponsors publications, public meetings, filmstrips, tours, and other educational and informational activities; regularly publishes ISSUES; provides counseling and assistance to individuals and groups; evaluates public programs and confers with public officials; operates two area committees; and organizes extensive committee activities. In all of its efforts, the Association works closely with other social agencies and with public agencies responsible for carrying out housing and renewal programs.

A civic association is in a particularly advantageous position if its activity is believed to be instrumental to the attainment of *several* ends. Even if the ends are mutually incompatible, it will be supported by those who entertain the ends, provided, of course, that it does not foolishly specify which of the incompatible ends it is trying to attain. The Community Service Organization in Los Angeles, for example, has had extraordinary success in registering Mexicans as voters: turnout among Mexicans, many of whom are low-income immigrants, is now among the highest of any group in the country. The organization's supporters (competing politicians, labor unions, and church groups) have different and in some cases opposed interests in getting out the Mexican vote; they support the organization *because* its goal is purely instrumental.

Selecting ends that are both very vague and very worthy makes it especially easy for a civic association to claim accomplishment. It can make its claims "without fear of contradiction" because the very vagueness of the end guarantees that the specific activities it engages in cannot be shown to be ineffective.

Civic associations often impress their members with their prestige, power, and accomplishment by establishing their right to be consulted by public officials. A politician who wants an association's "support" (not necessarily a declaration by it in favor of his candidacy; perhaps nothing more than a favorable reference to him in its newsletter or an invitation to sit at the head table at its annual dinner) may defer publicly to its views before making important appointments or policy proposals in the subject-matter field that is of particular concern to it. The consultative role of the civic association has in many places been given legal, or quasi-legal, standing. For example, the mayor of New

York, in making appointments to the board of education, is required by state law to consider the recommendations of "representative associations, civil, educational, business, labor and professional groups active or interested in the field of education and child welfare." Whether formal or informal, such arrangements give an association something to point to with pride when the time comes to report some accomplishment to its members. To be sure, the politician may ignore the association's recommendation when he gets it and, even if he acts on the recommendation, the appointee does not necessarily take the policy positions that the association would like him to take. Nevertheless, it can claim—often with justice—that it has had some influence, albeit indirect, on events.

The Influence of the Professional Staff

A large and well-established civic association employs a professional staff to do research, maintain relations with government officials, the press, and other civic associations, put out press releases and publications, and prepare program material for the membership. Because the association represents a job to the professionals and only an avocation to the officers, and because the professionals are necessarily in much closer touch with the details of the association's affairs, *de facto* control is usually in the hands of the staff. By making recommendations as to who should be put on the board and "groomed for leadership," by "training" new board members to the organizational (i.e., staff) point of view, by selecting program material, by using "research" to influence policy, by writing speeches and press releases for uncritical and often uninterested officers and board members, the staff may—and indeed often must—play a principal part in deciding the association's character, style, and strategy. The civic leaders who are the nominal heads of the association can hardly prevent this if they try: they are too busy with more important (private-serving) activities to take charge and, moreover, they realize that the staff must have a considerable degree of freedom if it is to serve the association effectively.

The staff man, having a large personal stake in the maintenance and enhancement of the organization, is particularly sensitive to the dangers of controversy. He avoids doing anything that might split the association or impart to it an "unfavorable image." If a point is reached where some substantial achievement in terms of the association's ends can be made only at the cost of losing some membership support, he is likely to forego the achievement. Not to do so, he would say, would destroy the "effectiveness" of the organization in the long run.

The ideological bent of the staff man is often different from that of the civic leaders who comprise his board of directors. He is selected, usually on the recommendation of other staff people, for his ability to assemble facts, write memoranda on policy matters, get along with people (especially those in government, academic, and professional circles), and for his commitment to public-serving, as distinguished from private-serving, ends.[14] He is apt, therefore, to share the views—conventional wisdom, it may be—of the occupational groups in which he was trained, with which he works, and to which he looks for approval. Consciously or otherwise, he often "feeds" to the officers and members of the association a policy line which is different from the one they would choose for themselves and which may even run directly counter to their interests and views. In Boston, for example, an association of conservative Republican businessmen undertook to make recommendations with regard to local tax policy. The staff they employed—liberal Democrats, as it happened—submitted a report which recommended (among other things) a graduated income tax. The businessmen signed the report and published it as a matter of course, although none of them favored an income tax and although there were no grounds for supposing that the staff's view of what "the public interest" required was any more defensible than the businessmen's.

The Ineffectiveness of Associations

Civic associations are rarely effective in terms of their stated ends. Several reasons for this must be apparent from what has already been

[14] For example, in the fall of 1962 the Philadelphia Housing Association was seeking an assistant director for its professional staff of four (managing director, assistant director, research director, and community worker). The position paid $6,700 to $10,000, depending upon the experience of the person chosen. The qualifications were as follows:

Graduate study, preferably in government or public administration. At least three years of experience in a public or private agency involved in some aspect of urban renewal.

Commitment to the public interest and the objectives and program of the Housing Association.

General interest in urban problems and some knowledge of the literature.

Ability to gather information on specific topics quickly and accurately, and relate it to over-all policy considerations.

Ability to write easily and to speak with facility.

Ability to get along well with people of varying backgrounds and viewpoints.

said. The civic leader has no vital personal interest at stake; the association cannot give him orders; its ends must be vague or instrumental to give him the illusion at least of accomplishment. These circumstances tend strongly to prevent any concrete accomplishment. Even more important is the association's deeply ingrained fear of controversy. The larger and more "powerful" (prestigious and well-financed) an association and—what often goes with this—the more completely it is controlled by its staff, the less likely it is to risk any loss of support by taking up a cause that its members consider controversial. In his study of civic activity in Chicago, Clark found that the large, permanent civic associations were generally ineffective because, even in the matters that concerned them most, they would not do anything that might alienate some of their support. In some instances, Clark found, they "took ambiguous positions; they could not influence politicians because the politicians did not know what the associations actually wanted. On other issues the associations took no stands at all; they withdrew. In still other issues, when they did take positions they used ineffective tactics."[15]

Associations which make their appeal to some highly homogeneous—and therefore relatively small—sector of the public are in a very different position in these respects from associations which make their appeal to the whole public or to some large—and consequently heterogeneous—sector of it. For example, the Parent-Teacher Association, which wants a large membership drawn from all walks of life, must avoid anything deeply controversial. On the other hand the National Association for the Advancement of Colored People, which wants a membership that will fight for racial justice, must have an uncompromising commitment to ends that (from the standpoint of the community, but not of its membership) are "extreme" and controversial. The controversy that is poison to the large, broadly based association is the staff of life to the small, narrowly based one. The very smallness of an association tends to become a cause of its remaining small; for in order to maintain itself it must appeal to extremists or deeply committed persons, and by doing this it condemns itself to remain small. And smallness usually means that it is relatively poor and ineffectual as well.

A circumstance which has further tended to make civic associations ineffective is the practice, now widespread, of financing many of them

[15] Clark, "Chicago Big Businessman," p. 119.

partly from the receipts of united community fund drives. Since this money is given by the public at large, organizations receiving it are required to refrain from "political" (i.e., controversial) activities. Although the rule is probably seldom enforced, its effect is undoubtedly to make the recipient associations even more wary of controversy than they would otherwise be.

Civic associations could often accomplish more in terms of their stated ends if they worked together harmoniously. In fact they very rarely do. What Sayre and Kaufman say about civic associations in New York can be said about them elsewhere as well, that "they are incurably pluralistic, competitive, specialized in their interests, jealous of their separate identities."[16] This is to be explained by their peculiar maintenance needs. Since they must compete for resources (money, prestigious names, volunteer effort) and for program material ("safe" issues, workable projects), they are usually more concerned with establishing and preserving their separate identities than with achieving something by joint action. Organizational rivalry is most intense among associations with similar objectives, clienteles, and memberships. Many large cities, for example, have four different Jewish "defense" agencies —the Anti-Defamation League, the American Jewish Congress, the American Jewish Committee, and the Jewish Labor Committee. With memberships and goals that overlap to a great extent, much effort is put forth to maintain the identity of each association and to resist efforts at consolidation or joint action. Usually such agencies can make a good case for separateness. A merger, by reducing competition, would reduce the total amount of resources (members and funds) that they could raise without giving any assurance that the resulting unified association would be more influential than the several competing ones together.

MORE EFFECTIVE CIVIC ACTIVITY

The civic leader, when he does not have to take account of the maintenance needs of an organization, that is, when he acts "as an individual," is less reluctant to take a stand on controversial matters. For this reason and others, he may exercise a considerable influence when "on his own" apart from a civic association. He is likely then to be in one or another of three quite distinct roles: (1) He may advise the mayor on some particular subject matter, such as downtown redevel-

16 Sayre and Kaufman, *Governing New York City*, p. 80.

opment, and act as a go-between for the mayor and some group or sector of the public, such as downtown businessmen. (2) He may negotiate the terms on which conflicting interests will agree to some specific undertaking (e.g., the main outline of an urban renewal program) that will then be presented to the public authorities for action. (3) He may promote, publicize, or "sell" to the larger public some undertaking that has already been agreed upon by a small group of activists; he does this by arranging meetings, giving after-dinner speeches, and issuing statements to the press.[17] In order to be effective in any of these capacities a civic leader must have the respect of the leading politicians and businessmen, something which is fairly rare because of the differences in point of view and background between those two groups. Usually such a civic leader has little or no *partisan* political weight.

Civic leaders are also relatively effective when they act through *ad hoc* civic associations. Because it is brought into being for a particular purpose and is expected to pass out of existence when that purpose has been accomplished, the *ad hoc* association is not as preoccupied with its own maintenance as is the permanent association and therefore lacks the permanent association's motive to avoid controversy. Its membership and leadership, moreover, are recruited with its particular purpose in mind, and they are therefore relatively cohesive and highly motivated. Because it either has no staff or has one that has been recruited for temporary service, the *ad hoc* association is less likely than the permanent association to fall under staff control.

The limitations of the permanent association being what they are, it is not surprising that when "important" (and hence controversial) issues arise the almost invariable practice is to create *ad hoc* associations to do what the permanent ones cannot, or will not, do. There are scores of permanent associations concerned with housing in New York, but when some people wanted to persuade the City Housing and Redevelopment Board to build a middle-income cooperative apartment instead of a rental project in Brooklyn, they organized the Cadman Plaza Civic Association and required that each member deposit fifty dollars as evidence of his interest. With just one well-defined purpose to serve and with a membership that had a tangible stake in its affairs, the association was almost certain to be more effective than any of the big, well-staffed associations would be. The necessity of taking a stand

[17] See Banfield, *Political Influence*, pp. 279–283.

in favor of cooperative and against rental housing would have paralyzed them.[18]

Citizen participation, which as we have shown has always been characteristic of the highly decentralized governmental institutions of American cities, has in recent years come to be regarded in many quarters as a normative principle inseparable from the idea of democracy itself. Indeed, the spread of the doctrine that there *ought* to be "grass roots" participation in local affairs has largely coincided with a reduction in real opportunities for ordinary citizens to exercise influence in the matters of importance to them; for example, opportunity to "participate" in planning urban renewal projects has taken the place of opportunity to "fix" traffic tickets. Some efforts to stimulate "grass roots" community organization arise out of the need felt by elected officials to establish lines of communication with voters which will serve some of the functions formerly served by ward and precinct organizations. The decay or destruction of precinct organization has left the officeholder unable to mobilize neighborhood opinion in support of his program.[19]

Citizen participation has also been encouraged by certain national reform organizations. The National Municipal League and the American Council to Improve Our Neighborhoods (ACTION), for example, have published pamphlets telling how to start civic associations and how to lead them to success. Some advocates of citizen participation justify it on the theory, popularized by the TVA, that there ought to be "a democratic partnership" between government agencies and the people's institutions.[20] This view appeals at once to the popular opinion that government ought to be kept subject to constant citizen control and surveillance. It also appeals to the desire of the government agencies themselves to demonstrate the democratic character of their activities; the agencies, which are of course confident that they will be

[18] For other examples, see the cases described at length in Banfield, *Political Influence*.

[19] See, for example, A. Theodore Brown's account of the efforts of the reform administration in Kansas City to establish neighborhood councils, in Banfield (ed.), *Urban Government* (New York: Free Press of Glencoe, 1961), pp. 543–553.

[20] For a discussion of TVA'S doctrines and practice, see Philip Selznick, *TVA and the Grass Roots, A Study in the Sociology of Formal Organization* (Berkeley: University of California Press, 1949). For an application of the doctrines to urban affairs, see Coleman Woodbury (ed.), *The Future of Cities and Urban Redevelopment* (Chicago: University of Chicago Press, 1953), chap. iv. It is interesting that Woodbury refers specifically to the TVA experience.

the senior members in any "partnership," like to have groups that will share with them, or take from them, responsibility for decisions that may be otherwise indefensible.

Thus, federal housing policy requires that before a city can receive federal funds for urban renewal projects, a local citizens' association must participate in and endorse the final plan. The law requires that this involvement include not only ready acceptance of the plans by the organized public but also the active participation by the public in the planning activity.

The one elaborate study that has been made of a civic association created to give citizens opportunities to participate in planning affords little basis for encouragement about such ventures. The study, by Peter Rossi and Robert Dentler, concerns the part played by the Hyde Park–Kenwood Community Conference in the development of a thirty-million-dollar renewal project in the neighborhood of the University of Chicago.[21] The Conference put the "democratic partnership" doctrine to the test under highly favorable circumstances. It had a public that was used to community-serving activities, for the neighborhood had a high proportion of university professors, professional workers, and other upper-middle-class people. It could draw almost without limit on the services of experts in planning, law, architecture, community organization, and other related fields. By every standard except one the Conference turned out to be a great success; it was ably led, it raised an adequate budget and employed a competent staff, and it had genuine "grass roots" support, for there was widespread support for the idea of improving the neighborhood and for the idea of keeping it genuinely interracial. Nevertheless, "citizen participation . . . played a relatively negligible role in determining the contents of the Final Plan," Rossi and Dentler concluded, although it played a considerable role in winning acceptance for the plan. If, as seemed likely to them, the Conference represented the upper limit of possible citizen participation in such an enterprise, then the "maximum role to be played by a citizen movement in urban renewal is primarily a passive one."[22]

One body was effective in determining the content of the plan. This, it is instructive to note, was a pseudo-civic association, the South East Chicago Commission, established, financed, and used as a kind of

---

[21] Peter H. Rossi and Robert A. Dentler, *The Politics of Urban Renewal* (New York: Free Press of Glencoe, 1961). See also Julia Abrahamson, *A Neighborhood Finds Itself* (New York: Harper, 1959).

[22] Rossi and Dentler, *Politics of Urban Renewal*, pp. 5–12.

"secular arm" by the University of Chicago, which had a large, direct, material interest in the future of the neighborhood. The Commission did not have a mass membership, was not internally democratic, was not much interested in general principles; it was remarkably effective precisely because it was run by a man who knew exactly what he wanted and did not have to consult a membership. The Conference was in exactly the opposite position: its functions were mainly to bring about agreement by affording citizens opportunities to learn of the details of the proposed plan; to serve as a "lightning rod" to attract and ground dissent; and to impart to the plan a legitimacy which the Commission and the University, being "selfish" and "undemocratic" organizations, could not give it.

In New York, where Columbia University sought to rehabilitate its decaying neighborhood around Morningside Heights, no effective citizens' organization on behalf of the plan could be created at all. There a normal pattern was followed: The citizens organized on an *ad hoc* basis to *oppose* specific plans of the university as soon as these plans became known.

CHAPTER 18 · BUSINESSMEN
IN POLITICS

BUSINESSMEN (meaning here owners and managers of *large* enterprises) seldom run for local offices. It is possible to suggest several reasons why. Like most prosperous people, they live in suburbs and are therefore ineligible to run in the central city. Holding local office—even being mayor of a large city—may be no more exciting or prestigious than being head of a big business. Politics—so many businessmen seem to think—is both demeaning and frustrating. These factors all tend to keep the businessmen from running, no doubt. But in all probability, the really decisive consideration is that he could not get elected if he tried. If he is an Anglo-Saxon, a Protestant, or a Republican (and he is likely to be all three), he is in effect disqualified for a high elective office in many large cities.

Even though he does not hold office, a businessman may play an important, or even a dominant, part in city affairs. In some cases, the nature of his business virtually requires him to do so. Where this is the case, he is likely to conclude that in order to serve well the interest of his business he must join with others to serve the interest of "business" and also the interest (as he himself defines it) of the "city as a whole." As a rule, neither he nor anyone else can distinguish clearly between his business-serving and his community-serving activity. Since he stands in the midst of most of the city's volunteer civic activity, the last chapter dealt, albeit somewhat obliquely, with the community-serving side of his role. This one deals mainly with its company-serving side.

BUSINESS INTERESTS IN CITY AFFAIRS

The businessmen who are most active in city affairs are those whose companies are most directly affected by what the city government does. These include especially the department stores, utilities, real estate operators, banks, and (a special case to be considered in a later chapter) newspapers.

Typically department stores (especially those without suburban branches) want to increase the volume of trade coming into the central business district. This means that they want to encourage good customers to come there and to discourage "undesirable" ones, that is, people with little money to spend whose presence would make the shopping district less attractive to the good customers. Therefore, they are enthusiastic promoters of urban renewal projects that will displace low-income people, particularly Negroes, from close-in districts and replace them with higher-income (white) customers. They favor construction of expressways to bring suburbanites downtown, underground parking facilities to make it convenient for them to come to their stores, and (sometimes) the subsidization of commuter railroads. If an important new public building is to be built, they want it so placed that the office workers will shop in their stores during lunch time or that it will serve as a barrier against the entry of "undesirables."

Utility companies tend to favor measures to increase the city's population, employment, and income. Because of the large fixed cost of putting down mains and constructing other such facilities, they benefit from steady, predictable growth of the city. If there is a shift of population from one part of the city to another—say from an inner deteriorating area to an outlying fringe—the company is left with excess capacity in the old area and must provide facilities in the new one before there are enough customers there to make doing so profitable. For this reason, utilities are usually strong advocates of city planning and of land-use control. They are also usually in favor of the consolidation of local government units: it is easier for a utility to deal with one local government than with many. Because they are peculiarly subject to regulation (usually by the state, not the city) they tend to be public-relations conscious and anxious to avoid controversy.

The real estate operators fall into two main groups. One consists of brokers, who arrange sales and purchases, and make their money by turnover; sometimes this tends to make them not only willing backers of sweeping plans of all kinds but also the initiators of such plans. The other group consists of owners and managers of office buildings; these people are much interested in tax and assessment practices and in plans to stabilize or to raise property values. If a public building is to be built, each one wants it placed where it will enhance the value of his property. Architects and contractors have a community of interest with both groups of real estate operators. They too are active promoters of civic centers, industrial parks, urban renewal projects, and monumental undertakings in the name of city beautification.[1]

Banks often own office buildings in choice central-business-district locations. Where this is the case, their interest is to that extent the same as the second group of real estate operators. However, they have a more important, although less direct, interest in the growth and prosperity of the city as a whole, and particularly of those large enterprises (for example, department stores, newspapers, real estate operators, and manufacturers) which are their principal customers. Each of the big banks in a city is the center of a clique of business influence and it is part of the job of the head of the bank to act as leader of the clique and to represent it in its dealings with officialdom. Many banks are prevented by the terms of their charters from doing business outside the city; these banks naturally take a greater influence in local affairs than do those whose charters do not limit them in this way.

Railroads and manufacturing companies are sometimes active in city affairs. Usually, however, they are less so than are the other businesses we have listed. Their holdings lie outside the city for the most part, and therefore their stake in what the city government does is less.

Companies that sell on a regional or national market often take little or no interest in local affairs. Having its headquarters or a plant in a city is not enough to give a business firm an interest in it; usually any city in the same region or postal zone would suit the firm as well. The Ford, Chrysler, and General Motors corporations, for example, are probably less important in the affairs of Detroit than the J. L. Hudson Company department store. (The Ford *family* has done much for Detroit, but that is another matter.) "It makes little difference to us what happens in the city," the president of a great industry headquartered in Philadelphia told an interviewer. "We do not have our homes here; we have no large plants located within the city limits; we have only an office building that we can close at any time that conditions within the city become too oppressive."[2]

[1] Prior to the Second World War, when city planning was concerned mainly with zoning and city beautification, real estate men, contractors, and architects were heavily represented on planning commissions. See Robert A. Walker, *The Planning Function in Urban Government* (Chicago: University of Chicago Press, 1950), p. 150.

[2] James Reichley, *The Art of Government: Reform and Organization Politics in Philadelphia* (New York: Fund for the Republic, 1959), p. 61.

In El Paso, Texas, for example, businessmen are the most powerful interest group in the community, and the most powerful members of this group are known locally as the "Kingmakers." But the officers of the biggest corporations in the city—Standard Oil, Texaco, American Smelting and Refining, and Phelps-Dodge—are not considered to be among the Kingmakers because they are national firms with little interest in local politics.

Similarly, absentee-owned companies are less likely than others to participate in local affairs. A manager who expects to be transferred to New York in a few years identifies less fully with the local business community and with the city than does an owner who intends to live out his life in the city.[3] What is more, the manager does not have the owner's freedom and action. The break-up of large fortunes by inheritance and otherwise, and the removal of the heirs from the active management of companies, has therefore tended to reduce business influence in local government. In the South and Southwest, however, absentee ownership of large corporations is less common than elsewhere, and in cities like Atlanta, Dallas, and Houston, business influence is comparatively strong. Furthermore, in any city, when an absentee-owned firm is a public utility, a department store, or some other institution that exists primarily to serve local markets (rather than to produce in local plants goods and services for national markets), it will be more likely to participate in local affairs.

THE MODES OF BUSINESS INFLUENCE

Businessmen have usually had a principal say about the civic agenda and sometimes they have had *the* principal one. The vantage points from which they have spoken and the rhetoric they have used have differed, however, according to time and place. Several generations

---

[3] In a Michigan city, Robert O. Schulze found differences between "local businessmen" and the managers of absentee-owned firms; the managers were younger, better educated, more mobile socially and geographically, and less involved in civic affairs; they held no public offices and held fewer memberships in voluntary associations. See Schulze's "The Bifurcation of Power in a Satellite City," in Morris Janowitz (ed.), *Community Political Systems* (New York: Free Press of Glencoe, 1961), pp. 19–20. However, students of other cities who employed different research methods found executives of national firms participating fully in local affairs. See Roland J. Pellegrin and Charles H. Coates, "Absentee-Owned Corporations and Community Power Structure," *American Journal of Sociology*, March 1956, pp. 413–419. For reflections on the significance to the community of the growing separation between it and the large corporation, see Norton E. Long, *The Polity* (Chicago: Rand-McNally, 1962), chap. ix.

ago, businessmen occupied most of the elective offices in many cities. Where they did not occupy office, they sometimes bossed political machines.[4] Much more often, however, they stood in the shadows behind the political boss, supporting him and dealing with him as business required. Indeed, as Tom Johnson, the businessman-turned-reformer who was mayor of Cleveland, explained to Lincoln Steffens, it was the businessman—more particularly, the businessman who wanted privileges—who was the root of all evil in local politics.

"Oh, I could see," he [Johnson] said, "that you did not know what it was that corrupted politics. First you thought it was bad politicians, who turned out to be pretty good fellows. Then you blamed the bad business men who bribed the good fellows, till you discovered that not all business men bribed and that those who did were pretty good business men. The little business men didn't bribe; so you settled upon, you invented, the phrase 'big business,' and that's as far as you and your kind have got: that it is big business that does all the harm. Hell! Can't you see that it's privileged business that does it? Whether it's a big steam railroad that wants a franchise or a little gambling-house that wants not to be raided, a temperance society that wants a law passed, a poor little prostitute, or a big merchant occupying an alley for storage—it's those who seek privileges who corrupt, it's those who possess privileges that defend our corrupt politics. Can't you see that?"[5]

Once they got their privileges and had prospered from them, the businessmen who had corrupted politics (or, more likely, their heirs) embraced reform. Being well established themselves, they wanted to prevent others from buying the same privileges and competing with them. They wanted also to keep the cost of government down, and this was something that "good government" promised to do. Further, they wanted a stable, predictable governmental environment, and this could best be provided by a professionalized city bureaucracy. Generally speaking, local businesses were the chief supporters of reform. Manufacturers, wholesalers, and investment houses—in fact, all who depended upon a regional or national market—had not gained from local corruption in the first place and were not threatened by the continuance of it. Accordingly they often took little interest in reform.

[4] Two thirds of those elected to local office in New Haven in the period 1875–1880 were businessmen. Robert A. Dahl, *Who Governs?* (New Haven: Yale University Press, 1962), p. 37. For a brief account of a businessman-boss, see Constance M. Green, *Holyoke, Massachusetts: A Case Study of the Industrial Revolution in America* (New Haven: Yale University Press, 1939), p. 268.

[5] *The Autobiography of Lincoln Steffens* (New York: Harcourt, Brace, 1931), p. 479.

Outright bribery of local government officials by the heads of large, well-established businesses is certainly a very rare thing today. The only businessmen who would try to buy favors from local government nowadays are the heads of criminal syndicates (organized gamblers, for example) and, perhaps, of new enterprises trying to break into an established field. These latter—businessmen who are "on the make"— are viewed with pain and disgust (as of course they should be) by the owners and managers of businesses that were created in exactly the same way not many years ago.[6]

Today the respectable (established) businessman is likely to use political influence for purely private purposes only in what may be called defensive actions. He may try his best to prevent some disturbance to the *status quo* that would affect his company adversely, but he is not at all likely to try to upset the *status quo* in order to get a windfall for himself.[7] For example, he may pull wires at City Hall to block a change of assessment practices that would hurt his company but he would not think of soliciting a change to benefit the company. The reason he behaves as he does is perhaps not hard to find. Not being willing to resort to bribery, and dealing with an officialdom that is too large and too professionalized to be bribed, he must limit himself to demands which are in some sense legitimate. In short, defensive action, being easier to justify, is more likely to succeed.

Businessmen whose companies are sensitive to actions by local government—but apparently few others—contribute to local political campaigns. Some businessmen have reason to fear direct reprisals if they do not contribute; a contractor whose business is largely with the city, for example, may suspect that ways will be found of preventing him from bidding successfully if he does not show gratitude for past favors. Some business firms contribute not so much from fear of reprisal as from a sense of obligation to support an administration which has been "good for business" and "good for the city." Some of these contributors are trying to lay up good will in City Hall against a rainy day or to put themselves in line for appointment to an advisory committee of

---

[6] Cf. the essay by Daniel Bell on "Crime as an American Way of Life" in his *The End of Ideology* (New York: Free Press of Glencoe, 1959).

[7] This point is made and evidence for it supplied in Peter B. Clark, "The Chicago Big Businessman as a Civic Leader" (unpublished dissertation, Department of Political Science, University of Chicago, 1959). Dahl (in *Who Governs?*, pp. 79–84 and 241) concludes that the "economic notables" in New Haven do not receive (and presumably do not seek) special favors; their property seems to be somewhat overassessed.

some sort, either for business reasons (the committee may make recommendations touching the interest of the business) or for the sake of personal prestige and the fun of being a civic statesman. Others, however, contribute without even an implied *quid pro quo*. When someone suggested to a group of Chicago businessmen (Republicans) that they attach conditions to their support of Mayor Richard Daley (a Democrat), they replied indignantly that this would be "crooked."

Because of the respect in which they are held by newspapers and middle-class voters, the endorsement of leading businessmen is often worth more to a politician than their money. Businessmen who can be co-opted formally are especially valuable, provided, of course, that their standing in the community is unimpeachable.[8]

In the large cities, whatever support the businessman gives is likely to be at the expense of the Republican party. The great Democratic party strongholds in New York and Chicago, for example, are financed in part by businessmen who are staunch Republicans in state and national politics.

THE BUSINESSMAN AS CIVIC STATESMAN

After the Second World War, the leading businessmen of most large cities organized themselves to prepare ambitious plans for the redevelopment of the central business districts. The Central Area Committee of Chicago, Civic Progress in St. Louis, the Allegheny Conference in Pittsburgh, the Civic Conference in Boston, the Greater Philadelphia Movement—these and many more organizations were formed on the same pattern. The business elite of the city met privately, agreed upon more or less comprehensive plans for the redevelopment of the central city, and presented the plans to the press, the politicians, and the public as their contribution to civic welfare.

The committees were something new in business-government relations. Chambers of Commerce had long represented "business," but they spoke for it frankly as a "special interest," they spoke for small as well as large businesses, and they represented not only the central business district but also outlying districts, whose interest was generally opposed to that of the central area. The new committees were different

---

[8] For example: "Graham Aldis, a prominent real estate man generally regarded as a Republican, is heading up the citizens' advisory committee for the Democrat, Assessor Cullerton. As his friends say, Aldis is no fool. Cullerton hailed the committee members for their 'unselfish interest and knowledge' to achieve better assessments." *Chicago Tribune,* March 30, 1959.

in that they consisted of a few "big men" whose only concern was with the central business district and who, far from regarding themselves as special interests, insisted that they served "the public interest," often at a considerable sacrifice of private, business interests.

It was the flight of the middle class to the suburbs, the deterioration of the central business districts and, of course, the prospect of getting large grants of federal money for urban renewal that stirred the "big men" to action. They were the owners and managers of the big department stores, banks, and office buildings, and the trustees of colleges, hospitals, and museums, and they could see that unless they acted fast, and acted with the power of government behind them, the central business district was doomed.

To some extent also, the big businessmen's interest in civic improvements reflects a new view of public relations. To seek the advantage of one's own business, or even of "business" in general (as the Chambers of Commerce did), tends, it is now thought, to create an "unfavorable image." "Service to the community," on the other hand, creates a favorable one. As the Vice President for Civic Affairs and Real Estate (*sic*) of a large department store explained to an interviewer,

> Obviously a business of the stature I hope ours has should present a good face to the public . . . should be for constant improvement for the public. All through the years, this business has tried to achieve the feeling among the public that we are just a nice, fine, wonderful organization, and whatever it takes to achieve that, we are interested in.
> What it takes is to be just a plain, honest, good citizen—and fostering the kinds of things that are good for *everyone*.[9]

Another thing that turns the big businessman toward civic statesmanship is his belief that his company has a responsibility to the community which ought to be discharged even at some sacrifice of profits. Corporations have grown steadily more "soulful" as the separation between ownership and control has widened. In a good many cases, however, the talk about the corporation's responsibilities to the community may be mainly rationalization to hide the personal inclinations of managers who are bored with making heavily taxed profits and who

[9] Personal communication. Whether the community-serving endeavors of a business do in fact redound to its business advantage is of course open to question. Peter H. Rossi concluded from a study of such activities on the part of the American Telephone & Telegraph Company in a small city that the general public was indifferent to them or else felt that there were more important things that the company could do (National Opinion Research Center, Report no. 64, *Industry and Community*, October 1957).

find it more "fun" to work up grandiose schemes for civic improvement and to pull strings to get them accepted. The opportunity to do good in the name of the company and to be a civic statesman may be one of the fringe benefits that a large corporation gives its head.[10]

Often, the civic projects advanced by the committees of businessmen have been ill-conceived, overly ambitious, and politically unworkable. Typically a committee has hired consultants to perform some hasty rituals of "research," had an architect make some perspective drawings suitable for newspaper reproduction, and then revealed its vision of the new city in the banquet hall of the best hotel amid fanfares of press releases. Such plans usually call for huge federal expenditures for land clearance and redevelopment, for forcing low-income people out of the central city and attracting upper-income ones into it, and for building freeways, civic centers, exhibition halls, and anything else that might prop up property values and stimulate optimism. On awkward matters of detail—where to put the displaced Negroes, where to find equity capital for rebuilding once sites were cleared, how to raise the larger amounts of taxes that would be needed, and precisely where to put new buildings and highways—they are almost always silent. It is up to the politician, the businessmen think, to work out the details; they have done their part by "providing leadership."

It goes without saying that the politician is often less than enthusiastic about such plans. He is sensitive, even if the businessmen are not, to the many interests that will be disturbed and he knows very well that it will be he, and not the businessmen, who will be responsible if the plan fails. He is skeptical, to say the least, of the businessmen's claim to be serving "the public interest." It is his job to know who will gain and who will lose by public action, and he is well aware that the big businessman, although he may convince himself to the contrary by his after-dinner rhetoric, will be the principal beneficiary of the schemes for civic improvement and that the ordinary taxpayer, and especially the Negro slum dweller, will be adversely affected by it. Knowing all this, the politician, although he may pay glowing tribute to the statesmanship of the business leaders who sponsored the plan,

[10] These developments were remarked by John Maynard Keynes in 1926. See his *Essays in Persuasion* (London: Macmillan, 1931), pp. 314–315. On the "soulful" corporation, see Carl Kaysen, "The Social Significance of the Modern Corporation," *American Economic Review*, vol. XLVII (1957), pp. 311–319. See also Robert A. Gordon, *Business Leadership in the Large Corporation* (Berkeley: University of California Press, 1961), esp. the preface and chap. xiv.

is likely to be slow about endorsing it. In the end, he usually does endorse it, or something like it, however, for he too believes that something must be done to stop the decline of the central business district and his judgment tells him that whatever the leading businessman can agree upon is the most feasible place to begin.

Even if he did not share the businessmen's concern about the future of the central business district, the politician would as a rule take their plan seriously. To an increasing extent, he needs their financial and other support in order to be re-elected. He also needs accomplishments —the more visible the better—to point to with pride when addressing the voters. Projects for the rebuilding of the central business districts, even though they may make matters worse for the slum dweller by reducing the amount of housing available to him, can be offered to "liberals" as evidence of his profound concern for the underdog. And of course—a happy feature of the situation indeed—since most of the cost of the undertaking will be paid for by the federal government, he can take credit for having got the city something for nothing. In general, therefore, there exists a solid basis for a three-way alliance between the politician, the business elite, and the "liberal" groups that want the city rebuilt.

PHILADELPHIA: A CASE IN POINT

The changing pattern of business-government relations and nature of the big businessman's present role as civic statesman may conveniently be illustrated by reference to Philadelphia.[11] Beginning somewhat before the turn of the century, the city was dominated by a Republican machine supported by big business interests, especially the Pennsylvania Railroad (the headquarters of which were in Philadelphia), the brokerage firm of Drexel & Company, and several of the larger banks. Thomas Sovereign Gates, a partner in the Drexel firm and in the House of Morgan, and later the president of the University of Pennsylvania, was the principal spokesman for big business. He and his associates were the powers behind the throne, but they left the management of the city in the hands of the Republican bosses, the brothers Vare, who held graft to what was considered a reasonable level.

[11] This account is based upon Reichley, *Art of Government,* and Robert L. Freedman, *A Report on Politics in Philadelphia* (Cambridge, Mass.: Joint Center for Urban Studies, 1962, mimeo).

When Gates died early in 1948, the business elite's control of the city seemed to be at an end. The Republican ward leaders fell to factional fighting and to grafting indiscriminately. Scandal ensued. This gave the Democrats their chance. In 1949 the Democratic party slated two blue-ribbon candidates, Richardson Dilworth and Joseph S. Clark, members of the Main Line elite, as treasurer and comptroller respectively. Two years later Clark was elected mayor, and then in 1955 Dilworth succeeded him, Clark having left to run for the United States Senate.

The businessmen of the city—both the big ones who belonged to the Main Line elite and the small ones who belonged to the Chamber of Commerce—helped expose graft in the Republican machine and thus helped in the victory of the Democratic reform candidates. While reform was brewing, the big business elites, the inheritors of the financial power that had been held by Thomas Sovereign Gates and his associates, formed the Greater Philadelphia Movement (GPM). This consisted of thirty-one members, mostly corporation lawyers and bankers, and its initial budget was said to be $225,000.

GPM at once began making plans for improvement of the business district. One of its most ambitious plans (its ultimate cost would be $100 million, according to some estimates) was for moving the city's food produce center from Dock Street to a site in South Philadelphia that would be created by filling in a city dump. The Dock Street market, according to a GPM leader who was president of the N. W. Ayer & Company advertising agency, was crowded and unsanitary, and the public interest required that it be moved. Despite objections in city council, Mayor Dilworth loaned several million dollars of city money to a nonprofit corporation, the Food Distribution Center, that was organized by GPM. Some skeptics denied that the old market was a health hazard and pointed out that bankers, contractors, and real estate operators stood to gain large amounts from the change. N. W. Ayer & Company, for example, owned an office building adjacent to Dock Street the value of which would be enhanced by "getting the bums out of Washington Square."

The skeptics were very much in the minority, however. The newspapers and the mayor applauded the proposal vigorously.

Other nonprofit corporations inspired by GPM were heavily subsidized by the city and the federal government. In every case, the board of corporations, although including representatives of the public, was controlled by the big business elite.

Mayor Dilworth tried hard to get a federal subsidy for the Pennsylvania Railroad on the grounds that the public interest required improvement of commuter service. (Dilworth sought the help of Mayor Daley of Chicago in getting a subsidy for the railroad, but Daley, who was skeptical of the claim that the subsidy would serve the public interest and was much less dependent than Dilworth on big business support, flatly refused to do a thing.)[12]

Under Dilworth, the liberal reformer, the Main Line business elite was certainly better served than it had been under the Republican machine. (Dilworth, one commentator said, was the businessman's "able servant instead of [as were the old Republican ward leaders] their grafting, inefficient slave.")[13]

Philadelphia has provided in recent years examples of almost all types of business involvement in politics. When Gates and his colleagues were supporting the Republican machine of the Vare brothers, the Main Line social elite was a powerful, although behind-the-scenes, political force. These wealthy and socially irreproachable men were eventually replaced as bankers of the Republican machine by new, first-generation industrialists who were only wealthy. Perhaps the wealthy men of the Main Line had become rentiers, divorced from both business management and political intrigue, anxious to conserve rather than risk reputations. The long-dormant Democratic party had few wealthy men and almost no socially prominent ones; a Jewish realtor and two Irish contractors provided the financial backbone of the party. When members of old Main Line families once again entered politics, they came not as Republicans but as Democrats, and not as machine backers but as reformers, seeking to destroy the system their ancestors—not so many generations ago—had created.

TYPES OF INFLUENCE STRUCTURE

The ability of a business elite to win adoption of its proposals for civic improvements depends to some extent upon the general circumstances affecting the ease or difficulty with which action can be concerted. Proposals will be more readily adopted (other things being equal) to the extent that there exist "structures" of control in both the business and the political spheres and to the extent that those who

[12] Compare also Dilworth's handling of the Dock Street project with Daley's handling of the Fort Dearborn Project as described in Banfield, *Political Influence* (New York: Free Press of Glencoe, 1961), chap. v.

[13] Reichley, *Art of Government*, p. 61.

control the business structures have adequate means of influencing those who control the political ones.[14] At the turn of the century, according to Lincoln Steffens, these conditions were met to a high degree in most cities; there was a "boss" who controlled business and another who controlled politics, and the business boss could "buy" the political one.[15]

To Steffens, the most interesting feature of the situation was the illicit character of the inducements by which the structure of influence was maintained. Today outright bribery of politicians by businessmen (or, for that matter, of politicians by politicians) is, as we have said, comparatively rare. Structures of influence remain, however, other inducements having been found to take the place of the illicit ones. Six principal types of structure exist in American cities today:

1. *A high degree of centralization in both the business and the political spheres, and the two spheres controlled directly by the same (business) elite.* Dallas, Texas, provides an example of an influence structure of this type. The Citizens' Council, membership in which is limited to presidents or general managers of business enterprises ("boss men," they are called), speaks authoritatively for business. In the political sphere, there is also considerable centralization: the city has a strong city manager who is backed by a stable council majority.[16] The structure of business control is dominant, not simply because all nine members of the city council are businessmen, but more importantly because businessmen control those things (money, prestige, publicity) which would-be councilmen need to get elected. Another city of the same type may be Atlanta, Georgia. There, according to Floyd Hunter, "men of independent decision" are few and, almost without exception, businessmen.[17]

2. *A high degree of centralization in both spheres, the business elite controlling the political sphere not directly but through control of a political boss.* Many political machines began under these cir-

---

[14] The analytical framework of this discussion is from Banfield, *Political Influence*, chap. xi.

[15] *Autobiography of Lincoln Steffens*, p. 596.

[16] John Bainbridge, *The Super Americans* (New York: Random House, 1962), pp. 145–146.

[17] Floyd Hunter, *Community Power Structure* (Chapel Hill: University of North Carolina Press, 1953). We have grave reservations (mentioned in Chapter 17) about Hunter's method, but are prepared to accept his substantive findings *as they apply to Atlanta*. Further research suggests to us that Hunter may have been right for the wrong reasons.

cumstances. A powerful business leader (or coterie of leaders) would create, with their wealth and influence, a political boss who would mobilize for their ends the voters the businessmen either could not or would not mobilize by themselves. Philadelphia in the period when the Republican machine of the Vare brothers was subsidized by Gates and his associates was perhaps the most recent and conspicuous example. Such a relationship, however, is inherently unstable; if the political boss is strong enough to deliver the vote for his business backers, he usually is strong enough to deliver it for himself, making up for any threatened loss in income by the opportunities for corruption within the government which political power affords. What began as an employer-employee relationship often changed into an equal partnership, with both businessman and politician obliged to bargain with the other from positions of comparable strength.

3. *A high degree of centralization in both spheres, with neither the businessman nor politician able to impose his will on the other.* Such a structure of influence emerged in Pittsburgh. There, Richard Mellon, who by virtue of his great personal prestige as well as his ownership of a large share of the city's real estate and industry, was a powerful business leader able to speak authoritatively for other businessmen in negotiating with the equally powerful political leader, David Lawrence, the boss of the city's strong Democratic machine. Neither could command the other but each could commit his followers to whatever bargains were struck between the two.

4. *Moderate centralization in the business sphere but much centralization in the political one, the (relatively many) controllers of business having little influence over the (few) controllers of politics.* In Chicago, for example, the size of the city and the diversity of its business prevent a high degree of centralization of business influence; the Central Area Committee, although comprised of the business elite, lacks the unity and discipline of, say, the Citizens' Council of Dallas. Control over politics, on the other hand, is highly centralized in the hands of the Democratic boss, Mayor Daley. The relatively poorly organized business leaders compete with each other by advancing mutually incompatible proposals; under the circumstances they have little influence on Daley. In a particular matter (although not, perhaps, in *all* matters), he can safely ignore their efforts to influence him.[18]

5. *Much centralization in the business sphere but little in the political one, the business controllers thus being hampered in their efforts to*

[18] See Banfield, *Political Influence,* chaps, ix and x.

bring about political action. In Los Angeles, for example, business interests are fairly well-organized, but the political system is highly decentralized. The mayor has little power over the city council, which is not dominated by any single faction. Public questions of even small importance are decided by the voters in referenda. The business controllers therefore have no one with whom they can deal in the political sphere. If they are to get their proposals adopted, they must influence the electorate through the mass media—an expensive and unreliable procedure.

6. *Decentralization in both business and political spheres, and, consequently, minimal influence of business.* None of Boston's many businesses, nor any few of them, is large enough to dominate or "lead" the business community. The political sphere too is characterized by decentralization; the city is nonpartisan, and no politician or possible combination of politicians has enough prestige, or enough organization, to dominate the city. Between the Anglo-Saxon Protestant business elite and the Irish Catholic political elite, there is a long history of mutual hostility. If there existed a business boss and a political boss the two might very possibly come to terms despite this hostility. Given the existing decentralization in both spheres, however, the ethnic cleavage constitutes an additional obstacle to the exercise of business influence.

To sum up: the extent of business influence (and thus the extent to which one can speak of a business-dominated "power elite") in American cities varies with the degree of centralization in the political and economic spheres and with the extent to which economic interests control those resources (money, status, publicity, and legitimacy) which politicians may require in order to win and hold office. Businessmen are most likely to control those resources in relatively homogeneous, middle-class communities where the class basis for machine politics is absent, or in communities where changes in the formal structure of politics (the introduction of such systems as nonpartisanship, the short ballot, at-large elections, and the like) have made it difficult or impossible for politicians to win votes with organizations entirely of their own making.[19] If the class basis of the city or its formal governmental structure (or both) precludes the possibility that politicians will have an independent base of power, then the only thing that can prevent other, nonpolitical groups (usually businessmen) from wield-

[19] Peter H. Rossi comes to essentially the same conclusion in his article, "Power and Community Structure," *Midwest Journal of Political Science,* November 1960, pp. 390–400.

ing power will be disagreements among themselves. The larger and more diverse the city's economy, however, the greater the likelihood that such disagreements will arise. And many businessmen—particularly those whose firms are national rather than local in character—will have little interest in local political influence.

Thus at least three conditions are requisite to a high degree of business influence: (1) businessmen must have an interest in wielding local influence; (2) they must have a common set of goals, either because they agree or because they can be made to agree by some centralizing influence in the business community; and (3) they must control those resources valued by politicians and thus control the politicians. So little research has been done in large American cities that no general answer can be given to the question of how influential businessmen are. However, on the basis of what we know of such cities as Chicago, New York, Detroit, St. Louis, Cleveland, and others, we feel safe in surmising that it is the exception rather than the rule for all three conditions to exist in any large, diverse American city, particularly in the industrial North. Special conditions—such as the absence of an immigrant lower class, the preponderance of a few large local industries, and the prevalence of "good government" institutions—may make the incidence of business dominance higher in the large cities of the South and Southwest.

CHAPTER 19 · ORGANIZED LABOR

PERHAPS the most striking thing about the part played by organized labor in city politics is its variety. Some unions want nothing more from city government than assurance that the police will not interfere with pickets during strikes. Others aspire to take possession of the city government and to run it as an adjunct of the union. Between these extreme positions there are many intermediate ones. Which position a union takes depends upon many factors, including its organizational structure, the ideological bent of its leaders, the nature of the industry and of the local economy, and the structure of party competition within the city.

THE INTEREST OF THE UNION IN LOCAL AFFAIRS

The range of interests that unions have in local affairs is suggested by the findings of Joel Seidman and his associates in their study of six locals in and near Chicago.[1] All six of the locals wanted friendly treatment from police, courts, and city officials, especially in the event of a strike. Beyond that, their goals differed considerably. For example, one local of the United Mine Workers paid practically no attention to local politics; it was in a community consisting entirely of miners who could be depended upon to elect fellow miners to office. Although the leaders of this local were very much interested in politics in the state capital and in Washington—where crucial safety and work regulations were framed—they ignored city and county politics.

At the opposite extreme, locals of the United Steelworkers of America and the United Auto Workers (UAW) felt keenly the need for organized political action at the local level. The Steelworkers were engaged in collective bargaining with a powerful firm under conditions of mutual hostility and suspicion, and were therefore particularly anxious to retain political support from the local Democratic machine in order to ensure its sympathy or at least neutrality. Many local Steel-

[1] Joel Seidman et al., The Worker Views His Union (Chicago: University of Chicago Press, 1958), pp. 227–236.

workers leaders disliked the machine politicians but felt they could not defeat them or dare to risk alienating them. The UAW, on the other hand, did not need political reinforcement of its collective bargaining position because contracts were not negotiated locally, but nationally. At the same time, however, the UAW leaders desired broader political involvement for what were essentially reasons of ideology rather than union security. Since the motivation was ideological, the choice of party tended to be made on ideological grounds, without reference to what party or what party faction controlled local government.

A local of the plumbers' union, one of the nineteen craft unions associated with the building and construction trades department of the AFL-CIO, was vitally concerned with city political matters. Entry into, and the rewards of, the plumbing profession were crucially dependent upon the licensing regulations which control the apprenticeship program and upon building and housing codes. Plumbers, like other building trade unions, must work with whatever party or faction happens to be in power locally in order to get favorable codes and the appointment of sympathetic building and plumbing inspectors. Not infrequently the union approves city inspectors or even nominates them from its own ranks. Furthermore, the city and county government is a prime source of construction contracts. The building trades unions have in common with contractors an interest in seeing that these contracts are large and frequent and that the work is done by private industry rather than by municipal or county employees.

These studies and others lend general support to the familiar observation that with respect to political involvement there is a sharp difference between industrial and craft unions. Industrial unions, with a large membership of unskilled or semiskilled workers in nation-wide industries, are concerned about industry-wide or national wage contracts and with the state and federal welfare measures which redistribute income in favor of lower-income groups. Craft unions, with a membership of well-paid skilled workers in competitive local markets, are concerned about access to the local bureaucracy, sympathetic treatment from local police, and local wages and hours.[2] The industrial union finds itself drawn into national political alliances, in particular with that party which seems most favorable to certain welfare measures; craft unions can and must resist such alignments, for they must

---

[2] See Richard Baisden, "Labor Unions in Los Angeles Politics," unpublished dissertation, Department of Political Science, University of Chicago, 1958.

not allow ideology to prevent them from working with whatever party or faction is in power locally.

Differences in markets create other differences among union leaders. The heads of the state and national federations of unions involved in local markets (e.g., building trades unions) have few direct links with rank-and-file members. The local leaders negotiate contracts and service the members; the state and national leaders can maintain their position only by persuading union members that they have common interests which only state or national leaders can serve. Legislative campaigns waged in Washington, D.C., are thus often dictated not so much by the felt needs of the rank-and-file worker as by the maintenance needs of higher-echelon officials who lack any other relationship with the members.

Unions dealing with national markets, by contrast, are apt to vest a much higher degree of influence in state and national leaders. Industry-wide and nation-wide contract negotiations give national union officials considerable authority over the locals. This bargaining pattern, together with the importance of federal legislation for nation-wide and industry-wide markets, imbues the entire organization with a more "political" or even "ideological" tone. As a result, even the local officials of, for example, the United Auto Workers may have more comprehensive political goals than the national leaders of a building trades union.

Given these differences, however, it is nonetheless true that local union leaders are generally less ideological than national ones. Where the leader's contact with the members is direct, ideology is typically of minor importance. If the industry is still unorganized, the leaders will be absorbed in establishing themselves as the bargaining agents of the workers and in arranging for the security of the union. Once the industry and the city are organized, however, other activities must be found for local unions. In the case of many craft unions, these other activities consist largely in enforcing agreements and supervising work conditions and job assignments—particularly when, as with the building trades, work is done on widely scattered sites by small groups of workers hired on a contract basis by small, highly competitive contractors. In the case of industrial unions,[3] the leaders must devise other services.

These other services, while something more than a concern for wages

---

[3] Seidman *et al.*, *Worker Views His Union*, pp. 42–47.

280 · SOME POLITICAL ROLES

and hours, are usually a good deal less than an active involvement in local politics. Where industry-wide contracts have eliminated local wage negotiations, the development of local welfare services becomes even more important.[4] These day-to-day services—often of crucial importance in ensuring the re-election of local officers—include handling individual grievances, providing free legal advice, filling out workmen's compensation applications, dealing with eviction notices or medical needs, helping to get loans, interceding with the police, and arranging social events and beer supplies. Many of these activities, not unexpectedly, are of precisely the same kind as a political ward leader spends his time on.

Nonetheless, some unions do engage in a significant amount of direct political action. In most large cities, the AFL-CIO council has a Committee on Political Education (COPE) which participates in party conventions and in primary and general elections. Individual unions may also contribute money and manpower outside the framework of COPE. Normally these tasks are undertaken by a relatively small number of activists who are involved because of personal ties to some candidate. Even in the heavily "political" Detroit UAW, no more than 6 to 10 percent of a random sample of union members when interviewed recalled having participated in any way in the 1952 Presidential campaign.[5]

In many locals it would appear that the pressure for active local political involvement arises, not from the expectations of the membership as a whole, but from the requirements of the union activists from whose ranks officers are drawn and by whose standards those officers are judged. On the extent to which rank-and-file members approve of union political activity, the evidence is conflicting. One study of the UAW in Detroit showed that a clear majority of the members supported such activity.[6] A study of the International Association of

[4] See the account of the UAW in Windsor, Ontario, in C. W. M. Hart, "Industrial Relations Research and Social Theory," *Canadian Journal of Economics and Political Science*, February 1949, esp. pp. 60–63. Community involvement also emerged as a substitute for collective bargaining among the unions in Lorain, Ohio; see James B. McKee, "Status and Power in the Industrial Community: A Comment on Drucker's Thesis," *American Journal of Sociology*, January 1953, p. 367.

[5] Arthur Kornhauser *et al.*, *When Labor Votes* (New York: University Books, 1956), pp. 124–126.

[6] *Ibid.*, pp. 100, 104, 105. The same results appeared in a 1956 survey: Harold L. Sheppard and Nicholas A. Masters, "The Political Attitudes and Preferences of Union Members: The Case of the Detroit Auto Workers," *American Political Science Review*, June 1959, pp. 440–443.

Machinists in an Illinois area found that slightly more than half the members believed that the "union should take an active part in politics" although they were not so sure that politics should be discussed at union meetings and were quite opposed to the union's telling members whom to vote for.[7] The Teamsters in St. Louis were in favor of union political action so long as it did not involve telling members how to vote.[8] In the study of six locals by Seidman and others, however, a clear majority of the members of five of the six unions rejected union political-activity organizations, and most of them opposed such organizations when they were explained to them.[9]

Even among the union activists who share a belief in political action of some sort, the precise strategy to employ is often in dispute because of the conflicting roles of the union *lobbyist* and the union *campaign director*.

The lobbyist sees political action in terms of getting concessions from elected officials, particularly legislators. He works alone in attempting to influence a fairly small group of men whose primary concern is with getting re-elected. Often he needs the votes of men from both political parties; thus, he dare not risk aligning himself entirely with one party or faction. Ideally, he would like to be free to commit his union to whoever has helped him the most; this sometimes means supporting—or at least not opposing—a conservative politician not normally friendly to labor. He avoids making allies if by so doing he must take on his ally's causes—"don't get stuck with the other fellow's fights." He chooses his issues carefully and concentrates on specific goals.

The union's campaign director, on the other hand, sees the requirements of political action in entirely different terms. He desires to elect a slate of local candidates. To do so he must create an organization of volunteers. Because of their political convictions, these volunteers often insist on working entirely within one party—usually the Democratic. The campaign director must, therefore, reject "deals" with Republicans and he must avoid endorsing conservative candidates who are not likely to arouse volunteer enthusiasm. He is inevitably restless with prior union commitments for they deprive the volunteers of a sense of participating in making decisions about endorsements. He

[7] Hjalmar Rosen and R. A. Rosen, *The Union Member Speaks* (New York: Prentice-Hall, 1955), pp. 36–42.

[8] Arnold Rose, *Union Solidarity* (Minneapolis: University of Minnesota Press, 1952), pp. 83–84.

[9] Seidman *et al.*, *Worker Views His Union*, pp. 230–233.

must seek out allies from other liberal groups; this means he must make their causes his.

This tension means that the unions with the most to gain from local lobbying (like the building trades unions) will tend to reject political campaigns, while those with the least to gain by local lobbying (such as the UAW) will emphasize such campaigning. Between these extremes there are unions which are not infrequently split between the two strategies. Even within the normally "political" industrial unions formerly of the CIO, campaigning has often been undertaken half-heartedly.[10]

THE UNION AS AN AGENCY OF CIVIC LEADERSHIP

Leaders of organized labor do not appear as frequently as businessmen among the ranks of reputed civic leaders or on the rosters of important civic or governmental organizations.[11] It is customary to find in most large cities one or two "labor representatives" appointed to the board of education, the board of the Community Chest, and various public commissions. However, when the members of, say, the board of education are elected rather than appointed, and when—as in most nonpartisan cities—there is no powerful political organization which can draw up and elect a "balanced ticket" to such boards, labor is likely to be unrepresented. This seems to be the case in Detroit and Los Angeles, for example.

Furthermore, there appears to be a crucial difference between business and union membership on such bodies. Organized labor—even if it includes in its ranks the majority of all the adult citizens in the community—is generally regarded as a "special interest" which must be "represented"; businessmen, on the other hand, are often regarded, not as "representing business" as a "special interest," but as serving the community as a whole. Businessmen, in Peter Clark's term, often are viewed as "symbols of civic legitimacy." Labor leaders rarely have this symbolic quality, but must contend with whatever stigma

---

[10] For an account of the difficulties experienced in political campaigning in Chicago by certain CIO unions, see James Q. Wilson, *Negro Politics* (Glencoe, Ill.: Free Press, 1960), pp. 125–127, and Fay Calkins, *The CIO and the Democratic Party* (Chicago: University of Chicago Press, 1952), pp. 70, 77, 81–84.

[11] See the tables in William H. Form and Delbert C. Miller, *Industry, Labor, and Community* (New York: Harper, 1960), p. 43.

attaches to being from a lower-class background and associated with a special-interest group.[12]

This bias in favor of business and professional occupations among governmental agencies and civic associations does not necessarily mean that such organizations always serve "business ends" to the detriment of labor. Given the many opportunities for private intervention in public decisions, labor, like all other politically involved organizations, may find that it can attain its ends (or prevent others from attaining theirs) with minimal or even no representation on such bodies. Underrepresentation in the politics of large American cities probably does not prevent groups such as labor from blocking civic actions. But this underrepresentation, and the lack of civic status it implies, probably does make it more difficult for labor goals to be placed near the top of the civic agenda. To put it another way, organized labor probably has less influence than businessmen *collectively* over *what kind* of issues are taken seriously in the city.

Labor is handicapped not only by having imputed to it less civic virtue but also by a shortage of money and organizational skills. Unions at the local level often can donate relatively little money to civic projects. Craft unions particularly are likely to have a very small staff, and sometimes a staff which—because its recruitment and tenure are closely tied to the fortunes of particular officers in the annual union elections—is not as competent as it might be if the job were sufficiently secure to attract able men.[13] Large industrial unions, on the other hand, may have a sizable permanent staff at the district or regional level.

Nonetheless, certain public bodies and civic associations have—particularly in recent years—gone out of their way to enlist union leaders, if only to co-opt potential opponents and increase the agency's resources. William Form and Delbert Miller note the rise of labor representation on the board of the Community Chest in Lansing, Michigan. There were only representatives of "company unions" in 1933 but six union men (on a 36-man board) by 1953. Labor obtained this recognition after having won its organizing fights in the auto plants and after the Chest realized the fund drives among workers would benefit if conducted by the unions (labor now contributes 40 per cent of all

[12] One measure of this difference in civic roles is found in the underrepresentation of labor leaders among those given certain kinds of public honors, including citation in *Who's Who*. See Orme W. Phelps, "Community Recognition of Union Leaders," *Industrial and Labor Relations Review*, April 1954, pp. 417–433.

[13] Hart, "Industrial Relations Research and Social Theory," p. 70.

Chest funds). In an attempt to increase further its representation in community welfare agencies, labor once threatened to boycott an important fund drive.[14]

A similar increase in labor representation on the Chest was reported in a study of Lorain, Ohio. The invitation to join was extended in order to increase the contributions from workers. Paradoxically, however, the unions made no substantive demands once they were accorded representation. In this city, and probably in many others, labor's demand to be included in civic and welfare associations reflects not so much a desire to attain certain political goals as simply a desire to participate in a status-conferring civic venture. This desire, in turn, probably is based on labor's attempt to acquire the kind of civic legitimacy heretofore reserved for businessmen. "The CIO in Lorain," James McKee wrote, "wants to be regarded as concerned with the welfare of the whole community, not merely with the interests of labor, and views its participation in the Community Chest as demonstrating this concern."[15]

Labor's preoccupation with strictly labor goals and its concern for general civic legitimacy have combined to produce in many cities an antipathy between union leaders and municipal reformers. Although there are cases such as Detroit where the UAW and liberal and reform Democrats have joined forces, the more common pattern is that of New York, Chicago, Los Angeles, and other cities where reform efforts have had to deal with the indifference or active hostility of most unions.[16] To the extent labor is concerned with strictly union objectives —wages and hours, workmen's compensation, unemployment benefits, union security guarantees—it finds the programs of civic reformers largely irrelevant. To the extent labor is concerned with acquiring influence in the local political parties and legislature, it regards the reformers as a rival. And to the extent labor is anxious about its civic reputation, it often sees the liberal reformers as the source of extreme and politically damaging ideology.

Thus, the Los Angeles County Federation of Labor passed a resolution in 1961 opposing the right of the liberal California Democratic Council to make pre-primary endorsements in state and local contests.

[14] See Form and Miller, *Industry, Labor, and Community,* pp. 673–674. In San Diego—which is not a pro-labor city—a prominent union official was chairman of the 1961 Community Chest drive.

[15] McKee, "Status and Power in the Industrial Community," pp. 368–369.

[16] The discussion of unions and reform follows Wilson, *The Amateur Democrat: Club Politics in Three Cities* (Chicago: University of Chicago Press, 1962), pp. 273–277.

The New York Central Labor Council in 1961 was largely indifferent to the anti-Tammany campaign then being waged by the reformers in the New York Committee for Democratic Voters, although it joined with the reformers in backing Robert Wagner, the anti-Tammany candidate. In Chicago, with some minor exceptions, union leaders have publicly supported the candidates of the Democratic machine, not those of the reform-minded Independent Voters of Illinois. The Liberal Party in New York, largely backed by unions in the garment industry, has remained independent of the various reform movements in the city.

In those few cases in which there has been a labor-reform alliance (as in Chicago's Fifth Senatorial District in 1950[17]), the union involved has typically been the United Auto Workers. But even the UAW cannot always act independently, for it must consider the costs of political isolation from other unions in the city and from state federations as well as from the local Democratic party. The desirability of playing politics in city affairs must be measured against the necessity of playing politics within labor affairs. It probably takes an energetic and persuasive labor leader to make the advantages of independent civic action more attractive than its costs.

UNIONS IN URBAN POLITICAL PARTIES

The common view that "labor is tied to the Democratic party" requires much modification before it is accurate, particularly with regard to local politics. Unions have many different relations with local parties. In a very few cases unions (mostly the UAW) have attempted to take over the leadership of the Democratic party; with the help of allies, they succeeded in this in Detroit, in Gary, Indiana, and in Rockford, Illinois.[18] Or they may act in coalition with party leaders, as in the Democratic Farmer-Labor party in Minneapolis and St. Paul. They may stay aloof from local politics, as in Houston. They may confine themselves to seeking favors from local party organizations, as in Chicago. They may form independent parties to win votes and thereby bargaining power, as in New York City. They may, as do most CIO unions, carry over into city politics their national attachment to the Democrats; or they may, as do many AFL unions, support local politicians with little reference to national party labels. Where the city is

[17] See Calkins, *CIO and Democratic Party*, pp. 59–85.
[18] *Ibid.*, chaps. v and vi.

nonpartisan, unions may—as they have in the past in St. Paul—endorse and elect a slate of candidates. Or they may—as in Los Angeles—instinctively oppose, with meager resources, whatever candidate the *Los Angeles Times* supports. (Labor-*Times* agreement in backing Mayor Norris Poulson in 1961 was an exception. And he lost anyway.)

Some representative cases of labor involvement in party politics follow.

1. The Unions Capture a Party: The Case of Detroit

Beginning in 1948, the Wayne County CIO Political Action Committee (PAC), then made up almost entirely of UAW members, began, in alliance with certain liberal Democrats, an effort to take control of the state leadership of the Michigan Democratic party. State law required that precinct captains be elected directly by the voters. The PAC-liberal coalition elected 720 captains in Wayne County in 1948, about one third of the total. This was enough to give them control of the Democratic conventions in five of the six Wayne County Congressional districts; control of these, in turn, was enough to give the liberal coalition control of the state Democratic convention. After a bitter struggle with the party's Old Guard, this victory was repeated in 1950, and since then the liberals—dominated by the UAW—have controlled the state party.[19]

In the city of Detroit, however, elections are nonpartisan. Here labor's Committee on Political Education (the successor to the PAC since the AFL-CIO merger) functions directly as a political party.[20] The AFL-CIO Council, acting on COPE recommendations, endorses candidates and operates the strongest precinct organization in the city. Although the UAW has only slightly more than half of all union members in the city, it provides almost all the key COPE officials. In some cases, COPE is open to nonlabor Democrats, and some liberals from business and professional backgrounds participate. Most nonlabor liberals, however, work directly through the Democratic party rather than through COPE. About 40 percent of all precinct captains are COPE members; alliances with non-COPE but liberal captains give COPE clear control of the county and thus of the state party. In city elections, these same captains work on behalf of nonpartisan labor endorsees.

[19] *Ibid.*, pp. 112–146.

[20] This account follows Kenneth E. Gray and David Greenstone, "Organized Labor in City Politics," in Banfield (ed.), *Urban Government* (New York: Free Press of Glencoe, 1961), pp. 368–373.

The Detroit COPE has had imparted to it by the UAW a militant attitude toward political action. Kenneth Gray and David Greenstone offer several reasons to explain this militancy:

First, the union was organized and led for some time by radicals . . . who fought violently among themselves but who agreed on the crucial importance of programmatic political action. Second, a bitter and violent struggle for recognition left the UAW with a deep hostility toward management. This hostility was manifested in political action. . . . Third, the union sought to ease a serious problem of ethnic and racial hostilities among its own members by emphasizing class solidarity of workers against management. This emphasis on the members' interest as a class strongly implied broad political goals rather than an exclusive concern with collective bargaining. . . . Fourth, the automobile workers have a tradition of rank-and-file participation, which contributes to the intensity of their activity in COPE.[21]

Militancy may have contributed to the state-wide successes of the Democrats, but it has not produced comparable successes in Detroit. Between 1946 and 1955, CIO-PAC endorsees won 67.5 percent of all primary and 91.2 percent of all general elections for partisan offices at the state, Congressional, and county level, but less than 38 percent of all contests for nonpartisan municipal offices.[22] As observed in an earlier chapter, union members have not hesitated to desert labor nominees in nonpartisan local elections—if, indeed, these members have even known who the labor candidates were. The CIO failed three times (1943, 1945, and 1949) to elect a mayor of Detroit after bitter contests in which labor's political arm emphasized "liberal issues" —Negro rights, public housing, urban redevelopment, and the right of public employees to strike. In 1953, labor regarded opposition to the incumbent as hopeless and made no endorsement. By 1957 a new strategy was emerging: play down ideological issues, back a sure winner, and hope for favors if he is elected. That year COPE joined with business and newspaper groups in supporting the man who won. Pleased with their success, labor leaders tried again in 1961, only to have the noncontroversial incumbent, despite almost unanimous business, labor, newspaper, and civic support, lose to an unknown who had strong support from Negroes.

Despite the 1961 setback, it is unlikely that COPE will revert to the militancy of the 1940's. First, Detroit city government has begun to be responsive to the demands of lower-class and Negro voters even with-

[21] *Ibid.,* p. 370.
[22] Nicholas A. Masters, "The Politics of Union Endorsement of Candidates in the Detroit Area," *Midwest Journal of Political Science,* August 1957, p. 149.

out labor control of the city government. Second, labor has learned "to conform to the peculiar rules of the nonpartisan game" which require that it refrain from overly aggressive political behavior, that it stress the most widely shared community sentiments, and that it avoid the appearance of seeking to "take over" city government.[23]

Not all cases of labor dominance in local affairs are confined to industrial unions, however. For many years, the AFL unions associated with the "Labor Temple" in St. Paul (now the St. Paul AFL-CIO Trades and Labor Assembly) were continually successful in electing their candidates to office in that nonpartisan city. These labor leaders were conservative in temper, but eventually their influence was undermined by the rise of an aggressive coalition of CIO leaders and intellectuals which made up the Democratic Farmer-Labor Party (DFL) that emerged in 1948. After much controversy, an uneasy alliance between the DFL and the Labor Temple developed.[24]

In Minneapolis too the AFL craft unions were powerful. Between 1941 and 1957, they made the Central Labor Union (CLU) the most important political force in that nonpartisan city.[25] With the advent of the DFL, the CLU remained the dominant partner; no liberal candidate felt he could win without labor support. The terms of the DFL-CLU alliance allowed the DFL to nominate candidates for state and national office (where the liberal ideologies of the DFL intellectuals were engaged anyway) while the CLU elected candidates for city posts. After the defeat of labor candidates in 1957 (owing to scandals, indiscretions, and poor tactics), CLU strength began to decline.

2. Unions Defer to the Party: The Case of New York and Chicago

In large, industrially diversified cities such as New York and Chicago, where political parties have (or have had) power independent of the support of other organized groups, labor has had to be content either with bargaining with elective officials (usually after, rather than before, the election) from a position of relative weakness, or with forming third parties to strengthen that bargaining postion. In contrast with Detroit, unions have not attempted to take over party posts, and

[23] Gray and Greenstone, "Organized Labor in City Politics," p. 373.
[24] Alan Altshuler, *A Report on Politics in St. Paul* (Cambridge, Mass.: Joint Center for Urban Studies, 1959, mimeo) pp. II–3 to II–10.
[25] Alan Altshuler, *A Report on Politics in Minneapolis* (Cambridge, Mass.: Joint Center for Urban Studies, 1959, mimeo), pp. II–8 to II–9 and V–5 to V–7.

in contrast with Minneapolis they have not been able to make themselves senior partners in a labor-liberal coalition. Only very rarely have a few unions challenged the regular party leadership (the Democrats, of course) in primary contests.

In Chicago, labor needs the politicians more than the politicians need labor. Both sides know this, and a kind of half-hearted good fellowship results. The craft unions typically remain close to the party and attempt to share in the patronage, particularly in the licensing and building-inspection departments. The industrial unions—notably the steel, auto, and meatpacking workers—usually support regular party candidates. But occasionally they assert their independence in what they know in advance is a lost cause; for example, certain unions backed an insurgent candidate for the Democratic nomination for governor in 1960. He lost, but the result of the challenge was to increase somewhat the vigor with which the regular candidate attempted to meet union demands in order to arouse their enthusiasm for the general election contest with the Republican. Indeed, labor leaders can probably wield greatest influence by endeavoring to control rather precisely the ardor with which they help Democrats mobilize voters in the closely contested county and state elections. The few union leaders who have been successful at this and at the same time have stayed clear of charges of "left wing" leanings have become important forces in local politics. In case of a showdown with the party, however, there is not much doubt as to who would win.

New York's Democratic party has in recent years been much weaker than its counterpart in Chicago, and therefore labor has probably been more influential. First with the American Labor party and then (after 1944) with the Liberal party, certain New York unions—mostly those Jewish-led unions in the garment industry—have endeavored to act as a third force in city and state politics. The ALP was in 1937 and 1941 a crucial source of votes for Fiorello H. La Guardia. After it was destroyed by the struggle between Communist and anti-Communist factions, the Liberal party continued the strategy of always endorsing Democrats nationally but of playing one side against the other locally. It has always polled a substantial vote, and in 1951 it managed to elect, on its own, a city council president.

Most New York unions, however, have never had any association with either the ALP or the Liberal party. The AFL unions, organized into the Central Trades and Labor Council, followed an almost unvarying policy of supporting regular Democrats in city elections and expecting in return to be given certain assurances about police attitudes toward strikers and certain concessions on local codes, licenses, inspections, and prevailing wage rates on city construction work. The very size of the New York labor movement—the Council had over three quarters of a million members—made it exceptionally difficult for it to speak with one voice on even crucial matters, much less on the secondary issues of political participation. The building trades unions and the Teamsters had their own councils which were part of the larger Council, and union autonomy was jealously guarded.[26]

In 1959, the CIO and AFL unions in New York merged into a Central Labor Council, with a total membership of a million and a half workers. Such an organization, even if it did nothing in politics, would be a force to be reckoned with because of the vast audience it could provide politicians fortunate enough to enjoy access to it. Union meetings are one way politicians have of dealing with the perennial and insoluble problem of how to reach the people.

But the new organization set out to be something more than just an audience. Its first president, Harry Van Arsdale, was a vigorous exponent of union education and political action. In 1961, he persuaded the Central Labor Council to support Mayor Robert Wagner for re-election even though the mayor had broken with the regular party leaders, and to organize a new political force, the "Brotherhood party," which would do for unions generally what the Liberal party had done for the needle trades. At the time this new party was created, it was widely believed that Wagner would not win the Democratic primary and thus he would need such third parties as the Brotherhood to enable him to run as an independent in the general election. Instead, Wagner won easily in the primary and the immediate need for the Brotherhood party vanished. Though the party had a strong start, organizing political units in most assembly districts in the city, its future became uncertain.

3. The Dormant Unions: The Case of the Southwest

In the large cities of the Southwest, where strong political parties do not exist and where population and industry are rapidly expanding, labor has been a recent and still minor civic actor. An aggressive union

[26] This account follows Wallace S. Sayre and Herbert Kaufman, *Governing New York City* (New York: Russell Sage Foundation, 1960), pp. 508–510.

may be able to convert a one-industry town into a one-party town, as in Detroit. And unions may extract concessions from professional politicians in the old, stable cities of the Northeast and Midwest, such as New York and Chicago. But in such booming cities as Houston, Dallas, San Diego, and Los Angeles, where rapid growth is occurring, business (and, more generally, middle-class) influence is often such that organized labor (which, in most of these communities, is only a recent arrival) is lacking in either legitimacy or power.

Businessmen often dominate the politics of these cities (sometimes by default) so long as they can agree among themselves. Furthermore, business and conservative values are widely shared. Business leadership is not an imposition; it is generally accepted. In Houston and Los Angeles, strong anti-union feelings are still widespread among citizens. The absence of a mass production heavy industry (such as an auto plant) means the absence of a large pool of easily organized unskilled workers. The largest CIO unions are often found in the aircraft plants where there is a high proportion of skilled workers. In San Diego, for example, the largest local industrial union is the International Association of Machinists. As Table 15 shows, these are the cities with the largest percentages of white-collar workers in the labor force, and such workers are extremely difficult—often impossible—to organize.

TABLE 15. Cities over 500,000 population ranked by the percentage of employed persons in white-collar occupations, 1960

Rank	City	Percent white-collar	Rank	City	Percent white-collar
1	Seattle	47.8	12	Boston	35.5
2	Dallas	45.9	13	Pittsburgh	35.2
3	Los Angeles	45.0	14	Philadelphia	35.1
4	San Diego	44.8	15	Baltimore	34.2
5	San Francisco	43.0	16	Chicago	33.4
6	New York City	42.8	17	Detroit	32.1
7	Washington	42.7	18	Milwaukee	31.5
8	Houston	41.6	19	Buffalo	30.4
9	New Orleans	39.0	20	St. Louis	30.2
10	San Antonio	38.1	21	Cleveland	24.8
11	Cincinnati	36.8			

Note: "White-collar" refers to professional, technical, official, managerial, sales, and clerical occupations.

Source: 1960 Census of Population.

Despite such constraints, labor in these cities may be a major participant in at least state and national politics. In Houston and San Diego, for example, some labor unions are principal partners in a liberal-labor coalition which contests Democratic primaries. The very absence of a strong party organization, the result in part of nonpartisan, business-dominated city politics, often gives rise to intraparty factional warfare at the county and state level in which labor, albeit weak, is strong enough to play an important role.

CHAPTER 20 · NEGROES

IN FIVE major cities outside the South, Negroes comprise more than one fourth of the population; in two others, more than one fifth; and in five others, around one sixth. The number of Negroes in the larger central cities has been increasing rapidly. Between 1950 and 1960, the twelve largest had a net loss of more than two million whites and a net gain of nearly two million Negroes. In view of all this, one would expect to find Negroes figuring prominently in the political life of the city. They often do, but rarely because of the elective positions they hold. As Table 16 shows, remarkably few of them are elected to office.

Not only are few Negroes elected to office, but those who *are* elected generally find it necessary to be politicians first and Negroes second. If they are to stay in office, they must often soft-pedal the racial issues that are of the most concern to Negroes as Negroes. Of course, white politicians are not indifferent to the interests—or at any rate, the votes

TABLE 16. Negro representation on city councils in selected non-Southern large cities

City	Total city council seats	Seats held by Negroes in 1961	Percent of seats held by Negroes	Negroes as percent of population, 1960
Detroit	9	1	11.1	28.9
Cleveland	33	8	24.2	28.6
St. Louis	29	6	20.7	28.6
Philadelphia	17	1	5.9	26.4
Chicago	50	6*	12.0	22.9
Cincinnati	9	0	0	21.6
New York City	25	2	8.0	14.0
Los Angeles	15	0**	0	13.5
Boston	9	0	0	9.1

* Results of preliminary elections in 1963 indicated that Chicago would add one more Negro to its council.

** Results of preliminary elections in 1963 indicated that Los Angeles would probably elect two Negroes to its council.

—of Negro constituents, but to the extent that the Negro wants to be represented in the sense of "symbolized" rather than "spoken on behalf of," the white politicians are obviously unable to do it. Since the Negroes do not always represent Negroes as Negroes, and since whites can and do represent Negroes to some extent, the underrepresentation of the Negro is in some respects greater and in some respects less than the figures in Table 16 suggest.

The anomaly of the Negro's numerical strength and political weakness can be explained largely in terms of two interrelated factors: the class structure of Negro society and the character of urban political systems. Because of these factors, much of the Negro's civic action takes place, not in the city's electoral or legislative systems, but in the courts or (more recently) in the streets. And often even this "direct action" (e.g., protest marches and mass meetings), though it occurs in the cities, has the federal rather than the city government as its ultimate target.

NEGRO CLASS STRUCTURE

The most crucial fact about Negro class structure in the larger cities is that (as compared to white) the lower class is large and economically backward. So far as we are aware, no analytical comparative studies have been published in recent years. However, the Census figures in Table 17, which compare whites and nonwhites with respect to income and education, are indicative.

Lower-class people generally are withdrawn from politics, but lower-class Negroes may be especially so. To some extent, their failure to

TABLE 17. Distribution of income and education among whites and nonwhites in Chicago, 1960

	Whites	Nonwhites
Income of families		
Percent under $3,000 per year	9.9	28.4
Percent $10,000 per year or more	26.3	8.7
Education of persons 25 and over		
Percent with less than 1 year of high school	41.6	48.0
Percent with 4 years of college or more	6.6	3.6

Source: 1960 Census of Population, PC (1)-15C (Illinois).

participate can be explained by the uncertainties of their situation. Uncertainty about jobs and housing and in a good many cases fear of the police keep many Negroes on the move. It is instructive that many of the Negroes participating in the 1963 demonstrations in Birmingham, Alabama, and Greenwood, Mississippi, were unemployed and there-fore immune to economic reprisals by white employers. The high rate of turnover in lower-income Negro areas makes their full political mobilization particularly difficult.

More important than transiency, however, is the social disorganiza-tion which is characteristic of lower-class Negroes and which is reflected in their high rates of crime, delinquency, desertion, divorce, and illegitimacy. This is in great part the result of the weakness of the family unit. The plantation system during the period of slavery made it difficult to form stable Negro families; the continuing lack of economic opportunities since then has made it difficult for Negro men to acquire the economic self-sufficiency to become the head and breadwinner of a family. Female-centered households are common among Negroes, and the "wandering male" who is only a part-time worker and a part-time husband has contributed to the high per-centage of Negro families supported by either working mothers or welfare checks or both.[1]

The cultural and economic factors which make the lower-class Negro's family life so uniquely precarious also make his sense of at-tachment to the community uniquely weak. The attributes which com-munity life presupposes—education, self-respect, personal skills, a belief in the efficacy of one's own efforts, and a sense of attachment to social entities larger than oneself—are often in short supply because there is no strong family unit to inculcate them. Consequently, the social institutions of the city, and especially its government, are often looked upon by Negroes as (at best) remote forces to be ignored or (at worst) hostile forces to be reckoned with.

The inability to feel himself part of a larger community may extend to the neighborhood and "the race" as well; these may be no more able to command his loyalty than is the city. In such circumstances, it is not surprising that, however much a lower-class Negro may talk of abstract racial issues, they have a good deal less meaning to him than

[1] For vivid accounts of the lower-class Negro world and the family system see E. Franklin Frazier, *The Negro Family in the United States* (Chicago: University of Chicago Press, 1939); and St. Clair Drake and Horace R. Cayton, *Black Metropolis* (New York: Harcourt, Brace, 1945), chaps. xx and xxi.

specific material considerations—a job, a place to live, a bed in the county hospital, and help when he is in trouble with the police.

Like all people who respond to specific material inducements, the lower-class Negro is a natural potential supporter of the political machine. As we have explained, there are now few white neighborhoods where a ward leader's offers of jobs, favors, and patronage have much appeal. Among the large and relatively disadvantaged Negro lower class, however, the situation is still very much as it was among immigrant whites two generations ago. But there is one very important difference. Because most white voters have ceased to want the machine's favors and have even come to feel contempt for it, the machine is a thing of the past in most cities and the ward politician has few if any favors to offer. Not having the material wherewithal to organize lower-class Negro voters, many party organizations rely instead on generalized loyalties to party labels, on the attraction of well-known national candidates, or (in rare cases) on developing "race issues"—like allegations of "police brutality"—which are considered relevant by these voters.

Often, however, a party which has been stripped of patronage resources by the reform movement and therefore cannot offer specific material incentives will endeavor to woo the lower-class Negro vote with *general* material incentives—particularly welfare payments of various kinds. For example, Negroes are the prime beneficiaries of the program of aid to dependent children. To curtail (or even to re-examine) such programs carries the greatest risks for a party in power because Negro voters, rightly or wrongly, will interpret such actions as "anti-Negro."

There have been some efforts to organize the Negro lower classes. The most conspicuous of these is the Black Muslim movement which uses frankly nationalistic, racist, and antiwhite sentiments to instil a sense of self-respect in Negroes.[2] By persuading the Negro that he is superior to whites, the "Muslim" leaders give him a sense of his own dignity sufficient to make him behaviorally, if not economically, middle-class. And often this transformation in style of life is accompanied by an improvement in the Negro's material circumstances because he becomes more strongly motivated to acquire an education, useful skills, and a stable family. The Muslim movement disavows political

---

[2] See the account in E. U. Essien-Udom, *Black Nationalism* (Chicago: University of Chicago Press, 1962).

or civic action, however, on the grounds that it is demeaning and disadvantageous to participate in a political and civic system which is the creation of whites and which ultimately can only serve their ends. But even if the Muslims should seek to wield influence in the cities, the nature of the movement is such that its enrolled membership can never be large. The ideology on which its appeal is based is sufficiently esoteric, restrictive, and even absurd that it cannot enlist large numbers of members.

Thus the first and most important feature of Negro social structure is the predominance of a lower class lacking a strong sense of community. And a second feature is the relative inability, or unwillingness, of the middle class to identify with the lower class and to provide leadership for it. In any community, of course, it is the middle and upper classes who provide most of the civic and political leadership. But in this respect the Negro faces not only those constraints which affect any group seeking to wield influence, but an additional set which arises out of the particular nature of the Negro community.

A middle-class Negro wears a badge of color that is associated with lower-class status, and therefore cannot take for granted that the difference between him and the lower-class Negro will be appreciated. Close contact with the lower class tends to obscure the status difference which he has been at enormous pains to establish. To eat spareribs on the street would entail psychic burdens for the educated and well-to-do Negro of a kind which, it is safe to say, eating blintzes does not entail for Governor Nelson Rockefeller. At any rate, the Negro middle class conspicuously avoids contact with the lower class.[3] The Negro politician, when not a member of the lower class, tends to be drawn from among those members of the middle class who are least averse to such contact. He seldom is a member of the elite of wealth and education.

[3] The Negro middle class, according to Essien-Udom (*ibid.*, esp. p. 304), looks upon the Negro masses with contempt and shame, and the masses have no confidence in the middle class. "Most Northern lower-class Negroes do not share in any significant way the opportunities which integration 'victories' are supposed to bring them. Northern Negroes have the right to vote where they please; yet this has not brought them nearer to the 'promised land.' They are conscious of the inequality of fortunes between them and the Negro middle class and whites in general. A great many Negroes know (and are discouraged by this awareness) that they will live and die in the Black Belt. They are beginning to resent the Negro middle-class leadership. They even feel elation when a middle-class Negro is humiliated, harassed, or actually prevented by whites in his effort to enter the white society. They are indignant and humiliated when the 'exceptional' Negro marries a white person." Essien-Udom believes that a class struggle may impend between "a semisatisfied Negro middle class and the Negro masses."

Often he is a new recruit to the middle class; as a politician, his class standing is likely to be marginal.

The relatively small Negro middle class is separated from the lower by differences of interest and ethos. Whereas the lower-class Negro is concerned with "welfare" goals, the middle-class Negro is concerned with "status" goals.[4] He wants the opportunity to move into an unsegregated suburb, to send his children to an unsegregated school, to join an exclusive club, to patronize the better hotels and restaurants, to have equal opportunities in his profession (to practice in an unsegregated hospital if he is a physician, for example). Needless to say, these things that are so important to the middle-class Negro rarely enter into the life of the lower-class one at all.

In some matters there is a clear conflict of interest between the two groups. The middle-class Negro, for example, may oppose establishment of a public housing project which will bring lower-class Negroes into his neighborhood, or he may support (perhaps not in a very conspicuous way) an urban renewal project which will clear out lower-class Negroes and so "upgrade" his neighborhood.[5] Police activity which the lower-class Negro finds harassing may be vigorously supported by the middle-class Negro who wants to live in peace and quiet. Such conflicts of interest are multiplied and exacerbated by residential segregation, which forces the middle class to live in the high-density slum in close proximity to the lower class.

The Negro middle class, like the white, places a relatively high value on community-regarding goals. To many of its members the primary "community" is the racial one, not the city. The preoccupation of these Negroes with status is not simply with their individual status; it is also —and often primarily— with the status of the race. To vindicate the principle of equal rights is generally at least as important to the middle-class Negro as to win concrete benefits, especially benefits of the "welfare" kind. In Chicago, for example, "race men" opposed the building of a new county hospital in the hope that overcrowding of the old one would lead to the break-down of segregation in private hospitals. To them the most important thing was to destroy the principle of discrimination, not to provide better facilities for hospital care. Probably

---

[4] On this distinction, see James Q. Wilson, *Negro Politics: The Search for Leadership* (Glencoe, Ill.: Free Press, 1960), chap. viii.

[5] See Martin Meyerson and Banfield, *Politics, Planning, and the Public Interest* (Glencoe, Ill.: Free Press, 1955), p. 234.

most of the middle class—but very little of the lower class—agreed with this view.[6]

A third important feature of Negro social structure is the fairly large and growing number of young people who have more education than the job market enables them to use. Between 1940 and 1960 the Negro's education improved greatly. His relative income improved also, but by no means as much, and most of the improvement occurred as long ago as World War II. Table 17 (page 294) indicates that although Negro-white disparities in income are great, in education they are much less.

The consequence is that there are now a great many Negroes who are, so to say, half in and half out of the middle class. Some have college degrees but can find nothing better to do than work as postmen, clerks, and the like. Others find jobs in their chosen fields—they are lawyers, professors, and journalists, for example—only to discover that their employers will not promote them. Most of these young people live in the larger cities. Having plenty of time and nothing much to lose, they become the activists in Negro civic associations. As such they are dedicated, militant, and highly articulate.

A fourth important feature of Negro social structure is the relative fewness of entrepreneurs and the consequent importance of professionals. There are very few Negro-owned businesses of any size; most of the large businesses Negroes patronize—even illegitimate ones like "policy" (a form of gambling for small amounts)—are run by whites. Few Negroes, therefore, are wealthy enough to support large-scale political undertakings. Most of the proprietors are owners of very small retail stores and service establishments. The prosperous members of the middle class are mostly professionals. Negro professionals, like white ones, often tend to be antipolitical in outlook and to come under pressure from the institutions they work for—especially schools and government agencies—to stay clear both of partisan politics and of controversy of any kind.

A fifth feature of Negro social-structure is that many important individuals and institutions have a vested interest in the maintenance of discrimination and segregation. Negro churches, political organizations, voluntary associations, schools, and businesses—and therefore,

[6] See Banfield, *Political Influence* (New York: Free Press of Glencoe, 1961), chap. ii, esp. p. 43.

of course, the individuals whose jobs and status depend upon them—benefit from discrimination both because it is their reason for being and because it frees them from the necessity of competing on equal terms with whites. Residential segregation benefits them additionally by affording economies of scale: the more that members or customers are concentrated in one place, the better the opportunities to organize or serve them. "Had it not been for segregation," a Negro alderman in Chicago was quoted as saying, "Negroes would not have been able to advance politically here. It's the same with Negro business—segregation has been a Godsend to Negro business. It's nothing new. The Poles seek out the Poles, the Germans seek out the Germans. Why shouldn't Negroes seek out Negroes?"[7]

That Negro institutions and leaders have this vested interest does not mean, of course, that they can be depended upon to support discrimination and segregation. To do that would get them in trouble with the large sector of Negro opinion that is influenced by "race" men. As a rule, moreover, antidiscrimination and antisegregation measures take effect so slowly and incompletely as not to endanger them greatly anyway. The Negro politician or minister can support a bill for "open occupancy" secure in the knowledge that its passage (which in itself may be unlikely) will not precipitate a mass exodus from the slum to the white suburbs. The individuals and institutions with a vested interest in discrimination and segregation are seldom to be found among the most aggressive fighters for reform, but they are not likely to be open opponents of it either unless it touches them very closely.

Negro civic organizations are small in size and short on resources. This is a sixth feature of Negro social structure, and one that is to a large extent explained by the other five.

In most cities that have substantial numbers of Negroes there are only one or two permanent Negro civic associations. The National Association for the Advancement of Colored People (NAACP), a militant Negro-rights organization, has (as of 1959) 1,366 branches and about 350,000 members. The Urban League, which until a few years ago was mainly occupied in finding jobs for selected Negroes but which now concerns itself with a wide range of problems, exists in

---

[7] *Chicago Sun-Times*, Jan. 6, 1963, p. 36. The alderman, Kenneth E. Campbell, was described as the heir apparent to the political power of Congressman William E. Dawson.

most large cities. Although staffed and led by Negroes, it is largely financed by whites.

Recently four other organizations, all utilizing a protest strategy to advance their ends, have become an important part of Negro civic affairs. One is the Congress of Racial Equality (CORE); another is the Student Nonviolent Co-ordinating Committee (SNCC). Both utilize the "sit-in" and other forms of direct protest action. A third is the Southern Christian Leadership Conference (SCLC), the organizational extension of the personality of its founder, the Rev. Martin Luther King, Jr., the leader of the Montgomery, Alabama, bus boycott and later of the Birmingham protest marches. These three groups have been primarily (although not exclusively) active in Southern cities where the targets for protest are many and obvious and where little in the way of Negro political organization exists to impede them. The fourth group is scarcely an organization at all but rather a deliberately amorphous boycott movement led, in various Northern cities, by Negro ministers—a group which for many years has played a relatively small role in militant Negro civic action of this kind. The ministers have induced Negroes, often with surprising effectiveness, to boycott certain business firms which failed to respond to Negro demands for jobs or promotions. The movement, which began in Philadelphia, is called the "selective patronage campaign." It is a frank effort to compel businesses to re-divide the existing supply of jobs.

Lower-class Negroes play little part in most of these organizations. Nor can the middle class be said to support them very well. NAACP's membership is small (see Table 18). Moreover, of the few Negroes who contribute money to NAACP, still fewer contribute time and effort. A large NAACP branch is doing well if it turns out 10 percent of its membership for a meeting and 2 percent for active committee work. The average member contributes only his two-dollar minimum membership fee. Because of the indifference of most members, it is usually easy for a handful of militants to dominate the activities of a branch, at least until there is a general membership meeting. Then conservatives, who often control blocs of votes through affiliation with churches, businesses, labor unions, and ward political organizations, are likely to join forces to sweep the militants out.

The older, permanent Negro civic association, like the permanent white one, tends to be immobilized in matters of importance by conflict over the concrete meaning of its goals. The newer, often *ad hoc* organizations, the memberships of which are more cohesive because they are concerned with only one issue, are usually readier to take a stand and to act; however, they suffer the disadvantage of having few allies and little money.

TABLE 18. NAACP membership relative to Negro population in selected cities

City	NAACP membership, 1959	NAACP members as percent of 1960 Negro population
Boston	4,859	7.7
Cleveland	12,318	4.9
Detroit	16,746	3.5
St. Louis	7,234	3.4
Baltimore	8,830	2.7
San Francisco	1,583	2.1
Chicago	12,051	1.5
Los Angeles	4,328	1.3
Philadelphia	6,797	1.3

Source of membership figures: Files of national headquarters, NAACP (New York City). The figures above include a relatively small number of white members.

Negro civic associations, both permanent and *ad hoc* ones, are generally most effective (in the North) when acting as "veto groups," trying to block a measure harmful to Negro interests. They have succeeded in preventing transfers of children from one school to another, in stopping land clearance projects, and in checking mistreatment of individuals by the police. They have been least effective in initiating new policies and programs, particularly ones the importance of which is mainly symbolic or ideological and which would benefit not specifiable individuals but the "race" in general.[8]

Given all these circumstances, what is remarkable is that any effective Negro civic action occurs at all. Yet it does, and more so each year. The source of much of this activity can be found in the college-educated but underemployed young men and women who constitute in many cities the backbone of the Negro volunteer activists in the NAACP, the "selective patronage campaign," and similar movements. And the successes of this group have raised the level of expectations governing the behavior of other, more conservative Negroes, with the

[8] See on this James Q. Wilson, "The Strategy of Protest: Problems of Negro Civic Action," *Journal of Conflict Resolution*, September 1961, pp. 291–303.

result that the tempo and militancy of Negro civic action as a whole increases steadily. But because of the nature of these activists, the goals sought and methods employed are often of a special kind—status rather than welfare goals, protest rather than bargaining tactics, and with middle-class rather than lower-class backing. Institutions most susceptible to such campaigns are typically those such as city agencies which have legal power over some community activity and which in turn are vulnerable to lawsuits, political pressures, and adverse public sentiment. Thus, boards of education and police departments find themselves increasingly under attack in Northern cities by militant Negroes concerned about "*de facto*" school segregation and police treatment of minorities.

Finally, it must be said that the Negro middle class has always been the beneficiary of civic action undertaken in its behalf by white liberals (often Jews) whose political ethos is markedly Anglo-Saxon Protestant. In Chicago, agitation for a state fair employment practices act was for many years led almost entirely by Jewish organizations (even though few Jews expected to benefit from such a law); the campaign for integrated public housing projects was waged largely by an *ad hoc* group of white liberals; opposition to an urban renewal project (on the grounds that it was anti-Negro) was primarily the result of efforts of a Catholic monsignor and a few Jewish allies. In New York, where Jewish and liberal organizations are even more abundant, race relations have been even more an activity of whites. The organization which led the successful fight for various "open occupancy" laws to eliminate discrimination in private housing was created largely by Jews and (although it had several prominent Negro officers) relied on white financing and white staffs.

Many Negroes regard this assistance as a mixed blessing. No one likes to take advice or be placed in a subordinate position in a cause which he feels is peculiarly his own. But perhaps more importantly, Negroes are beginning to feel that their white allies will not go "all the way" with them in efforts (such as selective patronage campaigns and other direct action rather than legalistic programs) to attain something more than purely symbolic victories.

EFFECT OF THE POLITICAL SYSTEM

These features of the social structure set certain boundaries (so to speak) on the nature of the Negro's participation in the politics of the city. Within these boundaries, however, a considerable variety of styles of Negro politics is possible. Which style will exist in a particular city depends mainly upon the nature of that city's political system. In other words, the nature of Negro politics (within the bounds set by social structure) depends largely upon the nature of white politics.

We will amplify and illustrate this general proposition by characterizing briefly the style of Negro politics in cities whose political systems are of the following kinds: (1) ward-based,[9] machine; (2) ward-based, weak organization or factions and followings; (3) proportional representation; and (4) nonpartisan, at-large.

Ward-based, Machine

In a city with a partisan, ward-based machine, Negroes will be organized as a sub-machine and will have as many representatives in the council as there are wards dominated by the sub-machine. The councilmen will not (at least publicly) take a "race" point of view, however, or indeed any point of view not tolerated by the leaders of the citywide machine. Chicago is a case in point. Negroes there have long had machine-style politics.[10] For many years the most powerful Negro boss has been Congressman William L. Dawson, who controls five all-Negro wards and therefore a large contingent of ward committeemen, aldermen, and state representatives. Control of these wards gives Dawson a safe seat in Congress (he is chairman of the House Government Operations Committee) and a place in the high councils of the Democratic National Committee.

Dawson maintains his machine in the usual way, by exchanging jobs, favors, and protection for votes. Almost every weekend he flies to Chicago to sit in a shabby ward office in the midst of the slums and to listen to all who come to him. Where the direct, material interests of his constituents are at stake, he and his organization are ready to help; they will get a sick man into the county hospital, find out why an old lady's welfare check has not arrived, defend a beleaguered

---

[9] We use the word "ward" in a broad sense here to refer to any arrangement that enables a Negro candidate to face a geographically drawn constituency that is entirely, or mainly, Negro. The ward system is in contradistinction to the at-large one, in which the candidate faces the (predominantly white) electorate of the whole city.

[10] For the history of Negro participation in Chicago politics, see Harold Gosnell, *The Negro Politician* (Chicago: University of Chicago Press, 1935). For an account of contemporary Negro politics there and of Congressman Dawson in particular, see Wilson, *Negro Politics;* and Wilson, "Two Negro Politicians; An Interpretation," *Midwest Journal of Political Science,* November 1960, pp. 346–369.

homeowner against the urban renewal authority, and go to the police commissioner, and if necessary the mayor, to see to it that a case of alleged police brutality is properly investigated. Matters involving Negro rights in the abstract do not interest them, however. These concern the militants, but they are not the base upon which the machine builds.

In the realm of general principles, Dawson is virtually apolitical. He very rarely speaks in the House (although he is highly regarded by the House leadership). On occasion he has publicly opposed the "race" position on important questions and at least once he and his lieutenants packed a membership meeting of the Chicago NAACP chapter in order to unseat a militant officer. In the city council it is the Jewish alderman from the University of Chicago ward who takes the initiative in race relations. The Negro aldermen vote for the measures he introduces, but they do not fight for them.

The Dawson machine is only part of the larger one controlled by Mayor Daley. In order to maintain his sub-machine, Dawson has to depend on Daley for patronage. He and those whom he controls must therefore support the candidates slated by Daley and the legislation proposed by him. No Negro alderman connected with the organization would seriously propose any measure that had not been "cleared" with Daley, and no Democratic Negro precinct captain would fail to urge a voter to vote against a Negro and for a white if the white was the organization candidate. "Ticket splitting," a Negro ward leader explained in a newspaper interview, "weakens my force." He was quoted as follows: "When I report to the central committee that 15 to 20 percent of the people in my ward split their tickets, I'm not as strong as the man with 95 percent straight ballots. The Negro gains more by voting for a party and not for a Negro candidate. Candidates on a partisan ticket should get all of the votes of that party—not just the Negro ones, or the Irish ones, or those of some other group."[11]

Ward-based, Weak Organization

In a partisan city with ward constituencies but a weak party organization (e.g., a decayed machine) or a coterie of factions and followings, as many Negroes will be elected to office as there are wards in which Negroes are in a majority, and the Negro politicians will be those who can develop personal followings or take advantage of intra-

[11] *Chicago Sun-Times*, Jan. 6, 1963, p. 38.

party factionalism. Manhattan is one example. Its political system does not provide Harlem politicians with sufficient patronage and other resources to build strong organizations, nor does it give city-wide politicians sufficient resources to control the Negro leaders.[12] Because of the lack of party-controlled material resources, Negro politicians in Harlem compete with personal followings (sometimes based on racial demagoguery) and with club-based factions.

Congressman Adam Clayton Powell, Jr., the principal Harlem politician, is an example of the kind of politician such a system produces. For many years the pastor of a large and fashionable church, he is entirely without ward or precinct organization. A constituent would not go to him for a job or a favor (although they might go to one of his aides in his *church*). His appeal is almost entirely personal and ideological. He is handsome, eloquent, flamboyant and—at least as he appears to his public—passionately and uncompromisingly dedicated to the cause of racial justice. This being the basis of his power, Powell is beyond the reach of party discipline. Whereas Mayor Daley and Dawson can talk to each other as two executives of the same organization and whereas Daley as head of the organization can give orders to Dawson, Mayor Wagner can do little or nothing to influence Powell.

Also in Harlem is J. Raymond Jones, a Negro politician whose stock in trade is not ideology or racism but rather his exceptional ability to survive and even prosper in the bitter factional warfare of the community. He has usually been able, by carefully timed alliances, to obtain enough patronage, favors, and nominations for elective office to maintain a firm hold on one part of Harlem but not to dominate for long all parts of Harlem. He was almost the only Tammany leader who foresaw that Mayor Wagner was going to defeat Tammany in the 1961 primary and who joined with the mayor in time to take advantage of that victory.

The factional politics of Cleveland is somewhat similar. There, most of the eight Negro councilmen maintain followings in all-Negro neighborhoods by being good fellows, by providing the associational attractions of political clubs, and by distributing limited amounts of patronage and favors. A few, however, are race-conscious, issue-

---

[12] Elsewhere in New York City—Brooklyn, for example—there is a party machine, and Negro politics is much as it is in Chicago. See Wilson, "Two Negro Politicians: An Interpretation."

oriented leaders whose appeal cuts across neighborhood lines. If the neighborhood-based councilmen had more patronage and other resources at their disposal they would doubtless convert their followings into full-fledged machines and take the seats of the issue-oriented councilmen. By the same token, if their political resources were less, they would probably be supplanted themselves by the issue-oriented politicians. As matters stand, both lower-class and middle-class elements of the Negro community are represented in the council; for that very reason, of course, the Negro councilmen do not constitute a unified bloc.

Proportional Representation

Proportional representation deserves brief mention here (despite the fact that it is used in only one city) because it leads by a different route to a result like that just described. Under PR, a Negro candidate appeals to what is for all practical purposes an all-Negro constituency (election is at-large, but the Negro expects to attract mainly Negro votes). In a PR city, too, the candidate has no patronage or other political resources with which to build an organization; therefore he too must depend upon showmanship and racial ideology. In Cincinnati, PR produced a Negro councilman as militant as Congressman Powell (although neither as flamboyant nor as unpredictable). This, indeed, was the principal reason why it was abandoned there in 1957.[13]

Nonpartisan, At-large

In a city with a nonpartisan, at-large system the nature of Negro politics is radically affected by the fact that the candidate must face the whole (predominantly white) electorate and must do so without benefit of a party label. Detroit is a city with a system of this kind. In order to have any chance of success, a Negro candidate for the Detroit city council must have the support of a newspaper or of some important city-wide civic associations. This means that he must be acceptable to middle-class whites. A Negro who is light-skinned, Harvard-educated, and "reasonable" on racial questions stands the

[13] On Negro politics under PR in Cincinnati, see Ralph A. Straetz, *PR Politics in Cincinnati* (New York: New York University Press, 1958), esp. chap. viii. The circumstances under which PR was abandoned are described in Kenneth Gray, *A Report on City Politics in Cincinnati* (Cambridge, Mass.: Joint Center for Urban Studies, 1959, mimeo).

best chance. Although almost 30 percent of the people of Detroit are Negroes, there is only one Negro councilman among nine.

A Negro elected under the circumstances that prevail in Detroit is in an extremely difficult position. Without a strong Negro vote he cannot hope to be re-elected, and to get a strong Negro vote he must (since he has no jobs, favors, or other material inducements to offer) be aggressive on at least some racial issues. But he must also have the support of the press and the civic associations in order to be re-elected, and he will not have this unless he is "reasonable" from the standpoint of conservative, middle-class whites. Recently, Detroit's one Negro councilman narrowly escaped being crushed between these two forces. Charges were made of police brutality. The Negro councilman introduced a measure empowering the Human Relations Commission to investigate the police department. This became an election issue. Somewhat surprisingly, a newspaper supported him and he was re-elected. Whether he can survive many such issues is hard to say.

NEGRO POLITICS IN THE SOUTH

What we have said applies to Northern cities; the situation in the South is different. In the smaller Southern cities, Negroes have generally been denied the right to vote or to hold office, and consequently their influence in civic affairs has been negligible. This has not been the case everywhere, however. In Atlanta, where almost a third of the population is Negro, Negroes have voted for many years and they have often held the balance of power between white candidates.[14]

After the school desegregation decision of 1954, the race issue came to dominate the politics of many Southern cities and the power of the Negro increased. Negroes registered to vote in large numbers, partly because federal laws and court orders gave them protection at the polls and partly because the urbanization and industrialization of the South raised their income and educational level and made them more politically conscious and assertive. Today about 25 percent of the eligible Negroes in the South are registered to vote. These are heavily concentrated in the larger cities.

In these cities, Negro political associations are forming and growing at a rapid rate. In Florida, for example, where between 1944 and 1956 Negro registration rose from 5.5 percent to 37.5 percent of eligibles,

[14] See Floyd Hunter, *Community Power Structure* (Chapel Hill: University of North Carolina Press, 1953), pp. 49–50.

many political leagues, or voters' associations, have sprung up. In some instances these began under church auspices and then soon broke away. They have developed effective tactics for identifying to the Negro voter the candidates who are preferable without at the same time running the risk of hurting the candidates' standing with their anti-Negro white constituents, and they have organized the Negro voters to make their endorsements effective at the polls.[15] Unlike the ethnic associations that have long existed in the North, these leagues do not seek "recognition" by electing their own representatives to office. That is out of the question in most places, and therefore the Southern Negro political league concentrates on trading votes for commitments from white politicians. In the nature of the case, they cannot rely on financial contributions from Negroes who expect to be elected to office or who are already in office (there are too few of them); to a considerable extent, therefore, they get them from whites who want their endorsement.

In the North the goals of lower-class and middle-class Negroes are often in conflict and the political process tends to exacerbate the conflict. In the South, by contrast, Negroes of all social classes want very much the same things—especially desegregation of schools and public accommodations, access to buses and eating places, and voting rights —and their common struggle tends to unify them. In the South, too, the issues confronting the Negro are of a kind that lend themselves well to the use of the tactics of mass protest and litigation. There is evidence that Negro civic leaders in the South are more nearly in agreement on goals and have more support from their followers than in the North.[16]

HUMAN RELATIONS AGENCIES

More and more large cities have created, as either independent agencies or as committees under the office of the mayor, public human relations organizations whose task it is to supervise the enforcement of civil rights ordinances and to act as fact-finding and mediation

[15] H. D. Price, *The Negro and Southern Politics: A Chapter of Florida History* (New York: New York University Press, 1957), pp. 67–81.

[16] See M. Elaine Burgess, *Negro Leadership in a Southern City* (Chapel Hill: University of North Carolina Press, 1962). Compare the case histories of issues reported there with those discussed in Wilson, *Negro Politics*, which deals with a Northern city. More data will be available upon the publication by Donald R. Matthews and James W. Prothro of their large-scale study of Negro political participation and community action in the South.

agencies. The Chicago Commission on Human Relations, established in 1943, was the first of these and it is still one of the largest. It has a staff of about thirty professional and clerical employees, and a budget of about a quarter of a million dollars a year. As of 1961, forty or so other cities in the United States had created, by ordinance, such commissions. Fifteen of these are in Illinois. Comparable commissions can be found in New York, Detroit, Philadelphia, and elsewhere. In addition, there are committees—not endowed with statutory authority—which advise mayors on race matters. Because cities in many cases do not have the constitutional authority to enact laws in this field, legislation barring discrimination in public accommodations, housing, employment, medical facilities, and such areas has often been enacted by the state; and state agencies such as New York's State Commission Against Discrimination have been created to supervise enforcement.

Indeed, so many public and private agencies have sprung up in this field that the staff members of such groups have formed a professional society, the National Association of Intergroup Relations Officials (NAIRO), and are publishing a journal.

A public human relations commission occupies a crucial but ambiguous role in the politics of race relations. On the one hand, it is a staff agency created to advise the mayor; on the other hand, it is looked to for "action" by various individuals and groups who have grievances in this field. Furthermore, it has its own conception—ingrained in the staff—of its mission to remedy certain conditions even if no one organizes a formal complaint and the mayor does not ask for advice; in such cases, the human relations agency does not act as the transmission belt which carries reports of outrages suffered from the point of grievance to the mayor, city council, or city attorney, nor does it provide the mayor with advice on what remedial policies are needed and then sit back and wait while the mayor drafts an appropriate ordinance or executive order. On the contrary, the commission is usually engaged simultaneously in stimulating protest and then proposing solutions to the mayor to eliminate the protest thus stimulated. This, of course, entails an elaborate pattern of negotiation and an organizational ability to face in several directions at once.

The very structure of Negro civic life means that a public race relations agency, if it does anything at all, must act in part as a combination of NAACP and Urban League. When Negro organizations are prevented by internal constraints from pressing for a certain goal, the commission must organize pressure of its own. When the Negro organizations *are* spontaneously exerting influence, the commission often discovers that action in the particular area is not feasible and it thus must find some way of stopping or diverting the protest activity. At the same time, the commission must maintain good relations with affected private white organizations—businesses, labor unions, hospitals, schools, and so forth—so that it can negotiate some kind of acceptable solution to a given race problem which the mayor can then ratify. In the circumstances it is hardly surprising that city human relations commissions are seldom completely successful.

Race becomes an issue in other kinds of city agencies as well, not just in those primarily charged with human relations work. In most large cities, it is an unwritten but unbreakable rule that a Negro must be appointed to certain kinds of boards and commissions—the public housing authority, the school board, the urban renewal or land clearance agency, perhaps the police commission, and so forth. The extent to which such Negro "representation" has an effect on the substance of public policy in these areas is problematical; in any case, it is sure to vary greatly from city to city. Everything depends on the terms on which the appointment is made.

In a city such as Chicago, where the Democratic party is powerful and where politics controls rewards sought by many, the mayor can appoint a Negro almost on his own terms. There are plenty of lawyers who depend on the party for business, advancement, and judicial appointments, even though they may hold no public or party office. Their service on a public commission is shaped by their expectations of future rewards and penalties and—what is equally important—by habits and attitudes acquired over years of intimate acquaintance with political leaders and deep involvement in the party's style of life.

In cities where there is no controlling party, where politics is nonpartisan or factional, and where each person must build his own career on an individual basis, Negroes may be able to dictate the terms on which they will accept appointment. Every city administration needs to legitimize its decisions; every city administration resorts, in some measure, to group representation as a way of achieving this legitimacy; but cities vary greatly in the extent to which they really depend on this sort of "front." Where the city administration lacks other sources of authority—where it has no machine and no faithful followers—it may attach a very high value indeed to the legitimacy that group representation can confer. In such a case it must seek out those representatives, including Negroes and other minorities, who have the greatest prestige as a result of their participation in *nonpolitical* activities—voluntary associations, businesses, churches, education, and so forth. The price the city must pay to obtain such men, of course, is a willingness to alter substantive policies to take into account the objections and recommendations of the members of the commission.[17]

[17] Philip Selznick makes a similar argument when he distinguishes between "formal" and "informal" co-optation in the TVA. "Formal" co-optation reflects the need to establish the legitimacy of the institution without actually sharing power (this corresponds to Negro appointments in Chicago). "Informal" co-optation refers to the need to adjust the institution to specific centers of power in the community by actually sharing power. Selznick, *TVA and the Grass Roots* (Berkeley: University of California Press, 1953), pp. 259 ff.

CHAPTER 21 · THE PRESS

THE METROPOLITAN daily newspaper is one of the very few actors on the civic scene (the mayor or city manager is usually the only other) in a position both to take a comprehensive view of the public interest and to exercise a powerful influence upon all of the other actors. It is therefore a political institution of great importance. But it is also a business—a manufacturing company which must meet a payroll and return dividends to stockholders. To understand its civic role, one must keep these two functions in mind and be aware of the tension that exists between them.

THE NEWSPAPER BUSINESS

The circulation of daily newspapers is at an all-time high, whether measured absolutely (60,000,000 copies a day in 1962) or in relation to the number of adults in the population.[1] Except among the very poor, almost everyone who is old enough to read reads at least one paper—or some part of it. Although the number of daily papers declined sharply between 1925 and 1945, the number in 1962 (1,760 papers in 1,460 cities) was a little larger than it was in the 1940's. Very few cities now have two or more papers under competitive ownership, but 91 percent of the people living in metropolitan areas (in which two thirds of all Americans live) are served locally by two or more dailies, 43 percent are served by three or more, and 30 percent are served by four or more.

For the big metropolitan dailies, however, business has not been good. Although the population of the metropolitan areas has increased greatly, the central-city papers have not increased their circulation very much. Most of the gain in readers has gone to suburban dailies. The

[1] The data in this paragraph are from Leo Bogart, "Newspapers in the Age of Television," *Daedalus*, Winter 1963, pp. 116–117. See also T. J. Kreps, "The Structure of the Newspaper Industry," in W. H. Adams (ed.), *The Structure of American Industry* (New York: Macmillan, 1961).

seven New York City dailies gained only 1.1 percent in circulation between 1952 and 1957 while the suburban papers gained 26.6 percent.[2] In Chicago, the daily *Tribune* lost almost 100,000 readers between 1950 and 1961, most of them in the suburbs. In Los Angeles the metropolitan area population increased 59 percent in a decade but the circulation of the central-city newspapers increased by only 4 percent. Papers have merged in five big cities (Los Angeles, Pittsburgh, Boston, Cleveland, and Detroit) in the last few years, and other mergers appear to be pending. A new daily has appeared in only one major city (Phoenix), though new ones have sprung up in many small fast-growing communities.

Newspapers get two thirds of their operating revenue from advertising. In recent years this revenue, though declining as a percentage of all advertising revenues, has grown in absolute terms and still is larger than that of television, radio, magazines, and billboards combined. The cost of newsprint and labor, the two great expense items for the newspaper publisher, have increased steadily, however, putting some papers in a tight financial squeeze. The big papers which went out of business did so for lack of sufficient advertising; they had about as many readers as ever.

The number of television and radio stations competing with newspapers for advertising dollars and public attention has increased rapidly. (Los Angeles, for example, has seven TV stations and more than twenty radio stations, including one for Negroes.) Some cities have influential TV and radio news commentators. In general, however, newspapers are still by far the most important source of local news and comment. Perhaps this is because some special magic attaches to the printed word. More likely it is because the newspaper is centered on the community in a way that the broadcasting station is not. As Leo Bogart remarks, the broadcaster is not likely to have as deep roots in the community as the newspaper. "His network affiliation (which he almost surely has if he is in TV) gives him a feeling of being hooked onto the New York–Hollywood main line. A larger proportion of his revenues comes from the national advertisers than from the local merchants. Thus his orientation tends to be toward the

[2] W. Eric Gustafson, "Printing and Publishing," in Max Hall (ed.), *Made in New York* (Cambridge, Mass.: Harvard University Press, 1959), p. 161. The tabloids lost circulation (3.6 to 4.8 percent) while the *New York Times* gained greatly (22.8 percent).

airport and the long distance telephone rather than toward what is going on around the corner."[3]

The metropolitan daily's orientation toward the city—and above all toward its central business district—is to be explained, perhaps, by the fact that three fourths of its advertising comes from local sources, especially department stores.[4] Because of their close dependence on local advertisers, metropolitan papers have been seriously hurt by the flight of the middle class to the suburbs and the declining volume of retail sales in the central business district. That the loss of population to the suburbs is offset, or partly offset, by larger numbers of lower-class people does not help matters very much from the standpoint of the newspapers, for the lower class have less to spend in the stores and are more difficult for a newspaper to reach. Every paper has a more or less distinctive character, the product of a long process of selection by both editors and readers. In the nature of the things, a character which appeals to one social class will not appeal to a different one. The kind of advertising a newspaper gets depends, moreover, upon the income and status of its readers. For these reasons, it does not try to appeal simultaneously to two very different readerships (say middle-class whites and lower-class Negroes). There is not, therefore, much that a middle-class newspaper can do to adapt to the situation if the population of the city changes from predominantly middle-class to predominantly lower-class.

Suburban dailies and community weeklies are supported by advertising from neighborhood and small-city shopping centers, for which they are a cheaper advertising medium than is the metropolitan press.[5] Their audiences are relatively homogeneous, and their social function, which they more or less consciously pursue, is that of creating a sense of community by stressing matters that are noncontroversial and of common interest in the locality. Whereas the metropolitan paper is in

[3] Bogart, "Newspapers in the Age of Television," p. 121.

[4] *Editor and Publisher*, April 20, 1957, p. 18, and U.S. Bureau of the Census, *1954 Census of Manufactures*, vol. II, part I, table 6C, p. 27A–16.

[5] Suburban dailies are more numerous in the West than in the East or the Midwest. There are twenty-six in the Los Angeles area, which is served by two metropolitan-wide papers. There are seven in the Oakland, California, area, which is served by the metropolitan-wide *Tribune*. Around Chicago, on the other hand, there are few strong suburban dailies, although the Copley chain (Aurora, Elgin, and other places) is vigorous. On the community press in the Chicago area, see Morris Janowitz, *The Community Press in an Urban Setting* (Glencoe, Ill.: Free Press, 1954).

a position similar to that of a mayor elected at large, theirs is similar to that of a ward or district leader. Frequently they bitterly oppose the measures supported by the large dailies in the name of the metropolitan-wide general interest.

THE CIVIC ROLE OF THE NEWSPAPER

The newspaper makes its principal effect on local public affairs by reporting and interpreting the news. The amount of space a paper gives to news stories of all kinds (its "newshole") is fixed within narrow limits by previous policy decisions. Ordinarily it is only a fraction of the total paper, since most of the space is given to advertisements and much of the rest to regularly scheduled features such as editorials, "columns," comics, stock market prices, and sports pages. Editors decide on a day-to-day basis the relative emphasis to be given to local stories as against state, national, and international news. Every day brings a different mix of news, and furthermore every city room has its own set of predilections. Crime and disaster and "human interest" (treed cats, hero cops, pretty girls arriving from Hollywood by plane) are balanced against wars and the doings of governments and social and economic matters by editors who take into account not only what they think the paper's clientele wants to read but also what they think it ought to read. It is not unusual for a big-city paper to give local and metropolitan news about the same space as it gives to national and foreign news.

Few dailies assign more than one reporter to local government news; he usually covers the mayor's office, the principal departments and independent agencies, and some of the civic associations. He is seldom the liveliest reporter on the paper, and if he has covered city hall for many years he is likely to be in a symbiotic relationship with the politicians and bureaucrats whose activities he reports. He wants to get stories with minimal effort; the politicians want publicity. He knows more than he can safely publish: failure to "play ball" would cost him his inside track on the news and perhaps embarrass his publisher. The politician, on the other hand, is eager to cultivate the reporters; to do this he must feed them good stories from time to time and keep them supplied with "tips." He knows that some of his tips will backfire on him and that the reporter cannot be trusted completely. Some city hall reporters simplify their task by making collusive arrangements to ensure that no reporter will be embarrassed by another's getting an "exclusive." In many places, the reporters rely largely on mimeographed "handouts" from government offices. Here and there they are on the payroll of politicians or interest groups, sometimes with the tacit consent of their city editors.[6] The principal factor offsetting this tendency toward sloppy, uncritical, and fragmentary handling of the local news is the spirit of professionalism among reporters and editors; this is strongest on the staffs of big-city papers.

With rare exceptions (the *New York Times* is a conspicuous one) newspapers are given to crusading in their news columns as well as in editorials—some almost constantly, others in fits and starts. Crime and corruption in high places are the preferred targets, but inefficiency and favoritism will do. Editors believe, rightly or wrongly, that crusades help to sell papers, but this is not the only reason why newspapers undertake them. Publishers, editors, and reporters all believe that a free press is the best guardian of the people's liberties, and many of them are inclined to think that a conspicuous demonstration of the power of the press has a wholesome effect even when the people's liberties are in no immediate danger. In the popular mind, the crusading city editor is a folk-hero cast in the same mold with the crusading district attorney. Newspapermen tend to share this view, and whether they share it or not they are glad to propagate it among their readers. A successful crusade may get the newspaper a Pulitzer prize, the prestige value of which is high. This possibility in itself would be enough to encourage crusading.

In "clean" cities perforce and in others on occasion, the crusading impulse is turned toward the promotion of projects for civic improvement—expressways, civic centers, metropolitan planning, and the like. By boosting for such projects, a paper shows its readers and advertisers that it is powerful and public-spirited. Besides, if the projects are carried out, the effect is presumably to create a "more favorable climate for business," including of course, the newspaper business.[7]

Many newspapers participate actively in the choice of candidates for local office. Some limit themselves to publishing a sample ballot of endorsements the day before election. Others campaign vigorously

[6] A few such cases are reported by Peter Braestrup in E. C. Banfield and Martha Derthick (ed.), *A Report on the Politics of Boston* (Cambridge, Mass.: Joint Center for Urban Studies, 1960, mimeo). An abbreviated version of Braestrup's report appeared in *Harper's*, October 1960, pp. 79–94.

[7] See, for example, the testimony of the editors of the *Chicago Tribune*, in Banfield, *Political Influence* (New York: Free Press of Glencoe, 1961), chap. vii, esp. pp. 230–231.

for their candidates. Not uncommonly, a publisher or editor plays a leading behind-the-scenes role in the choice of candidates.

Newspapers, like other big businesses with manufacturing plants, real estate holdings, and hundreds of employees, sometimes want favors from the city government. Needless to say, they are in a much better position than others to get them, for no day passes without their having an opportunity to give or withhold favors of their own. The use a paper will make of its "clout" depends to some extent upon the character of its management. But it depends also upon the nature of the city's political system. In a nonpartisan, council-manager city where economy, efficiency, and impartiality are the watch-words, a newspaper is not likely to ask for many favors. On the other hand, in a city whose politics is based on getting and giving favors, the newspaper is likely to be one of the principal getters. In such a city, it may (for example) ignore the setback requirements of the building code when it builds its new plant, get suits against itself expedited and criminal charges against one of its employees dropped, bring about the promotion of cooperative policemen and the transfer of uncooperative ones, and arrange to have its real estate under-assessed. (Incumbent assessors in such cities can almost always count on newspapers to support them for re-election.)

In cities where favors are to be had, newspapers are likely to seek them for their "friends" as well as for themselves. If a big department store's toes are being stepped on by the urban renewal agency, the newspaper will take the matter up with the mayor. Lesser interests may also turn to it for help in such routine matters as applications for liquor licenses, driveway permits, and zoning variations.

It is usually the reporter on the city hall beat who is expected to get things "taken care of" for the paper. Normally he asks the favor of the appropriate department head. "If his request is legitimate," a mayor's press secretary has written to the authors of this book, "the matter is expedited. In cases where requests are not legitimate, department heads make them look so. As for myself, if a favor is legitimate, I will unquestionably expedite it, and in many instances this will save the newspaper not only considerable time but also money. If it is not legitimate, I force the reporter to go to the Mayor, who usually sends him back to me. Then the publisher will step in, or one of his executives, and I don't know what happens."

It would be a mistake to assume, however, either that most newspapers are in the habit of asking for substantial favors or that those which do habitually ask for them value them highly enough to give editorial support to unworthy officials in order to get them. Some people assume that everything a newspaper does in local affairs is either a pay-off for a business advantage that has been given to the newspaper or else is somehow intended to increase the newspaper's profits.[8] This, in our opinion, is a great oversimplification. The newspaper's news coverage, crusading, electioneering, and favor-giving and getting are often self-serving, to be sure, but they are seldom so in a purely business way; any benefits to the paper are usually indirect and incidental and in terms of intangibles like power and prestige rather than in money.

The owners of newspapers do not think of them simply as businesses —i.e., as means of getting the largest possible money return on their capital. The newspaper owner wants to make a profit, of course, but not necessarily the largest one possible. He has his money in a newspaper rather than some other business (say shoe manufacturing) precisely because he wants nonmonetary as well as monetary returns. He may want prestige, power, and the opportunity to impress his personality upon public events. Or he may want to contribute to public welfare. It is probably because these nonmonetary returns are so important in the newspaper business that newspapers, to a greater extent than other business of the same scale, are owned by families, frequently by families that are enormously wealthy and imbued with a strong sense of "responsibility to serve the public welfare." (The *Washington Post*, the *Philadelphia Inquirer*, and the *Chicago Sun-Times–Daily News* are conspicuous examples).[9] The sense of "responsibility" is not, however, confined to those newspaper owners who are very wealthy. In varying degrees, it is felt by practically all of them.

[8] Cf. A. J. Liebling, *The Press* (New York: Ballatine Books, 1961), pp. 3–25.

[9] In recent years, a new type of publisher—typified by S. I. Newhouse—has come on the scene. These men look upon newspapers almost entirely as investments, judge them almost entirely on the basis of their profitability, and appear to be more or less disinterested in the paper's civic or political character. Editors are given even freer rein in forming the paper's "image" than is usual (subject, of course, to a profit constraint). Men such as Newhouse have a great advantage over rich families which own papers. Since they receive primarily material satisfactions from ownership, they are not deterred from reorganizing the management or altering the paper's character by fear of any loss in nonmaterial satisfaction.

That the newspaper is run to get nonmonetary, as well as monetary, returns and that it is generally a family affair are circumstances that tend to make its civic role somewhat hard to predict. The standard that is usually applicable in predicting the behavior of a business firm, namely the profit criterion, is more misleading than helpful. To the extent that the purpose of the paper is to provide an outlet through which the boss can "express his personality" or "do good," its civic role may be almost anything. And if, as is often the case, the paper is owned by several members of a family each of whom has a personality to express and ideas about what "doing good" consists of, the uncertainty is compounded.

It is not, however, as easy as one might think for a publisher to get his whims—or even his settled convictions—reflected in the columns of his newspaper. The editorial "side" of the paper has its own ideas. Editors and reporters are seized with enthusiasms which cause them to write features, interpretative pieces, and editorials which the publisher may not like. If he interferes too much in matters that they feel lie within their sphere of judgment and especially if his interference is of a kind that they feel comprises their integrity, their morale will suffer and they may leave. Replacing them does not solve the publisher's problem, for the replacements have ideas too. None of these difficulties is absolutely insuperable, of course, and a sufficiently determined publisher can get his way most of the time, as is proved by the existence of numerous papers with strong biases that are not generally shared by their employees.[10]

The money interest of the newspaper, moreover, is seldom seriously involved in the issues that are treated in its news and editorial columns. If, as is likely, the newspaper is a strenuous advocate of economy and lower taxes, the reason is not that its publisher wants to lower the taxes on his plant. Local taxes are a very minor part of his costs; newsprint and wages (especially those of printers) are vastly more important.

The newspaper does, however, have an *indirect* interest in many of the matters that it "pushes." It is of course eager to increase its circulation and advertising. Whatever will bring more people into its circulation area, whatever will increase the people's spending power, whatever will contribute to the prosperity of the department stores and other big advertisers, whatever will attract new businesses, and thus

[10] Cf. Warren Breed, "Social Control in the Newsroom; A Functional Analysis," *Social Forces*, May 1955, p. 333.

new advertising, to the city, is likely to have the ardent support of the paper.

The newspaper's interest in "creating a good climate for business" inclines it toward boosterism, and inclines it also, on occasion, to "play down" or even suppress news that would put the city in a bad light. Stories about racial strife, police brutality, bad management-labor relations, slums, high taxes, traffic congestion, smog and soot are often handled gingerly.[11] Some newspapers look the other way to avoid seeing vice and gambling. These are usually in convention cities. If they insisted upon putting an end to the illegal attractions which keep the hotels, restaurants, and nightclubs of the city jammed with free-spending convention-goers, they would not be showing a proper civic spirit.

Obviously the crusading impulse and the booster impulse come in conflict. The conflict is managed by crusading intermittently and by choosing targets circumspectly. In the usual case, a steady low paean of praise to the city is interrupted briefly by cries of alarm when the time comes once more to remind the citizens of their civic duties or to go to the aid of the beleaguered taxpayer.

THE NEGLECT OF CIVIC AFFAIRS

The question may be asked why, if editors and publishers regard the newspaper as a force for community improvement, they do not print more news of local government? And why is the news that they do print not more carefully and intelligently interpreted and analyzed?

A very general answer is to be found in the peculiarly public-private character of the newspaper. It must do more than serve the community; it must meet its payroll and make a profit as well. Most daily papers probably give more space to local government than they would if they acted in a purely businesslike (profit-maximizing) way. The cost of really covering local government and civic affairs is high, and the return in readership, and ultimately in advertising, is usually low. If a paper reduces its coverage of civic affairs to make room for another comic strip or for more "kitchen hints," it will ordinarily gain rather than lose circulation.

In short, it is the community-serving rather than the profit-making impulse that most often inspires the present policy. Editors give their readers as much news of local government as they do, not because the

[11] Reo M. Christenson, "The Power of the Press: The Case of 'The Toledo Blade,'" *Midwest Journal of Political Science*, August 1959, p. 238.

readers want it but because the editors think they ought to have it. Coverage of local government is to a large extent a luxury that the paper indulges in from public-serving motives. It follows, then, that the more prosperous the paper, the more of the luxury (up to a point) it will feel it can afford. In the cities where local government is especially well covered—for example, New York, Providence, Cleveland, Milwaukee, Louisville, Detroit, and St. Louis—the papers giving the good coverage are generally prosperous. In the few cities where papers are really competitive, the coverage of local government is conspicuously thin. Crime and sensation, human interest, and circulation-building contests tend to take the place of serious coverage of local news in these cities.[12]

Paradoxical as it may seem, it is partly because the newspaper regards its coverage of local government, and indeed any crusading for civic causes as well, as largely a community service that its treatment of them is often superficial and stereotyped. Civic affairs, although often taken seriously by particular editors and writers, are hardly ever among the main preoccupations of the people who run the newspaper. Out of a sense of duty and for public relations reasons these people want to display a community-serving attitude. To display the attitude is usually enough, however; the paper need not actually serve the community. Indeed, to do so would as a rule require incurring costs that even a large and prosperous newspaper would not be willing to afford in the name of public service, for it takes good reporters indeed to report the news fairly and interpret it intelligently, and it takes more than good reporting to arrive at realistic and constructive editorial positions on civic affairs.

Editorial conferences about civic issues tend to be perfunctory. Very often, a paper's position is formed, as well as expressed, in a few clichés. Reporters and editorial writers generally share the orientation of the civic association professionals, and the desire of the paper to maintain good relations with them (not to mention the convenience of the reporter, who would have to dig for himself if he did not depend upon them) leads to their getting sympathetic treatment almost automatically, especially if they take positions well known to be "sound."[13] The newspaper, accordingly, is apt to be in favor of metro-

[12] This point is documented to some extent by Braestrup, cited in footnote 6.

[13] Norton Long has remarked that for civic leaders, as well as newspapers, publicity tends to be a substitute for achievement, and civic reputation depends less on realizing goals than on being described in the press as a "civic leader." "For top influentials," he says, " . . . the news clips are an important way of

politan planning even if none of its editors has ever considered how in the absence of a metropolitan government a plan could be carried into effect. Similarly, it is apt to be in favor of urban renewal even if none of its editors has ever considered whether the housing supply will be increased or decreased thereby or where the slum dwellers who will be displaced are likely to go.

Three other factors tend to make newspaper treatment of civic issues superficial. One is the pace of newspaper work. The newspaperman's mind is geared to the clock—usually to its minute hand. He does not ordinarily plan much beyond the next day, and a matter which cannot be explained or analyzed quickly does not interest him. A second factor that tends to make newspaper writing superficial is its perfectly public character. There are some matters that cannot be discussed intelligently in the presence of the whole public, or at least cannot be discussed so within the space limitations of a newspaper. The newspaper writer who carries his analysis beyond what is merely plausible runs a very grave risk both of offending some readers and— what may be much worse in the eyes of the paper—of boring others. The third factor tending toward superficiality is its preoccupation with what is unique rather than what is typical. Particular circumstances of time and place are "interesting"; generalizations are not. But it is only in terms of the general that serious analysis can proceed. A reporter's vivid account of an angry confrontation between a police commissioner and the city council may make good reading, but as a description of political reality it is trivial as compared to a "trend" or "situation" story that plays down personalities and looks instead for some underlying logic that governs the relations between councilmen and department heads in general.

THE INFLUENCE OF NEWSPAPERS

When a newspaper really seeks to achieve an effect on public policy (and not merely to convey the impression that it is trying to achieve one), the degree of success that it has depends in large part upon the

keeping score. . . . It is not surprising that civic staff men should begin to equate accomplishment with their score measured in newspaper victories or that they should succumb to the temptation to impress their sponsors with publicity. . . . Many a civic ghost-writer has found his top leader converted to the cause by reading the ghosted speech he delivered at the civic luncheon reported with photographs and editorials in the press. This is even the case where the story appears in the top leader's own paper." Norton E. Long, "The Local Community as an Ecology of Games," *American Journal of Sociology*, November 1958, pp. 251–261.

structure of politics in the city. The more decentralized is authority in a city, the greater is the opportunity for unofficial institutions, especially civic associations, labor and business organizations, and newspapers to exercise influence. As we remarked in an earlier chapter, newspapers play a particularly important part in the electoral processes of nonpartisan cities, especially those so large that candidates cannot become known to the electorate through direct personal contacts.

The influence of newspapers is especially great among the middle class. "As one ascends the social scale," Bogart observes, "there is a greater sense of ease, intimacy, and personal relationship between the reader and his paper. It seems as though the better educated reader is more likely to view his hometown paper as an institution made up of people doing a job, subject to personal influences, and capable of rendering a service. For those lower on the educational scale, the newspaper as a major institution of power appears more remote and impersonal."[14] Where voters must choose among many obscure candidates or pass on a multitude of referenda issues, the newspaper acquires added influence. It acquires added influence also where they are given to split-ticket voting, unless, of course, the paper is undeviatingly partisan, in which case it will be ignored.[15] All of this means that the influence of an independent newspaper in a middle-class city is likely to be considerable.

The special place of the newspaper in the politics of the nonpartisan city may be seen in Detroit and Los Angeles. In Detroit, newspaper-backed candidates for city council have usually won, sometimes against labor-backed opponents, and the newspapers played an important part in the election of Mayor Albert Cobo, a conservative businessman, and his successor, Louis Miriani. The *Detroit News,* which assigns six reporters to the city-county building, is regarded as a "watchdog" of local government. In Los Angeles, the *Times* has long been regarded as the most powerful single political force in the city. Its influence arises partly from the involvement of its owners, the Chandler family, in a wide network of business and public affairs, but the highly decentralized nature of the city's governmental and party structure is an important element of the situation.

[14] Bogart, "Newspapers in the Age of Television," p. 124.
[15] See Banfield, *Political Influence,* p. 55. The first—and still almost the only—study of the influence of the press, Harold Gosnell's chapter on "The Relation of the Press to Voting," in his *Machine Politics: Chicago Model* (Chicago: University of Chicago Press, 1937), showed correlations between split-ticket endorsements by newspapers and split-ticket voting.

Chicago presents a sharply contrasting case. There, political power is highly centralized in the Democratic machine and the influence of the press is correspondingly weak. The *Tribune,* the largest and loudest of the Chicago papers, is unshakably Republican in everything and therefore has even less influence than it otherwise might. Although the Chicago papers are eager to exert influence in local affairs, they rarely have much effect. In three major civic controversies studied in 1957–58, the losing side had the enthusiastic support of all four newspapers. In three other controversies, the papers were on opposite sides or else not much involved.[16]

Cleveland's political structure is about mid-way between the extreme decentralization of Detroit and Los Angeles and the extreme centralization of Chicago. It has a party organization (Democratic), but a declining one. Its newspapers, the *Press* and the *Plain Dealer* (particularly the former), have elected mayors for about a quarter of a century with little help from the party and sometimes over its opposition. The mayors of Cleveland, accordingly, have been nonpartisan, good-government types, whereas the city councilmen, who have been chosen by the party and not the newspaper, have often been politicians of the old school.[17]

The influence of the newspaper with the voter is not to be taken for granted, however. Even in the cities where their influence is normally great, there are times when the endorsement of the newspapers seems to hurt a candidate more than help him. For example, in 1959 and 1961, Boston, Los Angeles, and Detroit elected mayors who had been decided underdogs as candidates, having no newspaper or other important support. In these cities the voters apparently grouped the newspapers, the professional politicians, and the business elite together as a "power structure" which they then repudiated—perhaps because of economic stagnation, accumulated grievances, or a general disaffection from local politics.

[16] Banfield, *Political Influence,* pp. 47, 86, 95, 131, 163, 182, 193.
[17] The situation in Toledo is apparently similar. See Christenson, "Power of the Press."

CONCLUSION

CONCLUSION · THE TREND
OF CITY POLITICS

OUR ACCOUNT of city politics has followed three main lines of analysis. One of them concerns the distribution of authority within the city, especially the effects of increases and decreases in the centralization of authority. A second concerns the various mechanisms by which power is accumulated and an informal centralization of influence established. And a third concerns the political ethos and emphasizes the fundamental cleavage between the public-regarding, Anglo-Saxon Protestant, middle-class ethos and the private-regarding, lower-class, immigrant ethos. In looking ahead at the changes that may be expected to occur in city politics over the next decade or two, these same lines of analysis appear to be relevant. What we have to say in this chapter will therefore carry forward some of the main implications of the analysis in the preceding ones.

THE GENERAL TREND

All three of these factors—distribution of authority, mechanism for centralizing influence, and political ethos—are of course changing in response to a variety of pressures. In our view, the changes that are occurring in political ethos are the most important. These to a large extent determine the nature of the changes in the distribution of authority and in the mechanisms by which influence is centralized.

The changes in political ethos are the product of changes in the class composition of the urban electorate. The immigrant lower class has been, and is still being, absorbed into the middle class at a rapid rate. This has profoundly affected the outlook of the electorate, for the middle class has always held to the Anglo-Saxon Protestant political ideal and those who have joined it have accepted this ideal along with others. The "new immigrant" (as Samuel Lubell has called these newcomers to the middle class) prefers political candidates who like himself have passed along the "tenement trail."[1] But increasingly

[1] Samuel Lubell, *The Future of American Politics* (Garden City, N.Y.: Doubleday, 1952), chap. iv.

the "new immigrant" has come to demand candidates who, whatever their origins, have the community-serving ethos and the public virtues that have long been associated with the Protestant elite.

The reader who has followed us this far will see that this shift from a predominantly lower-class to a predominantly middle-class political style is of pervasive importance. As we have said, the middle-class ideal sees local politics as a cooperative search for the concrete implications of a more or less objective public interest, an interest of the community "as a whole." The logic of the middle-class ideal requires that authority be exercised by those who are "best qualified," that is, technical experts and statesmen, not "politicians." The logic of the middle-class ideal implies also certain institutional arrangements (nonpartisanship, at-large election, the council-manager form, master planning, and metropolitan area organization); particular regard for the public virtues of honesty, efficiency, and impartiality; and a disposition to encourage the consumption of "public goods" like schools, parks, museums, libraries, and, by extension, urban renewal. In general, the tendency is toward what Benjamin DeMott has called "an apolitical politics, partyless and problemless."[2]

To be sure, middle-class families are moving toward the outskirts of metropolitan areas, and the populations of the larger, older cities are still heavily lower-class. Indeed, they may become somewhat more so in the next decade. The old-style politics of the boss and machine is, and no doubt will remain, highly congenial to the lower class. However, the nationally growing middle class has shown that it will use its control of state and federal governments—and particularly of law enforcement agencies and of special districts within the metropolitan areas—to withhold the patronage, protection, and other political resources that are indispensable to the growth of political machines in the central cities. This means that the lower class will have to play politics of a kind that is tolerable to the middle class or not play it at all.

SOME PARTICULAR TRENDS

The general trend toward local government in accordance with the middle-class ideal implies a great many particular trends, only a few of which can be mentioned here.

[2] Benjamin DeMott, "Party Apolitics," *The American Scholar*, Autumn 1962, p. 597.

One is a spreading and deepening popular hostility toward everything that has about it the odor of the smoke-filled room—toward such bosses and remnants of machines as still exist, toward all forms of professionalism in politics, and even toward politics itself. In many cities politicians find it easier to stir the electorate with charges of "bossism" and corruption, however little the grounds for such charges, than with discussion of matters that are more substantial and more pertinent. For example, in New York City, where many things of real and pressing importance need discussion, Governor Rockefeller and Mayor Wagner find it profitable to carry on their warfare mainly by exchanging charges and countercharges of "machine politics" and "bossism."

To regard politics as contrary to the public interest is consistent with the middle-class ideal; reformers have always taken this view. That the "new immigrants," once they have been assimilated into the middle class, should be contemptuous of politics is to be expected. There are indications, however, that their contempt for it is stronger than can be accounted for on these grounds alone. Perhaps it is in part symbolic —a gesture meant to repudiate not the style of politics alone but also, and perhaps mainly, the inferior class and ethnic status from which it sprang.

The old style of politics was not at all concerned with principles or ideology, and characteristically it took account of policy issues only as they promised to afford some private advantages. The new style, although highly principled and the expression of an ideology of sorts, is much more concerned with *how* things are done than with *what* is done. By an altogether different route, then, it arrives at a politics which is almost, if not quite, as problemless as the politics of the machine and the boss. In this, perhaps, is to be found another reason for the growing popular dissatisfaction with local politics in general. The tendency of the new style is to produce cynicism and boredom— cynicism because its procedural principles can never be fully lived up to and boredom because, when self-interest is excluded and the public interest is understood in procedural rather than substantive terms, nothing of much importance remains. Politics was more exciting as a "game" than it is as "service" to the community.

The ascendancy of the middle-class ideal will have an effect on what kinds of people enter local politics and rise through it. Without "gravy" with which to build machines and large followings, opportunities for political entrepreneurs to appear from within the lower class and to rise in the world through local politics will be few. The present lower class in many of the central cities and older suburbs is largely Negro, and the disappearance of this time-tested route of social mobility will doubtless have importance for the status of the race. If able and ambitious young men cannot get ahead through local politics (and therefore not through illicit enterprises either, since these enterprises cannot prosper in the atmosphere of the middle-class ideal), the assimilation of the whole minority may be retarded. Doubtless the most able and ambitious individuals will find other routes by which to climb; even so, the total amount of mobility—the number who rise multiplied by the distance that they rise—will be reduced.

Another effect of denying to the lower class the opportunity to play the only kind of politics that it knows how to play, or wants to play, will be to slow down the rate at which it acquires political interests and skills. The old style of politics gave the European immigrant a sense of belonging to a political community. The most recent immigrants to the cities, rural Negroes mainly, are unfortunate in having come just after the earlier immigrant groups, having learned their first lessons, have declared the old elementary school of politics—the ward-based machine—obsolete and anachronistic. To some extent, the Negro's segregated position may exempt him from this effect. Just as segregation and the alleged inferiority of the Negro make it possible for "policy" and other illicit activities that would not be so easily tolerated among whites to flourish in the Negro community, so the same causes may allow the old style of politics to continue there after it has been proscribed elsewhere. This is likely to happen only insofar as the Negro political world does not intrude upon the white one, however, and this, because of forces operating in both the Negro and the white political worlds, is not likely to be very far. Where the white majority has something to gain or lose from the existence of lower-class Negro organization, it may be expected to intervene and, ultimately, to set the rules within which Negro politics must be carried on. Moreover, even where Negroes are permitted to play the old style of politics, those of them who are most successful at it will not be permitted, as quite a few of the last generation were, to become respectable and to move into (predominantly middle-class) state and national politics. Such Negroes as manage to enter state and national politics will almost certainly have to do so by some route less offensive to the middle class than the old-style, necessarily corrupt machine.

If the middle-class ideal will exclude some types from politics, it will bring others into it. There will be a constant demand for "fresh faces"—for candidates who at least *seem* free from the taint of professionalism and who have the technical qualifications and the disinterestedness that the new style of politics calls for. The ideal, of course, is government without politics or politicians—real nonpartisanship. Even where partisan forms are retained, politicians will find it increasingly necessary to pretend to be nonpartisan—to play "party apolitics" as DeMott calls it. Mayor Daley of Chicago, for example, makes no mention of his party affiliation in his campaign literature; he presents himself as an efficient, impartial, and expert administrator. As the political weight of the middle class grows, politicians will try to look more and more like city managers.

The same forces that push the politician in this direction will draw professional administrators into politics. Here the example from Chicago can be balanced by one from New York. Paul R. Screvane, a career civil servant in the sanitation department who was elected to public office for the first time in 1962, was being written about in the spring of 1963 as a likely successor to Mayor Wagner.[3] A professional administrator like Screvane who wishes to pass for a politician needs some disguise, just as the politician who wishes to pass for a city manager needs some, for there are still many in the party and in the electorate who would not be satisfied with an administrator pure and simple. In general, however, it will probably be easier for the administrator than for the professional politician to acquire the right "image."

To an increasing extent, the issues of city politics will be connected with the larger, ideological ones of national politics. Urban renewal projects, for example, are very likely to raise the national and ideological issue of race. Because of this close connection with larger issues, local politics will be of increasing interest to those people whom Robert K. Merton has described as cosmopolitans rather than locals. It is altogether unlikely, however, that the locals will lose their near monopoly on city politics. City government will always be mainly a

[3] See Marion K. Sanders, "The Next Mayor of New York?" *Harper's*, February 1963. Screvane is described as "a kind of one-man balanced ticket—half Italian, half Irish, and he speaks Yiddish." But the writer attaches great importance to the "vigorous public commitments" he has made to "good government" goals.

matter of finding concrete solutions for practical problems, a task not congenial to the cosmopolitan. If here and there ideologues acquire power, they will have to find ways of coping with real problems; and that—as we observed in our account of the Manhattan reformers— will not be easy.

The circumstances that give an advantage to "fresh faces" (whether faces of politicians made up to look like city managers or of city managers made up to look like politicians) will tend also to increase the influence of the press, the civic associations, and lay civic leadership in general. These institutions speak (or claim to speak) from expertise and with regard to "objective facts," and to represent a conception of the public interest. To the extent that they supplant the parties in the management of the local electoral process, candidates will have to take their cues from them.

Much of this gain in influence will accrue to the paid executives who run the larger civic associations. Newspaper editors may have the final say about what candidates and issues are to be "pushed," but they will make their decisions largely on the advice of the civic association executives. As we have pointed out, most editors do not follow civic affairs closely enough to have a basis for independent judgment. Apart from the professional politician, the civic association executive is the only one in the city who does.

There is a tendency also for the activists in local government—espe- cially civic association executives, but many bureaucrats and some newspaper editors as well—to take their general policy lines from the executives of the national foundations, from federal agencies, and from such national bodies as the International City Managers' Associa- tion, the National Municipal League, the National Association of Hous- ing and Redevelopment Officials, and the American Institute of Plan- ners. The agenda of city government is being determined more and more by professionals within such bodies and less and less by the needs and problems of the particular city. This is not to say that cities are likely to do all, or even very much, of what the national "experts" say they should do. It is the subjects to be discussed, not the actions to be taken, that will be decided nationally. If the national "experts" stress the need for, say, metropolitan area organization, this need—whether real or imaginary—will preoccupy local civic associations and editorial writers; but it may not lead to acceptance of any plan for reorganiza- tion. When considered concretely, such matters are likely to be decided in the light of particular needs and interests, not of general principles.

The changes that *are* produced by the orthodoxy of the national "experts" may be more symbolic than real. The immediate purposes of the executives in the national organizations may sometimes be served as well by nominal changes as by real ones. If, for example, the officials of federal agencies are keen to have the cities engage in master planning because it gives them (the federal officials) grounds on which to claim that federal assistance is being used wisely, it matters little that the plans have no real validity; it is enough that they exist on paper. And if master planning can be accepted by the cities in principle and rejected by them in practice, other reforms prescribed by the national orthodoxy probably can too.

In an earlier chapter we remarked upon the tendency toward centralization of authority in the hands of the executive (mayor or manager). This tendency will doubtless be more marked in the next decade as the demand for more and better city services mounts. Independent and semi-independent boards and commissions (civil service agencies, for example) will be brought under the authority of the executive, and the amount and quality of technical aids and staff services available to the executive will be increased. All the recommendations of the national "experts," it is safe to say, will tend in this direction.[4]

The decay of the old style of politics will hasten the process of centralization. When there were many jobs and favors to be dispensed and much money and power to be acquired by dispensing them, a horde of local politicians had a powerful incentive to maintain the decentralization of authority that gave each his bailiwick.[5] As the number and value of jobs and favors has declined, so has the number of old-style politicians. The relatively few who remain will resist losing their bailiwicks, no doubt, but their resistance will not be as strenuous or effective as it was when there was more at stake.

The middle-class ideal favors centralization of authority in an ever-

[4] For example, these changes are recommended by the Municipal Manpower Commission, which was created by the Ford Foundation through the vehicle of the American Municipal Association, the American Society of Planning Officials, and the American Institute of Planners. The Commission is a good example of the kind of body that produces the orthodoxy referred to in the text; it describes its recommendations as "An Agenda for Metropolis," incidentally. See Municipal Manpower Commission, *Governmental Manpower for Tomorrow's Cities* (New York: McGraw-Hill, 1962), chap. iv.

[5] The Municipal Manpower Commission quotes an administrator as saying that "cities are too hemmed in by checks and balances to make it possible to deal effectively with the types of problems which now confront cities." *Ibid.*, p. 48.

wider sphere. In order to treat all elements of a situation in a coordinated way—"as a single whole"—the city manager, planner, or other administrator must cross over any jurisdictional boundary. For example, a housing program for a central city cannot be planned apart from related facilities like schools, transportation lines, and parks. These, it will then appear, cannot be planned on a purely central-city basis; if the situation is to be treated "as a whole," the planning must be as broad as the metropolitan area. But even this is not enough; there are always some features of the situation which can be treated only on a state, regional, or national, indeed a world, basis.

Although the centralizing tendency has been at work in most cities for a long time, it has not gone far enough to offset the loss of power occasioned by the decay of the machines and, more generally, the decay of the style of politics based upon specific, and usually material, inducements. A mayor or party boss who had plenty of "gravy" to pass out could get along with little *authority* or (in the case of those bosses who did not hold office) none at all. As reform slashed the number of jobs, favors, and other rewards at the politician's disposal, it reduced his power. It compensated for this to some extent by increasing his authority. But, because the increase in authority was usually not enough to make up entirely for the loss of power, the politician's total influence declined. While this was happening, more and more accomplishment was being expected of public officials (i.e., politicians in office); both the quantity and the quality of public services being demanded increased. This left elected officials in a difficult position: as their need for influence increased, their supply of it declined.

Persistent as are the forces tending toward centralization of authority, it may be doubted that in the next decade or two they will produce city governments as strong as were those run by the old machines. The American people seem to have a deeply ingrained reluctance to centralize authority, as contrasted with power. In this respect, at least, the logic of the Anglo-Saxon Protestant political ideal has not prevailed. It seems unlikely that measures to strengthen the authority of the executive, numerous and extensive as they will probably be, will catch up with the need for greater influence that is being generated by the new demands for service. New York City is perhaps the paradigm of what may be expected. As we explained, the authority of the mayor of New York is relatively great; but his power is small, and the city government, measured against the tasks that are given it, is weak.

The shift from "ward politics" to "city administration" will be a cause, as well as an effect, of ambitious and expensive public programs. The old-style politician had no incentive to try to confer benefits on the public at large. So long as he gave jobs and favors to the right people he could maintain his organization and get the votes he needed. The new-style, "good government" politician must employ other means. Insofar as he cannot persuade people to vote for him on purely rational grounds, he must use charm and salesmanship or else offer inducements to large classes of people or to the whole public. This will cause him to think of big undertakings—generous welfare and housing programs, civil rights campaigns, transportation subsidies, and the like—which he can offer to the mass of voters in place of the "friendship" that they used to get from precinct workers. In the nature of the case, these undertakings are likely to be costly and to entail many large and unintended consequences for the life of the city. In the nature of the case, too, "general" inducements will prove less reliable in their operation than did the "specific" ones of the machine. The new-style politician's position will therefore be relatively unstable. Whereas the old-style politician could withstand almost anything except an organization stronger than his, the new-style one may disappear from the scene the moment his charm ceases to work or his general inducements cease to appeal.

Insofar as he must rely upon general inducements, there will be sharp limits on the amount of power that the new-style politician can acquire. If the benefits of a public project will be accompanied by a perceptible increase in the tax bill, the voter may decide to forego them. The politician is then in difficulty. He may get out of the difficulty by offering programs which will confer benefits on some people while putting the costs on others. He may, for example, offer the voters of his city a new sewage disposal plant which is to be paid for by the federal government—that is, by taxpayers who cannot vote against him. The need of most local politicians to offer inducements of this kind accounts in large measure for the steady enlargement of the federal, and to a lesser extent the state, government's role in local affairs.

The politician's difficulty in finding inducements to offer his constituents is increased because a program which confers a net benefit on a large majority may nevertheless decrease his vote. This is likely to happen if the benefit to the average member of the majority is rather small or intangible and if the cost imposed on the average member of a minority—even a very small minority—is large. Suppose, for example, that hundreds of thousands of voters mildly favor fluoridation of the city's water supply ("it would be a good thing on the whole") and that a few hundred are strongly opposed to it ("it is a menace to health"). In such a case, a politician may decide that supporting fluoridation will bring him no votes, since no one will vote for him for that reason alone, and will lose him some, since a few will vote *against* him for that reason alone.

In several cities mayors have set up special "citizens' relations" bureaus to help them evaluate the intensity of voters' feelings on neighborhood issues. Thus they have incorporated into the formal governmental structure mechanisms for gathering and evaluating information that used to be part of the precinct and ward organization of the party. Some mayors have tried to encourage the growth of neighborhood associations by tacitly giving them power to modify, or veto, policies that affect their neighborhoods in return for support at election time. It is too early to judge how well these arrangements will serve the purposes of the voters or the politicians. Obviously the fundamental difficulty cannot be got around altogether. The more aware city hall is of intensely moved voters, the better it can pick its steps around the danger spots; but it must step somewhere, and so it is bound to suffer the wrath of some of the intensely moved.

The reason why city hall must step somewhere is, of course, that inducements must continually be offered to the mass of voters. It might possibly "pay" a politician to favor an intense minority over a not-intense majority on every issue if issues are considered separately. But it will not "pay" him to favor the intense minorities on all issues if issues are considered—as they must be—for the aggregate effect that they will produce. Unless a politician has "accomplishments" to point to, the majority will forsake him. If a mayor has his eyes too much on the intensely moved minorities and not enough on the not intensely moved majority, a sudden groundswell of opinion is likely to sweep him out of office in favor of an unknown who has promised to "get the city moving again."

Something fairly close to the style of politics toward which the cities are tending is to be seen in the case of Washington, D.C., a city which carries "nonpartisan apolitics" to its logical extreme, there being no local electorate and the conduct of affairs being largely in the hands of professional managers. These peculiarities of Washington's governmental structure have led, according to Martha Derthick, to a characteristic style of politics: one which encourages debate on issues rather than competition for public jobs or ethnic recognition or personal publicity, and is therefore "biased in favor of both 'liberals' and 'conservatives' at the expense of people who are neither." Ideologues and representatives of organized interest groups (the latter often in association with bureaucratic allies), Miss Derthick says, are especially important in the politics of Washington because the system tends to exclude from it those who would seek patronage and public recognition. Where there is no competition for election to office, programmatic —or at least ostensibly programmatic—goals become more important.[6]

THE SIGNIFICANCE OF THE CHANGES

If one asks whether on the whole these changes are for the better, the answer is by no means obvious. Perhaps the safest statement that can be made is that the routine business of the cities will be better administered. The old-style politician got his power in part by deliberately sacrificing the efficiency and integrity of city services. He could ignore intensely moved minorities because he used jobs, favors, and protection to maintain his organization and get the vote. This, of course, made for bad administration. The new-style politician, whose power—such as it is—arises from other sources, is not under the necessity to interfere with the processes of administration. On the contrary, he wants the approval of middle-class voters who regard good government and good administration as practically synonymous, and therefore he has the strongest incentive to search out and eliminate inefficiency and corruption.

It does not necessarily follow, however, that the new style of administration will be much better—or indeed any better—than the old. Its virtues have their corresponding defects, and these, although very different in kind from the defects of the old style of administration, may—even if the quality of government services is better than before— produce a ratio of costs to benefits that is every bit as bad and perhaps even worse. If in the old days there was waste and lack of coordination for want of technically trained supervisory personnel, now there is waste and lack of coordination because of the very profusion of such personnel. If in the old days city administration was biased in favor

---

[6] Martha Derthick, "Politics in Voteless Washington," *Journal of Politics,* vol. XXV (1963), pp. 101–102.

of the tastes of the lower class as made known by ward politicians, now it is biased in favor of the tastes of the middle class as made known by newspapers, civic associations, and, especially, professionals in various bureaucracies. If in the old days authority was overly decentralized because great numbers of politicians clung to their separate scraps of it, now it is too decentralized because great numbers of bureaucrats cling to their separate scraps of it. If in the old days specific material inducements were illegally given as bribes to favored individuals, now much bigger ones are legally given to a different class of favored individuals, and, in addition, general inducements are proffered in packages to every large group in the electorate and to tiny but intensely moved minorities as well.

The difference seems to be not so much in the effect produced as in the motives leading to the production of it. The motives that produced the faults of the old-style administration were reprehensible, and this made the faults readily identifiable as such, not only by the press and public but even by those who committed them. The faults of the new style of administration arise from motives that are respectable, often even admirable, and therefore they are not usually regarded as faults at all. If by zealously protecting the tenure of city employees an independent civil service commission fills the bureaucracy with hacks, the effect of its actions, although objectively no different from that which was produced by a machine politician, escapes notice because the intentions of the civil service commissioners were good. Similarly, if a downtown merchant, by promising election support to a mayor who "does things for the city," initiates a vast urban renewal project, he may enrich himself and impoverish others more than any businessman ever did by carrying a black bag to a boss's back room; but urban renewal rarely shocks anyone's sensibilities, for the intention of the merchant is good ("in the public interest," as he would say) even though the economic consequences of his actions may be no different, except in the larger dollar values usually involved nowadays, from those of the actions of the "boodlers" whom Lincoln Steffens excoriated.

It will be understood, of course, that this evaluation says little about the authors' own preferences in the matter. Speaking for ourselves, we would prefer (other things being equal) to live in a "good government" community where the service function is honestly and efficiently performed, provided this does not prevent the government from attending to more important matters.

One might expect a city with a nonpartisan, council-manager form of government and a long "good government" tradition to provide more and better services, and to provide them at lower unit cost, than a city which has long been governed by a corrupt machine. Although this may actually be the case, there is no evidence to prove it. Measurements of governmental efficiency are seldom possible, because the services supplied by different cities are never identical and because the tastes of taxpayer-consumers differ from city to city.[7] If the people of city "A" want their rubbish collected once a week and those of city "B" want theirs collected once in two weeks, any statement about the relative efficiency of the two sanitation departments must be extremely hazardous.

Although the spread of the middle-class ideal may reduce local government's ability to manage conflict, it will also reduce the amount of conflict requiring management and make easier the management of such conflict as there is.[8] Where the electorate is divided along class lines into two camps of approximately equal size, the political problem is severe: whatever one camp favors the other opposes and neither is strong enough to have its way. This has been the situation in many cities for two or three generations. The assimilation of the lower class to the middle is upsetting the balance, however, and as the middle class achieves a large majority the old lines of conflict will disappear because the middle class will be under no necessity of making concessions. There will still be conflicts, but they will tend to be within the majority rather than between the majority and the minority. They will be relatively easy to manage, too, because they will concern the merits of concrete issues, not generalized class antagonisms. What is more, the content of the middle-class ideal is such as to make the management of conflict easier, for the ideal includes willingness to settle matters on the basis of reasonable discussion and to make sacrifices of immediate and private interest for the sake of the longer-run "larger good of the community as a whole."

It does not follow from this, however, that as the cities become "less political" they will deal more effectively with their larger problems. It is not without significance that Washington, D.C., the voteless

---

[7] See Alice Vandermeulen, "Guideposts for Measuring the Efficiency of Governmental Expenditure," *Public Administration Review*, Winter 1950, pp. 7–12.

[8] This argument is developed by Banfield, "The Political Implications of Metropolitan Growth," in Lloyd Rodwin (ed.), *The Future Metropolis* (New York: George Braziller, 1960).

and pre-eminently apolitical city, has not been notably more successful in coping with its major problems than have other large cities. Indeed, according to Martha Derthick, it is the *style* of politics ("the way in which competition proceeds") and not the *substance* of it ("the outcome of political action") that is chiefly affected by Washington's special governmental structure.[9]

One might expect that the character of a city's government would be reflected in the scope of its activities and ultimately in the income, education, and living standards of its people. Actually such fragmentary evidence as exists suggests that the more middle-class a city the less likely it is to carry out what are generally considered to be progressive undertakings. Amos H. Hawley, for example, has shown that the higher the proportion of managers, proprietors, and officials in the employed labor force of a city, the *less* likely the city is to have undertaken an urban renewal project or, if it has undertaken one, to have carried it to the execution stage. Hawley found that this correlation persists even when one holds constant such variables as region, city size, age of housing, extent of dilapidation, size of planning budget, central city or suburban character, and form of city government.[10] Similarly, Maurice Pinard has found that the higher the proportion of employed males in managerial or professional occupations in a city, the *less* likely the city is to have voted favorably on the question of fluoridation of its water supplies.[11] Our explanation of these anomalies is that the political and governmental arrangements to which the middle-class ideal gives rise tend to emphasize procedural matters (honesty, efficiency, and impartiality) at the expense of substantive ones, and are in fact often incapable of assembling the amounts of influence necessary to carry out a large undertaking. Perhaps this is because their preoccupation with procedural proprieties makes it impossible for them to offer specific inducements in the right kinds and

[9] Martha Derthick, "Politics in Voteless Washington," p. 100.

[10] Amos H. Hawley, "Community Power and Urban Renewal Success," *American Journal of Sociology*, January 1963, pp. 422–431. See also the evidence that variations in the form of city government make no difference in the likelihood of a city's having a successful renewal program, in George S. Duggar, "The Relation of Local Government Structure to Urban Renewal," *Law and Contemporary Problems*, vol. XXVI (1961), pp. 49–69.

[11] Maurice Pinard, "Structural Attachments and Political Support in Urban Politics: The Case of Fluoridation Referendums," *American Journal of Sociology*, March 1963, pp. 513–526.

amounts. (Pinard, it is interesting to note, remarks that middle-class *individuals* tend to be more favorable to fluoridation than lower-class ones, whereas middle-class *communities* tend to be less favorable to it than lower-class ones. This, he thinks, may be explained "by different structural arrangements within the elites and between the social classes.")[12] Whatever may be the effect of city politics on the scope and character of local government activities, it seems to make little or no difference in the general standard of living. If one compares a few notably "good government" cities with a few notably "not good government" ones (eliminating from consideration all those that differ greatly in size, racial composition, and geographical location), the differences in median education, in median income, and in median rents will be found to be greater among cities in the same category ("good government" or "not good government") than among those in different categories.

It is our impression that the character of a city's politics affects the amount and manner of law enforcement more than it does anything else in the city. "Good government" cities are never "wide open," and their policemen and courts are relatively honest and impartial. So far as we know, the police forces with national reputations for competence and integrity are all in cities dominated by the middle-class ideal. Beyond this, however, it is very difficult to generalize. Cities with similar political styles differ greatly in their treatment of the various forms of vice. We suspect that cities which are markedly new-style in their politics, although in general much less tolerant of vice than other cities, are nevertheless relatively tolerant of those forms of it—obscenity, for example—that are peculiar to the middle class. Moreover, among the cities that retain the old style of politics, some are much less tolerant of vice—or in some cases of certain vices—than others. The notorious Hague machine, for example, was puritanical in its enforcement of laws against prostitution and dope peddling, and it kept the Prohibition mobs and later the Syndicate out of Jersey City.

It would be easy to overestimate what even strong city governments could do about the most important problems of the cities nowadays. The city, it should not be forgotten, is legally and in fact the creature of the state. In some places, to be sure, "home rule" has lengthened the leading strings on which the city is held; nevertheless the critical de-

12 *Ibid.*, p. 525.

cisions will be made mostly by governors and legislatures, not mayors and city councils. If the control over the cities is taken from the states, it will be taken by the federal government, not the cities.

The most fundamental problem of the central cities and of the older suburbs—one that constitutes a life-and-death crisis for them—is of such a nature that it cannot be "solved," or even much relieved, by government action at any level—local, state, or national. As we explained near the outset of the book, a large part of the housing in these cities, although built not very long ago and still structurally sound, has become obsolete by the rising standards of the middle class. It is cheaper to build new communities on farm lands beyond the city's borders than to remodel, or to tear down and rebuild, the old housing in the cities. (Even in the most congested metropolitan areas, including the one centering on New York City, there is enough vacant suburban land to meet the probable demand for another generation at least.) The middle class steadily moves out of the unpromising "gray areas" lying between the central business district and the suburbs. Therefore it is to be expected that the lower-class people—many of them Negro —who have been living in the high-density slums will spread out into those "gray areas" and will convert them into low-density slums. With few exceptions (such as midtown and lower Manhattan, Chicago's Loop and lakefront, and San Francisco) the downtown districts of the older cities will decline as centers of commerce, entertainment, and culture. There is little that government can do about this. The forces that are at work—especially changes in technology, in location of industry and population, and in consumer tastes and incomes—are all largely beyond the control of government in a free society. Given these constraints, the future of the cities is probably beyond the reach of policy.[13]

If trends in city politics do not make as much difference as one would expect in some matters, they may make far *more* difference than one would expect in others. Changes in the city's politics may have profound consequences for the national parties and thus indirectly for the

---

[13] This seems to us to be the clear implication of the position taken by Raymond Vernon in *The Myth and Reality of Our Urban Problems* (Cambridge, Mass.: Joint Center for Urban Studies, 1962). Anthony Downs takes a contrary view in "The Future Structure of American Cities," a paper presented at the Conference on Transportation of the National Academy of Sciences at Woods Hole, Massachusetts, August 1960 (mimeo).

whole governmental system. To the extent that national leaders—the President above all—cannot draw upon reservoirs of political power that are created out of, and maintained as adjuncts of, local politics, they must either make up for the loss by appealing directly to the electorate or else be weaker in consequence. President Roosevelt depended heavily for support at crucial times on Boss Kelly, Boss Flynn, Boss Crump, Boss Hague, and, for a time, Boss Pendergast. No President will ever again find such support in city politicians. Now that a national leader cannot expect to have large blocs of votes "delivered" by city bosses, he must get them for himself; to do this he may have to pay a higher price than was paid before, and a higher one, perhaps, than the nation can afford. To the extent that he cannot count on the "delivery" of votes, he is less free to disregard public opinion at crucial moments when public opinion, or intensely moved parts of it, is out of line with long-term national interests. He is under a greater necessity to offer extravagant bribes to large classes of voters—farmers, homeowners, manufacturers, and so on. And he is more dependent on the arts of charm, salesmanship, and rhetoric, and on the appeal of ideology. As the sources of power change, so will the kinds of men who are adept at getting power and so also will the uses to which power is put.[14]

The changes that are occurring in city politics will have an effect upon character also. From Aristotle through Tocqueville, theorists have explained that the individual is formed in and by the local community and that his attachment to it influences profoundly his outlook and morality. In the long run, this effect upon character may be the most important of all. It does not follow from this, however, that we can judge what the nature of the effect is likely to be; relations between cause and effect in these matters are far from straightforward. Machine politics, although corrupt and selfish, may not have had a generally detrimental effect upon character. (Machine politics "left no moral scars on my generation," writes Thomas J. Fleming, a novelist whose father was one of Mayor Frank Hague's ward leaders in Jersey City. "Instead, we all nourished respectable nonpolitical ambitions, and most of us have realized them. My block has produced two engineers, a

---

[14] For a fuller discussion of these matters see Edward C. Banfield, "In Defense of the American Party System," a paper appearing in a symposium edited by Robert C. Goldwin and to be published by Rand-McNally.

Harvard Law School graduate, two stock brokers, a college professor.")[15] Similarly, it cannot be assumed that the more democratic and community-regarding new style of local politics will have a generally ennobling effect upon character. Important long-run effects there will undoubtedly be, but about their nature we can say nothing even in retrospect.

What is true about effects on individual character is true about other effects as well. Probably all of the effects of changes in city politics that make the most difference in the long run will occur in ways so indirect as to make their identification unlikely or impossible. Some ultimate effects will occur because of intermediate changes that are brought about in the functioning of political institutions; conceivably, for example, changes in the style of city politics, by affecting the national party system and thus the Presidency, may affect the peace of the world and the future of mankind. Other ultimate effects may be produced in ways that are remote from government and politics; if, for example, the new style of politics is less able than the old to contain and give controlled release to popular restlessness, energy, and emotion, these may break out at unexpected times and places and in forms —fads and fashions, religious revivals, or new social movements—that are as remote from politics as it is possible to imagine. Among these indirect effects there may be some that are more dangerous to the well-being of the society than any of the ills that municipal reformers have ever contemplated. There is, of course, nothing to be gained from speculating about these matters since in the nature of the case nothing much can be known about them. It is well to recognize, however, that the common-sense view of things is probably wrong both in attributing to city politics an importance that it does not have in matters that seem to be obviously connected with it and also—perhaps especially—in failing to attribute to it a much larger, although unspecifiable, importance that it has in matters that seem to bear no relation to it whatever.

[15] Thomas J. Fleming, "City in the Shadow," *Saturday Evening Post*, Jan. 6, 1962, p. 82.

INDEX

INDEX

EDWARD C. BANFIELD is the author of *Political Influence,* the editor of *Urban Government: A Reader,* and the co-author, with Martin Meyerson, of *Politics, Planning, and the Public Interest.* He is Henry Lee Shattuck Professor of Urban Government at Harvard University.

JAMES Q. WILSON, Associate Professor of Government at Harvard, is the author of *Negro Politics: The Search for Leadership* and *The Amateur Democrat: Club Politics in Three Cities.* Since July 1963, he has been Director of the Joint Center for Urban Studies of M.I.T. and Harvard.

VINTAGE HISTORY—AMERICAN

VINTAGE POLITICAL SCIENCE
AND SOCIAL CRITICISM

A free catalogue of VINTAGE BOOKS *will be sent at your request. Write to* Vintage Books, 457 Madison Avenue, New York, New York 10022.

VINTAGE WORKS OF SCIENCE
AND PSYCHOLOGY

A free catalogue of VINTAGE BOOKS *will be sent at your request. Write to* Vintage Books, 457 Madison Avenue, New York, New York 10022.